The Letters and Diaries
of
John Henry Newman

The Letters and Diaries

of

John Henry Newman

Edited at the Birmingham Oratory
with notes and an introduction

by

Charles Stephen Dessain

of the same Oratory

Volume XXII
Between Pusey and the Extremists
July 1865 to December 1866

NELSON

THOMAS NELSON AND SONS LTD
36 Park Street London W1Y 4DE
PO Box 18123 Nairobi Kenya

THOMAS NELSON (AUSTRALIA) LTD
597 Little Collins Street Melbourne 3000

THOMAS NELSON AND SONS (CANADA) LTD
81 Curlew Drive Don Mills Ontario

THOMAS NELSON (NIGERIA) LTD
PO Box 336 Apapa Lagos

THOMAS NELSON AND SONS (SOUTH AFRICA) (PROPRIETARY) LTD
51 Commissioner Street Johannesburg

First Published 1972

Nihil obstat
John M. T. Barton, S.T.D., L.S.S.

Imprimatur
✠ Victor Guazzelli, V.G.
Westminster, 6 December 1971

SBN 0 17 135052 9

Printed in Great Britain by
Cox & Wyman Ltd,
London, Fakenham and Reading

Preface

WITHOUT the gradual building up at the Birmingham Oratory of a very full collection of Cardinal Newman's correspondence (an account of which will be found in the Introduction to Volume XI), the present work could not have been undertaken. Its aim is to provide an exhaustive edition of Newman's letters; with explanatory notes, which are often summaries of or quotations from the other side of the correspondence. Some of these letters *to* Newman, when they appear to have particular importance, or to be necessary for following a controversy, are inserted in the text. Every one of the letters written *by* Newman is included there, in chronological sequence. Should there eventually be any of his letters, whose existence is known to the editor, but of which he has failed to obtain a copy, this will be noted in its place. On the other hand, no attempt has been made to include a list of letters written by Newman and now lost, nor the brief précis he occasionally made of his reply, on the back of a correspondent's letter, although these are utilised for the annotation.

In order that the text of each letter may be as accurate as possible, the original autograph, when it still exists, or at least a photographic copy of it, has been used by the editor as his source. (The very few cases in which he has been content with an authenticated copy will be noted as they occur.) Always the text of the autograph is reproduced, or, when the autograph has disappeared, that of the copy that appears most reliable. When only Newman's draft exists, that is printed. The source used in each case is to be found in the list of letters by correspondents.

Such alterations as are made in transcribing the letters aim, without sacrifice of accuracy, at enabling them to be read with ease. Newman writes simply and has none of those idiosyncracies which sometimes need to be reproduced for the sake of the evidence of one kind or another which they provide.

The following are the only alterations made in transcription:

ADDRESS AND DATE are always printed on the same line, and at the head of the letter, even when Newman puts them at the end. When he omits or gives an incomplete date, the omission is supplied in square brackets, and justified in a note unless the reason for it is obvious. The addresses, to which letters were sent, are included in the list of letters by correspondents. The information derived from postmarks is matter for annotation.

THE CONCLUSION of the letter is made to run on, irrespective of Newman's separate lines, and all postscripts are placed at the end.

NEWMAN'S CORRECTIONS AND ADDITIONS are inserted in their intended place. His interlinear explanations are printed in the text in angle brackets $\langle\rangle$, after the word or phrase they explain. His erasures are given in footnotes when they appear to be of sufficient interest to warrant it. Square brackets being reserved for editorial additions; all Newman's brackets are printed as rounded ones (the kind most usual with him).

NEWMAN'S PARAGRAPHS AND PUNCTUATION are preserved, except that single quotation marks are printed throughout, and double ones for quotations within them. (Newman generally used the latter in both cases.) Further, a parenthesis or quotation that he began with the proper mark but failed to complete, or completed but did not begin, is supplied. All other punctuation marks supplied by the editor are enclosed in square brackets. Newman's dashes, which frequently do duty either for a full stop, a semicolon or a comma (especially when he is tired or writing hurriedly), are represented by a '—' with a space before and after. His spelling and use of capitals are left unchanged, but 'raised' letters are lowered in every case.

NEWMAN'S ABBREVIATIONS are retained in the case of proper names, and in the address and conclusion of each letter, since these are sometimes useful indications of his attitude at the time. In all other cases, abbreviations are printed out in full, where Newman employs them.

When he uses the initials of proper names, the full name is normally inserted in square brackets after the initials, at the first occurrence in each letter, and more often if it seems advisable in order to avoid confusion. No addition of the full name is made in the case of Newman's correspondent, whether his initials occur at the beginning of the letter or in the course of it.

When Newman uses only a Christian name, the surname is sometimes added in square brackets for the reader's convenience. The Christian names of members of the Oratory, since they are of frequent occurrence, are listed in the index of proper names and the reader is referred to surnames.

When transcription is made from a PRINTED SOURCE, typographical alterations clearly due to editor or printer are disregarded.

Sometimes Newman made HOLOGRAPH copies of his letters or of portions of them, when they were returned to him long after they had been written. In order that the reader may be able to see how much he copied and what changes he introduced, the copied passages are placed in quarter brackets ⌐⌐, and all additions of any importance included in the text in double square brackets, or, where this is impracticable, in the annotation.

Newman's letters are printed in CHRONOLOGICAL ORDER, with the name of his correspondent at the head (except that those of each day are arranged alphabetically), and, when more than one is written to the same person on the same day, numbered I, II. In the headings the name of the correspondent is given in its most convenient form, sometimes with Christian names in full, sometimes only with initials.

THE LIST OF LETTERS BY CORRESPONDENTS, at the end of each volume, shows whether the source used was an autograph, draft, printed source or copy, and in the last case, whether a holograph made by Newman later; and gives the present location of the source, as well as of any additional holograph copies or drafts. When a letter, or a considerable portion of it, has been printed in a standard work, references are given; but mistakes or omissions in these previous publications are noticed, if at all, in the annotation.

THE LETTERS WRITTEN TO NEWMAN, when inserted in the text, are printed in type smaller than that used for Newman's own letters, and headed by the name of the correspondent. These letters are not arranged in chronological order, but are placed either just before or just after the letter of Newman to which they are related. A list of them is given at the end of each volume in which they occur. These and the quotations from letters in the annotation are always, unless otherwise stated, printed from autographs at the Birmingham Oratory, and are transcribed in the same way as Newman's letters.

NEWMAN'S DIARIES COVER THE YEARS 1824 to 1879 (with a gap from July 1826 to March 1828). They are written in a series of mottled copy books, 12 × 18½ centimetres, printed for a year each, and entitled *The Private Diary: arranged, printed, and ruled, for receiving an account of every day's employment . . .*' with the exception of the four periods July 1847–May 1850, January 1854–January 1861, January 1861–March 1871, March 1871–October 1879, each of which is contained in a somewhat thicker copy book.

These diaries are printed complete for each day in which Newman has made an entry, except that the lists of people to whom he has written or from whom he has received letters are omitted, as not being of sufficient general interest. The original diaries are, of course, available for consultation. At the end of each diary book are various notes, lists of addresses, of people to be prayed for, accounts, etc. These, also, are omitted, except for occasional dated notes of events, which are inserted in their proper place. Of the rest of the notes, some are theological and will be reserved for a volume of Newman's theological papers, and others will perhaps have room found for them in any fuller edition of *Autobiographical Writings.*

Newman compiled with his own hand, on quarto sheets sewn together, a book of *Chronological Notes*, drawn largely from the diaries. Any new matter in these *Notes* is printed in italics with the appropriated iary entry. (It should be noted that the diary entries themselves were sometimes written up considerably later than the events they record.)

Each volume is preceded by a brief summary of the period of Newman's life that it covers. Summary, diaries and annotation give a roughly biographical form to the whole, and will, it is hoped, enable the ordinary reader to treat it as a continuous narrative.

THE BIOGRAPHIES OF PERSONS are collected in the index of proper names at the end of each volume, in order to simplify the annotation of the letters. Occasionally, when a person is mentioned only once or twice, and a note is required in any case, biographical details have been given in the notes, and a reference in the index. Volume XXI, being the first of a new period in Newman's life, contains an account of every person mentioned, with the exception of a few for whom a notice seemed unnecessary, and of still fewer who have not yet been identified. The indexes of Volume XXII and of subsequent volumes will contain notices of persons who appear in them for the first time, and references back, in the case of those who have been noticed in an earlier volume. (The editor will be grateful for information as to persons not identified.)

These notices have been compiled from such various sources — books of reference, letters at the Oratory, information supplied by the families or religious communities of the persons concerned, and by librarians and archivists — that the giving of authorities would be a very complicated and lengthy process. Like others faced with the same problem, the editor has decided usually to omit them. References are given, however, to *The Dictionary of National Biography*, or *The Dictionary of American Biography*, in all cases where there is an article there, and failing them, to Boase's *Modern English Biography* or Gillow's *Bibliographical Dictionary of the English Catholics*. When all the volumes of letters have been issued, a final index volume will be compiled for the whole work.

Contents

Acknowledgements

THE encouragement and help of John Tracy Ellis, professor of church history in the University of San Francisco and lecturer in church history in the Graduate Theological Union, Berkeley, California, have been invaluable ever since the project of publishing Newman's letters and diaries began. And now the publication of this present volume has been made possible thanks to his generosity.

The editor also wishes to thank the Father Provincial of the English Province of the Society of Jesus for enabling the Reverend Thomas Gornall to assist in the preparation of this and future volumes of *The Letters and Diaries of John Henry Newman*.

Abbreviations in Volume XXII

THE abbreviations used for Newman's works are those listed in Joseph Rickaby, S.J., *Index to the Works of John Henry Cardinal Newman*, London 1914, with a few additions.

References to works included by Newman in his uniform edition are always, unless otherwise stated, to that edition, which was begun in 1868 with *Parochial and Plain Sermons*, and concluded in 1881 with *Select Treatises of St Athanasius*. From 1886, until the stock was destroyed in the 1939–45 war, all the volumes were published by Longmans, Green and Co. They are distinguished from other, usually posthumous, publications by having their date of inclusion in the uniform edition in brackets after the title, in the list of abbreviations below. The unbracketed date is, in every case, the date of the edition (or impression) used for giving references. (Once volumes were included in the uniform edition the pagination usually remained unchanged, but there are exceptions and minor alterations.)

Add.	*Addresses to Cardinal Newman with His Replies etc. 1879–82, ed.* W. P. Neville, 1905.
Apo.	*Apologia pro Vita Sua*, (1873) 1905.
Ari.	*The Arians of the Fourth Century*, (1871) 1908.
Ath. I, II	*Select Treatises of St Athanasius*, two volumes, (1881) 1920.
A.W.	*John Henry Newman: Autobiographical Writings*, ed. Henry Tristram, 1956.
Call.	*Callista, a Tale of the Third Century*, (1876) 1923.
Campaign	*My Campaign in Ireland, Part I* (printed for private circulation only), 1896.
D.A.	*Discussions and Arguments on Various Subjects*, (1872) 1911.
Dev.	*An Essay on the Development of Christian Doctrine*, (1878) 1908.
Diff. I, II	*Certain Difficulties felt by Anglicans in Catholic Teaching*, two volumes, (1879, 1876) 1908.
Ess. I, II	*Essays Critical and Historical*, two volumes, (1871) 1919.
G.A.	*An Essay in aid of a Grammar of Assent*, (1870) 1913.
H.S. I, II, III	*Historical Sketches*, three volumes, (1872) 1908, 1912, 1909.
Idea	*The Idea of a University defined and illustrated*, (1873) 1902.
Jfc.	*Lectures on the Doctrine of Justification*, (1874) 1908.
K.C.	*Correspondence of John Henry Newman with John Keble and Others, 1839–45*, ed. at the Birmingham Oratory, 1917.
L.G.	*Loss and Gain: the Story of a Convert*, (1874) 1911.
M.D.	*Meditations and Devotions of the late Cardinal Newman*, 1893.
Mir.	*Two Essays on Biblical and on Ecclesiastical Miracles*, (1870) 1907.
Mix.	*Discourses addressed to Mixed Congregations*, (1871) 1909.
Moz. I, II	*Letters and Correspondence of John Henry Newman*, ed. Anne Mozley, two volumes, 1891.
O.S.	*Sermons preached on Various Occasions*, (1870) 1927.

P.S. I–VIII	*Parochial and Plain Sermons,* (1868) 1907–10.
Prepos.	*Present Position of Catholics,* (n.d. 1872) 1913.
S.D.	*Sermons bearing on Subjects of the Day,* (1869) 1902.
S.E.	*Stray Essays on Controversial Points,* (private) 1890.
S.N.	*Sermon Notes of John Henry Cardinal Newman, 1849–1879,* ed. Fathers of the Birmingham Oratory, 1913.
T.T.	*Tracts Theological and Ecclesiastical,* (1874) 1908.
U.S.	*Fifteen Sermons preached before the University of Oxford,* (1872) 1909.
V.M. I, II	*The Via Media,* (1877) 1908, 1911.
V.V.	*Verses on Various Occasions,* (1874) 1910.

*   *   *

Boase	Frederick Boase, *Modern English Biography,* six volumes, Truro 1892–1921.
Butler	Cuthbert Butler, *The Life and Times of Bishop Ullathorne,* two volumes, London 1926.
de Lisle	E. S. Purcell, *Life and Letters of Ambrose Phillipps de Lisle,* two volumes, London 1900.
D A B	*Dictionary of American Biography,* London, 1928–36.
D N B	*Dictionary of National Biography,* to 1900, London, reprinted in 1937–8 in twenty-two volumes, the last being a Supplement, *D N B,* Suppl.
D N B, 1901–11	*Dictionary of National Biography,* 1901–11, three volumes in one.
D R	*Dublin Review.*
D T C	*Dictionnaire de Théologie Catholique,* Paris 1903–50.
Gillow	Joseph Gillow, *Bibliographical Dictionary of the English Catholics,* five volumes, London 1885 and later.
Harper	Gordon Huntington Harper, *Cardinal Newman and William Froude, F.R.S. A Correspondence,* Baltimore 1933.
Liddon's *Pusey* I–IV	H. P. Liddon, *Life of Edward Bouverie Pusey,* four volumes, London 1893–7.
MacDougall	Hugh A. MacDougall, *The Acton-Newman Relations,* New York 1962.
Newman and Bloxam	R. D. Middleton, *Newman and Bloxam,* London 1947.
Purcell	E. S. Purcell, *The Life of Cardinal Manning,* two volumes, London 1895.
Trevor I	Meriol Trevor, *Newman the Pillar of the Cloud,* London 1962.
Trevor II	Meriol Trevor, *Newman Light in Winter,* London 1962,
Ward I, II	Wilfrid Ward, *The Life of John Henry Cardinal Newman,* two volumes, London 1912.

Introductory Note

THE earlier part of 1865 had seen the defeat of Newman's first attempt to cater for the higher education of English Catholics, by the foundation of an Oratory at Oxford. Had he been there to provide for their religious needs, parents would have been able to send their sons to the University. This had been prevented, against the wishes of the majority of the laity interested, and instead, Catholics were to be dissuaded from making use of the universities, without any alternative being offered to them. After this first failure there was a lull, although Bishop Ullathorne did again propose to Newman in August 1865 that he should eventually take over the Catholic mission at Oxford and bring the Oratory there.

The lull in Newman's activity was, however, soon ended, as a result of the controversy between Pusey and Manning. To the latter's *Workings of the Holy Spirit in the Church of England, a Letter to the Rev. E. B. Pusey*, there came the reply, *An Eirenicon in a Letter to the Author of 'The Christian Year'*. The copy of his *Eirenicon*, which Pusey sent to Newman, arrived early in September 1865. Among Pusey's chief targets were Catholic doctrine and devotion concerning the Blessed Virgin, and the infallibility claimed for the Papacy. Although from the first he considered Pusey's attack less than fair, Newman hoped that he would not be called upon to intervene in the controversy. It was gradually brought home to him that Pusey had criticised the views of the extremist and ultramontane Catholics, notably Faber, Manning and W. G. Ward, as though they were the acceptable Catholic ones. Someone must explain that more moderate views were not only permissible, but represented the traditional, the normal teaching.

Before all this, in the middle of September 1865, Newman and Keble met for the first and only time after the separation in religion between them, at Keble's Hursley vicarage. Pusey was visiting there at the same time and with him Newman conversed at length. But between himself and Keble there passed a current of strong though more silent sympathy. A month later Newman wrote to Keble a complaint of the unfairness of Pusey's *Eirenicon*, and then gently but firmly to Pusey himself. Towards the end of November Newman was telling Hope-Scott, 'Many persons wish me to write on the subject of Pusey's book, and it has struck me it will be the most inoffensive way of alluding to Faber and Ward, if I can write without hurting Pusey. I am in constant communication with him.'

Begun in the latter part of November, *A Letter to the Rev. E. B. Pusey*,

D.D. on his recent Eirenicon was finished on 8 December, and although he was seriously ill at this time with the stone, Newman was able to see it through the press. He confined himself to the one subject of Catholic belief and devotion concerning our Lady, and appealed to the witness of the primitive Church. The work was published on 31 January 1866, and two thousand copies were sold in a fortnight. It was meant to be a real Eirenicon and to remove obstacles to unity. Keble and Pusey welcomed the Letter. *The Times* devoted the whole of one page to a sympathetic review, the author of which was R. W. Church. Newman declared his preference for 'English habits of devotion to foreign', and rejected the exaggerations brought in by Faber and Ward. Various representative old Catholic priests wrote their approval of the line he had taken.

But Newman was engaged in a battle on two fronts, and the chief attacks came from the Catholic side. Against a violent one by E. R. Martin, correspondent of the *Tablet* in Rome, Newman was forthrightly defended the following week by Bishop Clifford of Clifton. Ward and Manning proceeded more circumspectly. An article was drawn up and printed by Ward, for insertion in the *Dublin Review*, which criticised Newman's 'slur' on foreign Catholics, and corrected several 'anti-Catholic statements' in his 'Protestant' letter. By Manning's advice it was sent to Ullathorne for revision. This he refused to undertake, on the ground that, as Newman's bishop, he would be his judge. He, too, wrote to the *Tablet* in vindication of Newman's devotion to our Lady, a letter reproduced as an appendix to this volume. Bishop Clifford was next approached, but declined to revise the article, because he thoroughly approved of Newman's *Letter*, and rejected the criticisms as without foundation. Ward and Manning then abandoned what they had prepared. They had wanted to preoccupy the ground against Newman, and mark him with a kind of censure, for which episcopal approval would have been obtained in advance.

In view of the opposition to his *Letter to Pusey* Newman decided not to write on the other questions raised by Pusey, the development of Revelation and papal infallibility. A beginning had been made in checking the extremists, a wedge inserted, and the wise plan was, not to stir up further animosity, but to allow the good already achieved to work itself out quietly.

At the end of March 1866, Ullathorne again pressed Newman to undertake the Catholic mission at Oxford, where Catholics there were still using a tiny chapel in a back street. With Newman and the Oratory at Oxford all this would be changed. Ullathorne does not appear to have realised the strength of Manning's determination that Newman should not go to Oxford. The plan of inserting an episcopally approved censure of Newman into the *Dublin Review* had aimed at making him *persona non grata*, when it came to establishing a Catholic representative at Oxford. As to Newman, he saw in the request of his lawful superior a definite call to undertake a work of great importance. He insisted once more to Ullathorne that he went to Oxford for the sake of the Catholics at the University. But after the lesson of his first attempt to found an Oratory at Oxford, he saw that he must have a guarantee from Cardinal Barnabò at the Congregation of Propaganda. Newman feared that after he had bought land and just as he was building or had completed a church at Oxford, his plans might be upset by some decision from Propaganda, which would hinder him from continuing his work, perhaps from remaining in Oxford at all. But if the church and house to be built at Oxford were to form an integral part of the Birmingham Oratory during Newman's lifetime and for three years after his death, there would be security of tenure. So for this permission Ullathorne was to petition. Unfortunately when writing to Rome he managed still further to prejudice Newman there. He declared that in 1864 Newman had proposed to engage in educational work at the University, and that he, Ullathorne, had restrained him from this dangerous involvement in 'mixed' education. Newman was in Switzerland, where he spent the month of August 1866, when this unfounded charge reached him. He wrote candidly to Ullathorne pointing out the damaging mistake that had been made, and how throughout his purpose had been to undertake the spiritual care of Catholic undergraduates. He was told airily that the matter would be set right in due time. All along Newman's friends insisted that a work of high importance had been entrusted to him, and that, no matter how frustrating the opposition, his must not be the responsibility for ending it. At the end of 1866 the permission from Propaganda reached Ullathorne, but it contained a secret instruction against Newman's residence at Oxford. The revelation of this in the following year led to the defeat of the second attempt to found an Oratory there, and with it the opportunity of university education for Catholics in Great Britain.

Besides correspondence on devotion to the Blessed Virgin and on papal infallibility, this volume contains forceful letters to Henry James Coleridge, editor of the *Month*, blaming him for his harshness in controversy with Anglicans, and others to Ambrose de Lisle on the question of corporate reunion. It also contains a remarkable one on the same subject to Bishop Dupanloup, who had asked Newman's advice on how best to meet Pusey's advances.

1865
26 August	Bishop Ullathorne again proposes to Newman that he should take the Oxford mission, and found an Oratory there.
4 September	Pusey offers to send Newman his *An Eirenicon in a Letter to the Author of 'The Christian Year'*.
12 September	Newman visits John Keble at Hursley. Pusey is also there.
8 December	Newman finishes writing *A Letter to the Rev. E. B. Pusey, D.D. on his recent Eirenicon*.

1866
17 January	End of Newman's serious illness, which began before Christmas.
31 January	*A Letter to Pusey* is published.
10 March	Attack in the *Tablet* on *A Letter to Pusey*. Ward and Manning prepare a critical article for the *Dublin Review*.
25 March	Bishop Ullathorne again asks Newman to undertake the Oxford mission.
29 March	Death of John Keble.
June	Newman's review of J. R. Seeley's *Ecce Homo* is published in the *Month*.
8 June	The Birmingham Oratory finally resolves to undertake the Oxford mission.
30 July	On medical advice Newman spends a month in Switzerland. He works on the problem of certitude, in preparation for *A Grammar of Assent*.
12 August	Letter of protest to Ullathorne. Newman accepts the Oxford mission 'with reluctance'.
7 September	Newman returns to Birmingham.
7 October	Newman preaches his sermon *The Pope and the Revolution*. It is published on 26 October.
21 October	Newman receives Gerard Manley Hopkins into the Catholic Church.
26 December	News of permission from Propaganda for the erection of an Oratory at Oxford, dependent on that of Birmingham, reaches Newman.

The Letters and Diaries
of
John Henry Newman

TO RALPH TURNBULL

(sent in substance but civiller)   July 1/65
Dear Sir,

I thank you for the terms in which you speak of me in your letter to the Shields Gazette.[1] However, I don't profess to be a politician, and don't see how it is possible to side with the Tories, while they are hand and glove with the Orangemen. Nor can I justify or admire the Church Establishment of Ireland

J H N

SATURDAY 1 JULY 1865   walked in to Edgbaston   weather clearing
SUNDAY 2 JULY   began to take part in the boys' concerts.

TO MISS HOLMES

The Oratory Bm July 2. 1865
My dear Miss Holmes,

I wish I had more power of serving you. It is not for want of thinking of you. I have given you and some other ladies 14 Masses since January, and it is to me a continual trouble that you should not have a clearer prospect before you. I heartily wish you could give up governessing; nor have I ever understood why your Music plans have so utterly failed. Of course it is most difficult to persevere without capital — but, if I may judge (I dare say on insufficient grounds) I think your fault is want of perseverance. It is to me wonderful what a unanimity there seems to be, among the familes you have been in, that you are a treasure to them, and that they are *sorry* to part with you — and how many are there whom you still know as friends! Tho' I dare say it was their *fault,* still it was not their *wish* to lose you. Yet what has been the *average* length of your stay in each place? I suppose there is nothing more irksome than to be a governess or tutor in a family. For myself I know little indeed about it — few persons consult me about Tutors, and none about governesses. Had I the means of serving you that way I would — but I would much rather hear that you saw your way to give up the occupation altogether. I have before now felt so strongly about it that I have been much tempted to write

---

[1] Turnbull wrote from 43 Tyne Street, North Shields, on 27 June, 'I enclose an extract from a letter of mine in the Shields Gazette of today to let you see that the good seed you have been sowing broadcast is not without fruit in the border country.' Turnbull's letter in the *Shields Gazette and Daily Telegraph,* (27 June 1867), signed 'A Roman Catholic Elector,' said that Catholics would vote conservative in the general election. 'Father Newman has in his last work stated that the Established Church has now become a breakwater for the protection of much Scriptural Catholic truth against infidelity and fanaticism,' hence a number of Catholics in Tynemouth would vote for the conservative candidate, 'believing that to do so at this moment will be best for the future of our still long-persecuted and down-trodden countrymen in Ireland, the old land of Erin, and for the freedom and protection of Catholic opinions.'

confidentially to some of your true friends on the subject. Nothing is so weari-
some as change — if I were you (tho' I dare say I am talking of what I cannot
conjecture at all about myself) I should make a resolution, as a matter of
conscience, that, when I got a situation, for at least two years I on my part
would do nothing indirectly or directly calculated to close the engagement.
Now you must pardon me, if I seem cruel — but I am cruel from the very
sincerity with which I am

Ever Yours affectly in Xt John H Newman of the Oratory

Miss Holmes

TO JAMES LAIRD PATTERSON

The Oratory, Birmingham. July 2nd. 65.

My dear Patterson,

I have been away from Edgbaston, or should have answered your kind
note sooner. I am sure, after the whirl I was in when last you came here, I had
no right to expect you would be so kind as to come up all the way again. The
Breviary has not yet got to me, but I suppose in due time it will make its
appearance. Thank you for saving it for me. You know I have one of Scott's
books for you which he specifies in his will.[1] His books were in a sad state —
many not forthcoming, including one or two left to individuals — many spoilt
by wet — some odd volumes.

I am sure that, as regards my seat at the consecration, everything was done
with the kindest intent — and the most provident exactness — but on such an
occasion the enthusiasm of individuals overrides propriety.[2]

I hope the Archbishop will return restored by his excursion.[3]

Ever yours very sincerely in Christ, John H. Newman, of the Oratory

Rev. J. L. Patterson.

TO J. WALKER OF SCARBOROUGH

The Oratory Bm July 2. 1865

Mr dear Mr Walker

I was amused at having at length caught it from the Saturday. Of course it
must have come sooner or later. I wonder whether the wounds I have received

[1] Patterson wrote on 24 June that he had been in Birmingham the previous week, and had
left there W. H. Scott's breviary for Newman, but had not had time to visit the Oratory. In a
later letter Patterson described a letter of 14 Oct. 1864 from Newman, who spoke of 'the book
which Scott left you by will — Lord Dudley's letters . . . I have kept it safely.'
[2] Patterson wrote, 'I wished particularly to see you also on account of the dismay and
annoyance I felt at the Consecration [of Manning in St Mary, Moorfields, on 8 June] in seeing
you towards the end of the long function, detruded from your modest nook and standing
merged in the sea of priests who, in unexpected numbers, encumbered the Sanctuary.'
[3] The day after his consecration Manning left for a month's holiday in France.

will do me any good with the people in London who go about saying I am a liberal. As they have said this up to now, in spite of my Apologia, I suppose the testimony of the Saturday in my favour may go for nothing — still it ought to tell.[1]

I suppose the Archbishop has got into the foreign way and does it naturally — but, with you, I feel awkward. He practised it with me before, that morning, but I had not improved. I believe it is usual with him in the case of most people. I never saw the Cardinal do it. I always feel ashamed, like a John Bull who does not know manners.[2]

Thank you for the good nature of your recipe of spears and pitchforks for improving my general health

Ever Yours very sincerely John H Newman of the Oratory
The Very Revd John Can. Walker

TO MESSRS ALLCOCK AND MILWARD

July 3. 1865

Dear Sirs

I do not like to relinquish the condition which Mr Hanley granted me when I offered to purchase his premises. It is a great inconvenience to me that there should be this delay in the negociation. I have bonâ fide wished to conclude it. The £2000 has been lying at my Banker's these three months, and shall lose, I suppose, so much interest.

I will draw out for you the state of the case. On January 12. I wrote to him 'I will purchase your ground at once. In that case I should (next week) send a surveyor from London for form sake, to look at the property and to report to me upon it, and should purchase it of you without delay.'

I said 'for form sake,' because it had been told me by friends who had seen the property that it was in good condition on the whole.

The surveyor made his report — said it was not favourable and you yourselves confirmed his judgment.

This did not move me in my wish to buy the land at once, though I had no intention of building at once. That I had no such intention, I know myself quite well; my friends have known it; the gentlemen at a distance who gave me

---

[1] The *Saturday Review*, (24 June 1865), (pp. 768–70), devoted a long article 'Dr. Newman and Liberalism,' to a review of *History of My Religious Opinions*. The article, by James Fitzjames Stephen, was a sustained attack on 'Note A,' 'Liberalism,' which Newman had added to *Apo.*, pp. 285–97. See note to diary for 13 Oct. 1865.

[2] Sibthorp wrote to Bloxam on 22 June about Manning's consecration, at which he was present, 'Now I kneel, and kiss his hand as Primate of the Roman Catholic Church in England! ... Dr Newman was there, and I just saw him to shake hands with him. As his manner is, he kept retired, but had come up for the ceremony, and immediately afterwards was seen in the sacristy on his knees before the archbishop, who hastened to raise him up and embrace him.' J. Fowler, *Richard Waldo Sibthorp*, London 1880, p. 173.

money in December last know it [,] nor did I say a word to Mr Hanley implying the contrary. So far from it that in the letter quoted above of January 12 I
said 'My next point is to ask you to set about inquiries as to the chance of
getting land *adjacent* to yours — My offer to *buy* at once, was, not to build at
once, but because other persons, Mr Hanley said, were after the land, and he
gave me about 8 days (I think) to make up my mind.

However, though the Surveyor's report did not alter my wish to buy Mr
Hanley's premises, it made me anxious about the management of them, the
rent etc. And I therefore caught at the offer which Mr Hanley proceeded to
make me to give me £100 for the premises *till I required them*. And I had nothing more to say till you yourselves brought before me the fact that Mr Hanley
meant to get rid of any such arrangement as soon as he could. Then I spoke
of a lease for seven years, but any other way of his fulfilling his offer, which you
can suggest, is the same to me.

The letters in which these circumstances are brought out are of the dates
of February 14 and 18.[1]

TO MRS PETER BRETHERTON

The Oratory, Birmingham July 3. 1865

My dear Mrs Bretherton

Your letter of the 30th has only arrived here this morning. I am deeply
concerned at what you say about dear Eleanor, but do trust that your own
natural anxiety makes you fear more than you have need to fear. No letter has
come from you of yesterday's date (Sunday) as you intended; and this letter
of June 30 has the post mark 'Bromsgrove July 2.'

I trust to say Mass for her the three next days — but before then I hope
you will write me word that all anxiety is over.[2]

Give her my love

Ever Yrs affly John H Newman of the Oratory

TUESDAY 4 JULY 1865 Bishop came up to Oy[Oratory] to confirm boys. I went to
Rednall and Henry in evening

WEDNESDAY 5 JULY Penny came to examine boys Henry returned to Oy

THURSDAY 6 JULY Parliament dissolved. Penny came over to see me with Wm
[William] Thunder

FRIDAY 7 JULY cloudy but good day

[1] See diary for 23 Aug.
[2] Mrs Bretherton's daughter was ill.

TO COURTNEY KENNY

Rednal. July 7. 1865

Dear Sir,

I thank you for your anecdote from Dean Swift's Life, which was new to me, and is exactly to the purpose of my discussion which you refer to.[1]

I recollect, when I was an Undergraduate, debating the point with a friend, and he gave the same solution, in substance, of the difficulty, as Swift's. He said, 'I should say to my questioner, "No — I did not write the book — but I tell you fairly, that, if I *had* written it, I should say, No, I did not write it."'

Thank you for the kind tone in which you speak of me and believe me to be, Dear Sir,

Very faithfully Yours John H Newman

Courtney Kenny Esqr

TO WILLIAM NEVILLE

Friday July 7/65

My dear Wm

Will you send tonight several copies of the Prospectus (they are on my round table) to the inclosed Mrs Fergusson, with my compliments, and in your politest few words answering her question.

And give the card to whoever wishes to go to Oscott, *who must answer it*.

And the unintelligible letter to Fr Henry.

Ever Yrs affly J H N

Dr Russell comes tomorrow.

SATURDAY 8 JULY 1865 Penny went. Walked in to Oy[Oratory] after the storm caught in the wet serious thunder storm Dr Russell came

---

[1] Kenny wrote from Halifax on 5 July of his interest in *Apo.*, and in reference to the discussion on truth, recounted: 'Dean Swift, having lampooned a Serjeant Bettesworth, was asked by the latter if he were the author of the attack: whereto, the Dean replied — 'I was advised in my youth that if ever any scoundrel or blockhead whom I had satirized should ask if it were I who attacked him, I should deny it; and *therefore* I tell you, Sir, that I am not the author of this book."'

Kenny, who asked for Newman's autograph, and wrote in a youthful hand, appears to be Courtney Stanhope Kenny (1847–1930), at this time articled to a Halifax firm of solicitors. In 1871 he entered Downing College, Cambridge, became a Fellow in 1875, and was called to the Bar in 1881. He sat in parliament as a liberal 1885–8, and in 1888 was made University Reader in English Law at Cambridge. In 1907 he succeeded F. W. Maitland as Downing Professor of Law, and held the chair until his resignation in 1918.

Rednal July 8/65

My dear Wetherell

I will return your masterly statement from Birmingham. I have little to criticize.[1] The paragraph p 5 is a bold one. It is taking the bull by the horns, and you should be sure that you have got tight hold of them.[2] The great difficulty is now to alter without disturbing the run of the type — so that I don't think it worth while to go out of the way to guard the passage. The fact *is*, that there is a *great* deal of distinct scepticism at both Universities — perhaps more at Cambridge. There is some little re-action at Oxford. I don't think we can say that it has set in. 'the last half century is beginning,' might stand 'late years is now at length beginning' — this will be taking out 18 letters and putting in 20. But I set this down to illustrate what I mean, rather than as positively suggesting it. In page 19 is an awkward sentence 'assurance' at first sight seems governed by 'felt' — it is so far from 'expressing.'[3]

There is no doubt at all, your facts will be disputed. Great people will say 'This gentleman has not had access to the best information — the *fact* is etc.' or 'he has coloured this very adroitly etc' But that will always be said, and your paper will stand, and, I trust, do its work

Very sincerely Yours John H Newman of the Oratory

T. F. Wetherell Esqr

July 9/65

My dear Mrs Bretherton

I am glad to have your account of Eleanor. She wishes me to meet Mr F. W.[4] I know how anxious you are — and I now shall make you more so — but I really cannot help doing so. The truth is that my general impression about him is so far from what I wish it to be, that I really do think it ought to be removed, before I seem by being introduced to him to countenance his having a place among you which from what I think he cannot believe that he deserves.

This is a most serious matter — Eleanor's whole future etc

[1] On 6 July Wetherell sent Newman a proof of *A Statement of Facts connected with the Memorial recently presented, by certain laymen to the Sacred Congregation of Propaganda, relative to the Education of Catholics at the Universities of Oxford and Cambridge.* Cf. letters of 4, 5 and 21 June, and 15 July to Wetherell.

[2] This paragraph eventually began: 'Meanwhile, outside the Universities the advance of unbelief has been continuous and rapid. And while in the great seats of learning themselves the dissolving criticism of late years is now at length beginning to be superseded by a reconstructive method, its results are descending through a more and more popular literature, and already permeate the higher and upper-middle classes of general English society.' The *Statement* went on to argue that contact with scepticism could not be avoided, but could be met by the higher mental training at the universities.

[3] This sentence was re-written.

[4] Frank Watt, to whom Mrs Bretherton's daughter Eleanor was engaged. Newman had received unfavourable reports about him. See letter of 17 May 1865 to Mrs Bretherton.

MONDAY 10 JULY 1865   Dr Russell went.   Ornsby came to examine the boys
TUESDAY 11 JULY   Mr E. Coffin came.   Elections for Parliament going on[1]

TO R. W. CHURCH

July 11 [1865]

My dear Church,

I have delayed thanking you for your great kindness in uniting with Rogers in giving me a fiddle, till I could report upon the fiddle itself. The Warehouse sent me three to choose out of — and I chose with trepidation, as fearing I was hardly up to choosing well. And then my fingers have been in such a state, as being cut by the strings, that up to Saturday last I had sticking plaster upon their ends — and therefore was in no condition to bring out a good tune from the strings and so to return good for evil. But on Saturday I had a good bout at Beethoven's Quartetts — which I used to play with poor Blanco White — and thought them more exquisite than ever — so that I was obliged to lay down the instrument and literally cry out with delight. However, what is more to the point, I was able to ascertain that I had got a very beautiful fiddle — such as I never had before. Think of my not having a good one till I was between sixty and seventy — and beginning to learn it when I was ten! However, I really think it will add to my power of working, and the length of my life. I never wrote more than when I played the fiddle. I always sleep better after music. There must be some electric current passing from the strings through the fingers into the brain and down the spinal marrow. Perhaps thought is music.

I hope to send you the 'Phormio' almost at once.

Ever yrs. affly., John H Newman

TO T. F. KNOX

The Oratory Birmingham July 11. 1865

My dear Father Knox

We have received your news of the death of your Father, Fr Gloag, with very deep concern — and we shall lose no time in saying the Masses for him We beg to send your Fathers our sincere condolements[2]

Yours affectionately John H Newman of the Oratory

WEDNESDAY 12 JULY 1865   Mr E. Coffin went   rain

[1] The new Parliament, in which the Liberals increased their majority to sixty-seven, was not opened until Feb. 1866.
[2] Thomas Dominic Gloag, who joined the London Oratory in 1850, died on 5 July at Florence.

The Oratory, Birmingham. July. 12th. 1865

My dear Lady Charles,

I have been at Rednal — which must be my apology for not sending you the enclosed sooner.[1] I was very sorry that in consequence I lost taking leave of Charlie. Give him my love, and tell him I hope he will go on with the violin, in which he is making so good a beginning. The last time I saw him was with the fiddle on his shoulder — and his bow arm promised to be a very good one.

With my best rememberance to Lord Charles, I am,

My dear Lady Charles, Sincerely yours in Christ,

John H Newman of the Oratory.

The Lady Charles Thynne

THURSDAY 13 JULY 1865 Ornsby went. I went to Rednall with Wm[William]
FRIDAY 14 JULY beautiful weather

TO H. LA SERRE

Rednal, July 14th. 65.

My dear M. La Serre,

I have to acknowledge the receipt of your Paper, and am sorry for the pain which it must have given you to write it.[2]

It will be a relief to you to be told that no one has made to me any accusation against you, as you suppose, so that it is not at all necessary that you should defend yourself. As to Father Prefect, he entertains, I know, a warm sense of your services to the School, while you have been here, as indeed we all do.

Be sure, my dear M. La Serre, that, in parting from us, as you now have determined, you carry with you our best and most friendly wishes for your welfare; and you leave with us the most pleasant remembrances of one who has ever been exemplary in his general conduct, and most zealous in the discharge of his School duties.

I hope you will not forget us, especially in your good prayers, and that you will acquaint us with the successive steps of your ecclesiastical course, and your eventual position among the Clergy of your great and truly Catholic country.

I am, My dear M. La Serre, Sincerely yours in Christ,

John H. Newman of the Oratory.

M. La Serre.

[1] Charles Thynne had left the Oratory School for good, and his parents had asked for specimens of his work, to show to his prospective tutor, Nicholas Darnell.
[2] La Serre, a priest from St Omer, and the French master at the Oratory School, had decided to leave. See also end of letter of 7 Aug. to him.

SATURDAY 15 JULY 1865   returned to Bm [Birmingham] to [sic] cab with my violin

TO T. F. WETHERELL

Rednal July 15. 1865

My dear Wetherell,

I did not receive your letter at this place till yesterday evening — so you will not get this till Monday. The proof shall get to you at the same time.[1]

First, I will set down, but merely as an illustration, how I should write your sentences, had I to do so myself, adding, that I think your proposed alteration of them 'This document etc' better than 'In this document etc' as they are printed, and that, as to my own, I know there is much awkwardness of expression etc in it.

'This document distinguishes clearly between the case of an educational institution which comes within the sphere of episcopal cognizance, and the acts of parents, in the education of their children, done on their own natural responsibility. And, while it states, that, in the question of a Catholic College, the disapproval of the Bishops is decisive and unanimous, on the other hand, instead of pronouncing a direct judgment ⟨(on the use of the existing Protestant Colleges for Catholic youth)⟩ on Catholics who make use of the existing Protestant Colleges, it goes no further than to 'dissuade' such a course ⟨(it)⟩, and (though that, strongly, yet) in terms which admit of the interpretation that the Bishops have but an opinion on the subject, perhaps not an unanimous opinion. Nor does it address either parents or children at all, except indirectly; it addresses the clergy; but even to the clergy it does not address a formal injunction, but it speaks ⟨comes presents itself⟩ to them in the shape ⟨on the footing⟩ and spirit of such opinions as are found in authoritative works on moral theology, St Alfonso's or Archbishop Kenrick's, which are decisions indeed of great weight, but, as applied to individual cases, are ever to be handled with discretion, and according to the best judgment of each priest to whom such individual cases *hic et nunc* are submitted, as being intended, to use the very words of the episcopal document, specially for his 'guidance.'[2]

---

[1] *A Statement of Facts connected with the Memorial to Propaganda* was about to be sent to all who had signed the Memorial, with a covering letter from Lord Castlerosse, chairman of the committee that had promoted it. Before signing the covering letter he consulted R. G. Macmullen, who, with J. W. Roberts, had been helping to revise the *Statement*. Macmullen thought its final paragraph minimised the unanimity of the English bishops in their decision about university education, and might provoke further action on their part. He suggested that Newman should settle whether the final paragraph should stand, and Wetherell wrote to him on 13 July.

[2] These sentences in explanation of Bishop Ullathorne's letter promulgating the English bishops' decision of 24 March (see note to letter of 31 March 1865 to Emily Bowles), were reproduced in the final paragraph of the *Statement*, as follows: 'The document agreed upon by the Bishops distinguishes clearly between the case of an educational institution which comes within the sphere of episcopal cognizance, and the acts of parents, in the education of their

Secondly, as to the question of expedience.

1. The very fact of Macmullen objecting gives ground for thinking that others may object also, not of the Memorialists merely, but of the 'promoters' of the Memorial; and as you and he are the only two representatives of the promoters, (Roberts being apparently neuter) I think this decides the question of prudence at once, viz. that you must carry him with you in what you publish. I don't see how Macmullen *can* agree simply to stand by my decision, when he represents a larger fact than his own opinion.

2. I think a Newspaper attack is inevitable, (unless they hope to ignore you) and it is well not to give unnecessary openings.

3. And the Bishops, or at least the Archbishop or Propaganda, *are* prepared to bring out something stronger. The Archbishop will go as far as ever he can prudently; and he feels this is the moment to strike, both because he is strong now, and because we are aiming to get the edge of the wedge in.

4. I don't think your Pamphlet can end with a bare insertion of the Bishop of Birmingham's letter. Surely the promoters are bound to say how they interpret it. Silence is a confession that it is dead against you. You should carry Macmullen with you here. You have only alluded to the agreement of the Bishop's Letter with Cardinal Barnabò's assurances — as far as *non-prohibition* goes; should you not say more distinctly that in other respects the Letter fulfils Cardinal Barnabò's account of it? there is no editto, no ezecuzione.[1]

5. I can't believe that the words of the (Bishops) Letter are not carefully chosen, and ought not to be taken in the letter. It seems to me striking that the word 'unanimous' is left out before 'opinion,' but it is another thing whether you will carry the world with you in saying so.[2] I am prepared to think that most men will agree with Macmullen, tho' I don't myself. And therefore I think it imprudent to put out such an interpretation except with a qualification. It will look like special pleading.

6. I fully believe the Bishops are not unanimous, except with that unanimity which is the expression of submission and obedience. By the bye, how many of them have published the document besides our Bishop? Why not?

children, done on their own natural responsibility. And, while it states that in the question of a Catholic College the disapproval of the Bishops is decisive and unanimous, it goes no further with regard to the use of the existing Protestant Colleges for Catholic youth than to speak of parents being "dissuaded" from it; and it does this in terms which admit of the interpretation that the Bishops have only an opinion on the subject, – perhaps not a unanimous opinion. Nor is it directly addressed to either parents or children at all: it is addressed to the clergy. And even on the clergy it lays no formal injunction, being only provided "for their guidance" in dealing, according to their own judgment and discretion, with such individual cases as may be submitted to them for advice.'

[1] *A Statements of Facts,* after inserting Ullathorne's letter, immediately commented, 'The course thus taken is in accordance with Cardinal Barnabò's assurance that no "edict" had been given, and that no "carrying out" was to be apprehended. The document agreed upon by the Bishops distinguishes clearly . . .'

[2] Ullathorne's Letter stated that the Bishops were 'unanimous in their disapproval of a Catholic College at any of the Protestant Universities. And they are further of opinion that parents ought to be in every way dissuaded from sending their children to pursue their studies at such Universities.'

7. Do what you will, I expect the document or parts of it will be in the Papers sooner or later.

I have answered your sentences as they ran

Very sincerely Yours John H Newman of the Oratory

T F Wetherell Esqr

P.S. You see then on the whole I am 1. distinctly for *some* comment on our Bishop's Letter. 2. one which commits you as little as possible,—paring down the meaning of the letter just as far as you can pare it without seeming to the world to be unfair.

SUNDAY 16 JULY 1865   Mrs Burmiston died[1]
MONDAY 17 JULY   Sir H. Pollen came   Examinations of boys   Austin and Stokes returned
TUESDAY 18 JULY   Sir H. Pollen went   Prizes given out   Concert etc in evening
WEDNESDAY 19 JULY   Boys went   Henry went away for holy day.   Ambrose's nieces came   Went over with Wm[William] to the Brethertons at Bromsgrove to dinner a wet day

TO EMILY BOWLES

The Oratory Bm July 20/65

My dear Miss Bowles

I don't quite like the idea of Miss Wilson going to a family, since there are openings to her, to engage in religious work at home. And I was not prepared to hear that she was disposed to such an employment — however, I will write to her.[2]

You have not, I hope, been overcome with London heat all this time — but have you fulfilled your purpose of breathing other air?

Ever Yours affly in Xt John H Newman

P.S. I wish she would give her full direction. I have written 'Boulogne' but am not sure it is not Dieppe. It is a bad trick of ladies — I don't mean of you, to write their names unintelligibly, never to say if they are married or single, to leave out month and year, and to give half only of their direction.

[1] See letter of 21 July to Miss Giberne.
[2] Lavinia Wilson, the Anglican nun whom Newman had received into the Church on Good Friday 1865, was staying at Boulogne. Emily Bowles proposed that she should become governess to the children of the Duchess of Sora, but wanted Newman to decide whether she should accept the post. Emily Bowles wrote to Newman on 18 July, 'I thought to see Rome for nothing was worth having — Besides the life in the Villa Borghese and seeing all the best Romans.'
The Duchess of Sora was Princess Agnes Borghese (1836–1920), granddaughter of the sixteenth Earl of Shrewsbury. She married in 1854 Rodolfo Boncompagni-Ludovisi, Duke of Sora.
See letter of 27 Aug.

The Oratory Bm July 20/65

My dear Wetherell

I have just ⟨(7 P.M.)⟩ received by post your letter of the 17th. I ought to have told you always to direct to me *here*. Letters are forwarded to me almost daily when at Rednal — and I am rarely there many days running.

1. I understood you to say that Macmullen wished to *end* with the Bishop's document of March 24 — and this seemed to me impossible. You are bound to say how you consider matters to stand at present — and they stand thus, that Catholic Undergraduates are not prohibited at Oxford, yet there is no provision for them. I am not determining, however, *what* you shall say — but if you ended simply with the Bishop's document, it would seem mysterious. I don't see any objection to p. 24. If Macmullen meant that it is imprudent to advocate the Oratory's being at Oxford, the question comes, whether the Oratory now would *go* there, advocate or no advocate. Certainly I have not the most distant intention of going there. I suppose this is the point you mean in p. 24. After 'indirectly prevented' could you add 'and nothing substituted?'[1] Does he mean the words 'The limits within which etc' would 'divide the Memorialists'? *he* is a judge of this, and I am not.[2]

2. What I sketched myself was to be as a new edition of the alteration which you wrote down in your own letter — which was made in the passage in p. 23. I did not myself see any objection to the rest from 'A large number of them' to the end of p 24 — but, I repeat, I am no judge.[3]

3. I think your objection 'Considering the statement will appear as the work of laymen etc' has force — certainly, in respect to the mode in which I have spoken, the definiteness etc. Still, I think it might be *hinted*, for it concerns the laity much what their clergy are likely to recommend them, and how far they are *ordered* to advise in a particular way. But here I am no judge of the

---

[1] The final sentences of *A Statement of Facts,* p. 24, eventually ran: 'The foundation of an Oratory at Oxford, therefore, has been indirectly prevented; and Catholic undergraduates will consequently still remain without that special provision for their moral and spiritual needs, which it was hoped had been secured for them. But nothing has occurred either to weaken the force of those considerations by which the necessity of the higher education for English Catholics is established, or to indicate any method by which they can obtain that education, at the present time, except through the Universities of Oxford and Cambridge.'

[2] Wetherell, who wrote on 17 July that Macmullen considered 'p. 24 would divide the Memorialists,' thought the sentence to which Newman here refers, to be the offending one. On 23 July Wetherell wrote, that, in consequence of Macmullen's objection it had been struck out. It came after the passage quoted in the previous note, about the Oratory at Oxford, in which Macmullen saw no difficulty.

[3] In *A Statement of Facts,* immediately after the passage quoted in the second note to letter of 15 July to Wetherell, and before that quoted in the first note above, occurred the following: 'A large number of them [the clergy], however, probably concur in the view which prevails among the Bishops; and it is natural that those who do not should be indisposed to take a prominent part in any measure for the immediate furtherance of an end which is not acceptable to authority. Nor would such a measure at the present time, obtain even the tacit sanction of any English Bishop.'

expedience, for I don't know the Memorialists. I would, as you suggest, certainly leave out my words within brackets.[1]

4. Perhaps 'indirectly' is not the right word and 'nor does it address, either parents or children at all, *except as it addresses* the clergy, and even to the clergy it does not address a formal injunction, as being intended etc.' Perhaps you will not think this meets your difficulty.[2]

5. Your difficulty is, I think, just — would it be got over by 'unanimous, on the other hand it goes no further than to dissuade' the use etc.[3]

It is very unsatisfactory that you have such difficulties in determining an important passage at the last moment.

Very sincerely Yours John H Newman

FRIDAY 21 JULY 1865   La Serre went for good.   I in retreat

TO SIR JOHN ACTON

The Oratory Birmingham July 21. 1865

My dear Sir John

I congratulate you, or rather the Catholic body, on your election — but *yourself*, as far as this — that you are in your proper place, as Member for Bridgenorth, but you were not so exactly as member for an Irish Borough. It is pleasant too that you are the first to break through the impediment raised against Catholics since the Hierarchy Bill, — as Sir John Simeon will, I trust, be the next; and the event comes with a curious fitness after the recent decision about the Archbishoprick, which seemed to force the action of the Catholics of England into one only channel. I wish you and Sir John Simeon may be the rallying points of a party — and that you may hit upon some means of being represented in the Newspaper Press. You will be looked after very sharply, and your influence may be very great. I am not speaking of a political party in the house of course (which is absurd) but a party among Catholics.[4]

Very sincerely Yours John H Newman of the Oratory

Sir John Acton Bart MP

P.S. So Sir J. S. [Simeon] is elected.

[1] Since *A Statement of Facts* would 'appear as the work of laymen addressing laymen on a lay question' Wetherell proposed to omit Newman's references (in his letter of 15 July) to 'authoritative works on moral theology'.

[2] See Newman's letter of 15 July.

[3] Wetherell thought Newman's phrase about the Bishops' 'pronouncing a direct judgment' was too emphatic, and it was omitted. See letter of 21 July to Wetherell.

[4] At the general election, Acton, who had previously sat for Carlow, was elected for Bridgnorth, and Sir John Simeon for the Isle of Wight. After the restoration of the Hierarchy in 1850 the only Catholic member of Parliament outside Ireland was Lord Edward Howard, returned regularly for Arundel, thanks to the influence of his family.

Acton and Simeon were Liberals in politics and also liberal Catholics. In 1867 the *Chronicle*, a mainly political and literary weekly, was founded, with Wetherell as editor.

The Oratory, Birmingham. July 21. 1865

My dear Badeley

Thank you for your Pamphlet.[1] It is very good news of you — for, though I am not a judge of a legal question, yet any one can see it is well argued out, and difficult to answer your statements. I am glad too that the ipse dixits of great men and their extra-judicial political judgments should be brought to book. Of course your arguments will re-appear on both sides in the trial now immediately coming on; and I am glad you have got it out in time.[2]

What an eventful time it is! so eventful that, as a rough sea puts a party on ship board at all possible angles and in all possible relations towards each other, so one has not a guess how one's friend's opinions are going, and needs have a common observatory with constant telegrams to register their several variations. Now here is Gladstone's matter. I really have doubted how I should have voted, had I had a vote — on this ground, not the Anglican,[3] but the political — for he seems disposed to open a door to reform, which cannot be shut till we are democratized. On the other hand I have had my sympathies so go along with him, and am so sorry at his defeat, both for his sake and for that of Oxford, that I suppose, after all, I should have voted on the side of Keble, Pusey, and my other old friends.

Then again the event previous to this, and its pendant, though so different, the elevation of Gladstone's old friend, the new Archbishop — how marvellous this is. I think all Oxford men (Anglicans I mean) must have a secret satisfaction that one, taken from the gremium Universitatis, should be the winning horse at Rome. And as to Catholics, why whatever is, is right — and I suppose he will do a great deal of good in his generation, if he has life.

Then again what is coming off at Rome? Spain, the spes ultima of a system which emphatically rests itself upon the Kings and governments of the earth, has changed her policy — and how is the Pope to keep his sovereignty, unless his people pronounce in his favour?[4] Perhaps they will — if they will not, it seems likely they would, at least after a while, did he leave them — and certainly to me, cogitanti sæpenumero, as Lord Brougham is so fond of saying, it seems better to trust in the future contrition of the Romans, than in

---

[1] *The Privilege of Religious Confessions in English Courts of Justice, considered in a letter to a friend,* London 1865.

[2] Constance Kent went to confession to H. M. Wagner, the High Church Vicar of Brighton. He induced her to make a public avowal to the police that she had murdered her small brother, but he declined to say how he had persuaded her to come forward. Constance Kent was tried for the murder on 21 July at Salisbury, but, since she pleaded guilty, the matter of her confession to Wagner was not pursued.

[3] Newman wrote on the autograph, [[I said otherwise to Keble and Pusey in Sept 1865]]. Gladstone was defeated at Oxford University by a combination of Conservatives and of Churchmen disappointed at his support of Liberal governments and of measures against the privileged position of the Church of England. On the other hand, Keble, Pusey and others, who remembered his services to the Anglican Church, took his side.

[4] In July, Spain recognised the new Kingdom of Italy and sent an ambassador to Florence.

the present patronage of Gallic or Austrian or Spanish bayonets. And now I have no room to hunt out other events and am

Ever Yours affectly in Xt   John H Newman

TO MISS M. R. GIBERNE

The Oratory Bm July 21. 1865

My dear Sister M. Pia

By this time you must have heard of your dear Sister's death. Tho', as having given yourself to your Lord, you have died to the world, still it must pain you deeply, for invisible ties connect us with the earth while we are in it. To me of course, it is very touching as throwing me back to the thought of her husband, and snapping remembrances while it re-kindles them.[1]

I had heard from her lately. I sent her the part of the Apologia in which Mr Mayers was spoken of. She sent me a letter of a friend of my brother's upon it, Mr Capel, and a review in a very kind spirit from some Scotch Magazine. Then I sent her the whole work — but she has been from home, as she wrote me word, and had not had time to read it. I had said Mass for her the very day of her death — the feast of our Lady of Mount Carmel.

I hope you are well all through this hot weather — and that you are supported by the full consolations of the Almighty Paraclete amid the many privations and trials in which you live

Ever Yours most affctly in Xt   John H Newman of the Oratory

Sister M. Pia

TO T. F. WETHERELL

The Oratory Birmingham July 21/65

My dear Wetherell

In my hurry last night I left out the question of my word 'judgment.' Of course it must be altered, since the Bishops use the word of the whole passage.[2]

I hope you understood that in speaking of what I wrote as an 'illustration' I meant to bring out that it was my *interpretation* of the passage with reference to yours — not as if it could be used as it stood.

Very sincerely Yours John H. Newman

[1] In 1824 Sarah Giberne married Walter Mayers, who died in 1828. He had been a master at Ealing School, and in 1816 was 'the human means' of Newman's first conversion. Mayers was appointed Rector of Over Worton, near Banbury, and in the church there Newman preached his first sermon on 23 June 1824. Sarah Mayers married again, and became Mrs Burmiston. She died on 16 July 1865, and was buried in the grave of her first husband at Over Worton.
[2] See the beginning of Newman's letter of 15 July to Wetherell.

SUNDAY 23 JULY 1865   sultry weather
MONDAY 24 JULY   sang Lady A. Acheson's black mass — went to Rednal
TUESDAY 25 JULY   returned from Rednal   sultry

TO T. F. WETHERELL

Rednall July 25/65

My dear Wetherell

I am quite content with your final settlement of the troublesome passage[1]

Yrs very sincerely John H Newman

P.S. This is sad about Acton, if true.[2]

WEDNESDAY 26 JULY 1865   attended black mass at Cathedral for Mr Flanagan[3] admitted John Norris to his first Probation.

TO LADY CHATTERTON

The Oratory Birmingham July 27. 1865

My dear Lady Chatterton

I am greatly flattered by the message you conveyed to me from Mr Dering.[4] It has been only an accident, which has occasioned my not conveying to you and him my thanks with less delay. I shall read his poems with the truest pleasure. Pray be so good as to say all this to him from me, especially about the dedication.

Should any thing bring me into your neighbourhood, I will most gladly avail myself of the opportunity you give me to visit him and you. At present I have no prospect of leaving home, which I find it difficult to do on many accounts.[5]

I am, with many thanks, Yours, My dear Lady Chatterton

Very sincerely John H Newman

Lady Chatterton

[1] Wetherell wrote on 23 July that Macmullen had accepted it.
[2] Acton's election at Bridgnorth was disputed, and he was unseated on petition in 1866.
[3] Thomas Flanagan (1814–65), Canon of Birmingham and author of *A History of the Church in England, from the earliest times to the Re-establishment of the Hierarchy in 1850*, London 1857, died on 21 July. Cf. letter of 28 July 1857.
[4] Lady Chatterton wrote on 18 July to ask if she might send some poems written by her husband, Edward Dering. He wished to dedicate them to Newman and thus 'to ask shelter for a dwarf in a giant's house.' The poems do not appear to have been published. See letter of 10 Sept. to Lady Chatterton.
[5] When inviting Newman, Lady Chatterton explained that her husband was on the verge of becoming a Catholic, and wished for his advice. See diary for 20 Sept.

FRIDAY 28 JULY 1865   workmen, painters, bricklayers etc in the house   first change of weather

SATURDAY 29 JULY   fine and enjoyable

TO HENRY BITTLESTON

The Oy Bm July 29/65

Private

My dear Henry

I wish you would look at Ward's letter in the Register of this day.[1] I am much tempted, almost as a matter of duty, to write to the Editor as follows:-

'Sir, A sentence in a letter inserted in your Paper of last Saturday ⟨Saturday the 29th⟩ runs thus:- "The recent Encyclical and Syllabus are, beyond question, the Church's infallible utterance." I beg leave to say that I do not subscribe to this proposition

John H Newman'

My reason is, charity to a number of persons, chiefly laymen, whom such doctrine will hurry in the direction of Arnold.[2] There must be a stop put to such extravagances.

My difficulty is, lest to do so, should bring some blow on the Oratory.

I write to you, however, principally for this: viz I must have a good theological opinion on my side, and whom am I to consult? It strikes Ambrose, that Stanislas is the best person — but then, if he knows it is *I* who ask, he will not give me an unbiassed judgment.

So I want you to write to him calling his attention to the letter — and asking him whether it would be theologically safe for you (H.B.) or some other priest to put the above letter into the Paper. If he could be got to get Fr O'Reilly's opinion in confidence (not on the doctrine, but on the Catholic's liberty of denying Ward's proposition as it stands) so much the better. E.g. if Fr O'Reilly could see *my* letter, and were asked simply 'is that letter admissible Catholically, or is it not?'[3]

A more dignified way would be, if some layman wrote to me, calling my

[1] The *Weekly Register* had criticised W. G. Ward for supporting at the general election the 'no popery' conservative Sir Charles Locock, who made a bigoted speech about convents. Locock was standing for the Isle of Wight, where he was defeated by the liberal, Sir John Simeon. Ward wrote a long letter to the *Weekly Register*, (29 July 1865), p. 65, to defend himself. He disapproved strongly of Sir John Simeon's religious views. During the election, Simeon had explained that, although a Catholic, he was not a mere puppet, and had boasted that he was one of the very few who had declined to sign the memorial in favour of the temporal power of the pope, eighteen months earlier. Ward, after recounting this, said, 'Now the recent Encyclical and Syllabus are beyond question, the Church's infallible utterance,' and 'in the Syllabus the Pope expressly teaches that "all Catholics ought *most firmly to retain*" the precise doctrine which Sir John boasts of denying.' Ward thought a Protestant M.P. better than a Catholic one who acted upon principles which 'have been authoritatively condemned by the Church's infallible voice.'

[2] Arnold had left the Church on the ground that he could no longer believe in its infallibility. See letter of 4 June to him.

[3] See letter of 4 Aug. to Bittleston.

attention to the Proposition, and asking what I thought of it, and my writing my letter in answer to him, and *his* putting it in the Paper. But this is a matter for future consideration. Ignatius has had his liver wrong, but a dose of medicine, administered by Dr Evans, has set it right

Ever Yrs affly J H N

The Revd F Bittleston

SUNDAY 30 JULY 1865   Ignatius not well.

TO F. J. WATT

July 30/65

Dear Sir

I beg to thank you for your letter; and have no difficulty in answering the point to which you draw my attention and which is the cause of your writing to me[1]

To use your own words, you merely write to me to tell me that Miss Bretherton was fully aware of your antecedents. I assure you I knew this, and I do not think that I have said any thing to her or to Mrs Bretherton to imply that you had not been candid with her

I have the greatest good will towards you, and it would rejoice me to perceive that you are worthy of such a young lady as Miss Bretherton

J H N

MONDAY 31 JULY 1865   Painting and Washing the House began — and dividing Playroom. began fires cold wet. wind NW

TUESDAY 1 AUGUST   Ambrose and William set off for Scotland   a fire

WEDNESDAY 2 AUGUST   a fire   glass has fallen from about 75 to near 60

TO AMBROSE ST JOHN

The Oy Bm Aug 3/65

My dear Ambrose

I am glad you have such beautiful weather. I send the book by this post.[2] Stokes *is* in Mme de Mussy house, so it is all a maresnest.[3] Allday's letter has

---

[1] See letter of 9 July to Mrs Bretherton. On 24 July Eleanor Bretherton forwarded to Newman the letter of 21 July from Watt, to which Newman is replying. Watt spoke of his 'London dissipations', and explained that he had told her every fact of his past life. Only after this had they become engaged.

[2] St John was in Edinburgh, and asked for *Black's Guide through Scotland* to be sent to him, to the Royal George Hotel, Perth.

[3] John Scott Stokes had gone to France as tutor to Philippe de Mussy, a boy at the Oratory School.

come back to you from the dead letter office — so you are as you were. I inclose a letter which has come for you.

You don't suspect I can have much news. Mr Tylee, or whatever he [[is called is]] coming on Saturday in order to see Oscott etc. I suppose he must go into Miss Mitchell's, we are in such a state here. Mr Towneley has written to ask whether Richard will be able to pass the Balliol examination *next Easter*, if he goes to a private Tutor. I have said 'Yes, if he employs the interval here —' but *I wish you would* write me a line to tell me *how* (not relatively but positively) he got thro' the Norfolk examination — for the subjects were the same as the Balliol.[1]

The Seville Oratory has been burned — and they have written to us to subscribe on the ground that they *have no endowments*. Perhaps they will give *us* something for a Rednall school house on a like reason.

Love to William Ever Yours affly J H N

TO HENRY BEDFORD (ANGLICAN CURATE)

The Oratory Birmingham August 4. 1865

My Dear Sir

I feel the kind confidence you show me in sending me your most interesting and painful letter — but such pain as you are suffering is your price for that inestimable benefit which I doubt not God reserves for you, admission to Catholic communion.[2]

I cannot doubt that it is your duty to make up your mind on the subject without reference to worldly matters — though of course such uncertainty, as you describe, is part of your trial. You do not speak distinctly on the point, but I take you to imply, that, were it not for this difficulty, there is nothing strong enough to keep you back.[3]

It is easy to give good advice. I can only say, that, when I joined the Catholic Church, I had not so much as the sum you name as having yourself — nor would it be considered a small sum by most of my friends, *supposing* you have a vocation to the Priesthood. But no one can tell at present whether you will or will not have one — and I don't think it would be safe to take it for granted. And then, as to time of preparation, it varies with the individual. I was myself ordained within two years — but Dr Manning, I think, in only a week or two. So, I *believe*, was Mr Sibthorp. Others have been kept some years before they even had sacred orders. Some were found in the event to have no vocation.

---

[1] The Norfolk examination was for a prize of £20 in books, presented to the Oratory School by the Duke of Norfolk.

[2] Bedford, who took orders in 1854, and was Curate at Foxearth, Sudbury, had been a High Churchman for many years.

[3] In replying on 7 Aug., Bedford wrote anxiously about his prospects as a Catholic, 'if I had no Vocation to the Priesthood, or from illness could not study sufficiently, I might be left nearly destitute.' He concluded, 'Were I *sure* it was God's will, I should not hesitate a moment.'

I should have thought what you wanted was *rest*; and that it might really be of service to your health, to remain without work or prospect for a while — till your mind had recovered its tone. But of course I do not pretend to do more than make a conjecture. I am not sure that you could not get on fairly on the interest of £1200.

Certainly I will gladly remember you in my prayers — and shall be most glad to answer any other question you wish to ask me[1]

    I am, My dear Sir, Very truly Yours John H Newman

The Revd Henry Bedford

TO HENRY BITTLESTON

            The Oy Bm Aug 4/65

My dear H

Thank you for your and S's [Stanislas Flanagan] letters. Of course it puts an end to the whole scheme.[2]

1. As to my bringing out my views, it is absurd.

2. I fully think with S, and have ever said, that we must wait patiently for a re-action.

3. But if there are no protests, there will be no re-action.

4. I meant simply a Protest; and that, as one out of a number of accumulating pebbles which at length would fill the urna divina.[1]

5. I feel *extremely* (tho' I am only conjecturing) for a number of laymen, especially converts — and for those who are approaching to the Church — who find all this a grievous scandal

---

[1] See letter of 10 Aug.

[2] After receiving Newman's letter of 29 July, Bittleston wrote at once to Flanagan, who replied to him from Ireland on 1 Aug. that he had not been surprised at W. G. Ward's letter, which maintained the infallibility of the Encyclical *Quanta cura* in view of his articles in *D R*. 'In the last number he gives quotations from the "Mandements" of several French Bishops who seem undoubtedly to have adopted his views on the subject. Then Dr Murray of Maynooth in his new volume of the Tract "De Ecclesiâ" treats ex professo of this proposition and maintains (if I remember rightly) that though it is not precisely "de fide" it is as close as possible upon it, and is "definibilis de fide" — He says that Muratori and Chrismann are the only theologians who have been on the other side . . .

As to receiving and adhering to Ward's and Murray's doctrine in my own mind I find it, according to my present knowledge, quite impossible to do so, and I conceive that I am at perfect liberty to reject it without any temerity. However I believe the general feeling of the Bishops and others to be so much the other way just at this moment that a man who should openly assert his liberty to dissent from their (Ward's and Murray's) doctrine would be looked on with great suspicion . . .'

As to going into the matter for the sake of others, Flanagan added, 'It is of immense importance that some one should do it – up to this no one whatever (so far as I know) has attempted to answer Ward or Murray. On the whole, just at this time, I think it would be imprudent for you, as a Father of the Oratory, to write such a letter as you propose. If *I* could do it *well* I would do it — But even if *I* did it, all that know me, would be sure to say I was a pupil of the Father's [Newman] and make him answerable for my views. The only course I see is to be patient and wait for the day of reaction — In Ireland such questions trouble no one. They have no conception of the intellectual difficulties . . .'

[3] Cf. Horace, *Satires* I, ix, 30.

6. But further, which is a practical point, *if I am asked*, did this convert, that inquirer, or some controversialist appeal to me and ask me, *what am* I to say?

7. *What then am I to say?* This might come upon me any day suddenly.

It is best then to wait patiently and not to forestall a crisis but it is quite certain that *any day* I may be obliged to give an answer. I really do wish I had a distinct opinion given me as my safe guard, — in confidence of course.

But, after all, the priests all thro' the country will follow Ward, if he is let alone — and how much *more* difficult will a collision be ten years hence than now!

I may not see that time — and I should care nothing for any personal obloquy which might come on me now, *so that I were sure of my ground*. How very hard a man like Fr O'Reilly will not at least in confidence speak out! Unless he has changed, I *know* he could not simply subscribe that sentence[1]

Ever Yrs affly J H N

Ambrose and Wm [William] are in Scotland.

TO JOHN KEBLE

The Oratory Birmingham August 4. 1865

My dear Keble

You must not fancy I am forgetting to avail myself of your welcome wish, because I have not yet made my way to you. I find it very difficult to leave home — just now, impossible. As it is vacation time, most of our party are away — working hard, this is their only chance of a holy day in the year. I am one of the few, who are here to keep on the duties of the Church etc. Moreover, the house, as empty of its natural inmates, is filled with plasterers, bricklayers, painters, carpenters, who are having their innings — and it does not do to let the place be simply in the hands of Brummagem workmen.

I don't like to promise any thing — but it is my full intention, when relieved of all this superintendence, to move down to Hursley.

So Gladstone has left you — He came when I had ceased to be an Oxford man — so I never had him.[2] A very painful separation, certainly, both for him and for all of you. Yet, really, he does go great lengths — and I cannot help feeling that the anxiety to keep him, on the part of such persons as yourself, was quite as much on his own account as on account of the University. He has lost his tether, now that the Conservatives have got rid of him — and won't he go lengths? I was pained at his 'Keep moving' speech.[3] In saying all

[1] See *Diff* II, pp. 262–98 on the Encyclical and the Syllabus, and p. 338 for O'Reilly's opinion, given in 1874.
[2] Gladstone was Member of Parliament for Oxford University from 1847 until his defeat at the General Election in July 1865. Keble supported him to the last.
[3] Gladstone after his rejection at Oxford, was able to come forward as a candidate for South Lancashire, and as he declared in his election speech on 18 July, he was now 'unmuzzled.' In

this, I am putting myself in your place, (for I suppose he will do good to *us*) but I declare, I should have been in great perplexity, had I been an Oxford man, how to vote. I suppose I should certainly in the event have voted for him — but most grudgingly. None of his friends seem to trust his politics — indeed he seems not to know himself what are his land marks and his necessary limits.

Don't fancy I am saying this without the greatest respect and liking for him (though I scarcely know him personally) — All one can say is that the great deluge is pouring in — and his boat is as good as another's. Who *is* there to trust?

It is curious that both members for the University should be Oriel men — (for Sir W. is so, in spite of Allsouls) and the House has not one. One reason for taking Sir Robert Inglis, recollect, was his *being* Ch Ch[1]

Ever Yrs affly John H Newman

TO AMBROSE ST JOHN

The Oy Bm Augst 5. 1865

My dear Ambrose

I have come to one fixed opinion about the Eunuchus. It is no use attempting it, *unless we have a good Pythias.* She is the life of the play, the sustaining power, during the latter third part, and it will fall flat and be a failure unless her part is done well. This is my immoveable opinion. You have then to *find* a Pythias — *it must not be a tall boy* — and must be a lively one with the vis comica — it is *no use* to attempt it if you cannot find one. But what junior knows Latin enough? I have thought of Edward Bellasis. When put on his metal he can do a great deal. It must be a boy who can jump about the stage. She begins with 'O lepidissimum caput,' and almost drives thereby Chremes off it. I wish Pope senior could be got to throw off his woodenness and do it. But I should not dare to begin with any boy whom I could not cast off if he failed. Could Pope laugh without intermission for ten minutes? There is the test. You must take three or four boys together, and set them off as a trial one against the other.[2]

his speech after the results had been declared on 22 July, he said, 'If you ask me for a political motto, in my search for one I should be very apt to borrow it from . . . the policeman. When the policeman in London . . . finds a number of people blocking the footpath, he jogs them gently by the elbow, and just says, "Keep moving." . . . that motto . . . I presume to think is a sound motto in political affairs.'

[1] Christ Church, 'The House.' Newman is referring to the famous election in 1829, when Sir Robert Inglis was put up against Sir Robert Peel, and represented Oxford University until 1854. In July 1865 Sir William Heathcote was reelected and Gathorne Hardy took Gladstone's place. Both were Oriel men, and the former, who had been a Fellow of All Souls, was made an honorary Fellow in 1858.

[2] Terence's *Eunuchus* was adapted by Newman, and became *Pincerna*, 'The Cup-Bearer.' It was performed in May 1866, when Arthur Gould took the part of Pythias, and Archdale Taylor Pope that of Phaedria. St John replied to Newman on 12 August 1865 rejecting Bellasis as 'too flighty' to be Pythias.

Augst 8. I have kept this till I got your direction. We have a Gordon coming, half a Spaniard, age 14 — but I have taken all precautions before agreeing to it.[1] The confusion of the Corridors is at the height. Ignatius went yesterday. Henry returns on Saturday. Norris sends me a very pleasant letter, he stops till the 19th. Godwin is away. Bateman goes for a few days on Monday Love to Wm

Ever Yours affly J H N

SUNDAY 6 AUGUST 1865   Mr Tylee about this time for a day sleeping in Number 68.

TO R. W. CHURCH

The Oratory Birmingham August 6. 1865

My dear Church

I suppose the two little books will go to you by tonight's post. I have made a great fuss about them.[2] It is a sad thing that you have lost Gladstone — yet as much for his sake as for yours. He is a bold man — how could he expect to succeed after almost giving up the Irish Established Church? it was throwing down the gauntlet, and all that could be said was, that, as a sitting member had never been displaced, he did *not* give the University an opportunity of displacing him, or throw down the gauntlet, and that they might have let it alone. But then he knew that already on former occasions there had been an attempt to displace him and that therefore, as far as his re-election went, he was in the same boat with Sir R. Peel in 1829 — and so it *was* a challenge. And, pace tua, I don't see how any one, who wished the Established Church of Ireland to continue, *could* vote for him.[3] I am led on therefore to think that those who voted for him have no great love of the Irish Establishment, in spite of Archbishop Trench. And, should this be so, I should not wonder at it, for I really do think it does the Church of England harm, and that in fact it is the weak point of the Church of England — and the union between the two churches was made, without the latter being consulted, as a bribe to the Orangemen. In saying all this, I am without bias — for I doubt very much if Catholics would be benefited by the downfall of the Irish Establishment. It (The downfall) is very likely to weaken the attachment of the Catholic laity

---

[1] Arthur Leo Gordon came to the Oratory School on 12 Sept. 1865 and left in Dec. 1867.
[2] These were copies of Newman's edition of Terence's *Phormio*, and his English translation of it.
[3] Gladstone, who had previously been returned unopposed, was obliged to contest his Oxford University seat in 1859, when he joined the Liberals and became Chancellor of the Exchequer in Palmerston's ministry. On 28 March 1865, when a Resolution calling for the disestablishment of the Church of Ireland was proposed, Gladstone opposed it, but solely on the ground that the time was not yet ripe. Archbishop Trench of Dublin was a supporter of Gladstone, but thought the danger of disestablishment was remote.

in towns to their hierarchy. If then a man thinks all this, he need not quarrel with Gladstone on this score.

But his views on Reform are another hitch. If he really *had* views, it would be a relief to many who now look so anxiously at him — but he gives no indication of having a limit which he cannot pass.

Now in saying all this I am not saying I should not have voted for him, had I had a vote — but I should have done so with great grumbling. And I was very sorry to read his speech, since his severance with Oxford, about 'keeping moving,' which, if the real expression of his views, was most un-satisfactory.[1] All this is apropos of the Phormio.

Ever yours affecty John H. Newman.

MONDAY 7 AUGUST 1865   Ignatius off for his holiday? And Mr Stevens at Bosco

TO MRS WILLIAM FROUDE

The Oratory Bm Augst 7/65

I was with Rogers for two days on occasion of the Archbishop's consecra-tion. Church came up to meet me. We had a very pleasant time. It was always Rogers's fault; yet it is difficult to find fault with a high standard. But he seems to me softened with years. And then the development of liberalism, and the great divisions in the Anglican Church may make him more patient. His note of the Church is sanctity; and he has been accustomed to apply it savagely. Nothing could be more easy and familiar than his manner with me now. My surmise is, that he thinks me a profoundly sceptical thinker, who, determined on not building on an abyss, have, by mere strength of will, bridged it over, and built upon my bridge — but that my bridge, like Mahomet's coffin, is self suspended, by the action of the will — but I may be putting it too strong. He himself is not nearly so sceptical as I had feared. I like Lady Rogers very much.

Ever Yours affly John H Newman of the Oratory

Mrs Froude

TO H. LA SERRE

The Oratory, Birmingham, August 7th. 1865.

My dear M la Serre,

Some one told me the other day that you had done me the great compli-ment of translating a portion of my Apologia, and that it was done very well. But I did not at all understand, you seriously contemplated the work — else,

---

[1] See letter of 4 Aug. to Keble.

I should have dissuaded you. Not that I did not feel that you would make a very good translation, — (and this is a great praise to give to any one, for I think to translate an English style into French is one of the most difficult of works) — but because two translations are already made. One of them is already published at M.P.M. Laroche's 66 Rue Bonaparte.[1] The other is made from my second edition, and under my sanction, which I gave to the translator about a year ago. I am expecting to hear of its publication every day.[2] Under these circumstances, tho' I am truly sorry to lose the advantage of your skill in translation, I cannot advise you to continue this work.

I am perfectly sure that those boys, who gave you most trouble, will, as life goes on, repent of their boyishness, and feel that they owe you a good deal — and that, should they, when they grow up, ever meet you, it will be a very great pleasure to them, and be a very joyful day.

Father Mills and Caswall are the only two of our party here at present — and they desire their kindest regards.

Believe to be, my dear M. la Serre, Very sincerely yours in Jesus Christ,

John H. Newman of the Oratory.

M. H. la Serre.

TUESDAY 8 AUGUST 1865   Austin, I, and Edward the only three in the house   on the whole wet — some fine days

TO JOHN NORRIS

The Oratory Bm Augst 9. 1865

My dear John

I was very glad to hear from you — and that you had had so pleasant an excursion, and had gained so much good from it.[3] By all means stay till Saturday week, as you propose — and come back, as you are likely to do, strong, well, and happy.

Frs Edward and Austin are my only companions here now, besides plasterers, painters, bricklayers, and carpenters. It will be a difficult job to get it done by September 1. when there is to be a three day retreat for the servants etc. Fr Henry returns next Saturday, when Fr Edward goes. Your excursion was in the rainy week — but the pleasure of good company turns bad or good weather equally into pleasant

Ever Yours affectly in St Philip John H Newman of the Oratory

[1] *De l'Anglicanisme au Catholicisme ou histoire de ma vie et de mes croyances religieuses,* published by Casterman of Tournai in 1865, whose Paris agent Newman names.
[2] *Histoire de mes opinions religieuses,* translated by Georges du Pré de Saint-Maur, Paris 1866. Cf. letter of 12 Aug. 1864 to Monsell.
[3] John Norris had been touring the Lake District with friends from Ushaw.

TO HENRY BEDFORD (ANGLICAN CURATE)

The Oratory Bm Augst 10. 1865

My dear Sir

The books you speak of as having are very good ones. 'Grounds of the Faith' is the only one which I do not recollect having seen.[1] I would recommend you to get the Catechismus Romanus or Catechism of the Council of Trent. It is of the first authority — indeed, it is *authoritative*. It would show you what we do not hold, and would give you full instruction in what we do in preparation of your being a Catholic. You will be very glad to have mastered it. It is not controversial. The little Manual called 'The Garden of the Soul' would be very useful to you also.

When I spoke of your needing rest, I was thinking of your joining the Church — I meant to say that, though you did nothing at once and did not begin at once to ask yourself whether you had a vocation for the Priesthood, the quiet itself would be of great use to you. But I am far from dissuading you from giving up Anglican duty at once — indeed, I think it would be both natural and serviceable to you to be free from any such tie.

The climate of Rome is very peculiar. It has been almost a medicine to Brownlow — to others it is in one way or another almost poison.[2] I was never ill there — but I don't like the climate for all that. It would be a great thing for you to be near your friend. I doubt whether the living is cheap; and I know it is very bad. Robert Wilberforce was killed either by the climate or food, or both. A Milord Anglais *will* be served well — but seminarists, and persons who live quietly, are badly off. Could any medical man tell you whether Rome would suit you? there could not be a better plan, if it would.[3]

Very truly Yours John H Newman

The Revd H. Bedford

TO SIMEON WILBERFORCE O'NEILL

The Oratory Birmingham August 11. 1865

My dear Sir

I will answer your questions as distinctly as I can.[4]

---

[1] Bedford wrote on 7 Aug., 'The only Catholic books I have by me are as follows. Lockhart's Popular Lectures [on the Catholic Religion]. Clifton Tracts. Volume 1. [The Reformation]. Bossuet on the Church. Grounds of the Faith. Brownlow's Letter [*How and Why I became a Catholic*, Torquay 1864]. Missal.'

[2] Bedford was a friend of Brownlow, who was studying for the priesthood in Rome.

[3] Bedford, who was anxious about his health, held various curacies during the ensuing years, and did not go even physically to Rome.

[4] O'Neill had been assistant master at Eton, and curate to T. T. Carter at Cleaver, then to W. J. Butler at Wantage. He realised the need for missionary brotherhoods and early in 1865 went to live with R. M. Benson at Cowley. At the end of 1866 O'Neill became one of the three original members of the Cowley Fathers. On 8 Aug. 1865 he wrote from 3 Malcolm Street, Cambridge, to ask the questions which Newman proceeds to answer.

'In the case of an Anglocatholic Priest being received into the Roman Catholic Church,

1. must he be baptized and confirmed?'

Subject to the answer to the next question, I answer — Yes.

In baptism, however, the ceremonies, which are considerable, are all omitted — and nothing is necessary but the private use of the words, 'Ego te baptizo in nomine etc'

In confirmation the whole service is used, but it scarcely consists of more than the sacramental words.

2. 'Unconditionally.?'

With an expressed condition in baptism. 'Si non es baptizatus, ego te etc' — and without any expressed condition, in confirmation.

3. 'If he wishes to serve God as a priest, must he receive Holy Orders again at the hands of a R.C. Bishop?' he must.

4. 'are they conferred unconditionally?' there is no expressed condition.

5. 'Is he obliged to disbelieve in the Real Presence in the Eucharist of the English Church?' Certainly not.

6. 'And in the validity of the English Absolutions?' I cannot say that he is *obliged*; but, putting aside the question of the validity of Anglican Orders, comes the question of jurisdiction. We hold that orders confers the power of absolution, but this power cannot be exercised till subjects are given to the ordained person *in order to* the exercise of his gift; — so that his absolutions, till he has a people, are not only not licit, but not valid. The absence then of jurisdiction in a priest is an obex to the effect of his absolutions; and, I think I should say, more, viz that, not only the effect of the Sacrament is not present in such an absolution — but that the Sacrament itself non conficitur, even though the penitent had contrition and made confession. But this is a nice point, and I am not theologian enough to answer it. It might be objected, since there is both matter and form, and intention, and a priest really ordained, why is there not the Sacrament? but any how, without jurisdiction, that is, without power over subjects, the sacrament has not *effect*, as, e.g. the effect of baptism does not take place, (except as regards the character,) in the case of an hypocritical recipient. N.B. The words of the Council of Trent are '*nullius momenti*' absolutionem eam esse, quam etc[1]

I have now answered your questions as simply and exactly as I can, but perhaps some explanation is necessary – so I add the following:-

They are very jealous at Rome of any such custom of baptizing Protestants on their reconciliation. For the Church has right over all baptized persons; and, to say that the English are unbaptized would be to destroy those rights in their case. Accordingly great difficulty was made, when the Vicars Apostolic in England first wished [to] introduce conditional baptism. But it was simply necessary. I had quite abundant proof in the Anglican Church myself, of the

---

[1] 'nullius momenti absolutionem eam esse debere, quam sacerdos in eum profert, in quem . . . non habet jurisdictionem.' *Denzinger-Schönmetzer*, 1686.

extreme doubtfulness of many baptisms administered even by high churchmen — the cap, not the infant being baptized — and among the poor, no
distinction was made between Anglican baptism and a dissenting rite of
initiation in which no water was used — so that the poor always *said* they were
baptized, when on examination in various instances it was found out that they
were not. Since that time, Mr Goring's views (have I the right name?), then
extensively held, have been recognised as allowable —[1] And, as to great Towns,
I am afraid to think how large a portion of (e.g.) Birmingham people are
simply unbaptized. Now therefore the rule is that every convert is conditionally baptized.

Conditions in the Sacrament, as *expressed*, are not primitive. The first
conditional baptism on record occurs, I think, in the history of St Boniface,
Apostle of Germany. Conditional absolution was not known till the middle
ages. I am not speaking from book, but from memory. Yet from the first,
conditional administration must have at times been necessary. Hence it is to
be inferred that it was conditional in the *intention* of the administrator. So it
sometimes is in the case of other sacraments, as confirmation and orders, now.
This will appear if I mention what the late Cardinal Wiseman once told me.
Soon after I was received, I felt the objection to receiving ordination, which he
proposed to me, which was natural in one who could not say for certain that
the Anglican Orders were invalid. He asked whether it was not *safer* to be
ordained, if there was, as assuredly there ws, a doubt whether they were valid.
And then he told me the following story. Bishop Bramston, Vicar Apostolic
of the London district in the early part of the century, was a convert. After he
became Bishop, (or Priest, I forget which) doubt was thrown upon his baptism.
Either he had not been conditionally baptized, or (which is far less likely)
doubt was thrown upon some circumstance of his Catholic Baptism. He had all
the (Catholic) sacraments, i.e. Baptism, Confirmation, and the various Orders
repeated. Dr Wiseman said, we are not asking of *you* more than was asked of a
Catholic Ecclesiastic. His baptism being doubtful, all the Sacraments were in
his case doubtful. I asked, whether they were administered to him in a conditional form. He said, No, this was never done except in the case of Baptism
and Penance, and he gave as a reason, as regards Orders, the peculiarity of the
Service of Ordination for Priests, which is such, that the place in it could not
be fixed upon, where the conditional clause should be introduced. Then I
asked him, Did the ordaining Bishop make the *intention* of administering
conditionally? he said No; ⟨(We may say the Church makes the intention, as
we speak of children being baptized in the faith of the church.)⟩ but it was
open to the *recipient* (I *think* he said so) to do so — and he went on to state of
the case of Sir — Trelawney (I think) a convert at Rome, who, though he had
never received Catholic orders, — well, I must not finish my sentence, I am

[1] The decision of the Judicial Committee of the Privy Council in 1850, in the case of G. C.
Gorham, recognised that it was not necessary for a member of the Church of England to
believe in baptismal regeneration.

writing down a convers[at]ion which took place 19 years ago, and what I think he went on to say was so extraordinary, that I do not like to trust my memory.[1]

I should add a remark from what I have said above. Since Dr Bramston because of his doubtful baptism was re-ordained (conditionally) ⟨in intention⟩ after receiving even Catholic orders, it is quite clear that our Bishops would never be satisfied with Anglican Orders, from the very fact that they require conditional baptism in the case of all Anglicans. So that conditional baptism is ipso facto a practical disavowal of Anglican Orders. Excuse my hasty penmanship

I am, Dear Sir, Yours truly John H Newman[2]

SATURDAY 12 AUGUST 1865   Henry returned   glass keeping up several degrees above 60

TO JAMES PAGET

The Oratory Birmingham August 14. 1865

My dear Sir,

It has given me great pleasure to receive your letter. I ventured to send you my book, not as supposing you would have found time to read it, but as a satisfaction to myself in any way to show my sense of your kindness in having kept my name in remembrance after an accidental meeting with me so many years ago. I feel then the more the compliment of your having given your attention to it, and am gratified by your judgment upon its contents.[3]

Also I have to thank you for your important testimony on the question of

---

[1] Newman's conversation seems to have been that of 20 Nov. 1845 with Bishop Griffiths, Vicar Apostolic of the London District. On 18 April 1847 Newman wrote to Mrs Bowden, 'Sir H. Trelawny an English clergyman who joined the Church of Rome was ordained there on the admitted understanding that he considered English orders valid, and submitted to the form only for the greater satisfaction and security of other minds.' Volume XI, p. 151.

[2] On 12 Aug. O'Neill thanked Newman for his letter and said: 'I am a Catholic in heart and conviction and have been so since I first read some of your later books — some 15 months since. But imagining that if I should join the Catholic Church it would be necessary for me to deny the Presence of my Lord where I had so often worshiped Him, it seemed to me as if I should have to pass through infidelity to gain Rome and I resolved to put away the controversy from my thoughts, and to pray for the submission of the English Church to the Holy See.

Now I think my course is plain and that I ought to leave as soon as possible what I know to be a schismatical church. I have written to my spiritual director about it.' O'Neill then asked if it would be possible to make a retreat 'at some religious house at Birmingham before being admitted into the Catholic Church?' Newman invited him to come to the Oratory in Sept. and on 15 Aug. O'Neill accepted, adding, 'But it is very difficult to be so presumptious as to separate from a host of better and wiser friends. If God would put it into the hearts of one or two to come over with me, we could escape more easily.' On 21 Aug. he wrote that he could wait no longer, and since Newman could not yet give him hospitality, 'I have thought it better to go to London and ask the Fathers of the S. J. [Society of Jesus] to take me in for a time until I am admitted to the Catholic Church.'

After joining the Cowley Fathers O'Neill became an heroic missionary in India.

[3] For the first meeting with Paget see diary for 18 and 19 Nov. 1845. Newman sent him a copy of the second edition of *Apo.*, for which he wrote his thanks on 13 Aug.

the possibility of speech without the use of the tongue.[1] I wonder whether in many other languages besides Latin and its derivatives the word for 'language' is lingua. I forget what it is in Hebrew, but I see that the translation of Gen. xi 'The whole earth was of one language,' is in the Vulgate 'unius *labii*.' This, however, is nothing to the point. I am very glad to receive your information, and shall keep your letter as bearing on what I have written, quite understanding, at the same time, that you are speaking to a fact, apart from all other considerations.

As men get older, they are necessarily more dependent upon professional skill; and, though I am very well just now, yet I am neither unmindful of the chances of the future, nor insensible to your friendliness in offering me your advice, should I need it.

I am, My dear Sir, Very truly Yours John H Newman

James Paget Esqr

TO AMBROSE ST JOHN

⌜The Oratory Bm August 14/65⌝

My dear A

⌜The first principle in an excursion is to be a heathen (except half an hour on days of obligation) else, why do you excur? So did I cure Gulielmo 4 years ago — and it is the only way.[2] You can't have every thing in the world — stay at home and be sober[3] — or go abroad and be a savage. But this time two years you did the same at Treves [[and Mayence]] etc. Is Scotland less pagan than the Rhine?

I send you my Prologue[4] — which implies the work is done — and, while you have been paganizans in Scotiâ I have been Christianizans in Terentio.

Towneley is coming back, but on my *engagement* that, if he comes Sept 25 and stops with us over Christmas, he shall in *January* pass the Balliol examination. Am I rash? of course, he is to *work*.

⌜Painters, plasterers, carpenters, and brick layers are four out of the [[ten]] plagues of Egypt,⌝ the frogs, the lice, the flies, and the locusts. ⌜Their first throw off was to be found in our private rooms,[5] e.g. in mine, — they said,

---

[1] On pp. 306–08 of *Apo.* the miracle of the African confessors, who spoke after their tongues had been cut out, was considered, and evidence adduced to show that the tongue was not necessary for articulate speech. Paget, who was the leading surgeon of the day, wrote that 'the whole tongue may certainly be taken away, and, within even some days, intelligible speech may be regained.' He gave an example in the case of a man on whom he had recently operated, but quoted it 'as a bare fact' and not 'as having any general bearing on the evidence for miracles.'

[2] St John wrote on 12 Aug., 'Mass is a great difficulty in Scotland you have to arrange for it beforehand, and it ties you to a place; and knocks up fishing and that sort of thing.' The holiday with Neville was at the end of July 1861.

[3] [[pious]]

[4] i.e. the Prologue to *Pincerna,* which Newman had expurgated.

[5] [[niduli]]

32

'out of curiosity.' They come and go almost at their pleasure. One sends for drink from the Ivy Bush in the forenoon, tumbles off a ladder, and breaks his eyebrow. They stop up the drains, white wash the closet-seats — and they never will go.

I know with what a touchy man I have to do, and am in some alarm. The Choir has struck, at the presence of Mr Emma-Webb's Arnold — and I have been obliged to suspend his presence at the Music till your return. I doubt not you will tell me I am lowering your authority with Mr Delany, Miss Blackburn and Company — but I was doing what I wished to be done to me, ⌐ when for *your* sake I did not let them strike, and for their sakes I did not force on them a man from whom they shrank.

⌐Henry is back — and Edward goes in a day or so —⌐ Henry met Rowe and heard of Hope Scott and Grassmere I think it *is* odd — but all the king's horses and all his men (viz the London Oratory) cannot give N. the material establishment for a large school — if his Father has left £10.000 and he chooses to risk it all on, or at the bottom of, the Mere, it is another matter, of course.[1]

⌐Bateman has gone off for 4 days — and we are expecting Godwin back hourly.

You must not be startled at the *name* of the play I am substituting for Eunuchus. It is quite as good as many of the names given to the plays by Menander, Terence, Plautus etc e.g. Historiographus, Litigantes, Avarus, Thesaurus, Commorientes, Unctrix, Insatiabilis, Tutor, Hæres, Pictor, Fidicen, Puteus, Ira, Agricola, Auriga, Nutrix, Vidua, Mercator, Miles, Rudens, Truculentus, Fretum, Fæneratrix, Hortulus, Cæcus. Accordingly I shall call it 'Pincerna' or 'the Cup bearer.'⌐

Ever Yrs affly J H N

⌐Love to Wm [[William]] — who, from his silence, I suppose is getting up St Alfonso.⌐

TUESDAY 15 AUGUST 1865 Mr Lambert called and dined as did Fr Whitty and Fr K [Kingdon] to recreation   very wet in morning

WEDNESDAY 16 AUGUST   Edward went for his holiday

THURSDAY 17 AUGUST   chilly, wet, unpropitious weather with some better days

[1] J. B. Rowe of the London Oratory was visiting Hope-Scott in Scotland, and was then going to Grassmere, where Nicholas Darnell was tutoring boys. This work Darnell hoped to develop until it became a public school. His father, Rector of Stanhope, Durham, a living of £5000 a year, died on 19 June.

TO JOHN HOSTAGE

The Oratory Bm August 17/65

My dear Mr Hostage

We are very sorry to lose your son. He will leave a very pleasant impression on our minds, and I hope you will kindly allow and urge him to pay us a visit now and then. I trust he acquitted himself well in his Law examination. I examined him previously, and he answered well, but a youth never rises to his mark on a trying occasion such as that

with much respect, I am, My dear Sir Very faithfully Yours

John H Newman

J H Hostage Esqr

FRIDAY 18 AUGUST 1865   Miss Munro at Mrs Wootten's

SATURDAY 19 AUGUST   Brother John (Norris) returned   Stanislas [Flanagan] in Bm [Birmingham] and dined one of these days, perhaps the 22nd, with Henry, Austin and me in refectory   a thick wet mist.

TUESDAY 22 AUGUST   a beautiful day

TO ANNA SWANWICK

The Oratory Birmingham August 22. 1865

My dear Madam,

It is not often that I have a greater pleasure than I felt on reading your letter, and I thank you heartily for it. I wrote to you as a stranger, and you have answered me in words (if you will let me so speak) which are those of a friend.[1] I call it a very friendly act to bear so long a remembrance of me and my volumes; (for long ago it must have been,) and when I have no personal claim on you for such a favour. And I assure you I thank God, if so it be, as you kindly say, that you have received any benefit from me. That He, our Loving Father, may ever watch over and guide you, is the sincere prayer of

Yours very truly

John H Newman

Miss A. Swanwick

[1] Anna Swanwick sent Newman a copy of her *The Agamemnon, Choephori, and Eumenides of Aeschylus translated into English Verse*, London 1865, writing on the flyleaf 'By Mr F. W. Newman's desire to The Very Revd. Dr J. H. Newman.' Anna Swanwick, who was a Unitarian, wrote on 14 Aug. to thank Newman for his favourable criticism of her book. She added: 'Before bidding you farewell I would fain thank you for the spiritual benefit which in by gone years I have derived from the perusal of your Sermons, many of which appeared to me to embody, in language glowing with poetic thought, some of the profoundest truths of Christianity. One more especially, entitled, "The Church the Home for the Lonely" [*P.S.* IV, p. 185], notwithstanding the lapse of time, dwells vividly in my remembrance.

Though not a member of your church I have listened with deep interest to your voice, while you have spoken of things spiritual and eternal.'

WEDNESDAY 23 AUGUST 1865   Mr Milward went to Oxford with the £2000 to settle the purchase of Hanley's land.[1]   bad weather again (Mrs etc Wilkinson left for London)? painting in the first floor corridor finished — and new matting begun laying down. Ambrose and Wm[William] returned.

TO HENRY JAMES COLERIDGE

The Oratory Bm August 23. 1865

My dear Fr Coleridge

I enclose the 'Sayings.' They will be too late for this Month, I suppose — but they will do for one month as well as for another.[2] I hope you feel yourself to be getting on

Yours very sincerely in Xt   John H Newman of the Oratory
The Revd Fr Coleridge

FRIDAY 25 AUGUST   Ambrose went off again to the South

TO WILLIAM KIRBY SULLIVAN

The Oratory Bm August 25/65

My dear Professor Sullivan

If you are coming to the Meeting of the Association here in the beginning of September, and want a house, pray let us supply one. We are expecting you. I trust I shall personally be able to play the host some part of the time, but the only holiday I can get this year is between September 4 and September 25. However, you shall be well taken care of, to the extent of your wishes (for I know you have great expeditions and entertainments during the solemnity) whether I am here or not. I shall be much disappointed, if I am not here some part of the time[3]

Very sincerely Yours John H Newman of the Oratory

Professor Sullivan

SUNDAY 27 AUGUST 1865   Henry Bethell to dinner

[1] i.e. that opposite Christ Church. See letter of 3 Jan. 1865 to St John.
[2] Ten of this series of pithy maxims, entitled 'Fathers of the Desert,' and chosen by Newman, occupied a page in the *Month*, between Oct 1864 and March 1866. These Sayings of the Fathers came to an end, after they had been parodied in *Punch*, (10 March 1866), as 'Sayings of the Fathers of the Dessert, (Dedicated with feelings of the greatest possible respect to an eminent contributor to *The Month*).' The author of the good-humoured skit was F. C. Burnand. See the *Month* (Dec. 1902), pp. 565–6, and (Jan. 1903), p. 10.
[3] Sullivan replied on 30 Aug. that he would almost certainly not be able to attend the meeting of the British Association, which began in Birmingham on 6 Sept.

TO MISS HOLMES

The Oratory Birmingham[1]

My dear Miss Holmes,

I have been too busy to write. I shall be rejoiced to see you, as you propose — but from September 4th to (say) the 29th, I shall be away. Did you receive a letter from me a little time back on your telling me about Mr Hope Scott? I say it, because you speak as if I had been quite silent

Ever Yrs affectly John H Newman of the Oratory

Miss Holmes

TO MRS JOHN MOZLEY

The Oratory Bm August 27/65

My dear Jemima

Thank you for your letter. I saw Rickards's death in the paper, shortly before it came. It is strange indeed, that she should be the one left, who seemed so delicate. I am afraid her sister is dead — if so, I suppose her brothers are her only near friends. If you think she would like it, tell her how warm my recollections of her are, and how truly I condole with her. She was one of the most pleasing persons I ever saw; I don't forget her kind arrangements, when I took the duty at Ulcombe — and to this day I have serious annoyance with myself to think how I ate her marmalade.[2]

From what you say, I trust you are steadily getting well. You were kind enough to offer me a copy of Corelli's solos, were you not? were they mine? if not, they might be useful some day to those about you, and I think it would be a pity to send them. Otherwise, I should be obliged to you for them.

Ever Yours affectly John H Newman

Mrs J. Mozley

TO CHARLES BURTON REID

Aug 27/65

answered that I would gladly subscribe — if a trifle would do, as I am not rich — but I should not like my name to appear, as it might seem an incon-

---

[1] This letter has been dated 'probably Aug 27, 1865'.

[2] Samuel Rickards died on 24 Aug. He married in 1821 Lucy, daughter of Sir Robert Wilmot, Bart, of Chaddesden, Derby. Three of her brothers were still living, and one of her sisters.

For Newman's visits to Ulcombe, the first of which was in 1826, see *Moz.* I pp. 135–8 and 491; *Trevor* I, pp. 61–8.

sistency in me, and require explanation, if I was known to subscribe for a memorial in a Church of the Established Religion[1]

J H N

TO AMBROSE ST JOHN

The Oratory ⌜Augst 27/65⌝

My dear A

⌜Thank you for the remark about 'rem habere —' I deliberated, and thought the fact of its being a Euphuism[2] was sufficiently to excuse it. I should translate it 'When he perceived that I was carrying on a flirtation with you,' or 'that I was on terms with you.'

As to 'Modo ambiendi sponsam, non satis Attico,' I construe it, modo, by a fashion; ambiendi, of courting; sponsam, his love; non satis Attico, not quite in the Attic style.

We have in Livy — servorum modo, after the fashion of servants ⟨slaves⟩ — in Tacitus, pecorum modo trucidari, after the fashion of sheep — in Horace apis, modo — in Pliny, ignium modo, muricum modo, in Livy in vaticinantis modum; in Tacitus in nostrum modum — in Livy, hostilem in modum — in Livy, in modum fugientium — in Cicero, non in uno modo tractantur. Also modus will take a gerund genitive, for we have, lugendi modus in Cicero.[3]

The Bishop came yesterday. He asked me, if I still thought of Oxford. I said absolutely no. I added, I had bought some land, but for the chances of the future, not as connected with myself. He said he had heard so. Well, for the chance of things he should keep the matter open for a year. He said that Cardinal Barnabò had told the Archbishop that there would be a great meeting next year — time and subjects uncertain.[4] The Bishop said there was a great deal to do in the way of discipline, e.g. about nuns, parishes etc. He hoped they would be cautious of touching philosophy — said the Pope had some wish for one or two doctrinal decrees, but spoke as if others did not share in it; said he was sure the Bishops' voice would be heard — implied that the [[actual]] syllabus, was a great improvement on what it was to have

[1] Reid, who had been at Ealing School ten years after Newman, and was Army Chaplain at Hounslow Barracks 1853–67, wrote on 24 Aug. that a window in memory of Dr Nicholas was to be erected in the parish church at Ealing, by his former pupils. Reid wrote that he had been informed that Newman was 'very much attached to him and to his family.'

[2] [[its euphyistic character]] This was a phrase in the first act of Newman's adaptation of Terence, *Pincerna*, London 1865, line 93. The phrase which follows was in the Prologue.

[3] [['Modo ambiendi' — by a fashion — so, servorum modo, Livy — pecorum modo, Tacitus; apis modo Horace — ignium modo, Pliny — muricum modo etc etc Modus will take a gerund genitive, as lugendi modus in Cicero]]

[4] i.e. a great meeting of bishops at Rome. This took place in the summer of 1867, in celebration of the eighteenth century of St Peter's martrydom.

been, before the Bishops took it in hand, a year or two previous to its publication. I wonder what the Pope's doctrinal points are. The Bishop spoke of a meeting like that for the Immaculate Conception, which would be a serious thing, as being so unusual.[7]

Young Ricardo is coming — so you will have I am glad to say, a boy of eight in spite of you.[1] I inclose one letter — the other is from Wegg Prosser, whose boy is coming.

Ever Yrs affly John H Newman

P.S. You must ascertain HOW LONG Lord Edmund has been separated from his sisters who have the scarletina.[2]

TO FRANCIS RICHARD WEGG-PROSSER

The Oratory Bm August 27. 1865

My dear Mr Wegg Prosser

In Fr St John's absence I answer your letter to him. We shall be quite ready for your boy, and it is a great pleasure to me personally to have the charge of him. Our day of meeting is the 12th of September.

As to the whooping cough, from what you say, I think there would be no danger in his coming — and, if you and your physician are of that opinion, we are satisfied.

Fr St John would have great pleasure, I am sure, in availing himself of your invitation, were he in your neighbourhood, but he is out at Brighton and on the south coast.

Very truly Yours in Xt   John H Newman of the Oratory

F. R. Wegg Prosser Esqr

TO LAVINIA WILSON

The Oratory, Birmingham. August 27. 1865.

My dear Child,

I am very glad you are in England again — and, with you, have no wish you should ever leave it.[3] I am sorry to tell you, I cannot promise to be in Birmingham between September 4 and September 29. I am for months past

[1] William Percy Ricardo came to the Oratory School on 12 Sept. He joined the 9th Lancers and was killed in action at Cabul, 12 Dec. 1879, aged 22 years.
[2] Lord Edmund Howard, later Viscount Fitzalan, younger brother of the Duke of Norfolk, came to the Oratory School in May 1865.
[3] See letter of 20 July. Lavinia Wilson arrived at Mother Margaret Hallahan's Convent, Stone, on 25 Aug., and entered there as a postulant on 15 Sept.

due at Mr. Keble's, whenever I can leave home, and I am not able till September, and not after September. I grieve about Miss Kebbell[1]

Ever yours affectionately, John H. Newman .

P.S. My kindest respects to Mother Provincial, Mother Superioress and the good Nuns.

MONDAY 28 AUGUST 1865   Miss Monro went

TO MRS PETER BRETHERTON

The Oratory, Birmm Aug. 28. 1865

My dear Mrs Bretherton

William left this house sooner than I was told. I was engaged when he came, and merely shook hands with him — but was told that he was to stay till half past one. At that time I went to find him, and he was gone. This could not be helped, for he had many things to do.

I have only just got your letter, and inclose a letter of introduction.[2]

I am sorry dear Eleanor is not yet strong again. She must write to me before she comes, as I am due at Mr Keble's soon whom I have not seen these 22 years.

Ever Yours affly in Xt   John H. Newman of the Oratory

TO THOMAS JOSEPH BROWN, BISHOP OF NEWPORT

The Oratory, Birmm Aug. 28. 1865

My dear Lord,

I have just received a letter, which, if I do not misread the signature, is from your Lordship. It is a great gratification to me to receive your Lordship's approbation on any thing which I have written.[3] Begging your Lordship's blessing, I am, My dear Lord,

Your faithful Servt in Xt   John H. Newman of the Oratory

The Rt Revd The Bp of Newport

---

[1] Mary Kebbel had been corresponding with Newman in 1864, and was on the verge of becoming a Catholic. She wrote again on 29 March 1865, more hesitant, and saying that she could not become a Catholic during the lifetime of her father, Henry Kebbel (1772–1867), who was Perpetual Curate of Kilby, Leicestershire, from 1813 until death.

[2] Mrs Bretherton's son William was about to emigrate to New Zealand, and wanted a letter of introduction to the Bishop of Wellington.

[3] Brown, who prefixed no '✠' to his signature, and addressed Newman as 'My dear very Reverend Brother,' wrote from the Benedictine Priory at Colwich on 27 Aug. He expressed his admiration for *The Dream of Gerontius*, which he read aloud to the nuns, 'Many with myself shed tears ere we concluded it.' What Newman wrote 'On consulting the Faithful in Matters of Doctrine' had not received his Lordship's approbation, who, without telling the author, delated it to Propaganda.

TO W. J. COPELAND

The Oratory Bm August 28/65

My dear Copeland

We are employing the Vacation in painting etc. So I neither have been able to get away, nor to think of asking you here. It is impossible. And now the weather is so bad — or I should propose to pass a day with you Monday or Tuesday next, or Thursday or Friday, for I don't know when I shall be free here.

I think of being from home a week, and in that time to go to London, to you (if it suits you, to Hursley (whether you go or not) to the Bowdens at Ryde, to Sir John Simeon, also in the Isle of Wight, and so back home.

However, I never can fix my plans — so many unexpected difficulties arise — and I write this as a sort of first protocol — before we come to the stage of definitive treaties.

I saw Rickards's death in the Paper to my great regret. I should have liked to have seen him again. He was very fierce, however, and I don't suppose it was likely, had he lived ever so long. I have the pleasantest recollections of the days we passed together at his Parsonages, near 40 years ago. What a dream life is!

Who in the world is Mr Payne Smith who is made Regius Professor? I mean, who ever heard of him as a divine? Is he the negative result of contrary positive forces, representing an equilibrium, in which $x = y$ or $x - y = 0$? Scott of Balliol was named, I see — a safe man, siquis alius — but then how could he give up, and how could he retain, the Cathedra Jinksii?[1]

Ever Yours affectionately John H Newman

Revd W J Copeland

TO W. J. COPELAND

Aug 30/56

My dear C

To save the post, I write in a great hurry. We are always running foul of each other.

What I think would be best is this — Go to Cheltenham, Gloucester, etc as you propose. And, *if you will*, *then* go to Hursley

---

[1] Robert Payne Smith, an evangelical and a Syriac scholar, was sub-librarian of the Bodleian. His appointment as Regius Professor of Divinity in 1865 was due to the influence of the former Master of his Oxford college, Pembroke, Francis Jeune, Bishop of Peterborough, and of the Earl of Shaftesbury.

Robert Scott would have had to relinquish the Mastership of Balliol, where he had succeeded Richard Jenkins in 1854. Copeland replied on 29 Aug., 'The promotion of Scott would have involved the enthronement of Jowett in the Cathedra Jinksii!!' The *Guardian* wrote, (30 Aug. 1865), p. 877, '*The Times* vouches for the scholarship of the new Professor, and the *Record* that he is pious. We trust he may prove equal to his position.'

Meanwhile, I will start next week for Henry Bowden's at Ryde — and I will come over to Hursley thence, when I find that you are there. Or if you are not, I will go by myself.

Of course, it will be a great additional pleasure to me, if you are there, but don't by any means put yourself out to go there.

Drop a line to me by return of post, please

Ever Yrs affly John H Newman

Revd W J Copeland

THURSDAY 31 AUGUST 1865   Mr H. Bedford called in evening
FRIDAY 1 SEPTEMBER   In retreat   Miss Wilson in Edgbaston

TO W. J. COPELAND

The Oratory Birmingham Septr 1. 1865

My dear Copeland

If all is well, and if it suits Keble (to whom I have written by this post) I will be at Hursley on Thursday morning — stay the day — and leave for the H. Bowdens at Ryde

Don't put yourself out to come, if it is difficult

Ever Yrs affly John H Newman

The Revd W. J. Copeland

SATURDAY 2 SEPTEMBER 1865   The painting and new matting laying finished.

TO JOHN KEBLE

The Oratory Bm Septr 1. 1865

My dear Keble,

I have a great shrinking from pledging myself, for sometimes I cannot fulfil, and therefore disappoint the parties to whom I have pledged myself — but, please God, if all is well, *and if it suits you*, I propose to be with you on Thursday morning next, and spend the day with you. I leave you for the H. Bowdens at Ryde

Ever Yours affectly John H Newman

The Revd John Keble

41

TO W. J. COPELAND

Sunday Septr 3/65

My dear C

If all is well, and Keble wishes me, I shall be with him Thursday morning. Don't put yourself out.

Ever Yrs affly J H N

TO EDWARD BELLASIS

The Oratory Bm Septr 4. 1865

My dear Bellasis

Your letter of course made me very glad — and it is very kind of you to write it. *We* cannot, however, take more than a due portion of the credit as regards your boys, seeing the patterns and guidance they have at home.[1]

What pleased me especially in Richard was that the music had not interfered with his studies. I was very jealous as to the chance of it. To my mind music is an important part of education, where a boy has a turn for it. It is a great resource when they are thrown on the world — it is a social amusement — perfectly innocent — and what is so great a point employs their thoughts. Drawing does not do this. It is often a great point for a boy to escape from himself; and music enables him. He cannot be playing difficult passages on the violin, and thinking of any thing else.

But still there are more important things — and I had some fear that Master Richard might be neglecting his proper studies. Now since he has not, his music is all gain — and I may without reluctance say that he has made a good start in it. He plays *fluently*, so to say — by fluency I mean in time, in tune, and with execution. This is stage one — stage two is eloquence — by which I mean grace, delicacy and expression. To gain this, nothing is better than to accompany his sisters. A boy who always is first fiddle is in danger of artistic faults parallel to those which are implied in the metaphorical sense of the words. When he comes back, I think he has had enough of the music master, and I shall try to make him turn his thoughts to a higher school of music than is suitable to a beginner — but I cannot tell yet whether he is old enough to take to it. I recollect how slow I was as a boy to like the school of music which afterwards so possessed me that I have come to think Haydn, in spite of his genius, almost vulgar.

My love to him and his two brothers — and with kindest regards to Mrs Bellasis and all of you, and thanks for the invitation to the Lawn, which I shall not forget. I am

Ever Yours affectly in Xt   John H Newman of the Oratory

Mr Serjeant Bellasis

[1] Bellasis wrote from The Lawn, Putney, on 30 Aug., in praise of his sons, to thank Newman for 'the prudence and care with which the good points of their characters have been encouraged at Edgbaston. So far as I and mine have been concerned your school has been a great success.'

TO W. J. COPELAND

Sept 4/65

My dear Copeland

I grieve to hear that Mrs Keble is ill, and they are at Bournemouth. So I must delay my visit. All I have done is to spoil yours at Gloucester

Ever Yours affly J H N

P.S. My plans are quite uncertain

TO JOHN KEBLE

The Oy Bm Septr 4/65

My dear Keble

I grieve to hear your anxiety about Mrs Keble.[1] I will *delay* — for what I see, I need not be *fixed* here till about the 20th

Before that time your anxiety may be over and you may be back home — and then I will come to you.

If not, I will wait a better time. We must take it easy.

Ever Yrs affly John H Newman

TO J. SPENCER NORTHCOTE

The Oratory Birmingham Septr 5. 1865

My dear President,

We had no Bethell of the name of Hugh — but Robert and Gerald. They were both very good boys, and Gerald a clever one[2]

Very sincerely Yours John H Newman of the Oratory

The Very Revd The President &c

[1] Keble wrote on 3 Sept. from Bournemouth, 'I am vexed and troubled that I am not able to say at once, "Come, as you kindly propose —" but your letter finds us away from home to try if we can find more easy breathing for my wife.' He suggested that Newman might come to Bournemouth, 'Give us what you can of yourself . . .' On this letter Newman wrote 'N.B I went off to Hursley from Southampton on Tuesday September 12 where I found Pusey with Keble. I left in the evening for Ryde J H N.'

[2] Northcote was asked to take Hugh Bethell at Oscott, and his father explained that he had previously been at the Oratory School. Robert Victor Bethell, born in 1848, and his brother Hugh Nicholas Fitzgerald Bethell, born in 1849, came to the Oratory School in Sept. 1860. The latter was always known as 'Gerald.' Robert had already left the Oratory School and Gerald was taken away by his father at Easter 1865. See letter of 18 Sept. to St John.

TO E. B. PUSEY

The Oratory Birmingham Septr 5. 1865

My dear Pusey,

I shall be much obliged by your sending me your book. Somehow, outright controversy is more pleasant to me than such uncontroversial works as are necessarily built on assumptions which pain me.[1]

For myself, I don't think I have written anything controversial for the last 14 years. Nor have I ever, as I think, replied to any controversial notice of what I have written. Certainly, I let pass without a word the various volumes which were written in answer to my Essay on Doctrinal Development, and that on the principle that truth defends itself, and falsehood refutes itself — and that, having said my say, time would decide for me, without any trouble, how far it was true, and how far not true. And I have quoted Crabbe's line as to my purpose, (though I can't quote correctly):-

> Leaving the case to Time, who solves all doubt,
> By bringing Truth, his glorious daughter, out.[2]

This being so, I can't conceive I could feel it in any sense an imperative duty to remark on any thing you said in your book. I dare say there is a great deal in which I should agree. Certainly, I so dislike Ward's way of going on, that I can't get myself to read the Dublin. But on those points I have said my say in the Apologia, and, though I can't see the future, am likely to leave them alone. A great attempt has been made in some quarters to find (censurable) mistakes in my book — but it has altogether failed, and I consider Ward's articles to be impotent attempts to put down by argument what is left safe in the domain of theological opinion.

But, while I would maintain my own theological opinions, I don't dispute with Ward the right of holding his, so that he does not attempt to impose them on me — nor do I dispute the right of whoso will, to use devotions to the Blessed Virgin which seem to me unnatural and forced. Did authority attempt

---

[1] *The Church of England a Portion of Christ's One Holy Catholic Church, and a Means of Restoring Visible Unity. An Eirenicon, in a Letter to the Author of 'The Christian Year,'* Oxford 1865. It was a reply to Manning's *The Workings of the Holy Spirit in the Church of England, a Letter to the Rev. E. B. Pusey,* London 1864.

Pusey wrote on 4 Sept., 'I have not in all these sad years, sent you any thing which had any controversy in it. And in this too, though I have been reviving the mode of conciliation of Du Pin and Wake, I have had to deprecate the Ultramontanism, which, in the Dublin Review, goes beyond Bellarmine as to the Infallibility of the Pope, and the large development of the system as to the Blessed Virgin. There is, of course, no declamation; it is simply historical, I believe.

But now the object of this note is to say, unless you should otherwise read it, I should not send it to you. I should be sorry that you should have anything of mine from the booksellers; but still more sorry to be the occasion of your writing any thing against it by bringing it under your notice.' See also Liddon's *Pusey,* IV, p. 106.

[2] George Crabbe, *Tales of the Hall,* IX, 'The Preceptor Husband,'
> Leaving the truth to Time, who solves our doubt,
> By bringing his all-glorious daughter out —
> Truth!

This quotation comes near the middle of the poem; in the Oxford edition, p. 393.

to put them down, while they do not infringe on the great Catholic verities, I think it would act, as the Bishop of London is doing, in putting down the devotional observances of the Tractarian party at St Michael's and elsewhere. He is tender towards freethinkers and stern towards Romanizers. Dat veniam corvis, vexat censura columbas.[1] Now the Church of Rome is severe on the freethinkers and indulgent towards devotees

Ever Yrs affly   John H Newman

TO CHARLES RUSSELL

The Oratory, Bm Septr 5. 1865

My dear Dr Russell

Thank you for your inclosure, which I will forward to Mr Monsell. I will not forget your point, which is an important one.[2]

After all your kind trouble about the *Dublins*, I am sorry to say that they deny all knowledge about them at the railway station. This is very provoking. The Papers say that your Bishops have put aside the University Question for further consideration.[3]

Yours affly in Xt   John H Newman

TO T. F. WETHERELL

The Oratory Birmingham Septr 5. 1865

My dear Wetherell

I am glad to have your Pamphlet.[4] Should I want more copies, I will avail myself of your offer. I take it for granted you sent it to such as Hanmer, Allies, Monsell and Lord Dunraven. If not, I think I shall send it to them at once from myself.

I have seen one or two numbers of the Pall Mall Gazette lately. There are writers on its staff who know the state of Catholic matters well. If you don't

---

[1] Juvenal, *Satires*, II, 63. At the consecration on 24 Aug. of St Michael's, Shoreditch, the Bishop of London, A. C. Tait, insisted that the coloured stoles of the clergy should be removed, and objected to a crucifix and to other signs of ritualism.
[2] The enclosure concerned the plan for affiliating the Catholic University of Ireland to the Queen's University, or rather to a new University which would take its place. Cf. letter of 11 June to Woodlock. Russell wrote on 1 Sept., 'It strikes me that the provision about the election of a portion of the new Senate by the Graduates might be *expressly* limited to the Graduates of the new University. If those of the Queen's University were allowed to vote they would swamp the new men for years to come.'
[3] The meeting of the Irish bishops at the end of Aug. was adjourned until further information became available. E. R. Norman, *The Catholic Church and Ireland in the Age of Rebellion, 1859–1873*, London 1965, p. 208.
[4] *A Statement of Facts connected with the Memorial recently presented, by certain Laymen, to the Sacred Congregation of Propaganda, relative to the Education of Catholics at the Universities of Oxford and Cambridge.*

look sharp, they will get possession of your Statement. Their views are very liberal, and they have made remarks lately on the Oxford plan, which, though really in its favour, may easily be quoted against it, and I expect will. Would it not be possible, in the existing difficulty, to exert an influence upon its notices of Catholicism, so that it might not impinge upon the moderate Catholic party? Perhaps even more could be done with it. But of course I speak from my own nido, and know nothing of the parties and their currents in the great metropolis

Yours very sincerely John H Newman of the Oratory

T. F. Wetherell Esqr

TO CATHERINE ANNE BATHURST

The Oratory Bm Septr 6. 1865

My dear Child

Miss Wilson, I suppose, will try the Sisters of Penance. I was not neglectful of you — but the Bishop and she hit it off wonderfully from the first — she desired to go to Stone from the first — she has gone there straight, when she returned from France — and she has now resolved, if they will take her, to be taken.[1]

I hope you have got well through first the heat, and then the wet. I hear that your work thrives, and I trust you do also.

I suppose I am going to see Keble in a day or two. I have not seen him for 20 years and more. Dear Isaac Williams I saw for a few hours a day or two before he died

Ever Yours affly John H Newman of the Oratory

Sister M. Catharine

TO LADY CHATTERTON

The Oratory Bm. Septr. 6. 1865

My dear Lady Chatterton

I had first written and directed my letter to Mr Dering which goes by the same post as this, when your letter was brought me. I assure you, it is from no forgetfulness or negligence that he has not heard from me before — but I am full of work which only can be done now, and must be finished by a fixed day — that is between August 1 and September 12, and Mr Dering's MS came just on the 2nd of August, I think

I am very sorry that I have kept him in suspense. I rarely leave home, for it is an effort to me, and I had promised Mr Keble, whom I have not seen for

[1] See letter of 27 Aug. to Lavinia Wilson. Catherine Anne Bathurst hoped Miss Wilson might have joined her community of Dominican nuns in London.

more than 20 years, that I would go to him into Hampshire as soon as I was at liberty. It interests me extremely to think that Mr Dering should be so seriously directing his steps towards the Catholic Church — and I would do any thing in my power to serve him. I can say no more at this minute — but you must allow me to write again

I am, Dear Lady Chatterton, Sincerely Yours John H Newman

P.S. I have not time or strength for so long a journey. If I go, I must go to Mr Keble — but my real rest would be to remain here, doing nothing. I hope to write to Mr Dering again in the course of a few posts.

TO EDWARD HENEAGE DERING

The Oratory Birmingham Septr 6. 1865

My dear Sir

I much fear you must be wondering at my silence, considering the time that has past since you were kind enough to send me your MSS.[1] But the truth is, I have been very busy, and not the master of my own time. I hope soon to be able to avail myself of the pleasure which I am sure I shall find in the perusal of it. And then I will write to you at once.

I am, My dear Sir, Very truly yours John H Newman

E Dering Esqr

TO PRINCE DORIA'S AGENTS

Sept 6/65

Gentlemen

Dr Newman requests me to inform the Prince, in answer to his Highness's question, whether 'the £12. 10., charged for Private Tuition by Mr Drew is for the entire year or only for the Term in which the charge appears, that it is, not for the year, but for the Term.[2] The Prince will observe, on referring to the Lent Term Account, that the same sum is charged there. This charge had in consequence the Prince's own sanction in the beginning of this year. Dr Newman wrote to him advising that Don Alfonso should have a private Tutor for two terms, Lent and Trinity, at an expence of £25 extra. The Prince replied at once in these words — 'Quando lei creda utile per il mio figlio Alfonso di farlo ajutare ne' suoi studi d'un particolare maestro, non v'*incontro difficoltà di qualche aumento di spesa,* essendo il solo mio desiderio di veder far profitto

---

[1] See letter of 27 July to Lady Chatterton.
[2] J. and R. McCracken, 38 Queen Street, Cannon Street West, London, 'General and Foreign Agents, Agents by appointment to the Royal Academy, the National Gallery . . . and Wine Merchants,' wrote on 5 Sept. questioning two items in Alfonso Doria's school bill for the preceding term.

di studii il mio figlio. Così faccia pure cio che meglia creda.[1] On this permission I have acted.

As to the expenses of Mr Pope's journey, Mr Pope conveyed one other boy besides Don Alfonso to Paris, not more. There were two others from this place in the train, but they had already on former occasions gone by themselves, and Mr Pope had no charge of them. He did take off a portion of his whole travelling expenses as a charge for this one boy. Don Alfonso's expenses were £13. 3. 9 His own, to France and back, would be double viz £26, whereas he has charged only £21. 0. 0. He could not take a return ticket, for I believe he had reason to think that the Prince meant to retain him with Don Alfonso.

J H N

THURSDAY 7 SEPTEMBER 1865 Wm Froude and Eddy to Breakfast. went off to Rednall

TO W. J. COPELAND

Septr 7/65

My dear Copeland

It is unfortunate — but *don't dream* of going *again* to Keble. Pusey is going to him I think next Monday or Tuesday. In which case I should not go

Ever Yrs affly John H Newman

TO JOHN KEBLE

The Oratory Bm Septr 7. 1865

My dear Keble

I am glad Mrs Keble is so much better.[1] As I have no Bradshaw here (Rednall) I can't fix on a train — but, if all is well, I shall go straight to Southampton, on Monday afternoon — sleep there — and leave my baggage — and come over to you on Tuesday morning. But, it is so difficult to go into Birmingham without falling in and being detained by people (especially as our School is just re-assembling and the British Association is going on), (this has taken me out here) that I don't like to promise.

There is another difficulty. *I wish you would put me off*, if Pusey is coming to you. I say so merely, as you must feel, because to meet two friends is not to meet one. Copeland is another matter, for I have seen him so often. Pusey

---

[1] 'If you think it advisable that my son Alfonso should have the help in his work of a private tutor there is no difficulty about incurring some extra expense, for my only wish is to see my son profiting by his studies. So please do what you think best.'
[2] Keble wrote on 7 Sept. that he and his wife would be returning next day to Hursley, 'and any day after, that may suit you, will as far as we know suit us. I do hope that nothing may happen to hinder our meeting, too long deferred.'

has *told* me he is going to you next week. To put me off would only *postpone* me — for, please God, *I will come.*[1]

Ever Yrs affly J H N

P.S. I consider this will get to you tomorrow noon — so you will have time to put me off. (direct to the Oratory) Or you might write to me '*Railroad Hotel — Southampton.*' If I found Pusey was with you, I should go on to the Bowdens for a day or two.

SUNDAY 10 SEPTEMBER 1865   the servants had a day at Rednall

TO LADY CHATTERTON

Rednal Septr 10. 1865

Dear Lady Chatterton,

I prefer to write to you about Mr Dering's Poems, which I have read with much interest. They abound in beautiful and striking thoughts, and evidence great depth of feeling. And I found myself carried on by his Irish story, as a poet would wish his reader to be. Also, I think he has a just and original idea of the contrasts afforded by varieties of metre, and of the mode of turning them to artistic purposes. As it seems to me, his execution, that is, his versification is not equal to his conception and his taste. I think this distinctly. And in consequence, considering our language has now been elaborated in a succession of centuries, and readers are unreasonably impatient of any thing that is obscure, or gives trouble, or offends their notions of taste, I am not sure that the literary public will give itself the opportunity of entering into the spirit of poems, which from their intrinsic merit have such claim on its attention. But if there is one species of composition above others, about which I always profess to speak diffidently, it is poetry — for its popularity seems to me to depend on the accident of the age, or the day.

And now as to the subject which you suggested apropos of the Poems. It is quite plain to me, as far as one can judge from writings, that Mr Dering ought to be a Catholic. I doubt not he knows the Catholic Religion well enough to need no information about its doctrines; and he shows, I think, that he has mastered its main principle, viz that the Church is the infallible interpreter of the old Apostolic doctrine. It seems to me the only question is, how is he to be received? At Tunbridge Wells there is a Jesuit Mission — and the Jesuits are men of education and refinement. They would doubtless attend to him, if he wished it. For myself, I would most gladly receive him into the Church, if he wished it; but *I* could not do so without writing to the Bishop of the Diocese for special faculties, which I have not at present.[2] Tomorrow I go

---

[1] Pusey told Newman on 4 Sept. that he was about to visit Keble.
[2] In his draft Newman wrote here, 'Should Mr Dering wish it, I should think it a duty to ask for those faculties, and I would do so at once.'

to Southampton on my way to Hursley. Would you be kind enough to write to me by return of post, directing, 'Revd John Keble, Hursley, Winchester?' From him I go to friends in the Isle of Wight and return home by the end of the week: but should Mr Dering make up his mind to be received, I will go from the Island to Finchden and so home. Excuse the abruptness of this letter and with my best respects to Mr Dering,

believe me to be Very truly Yours John H Newman

P.S. If Mr Dering wishes for a small catechism, he can get from Messrs Burns 17 Portman Street W, 'Doyle's Abridgement of the Douay.'[1]

TO WILLIAM NEVILLE

Rednall Sept 10/65

My dear W

Thanks. Yes, please.

1 Write to Mr Boyle that you have sent me his letter. 'Revd G. D. Boyle, Handsworth, Birmingham.'[2]

2 And the same to Mr Kidd. I sent a prospectus to Mrs Montray some fortnight back. Send another. I am disgusted to find her boys are 14 or 15! *And I don't like it.* Send my sorrow that I was not at home, and my thanks, 'Revd J. Kidd, Halesowen.'[3]

3 To Meyrick 'Revd Fr Meyrick, Beaumont, Old Windsor,' with a good word for Safe, and only one of them.[4]

4 To Lady Hatherton, that Doria is away. I inclose her letter.[5]

I suppose I come in by 11 or 12 tomorrow don't tell — except that I shall want dinner at one.

As to Mr Fitzgerald, Ambrose must give letters to his Professor friend and to Baron Wurtzburg.

Ever Yrs affly J H N

[1] Dering replied on 11 Sept, 'I cannot sufficiently express my gratitude for your kindest of offers . . .
Only name the day which best suits you, and the carriage shall be at the station.'
[2] See letter of 15 Sept.
[3] Kidd, who was the Anglican curate at Halesowen, wrote on behalf of Mrs Montray, of Kilmainham, Dublin, the widow of an officer. Her sons did not go to the Oratory School.
[4] Thomas Meyrick asked for a report on two boys of the name of Safe, who had applied to go to school at Beaumont. One of them, James, was at the Oratory School in 1863.
[5] Lady Hatherton wrote asking if she might visit Prince Alfonso Doria.

TO J. SPENCER NORTHCOTE

Rednal Septr 10/65

My dear President

I fear I forgot to answer your question about the Phormio. I saw it on the London University List — and thought the selection of it atrocious.

I am sorry to say that my edition is not published — and, since it is very free in its corrections, the Authorities in London might prefer to criticize the Latin to granting your wish. Professor Key, I believe, is great in Terentian Metres[1]

Very sincerely Yours John H Newman

The Very Revd The President

MONDAY 11 SEPTEMBER 1865   came back to Bm[Birmingham] and went off to Southampton where slept

TUESDAY 12 SEPTEMBER   went to Keble's, where Pusey — dined with them — then to Ryde to the Bowdens

TO AMBROSE ST JOHN

⌜Buckland Grange Ryde Septr 13. 1865⌝

My dear A

⌜Here I am, very comfortable and, if I had my dear fiddle with me, I might sing and play recubans sub tegmine fagi[2] in full content. Scarcely had I left Birmingham, when it struck me that, since Pusey was to be at Keble's that evening, there was no manner of doubt that he would get into my train at Oxford and journey down with me.⌝ I was sure of this. When he did not get into my carriage at Oxford, I felt sure we should recognise each other when we were thrown off the train at Reading — ⌜but no, he did not⌝ turn up — as it happened, he went by an earlier train. However, this expectation put me upon thinking on the subject — and ⌜I made up my mind to go to Keble's next morning and see him — and I did. I slept at the Railway Hotel at Southampton Dock — a very reasonable house, and good too —⌝ my bed only 2/6 — ⌜(they are building close by a grand Imperial Hotel) and then yesterday morning (Tuesday) I retraced my steps to Bishopstoke, left my portmanteau there, and went over to Hursley. I had forgotten the country

[1] Terence's *Phormio* was the play chosen by London University for the first B.A. examination in 1866. Northcote asked on 6 Sept. whether Newman's expurgated edition had been 'really *published*,' so that he could use it for his students at Oscott.

Thomas Hewitt Key (1799–1875), was Professor of Latin in London University, 1828–42, and Headmaster of the University School in Gower Street from 1833 until his death. He had made a minute study of Plautus and Terence.

[2] Virgil, *Eclogue* I, i.

and was not prepared for such beauty, in the shape of Woods. Keble was at the door, he did not know me, nor I him. How mysterious that first sight of friends is! for when I came to contemplate him, it was the old face and manner, but the first effect and impression was different. His wife had been taken ill again in the night, and at the first moment he, I *think*, and *certainly* I, wished myself away. Then he said, Have you missed my letters? meaning Pusey is here, and I wrote to stop your coming. He [[then]] said I must go and prepare Pusey. He did so, and then took me into the room [[where Pusey was]]. I went in rapidly, and it is strange how action overcomes pain. Pusey, as being passive, was evidently shrinking back into the corner of the room — as I should have done if he had rushed in upon me. He could not help contemplating the look of me narrowly and long — Ah, I thought, you are thinking how old I am grown, and I see myself in you — though you, I do think, are more altered than I am. Indeed, the alteration in him shocked me[1] (I would not say this to every one) — ⌜it pained and grieved me.[1] I should have known him any where — his face is not changed, but it is as if you looked at him through a prodigious magnifier. I recollect him short and small — with a round head — smallish features — flaxen curly hair — huddled up together from his shoulders downward — and walking fast. This was as a young man — but comparing him even when last I saw him [[in 1846]], when he was slow in his motions and staid in his figure, still there is a wonderful change. His head and his features are half as large again — his chest is very broad ⟨(*don't say all this*)⟩ — and he has, I think, a paunch —[2] His voice is the same — were my eyes shut, I should not have been sensible of any lapse of time.[3] As we three sat together at one table, I had as painful thoughts as I ever recollect, though it was a pain, not acute, but heavy.[4] There were three old men, who had worked together vigorously in their prime. This is what they have come to — poor human nature — after 20 years they meet together round a table, but without a common cause, or free outspoken thoughts — but, though kind yet subdued, and antagonistic in their mode of speaking, and all of them with broken prospects.[5] Pusey is full of his book[6] which is all but out — against Manning; and full of his speech on the relations between physical science and the Bible, which he is to deliver at the Church Congress at Norwich. He is full of polemics and of hope. Keble is as different as possible; he is as delightful as ever — and, it *seemed* to me as if he felt a sympathy and intimacy with me which he did not find with Pusey. At least he spoke to me of him — and I

[1] [[the alteration in him startled, I will add, pained and grieved me.]]
[2] [[his chest is very broad, and he is altogether large. (Don't say all this to any one) and he has a strange condescending way when he speaks]]
[3] [[alteration]]
[4] [[I had a painful thought, not acute pain, but heavy.]]
[5] [[antagonistic in their language to each other, and all of them with broken prospects, yet each viewing in his own way the world in which those prospects lay.]]
[6] [[Irenicon]] For Pusey's Paper at Norwich, read on 5 Oct., see Liddon's *Pusey*, IV, pp. 79–81.

don't think in the same tone he would have spoken to him of me.[1] I took an early dinner with them, and when the bell chimed for evensong at 4 o'clock, I got into my gig, and so from Bishopstoke to Ryde, arriving here between 7 and 8. Only three girls are here — Harry is away. Willie grown prodigiously,⌐ but as soon as ever he begins to look at a book, his headaches return — and he is only well in the open air.

⌐I have settled with Keble to go to him next Monday, if his wife is well enough.⌐ As to Lady C. [Chatterton] I have not yet heard — but I find I could not well have heard at Keble's — and there has not yet been time for any letter to have reached me here, sent on from Hursley. My love to all of you

Ever Yrs affly John H Newman

The Revd Fr St John

TO EDWARD HENEAGE DERING

Buckland Grange Ryde — Isle of Wight Septr 14/65

My dear Mr Dering

I thank God to find from your letter that you have made up your mind to take the step, to which I feel you are so distinctly called by Almighty God, and which will be in all respects so happy for you. My plans have been disarranged by Mrs Keble's illness. I was with him on Tuesday — and am to go to him again next Monday, unless he puts me off in consequence of a return of her indisposition. I have come to the resolution of breaking the journey between Hursley and Finchden — and am writing by this post to a friend near Worthing to ask if he can receive me on Tuesday. If so, I shall come on to you on Wednesday morning — arriving at Appledore at 4.25 PM. If all is well I will hear your confession, administer conditional baptism, and receive you into the Catholic Church Wednesday evening and Thursday morning. I have to get back to Birmingham by Thursday evening.

I am writing by this post to the Bishop for Faculties. I take it for granted that you were baptized in infancy. In such cases, which are the usual ones, the rite is conditional baptism which is completed in less than a minute — but where baptism has to be administered without condition, it must be administered in Church with the full ceremonies. In which case I could not receive you at once.

I should like a line in answer to this letter, to say that you approve of my arrangements — but the difficulty is to give you a direction which will be sure

---

[1] [[which he did not show towards Pusey. I judge by the way and tone he spoke to me of him.]]

In a letter to Church about his visit to Keble, Newman wrote, 'As hours went on, the *nota facies* came out upon his countenance, as if it were the soul showing itself in spite of the course and change of time. He always had an expression like no one else, and that sweet pleading earnestness never showed itself to me as piercingly as then, in his eyes and in his carriage.' *Ward* II, p. 96 note. For another account of the visit, see letter of 17 Sept. 1868 to Sir John Coleridge.

to find me. I cannot be sure, — but I expect to leave this place on Saturday for Sir John Simeon's Swainston, Isle of Wight — If I go to him, I shall leave him before post time Monday morning for Mr Keble's — but if Mr Keble could not receive me, I think his place must still serve as my direction for *Monday* — since I must wait in this neighbourhood, till I get the Bishop's permission.[1]

Praying God would bless and preserve you, and strengthen you especially at this time, and with my best respects to Lady Chatterton,

> I am, My dear Mr Dering, Sincerely yours
> John H Newman of the Oratory

E Dering Esqr

TO J. R. BLOXAM

> Buckland Grange, Ryde, Isle of Wight Septr 14. 1865

My dear Bloxam

I write on the *chance* of your being able to receive me next Tuesday, to go away next morning. If so, I would be at Bramber by the 2.45 PM train.

My address is, till noon on Saturday *here*, on Sunday morning at 'Sir John Simeon Bart M P. Swainston, Newport, Isle of Wight.' On Monday morning at 'Revd John Keble's, Hursley, Winchester.'

> Ever Yours affectly John H Newman

TO G. D. BOYLE

> Ryde, Isle of Wight Sept. 15. 1865

My dear Mr Boyle

I hope you will excuse my silence of so many days, after your very kind invitation came to me — but I was out of Birmingham at the time and have been moving about ever since, so that I have not been able to find the leisure to write to you.[2]

I felt your letter as a very friendly one — and, were it not that I am too old now to be able to avail myself easily of opportunities such as that you gave me of meeting men of celebrity, it would have been a great pleasure to me to accept it — but I am out of the habit of going from home.

I came into this part of the world to see Mr Keble at Hursley — whom I had not met for at least 21 years — there I found Dr Pusey whom I had not seen for nearly as long a time. And, Mrs Keble being ill, we three dined tête à

---

[1] Dering replied next day, 'I have just received your most welcome letter. I have been baptised . . .'

[2] G. D. Boyle, Vicar of St Michael's, Handsworth, Birmingham, wrote on 8 Sept., inviting Newman to breakfast on 11 Sept. Owing to the meeting of the British Association he had 'Dr Henry Acland and his wife, Lord Stanley, Professor G. Rawlinson, Professor H. J. Smith of Oxford, all staying with me, and to all of them it would be a true pleasure to meet you.'

tete together, a thing which perhaps we never did before in our lives. His wife, I am sorry to say, was too ill for me to stay, but, if all is well, I am going to him again next Monday.

Again thanking you for your kindness,

I am, My dear Mr Boyle, Very truly Yours John H Newman

The Revd G. D. Boyle

TO MISS HOLMES

Ryde. Isle of Wight Septr 15/65

My dear Miss Holmes,

I came into this neighbourhood to see my dear friend, Mr Keble, whom I had not seen these 22 years. When I got to Hursley, his wife had fallen ill — so I am going to try again next Monday. Meanwhile, I have come to the Island to my old friends, the Bowdens, and to Sir John Simeon. From Keble, I am going into the depth of Kent for a day, and am to take Mr Bloxam in the way.

I was at Mr Keble's some hours last Tuesday, and Pusey had come there the night before whom I had not seen since 1846 — so there were we three dining tête a tete, which perhaps had never happened before.

I expect to get back to Birmingham before this day week — but shall not be settled in the Oratory till the end of the month

Ever Yours affecty in Xt   John H Newman of the Oratory

Miss Holmes

TO AMBROSE ST JOHN

⌜Buckland Grange Ryde Septr 15/65⌝

My dear A

I have nothing to say but you may like to know my movements. This is John Bowden's Anniversary, and I have been saying Mass this morning for the intention which it suggests, all the Bowdens present at it.[1]

⌜I am to leave this place tomorrow for Swainston. Monday morning *early* for Hursley — Tuesday morning *early* for Bloxam's⌝ (Beding Priory Shoreham?) *if* he can receive me. ⌜Wednesday morning *early* for Finchden. Thursday for Birmingham —⌝ where I hope to arrive in the evening. I thought we might have a Congregation Friday morning (the 22nd) and then I would go to Rednall.

Harry Bowden has been away — but returns here today. ⌜The weather splendid.

Keble asked particularly after you. Adding something about his doing so, because you had been so kind to me.⌝

Ever Yrs affly John H Newman

---

[1] John William Bowden died in 1844.

SATURDAY 16 SEPTEMBER 1865   left the Bowdens for Sir John Simeon's   where Mrs Roberts and another Lady

TO J. R. BLOXAM

Swainston Isle of Wight Septr 17. 1865

My dear Bloxam

Keble's wife, alas, is ill and I cannot go to him. Will you send me a line to Shoreham at once, either to Telegram Office or Post Office, to say whether you can receive me on Tuesday. I shall be at Bramber at 2.45 PM, if you can. If you can't, the fates are against us

Ever Yrs affly John H Newman

Revd John Bloxam

TO EDWARD HENEAGE DERING

Swainston, Isle of Wight. Sept 17. 1865

My dear Mr Dering

Excuse great haste to save the post. I do not like to say no to such a proposal — still I am *obliged* to say no.[1] I must go to Town on Thursday, for I have an engagement in Town, and then in the same evening must be at Birmingham. It is very kind of you

and I am, Sincerely yours John H Newman

TO AMBROSE ST JOHN

Swainston, Isle of Wight. Septr 18. 1865

My dearest A

I am glad of course of Mrs B's letter, and have answered it — I have no doubt that a certain other party is a brute, and that she has a great deal to bear — however, we must get our money, if we can, — on the prospect of which her letter seems to me to shed a perplexed light, I confess.[2]

Mrs Keble is too ill for him to see me — he has put me off and I am stopping a day longer here. They are as kind as possible and I have had a great

[1] Dering wrote on 15 Sept., asking Newman to stay a second night at Finchden, because 'three Anglican clergymen are excessively anxious to meet you; and I am deceived *if* their desire be not something *more* than the wish to stare.'

[2] Mrs Bethell on 13 Sept. expressed her sorrow at the removal of her son Gerald from the Oratory School. Cf. letter of 5 Sept. to Northcote. She wrote that 'Mr Bethell is under the impression that a *rougher* school would be more useful to Gerald, who is so very shy and retiring.' Bethell also thought the boy was backward, but this Mrs Bethell said had been disproved, and she added that having such a strong tie with the Birmingham Oratory since its establishment 'I feel deeply being now cut off from it . . . My four Boys, and *I* in them — owe you so much gratitude.'
Mr Bethell had not yet paid fees due to the Oratory School.

deal of pleasant talk with both of them. Mrs Roberts too is here, Fr R's mother — which has been very pleasant.

From the time I came here, I have been pulled down — pains within me — little sleep — dizziness and deafness. I say it, because I wish to record how little of a recreation it really is to go from home. I am very comfortable here, and at the Bowdens — but, when I have been most so, as when I wrote to you before, I ever have had a secret desire to get back. Do recollect this — when I return I must have a week at Rednall, to recover this fatigue.

Tomorrow I go to Bloxam, but, owing to this change of route, from K's inability to see me, I have not got his answer to my letter, and shall not know till I get to Shoreham, whether he can receive me or not. I shall not be sorry if he can't, and I have a day at Worthing or Brighton to get right in. I am due on Wednesday at Finchden — and hope to get home Thursday night.

No news — Harry Bowden returned the day after I left them — and came over here yesterday to see me. Here I have heard some good mots of W. G. Ward's — One is a recent one 'As to Manning, it is quite wonderful what little ability he has.' They heard it from the person he said it to.

Ever Yours affly J H N

TUESDAY 19 SEPTEMBER 1865   left Sir J Simeon for Bloxam's — where slept

WEDNESDAY 20 SEPTEMBER   went on to Mr Dering's, Finchden, where I received him, Lady Chatterton, and Miss Orpen[1]

THURSDAY 21 SEPTEMBER   left Finchden for Bm[Birmingham] calling in London on Mr Clutton and Lintott

FRIDAY 22 SEPTEMBER   went to Rednall

TO EDWARD HENEAGE DERING

The Oy Birmingham Septr 22. 1865

My dear Mr Dering

I got home quite safely at 8½ last night, and write this, as you so kindly wish, to tell you so.

[1] Bishop Grant had given Newman faculties for the reception of converts, not merely of Dering, during his visit to the diocese of Southwark. On 22 Sept. Grant wrote, 'Will you offer my sincere congratulations to the three whom you have so happily received into the Church? I was right in giving you power to receive several . . .'
   Although Dering said that his wife, Lady Chatterton, had led him on towards the Church, she was still filled with doubts. Cf. letter of 29 March 1866 to her. By 1873 she seems to have given up practising as a Catholic. See letter of 10 March 1873 to Mrs Ferrers. By the end of Aug. 1875 her faith was sufficient ro enable her to live fully as a Catholic, for the last months of her life. See *Memoirs of Georgiana, Lady Chatterton,* second edition, London 1901, by Edward Heneage, Dering, who avoids mentioning his wife's reception in 1865.

Tell Miss Orpen that her sanwiches and wine were most acceptable — for I had no opportunity of eating and drinking till I got here — and I made a clearance of the whole with a very good appetite. I shall soon be writing to Lady Chatterton.

Very sincerely Yours John H Newman

E Heneage Dering Esqr

TO WILLIAM NEVILLE

Rednall Sept 24/65

My dear W

1. Without delay, make experiments on leather blinds for the discipline.[1]

2. I inclose a letter for Miss Whately for the foreign post, it should go without delay. But I can't read her address — so I inclose her letter too — keep her letter for me.

3. On Friday, before coming off, I sent Godwin to you for a postage stamp, and *two letters for the postbox*. He is so uncertain, that I want to make sure he *did* put them into the box.

4. I inclose a letter *to Mr Shaw* for Fr Ambrose's etc approbation. If there is no objection, let it go. The sale of More's goods comes off in 10 days — so no time is to be lost[2]

Ever Yrs affly J H N

Fr Wm Neville

Beware of my letter to Mr Shaw going to Miss Whately.

TO E. JANE WHATELY

Rednall. Septr 24/65

Dear Miss Whately

I have been away from home, indeed I have not yet returned to it — and this must be my apology for not having answered your letter, which as I was moving about could not be forwarded to me

I wrote out for you one, perhaps two letters of the Archbishop's of about the date of 1832 — And a correspondence, which I suppose is the same as that which you have otherwise in your possession. But it consists of *four* letters, two of the Archbishop's and two of mine. Of course I can see no

---

[1] i.e. leather blinds for the windows of the oratory in which the discipline was taken.

[2] This refers to a farm at Rednal, leased by Charles J. Shaw to Mr Moore.

Newman's draft ran: 'Dear Sir I hope you will not think I am taking a liberty in writing to you on the following subject.

There is a report that our immediate neighbour here, Mr More, is giving up the farm which he holds of you. We fear it would be too formidable a concern for us to ask to rent of you, but it is so convenient for the purposes of our School to have ground at Rednall, that we should wish very much to be allowed to treat with you for it J H N '

Shaw replied on 27 Sept. that his tenant was not leaving Rednal.

difficulty whatever in your publishing the Archbishop's two and not mine —
but if one of mine is published, I should like the other published also. I will
send them to any place which you tell me. My direction is not Oscott (which is
some miles from us) but the Oratory Bm [Birmingham][1]

J H N

TO JAMES HOPE-SCOTT

Rednall ⌐Septr 25/65

My dear Hope Scott⌐

I have said Mass for Lady Victoria and your little child this morning. Last
week I passed by you, and heard the news.[2] I left home, first to see Keble, then
to receive some people in Kent, and my passage lay along the coast line. I
stopped a night with Bloxam near Bramber, but otherwise went straight
ahead. Thank you for your letter, and for your account of those so dear to you.

⌐I have bought a property at Oxford opposite Ch Ch [Christ Church],
quite large enough for an Oratory, not large enough for a Mission Church.
The adjacent houses may be bought too, — at a price; but I leave that to the
future. It has cost £2000. Also, friends have given me about £500 towards an
Oratory Church. Our Bishop has again brought the project of our taking the
Oxford Mission before me — but things are not yet ripe for it. Meanwhile
Catholic youths are going to Oxford — and it will be deplorable, if they are
under no guidance.

We have a number of foreign boys in the School; this has made us anxious
— but hitherto all has been well. One boy, some time ago, we quietly got rid
of, after he had been with us a few weeks — another we shall get rid of now,
without delay. Otherwise, they have been excellent boys. Our rule is, to take
them when *young*; but several, who have been past 14 when they came, have
gone on very satisfactorily. We are still thinking of a plan which I think I
mentioned to you in the Spring — viz of having a School House for the
summer term at Rednall.⌐ If we had ten or fifteen boys more, we should do
it — for then our two ends would meet. ⌐At present, we are daunted by the
expense, and next by the Archbishop — lest, that is, he should have plans,
which he does not bring out, which will embarass our proceedings.⌐ It is a
great relief to us (pecuniarily) to have parted with Arnold. He, poor fellow,

[1] Miss Whately wrote on 15 Sept. that she had copies of only one correspondence between
Newman and her father after his departure from Oxford, consisting of two letters from her
father and one from Newman. These she published in her *Life and Correspondence of Richard
Whately, D. D.*, London 1866, I, pp. 223–6; second edition in one volume, London 1868, pp.
100–06. Newman published all four letters in *Apo.*, as the first of the 'Additional Notes,' pp.
380–7. See letters of 29 Nov. 1866 to H. Wilberforce, and 12 Feb. 1869 to Rogers.
[2] Hope-Scott wrote on 22 Sept. from Littlehampton to apologise for not having told him
sooner that his wife had given birth to a daughter, Theresa Anne, on 14 Sept.

went, because we could not give him *more*. He will not allow he has joined the Protestant Church.[1]

Ever Yours affectly John H Newman

So, Mrs Beadon Heathcote is a Catholic.[2]

P.S. I am short of paper, but ⌐I wish to add a line about my visit to Keble. I attempted it in the Spring and failed — then, when I was going now, Mrs Keble fell ill, and they went to Bournemouth. On their return to Hursley, I went, but found she had had a relapse. So I only saw him for a few hours, and retired to the Isle of Wight to Henry Bowden's and Simeon's. I was to go again this day last week, but at the last minute he wrote again to put me off on account of his wife — so I ran off into Kent to receive a gentleman and his wife, and came straight back here.

Though Keble knew I was coming, and he was at his door when I came, we did not know each other. In a very short time, the old Keble, that is the young, shone through the aged face. He is as sweet and tender, as he ever was to me. Pusey had written to me *he* was going to him, tho' he did not know that *I* was. So I met them both together — I had not seen them together for at least 23 years — and, as Mrs Keble kept her room, we three dined together — tête a tete — a thing we had never (I suppose) done in our lives before. You may think how piercing a meeting it was to all of us. Keble's speech is much affected by his illness.⌐ J H N

TO ROBERT WHITTY
(not sent)

Rednall. Sept 25. 1865

My dear Fr Whitty

Fr St John has reported to me the conversation about me which you had with him, in which your questions were so kind and his answers so explicit, that it might seem enough if I did but thank you for opening the subject, and leave it where he left it. Yet I think you may like a line or two from myself.[3]

You ask why I do not come forward at this time. This must mean, in *writing*; for, as to my position in Birmingham, I am where Providence has

---

[1] See letter of 4 June 1865 to Arnold.

[2] Mary Elizabeth Heathcote (1816–92), daughter of George Deane, Rector of Brighton, was the widow of William Beadon Heathcote, Prebendary of Salisbury, and a cousin of Sir William Heathcote, M.P. for Oxford University and Keble's squire at Hursley.

[3] St John wrote to Newman on the day of Whitty's visit, 17 Sept. The latter promised the support of the Jesuits if Newman would take the lead in meeting the infidelity of the day. St John pointed out that *D R* was covertly attacking *Apo.* which the Jesuits had examined and pronounced free from error, and when H. J. Coleridge undertook Newman's defence, Ward had stopped him. Whitty was unwilling to come forward against Ward. St John explained that Newman had found Manning could not be trusted, which Whitty had to admit, and concluded by saying all Newman wanted was to be left alone in his work of education, and for people to cease talking against the Oratory School.

placed me. Cardinal Wiseman from the first, when he called me from Little-more, marked out Oscott or Birmingham for me; it was he who led me to fix Birmingham for the site of the Oratory; he never at a later date asked me to leave Birmingham for London. On the contrary Fr Faber, with his sanction, Fr Faber, whom I had placed in London, gained a Brief from Propaganda, without a word to me, that no other Oratory should be within ten miles of his own London one.[1] Moreover, last year, when I attempted to gain a footing in Oxford, the Cardinal and other influential persons still alive, interfered, in spite of my Bishop, and hindered my doing so. You see then, that, in being content with Birmingham, I am but conforming myself to a higher will than my own.

Therefore, the only way in which you must wish me to have come forward whereas I have not, is theological or literary writing.

Why then do I not write more on subjects of the day? Simply, because I have not the gift of writing to orders. One of my first attempts thirty years ago was to write to order a History of the Councils; but it turned out to be a very different thing, a history of the Arians of the 4th century. This will serve as an illustration. If I attempted a work on the Pope's Temporal Power, it might turn out in the result a History of Charlemagne. Almost every thing that I have written has arisen out of the duties of the moment. Loss and Gain was the sudden result of a tale sent to me at Rome against Converts by a convert who had left the Catholic Church.[2] As soon as I had finished it, I at once attempted another story, but could not get on with it, though I strove hard. So it remained, one or two chapters alone written, for seven years. Then, in 1855, the Cardinal desired a library of light literature as a Catholic object; and I was able to take it up and publish it under the name of Callista. I cannot write by wishing; I can only write when power is given me to write.

Such I am at best, even though there be no discouragements in the way of my writing; but I have positive reasons against my writing, in consequence of what has happened to me. I have no desire at my age to get into controversy or dispute. I have no wish to be accused at Rome, or have to go there to defend myself. Some years ago the Cardinal and my Bishop wished me to interfere in the Rambler matter; and in consequence I got the Editor to put the Magazine at my disposal. The Cardinal thanked me for doing so. On the appearance of my very first number, I was at once remonstrated with by persons in authority, and recommended to give up the Editorship. I promised to do so after the appearance of the Second Number, which was in the Press. On its appearance, at once a theologian wrote to suggest to me that I had written heresy, and, on my protesting, would not go further in concession than to allow that I might be a material heretic.[3] And a bishop without delay brought the matter before the Holy See. Neither asked of me first for any explanation; and, as I gave up

[1] See letter of 15 Aug. 1856 to Barnabò.
[2] *From Oxford to Rome: and how it fared with some who lately made the Journey*, by a Companion Traveller, [Elizabeth Furlong Shipton Harris], 1847.
[3] Letter of 2 Sept. 1859 to Gillow.

the Magazine before the third number, I had no opportunity of explaining what I believe was altogether capable of explanation. Thus, after interfering at the Cardinal's wish in a matter not mine, by an act of great self sacrifice, I was left in the lurch.

Again, I undertook a translation of Scripture:- first the Cardinal threw all the financial matters on me. Next, when the American Bishops wrote to Propaganda and to him to protest in favour of Dr Kenrick's version, he, without answering their letter himself, simply sent it to me, with a verbal message (not one line in writing) through another Bishop, that I had better arrange the matter with the American Prelates. Thus too I was left in the lurch.

Moreover, to obey the Holy Father, I undertook to commence the Catholic University of Ireland. Here again, in the event, I was simply left in the lurch.

Last year, I bought a piece of ground for between £8000 and £9000 for an Oxford Oratory, first making it clear to my Bishop, who had taken the first step by offering me the Mission of the place, that I did so solely and simply in order to take care of the young Catholics at the University. When I had done so, Cardinal Wiseman interfered, and was very angry with me for presuming on such a step. And Cardinal Barnabò gave me a cheap consolation, by telling me that my good intentions would have their reward in heaven. He did not tell me how to get back my £8000.[1]

Since then I had no wish to disturb my quiet by bootless labours, by controversy with great men, by correspondence with Propaganda, by journeys to Rome, by anxieties, suspenses, disappointments, and scandals, I will not go out of my way to take an initiative, in the theological discussions of the day, which is both against my nature and against my antecedents.

J H N

TUESDAY 26 SEPTEMBER 1865   Boys came out to Rednall
THURSDAY 28 SEPTEMBER   Mr Monro met me at the Barnt Green Station for an hour[2]

TO J. R. BLOXAM

Rednall Septr 28/65

My dear Bloxam

Since I got home, I have been here, recruiting — after the fatigue which it generally is to me to move about. This must account for my not having yet made inquiries about the drawing of me which Miss Giberne made — but I will not forget to do so.

[1] Letter quoted in note to that of 17 Feb. 1865 to Ullathorne.
[2] P. G. Munro, tutor to Lord Campden's sons, was staying at the Oratory, and was anxious to see Newman. He said he owed everything to him, and was interested in his educational work, and wanted to be a priest and join the Oratory.

I cannot think of any thing to say to you, except that it was a great pleasure to me to see you in your home and that I am

Ever Yrs affly John H Newman

Revd J R Bloxam

TO JOHN KEBLE

Rednall. Septr 28/65

My dear Keble,

I wonder whether I wrote to you on receipt of yours.[1] On leaving Sir John Simeon's, I went to Bloxam, and so by Kent home. Being somewhat knocked up, I came here to recruit, and have been without letter paper, or I should have written to you before.

I shall be very grateful, if you will send me a couple of lines to say (if, as I trust, you can say it) that Mrs Keble is getting round.

It is a sad disappointment to me not having had a talk with you; but it is a great thing to have seen you.[2]

I hope Pusey will not be attempting too much in his Address at Norwich.

Ever Yrs affly John H Newman

The Revd John Keble

TO E. B. PUSEY

Rednall Septr 28/65

My dear Pusey

I hope you got the Patrizzi; I gave directions for it to be sent you — and Migne's volume of Treatises, though I dare say you have it.[3]

I suppose your Norwich's address will be in the Papers. I am rather anxious lest neither people's minds nor the subjects themselves are ripe for a discussion.

Ever Yrs affly John H Newman

The Revd E B Pusey DD

[1] Keble wrote on 17 Sept. to ask Newman not to pay a second visit owing to his wife's illness. 'But you must let us hold you engaged for a more favourable time.' He added, 'it was most pleasant your catching E. B. P. [Pusey] here, and will make the day a bright one to remember as long as one is to stay here. It so brought home to us the assurance of your sympathy, full sympathy, in almost all that one hopes and tries to be chiefly occupied in

Ever my dear old Friend most affly yours J. K.'

[2] Keble replied on 30 Sept., 'It was a real disappointment not to have a good talk with you, but a real compensation to hear so much of your talk with Pusey.'

[3] Francisci Xaverii Patritii, *De Evangeliis*, Freiburg-im-Breisgau 1853, and J. P. Migne's *Scripturae Sacrae Cursus Completus*, III, Paris 1842. These were to help Pusey in preparing *The Spirit in which the Researches of Learning and Science should be applied to the Study of the Bible*, his paper read at the Norwich Church Congress. See seventh note to letter of 13 Sept. to St John.

Rednall Septr 29/65

My dear Child

I did not get your letter till after the 15th — as I was moving about.

God speed you — I will say Mass for your tomorrow, if all is well[1]

Yrs affly J H N

SATURDAY 30 SEPTEMBER 1865 returned from Rednall for good — found Renouf in Bm[Birmingham] — and Harry Wiberforce came

MONDAY 2 OCTOBER Harry W. left. Miss Holmes dined in guest room.

TO EDWARD BERDOE[2]

Oct 2/65[3]

Before a person is a judge, whether our devotions to the Blessed Virgin and the Saints are idolatrous or not, he must place himself in the position towards them in which, as a matter of faith, we hold ourselves to be.

We believe in a family of God, of which the Saints are the heavenly members and we the earthly — yet one family embracing earth and heaven. We believe we have access to the heavenly members, and are at liberty to converse with them — and that we can ask them for benefits and they can gain them for us. We believe at the same time that they are so different from us, and so much above us, that our *natural* feelings towards them would be awe, fear, and dismay, such as we should have on seeing a ghost, or as Daniel's when he fell down and quaked at the vision of the Angel — these feelings being changed into loving admiration and familiar devotion, by our belief in the Communion of Saints. Moreover, we believe them present with us as truly as our fellow-men are present. Now consider the honours paid to monarchs on earth — men kneel to them, bow to their empty throne, pay them the most profound homage, use almost the language of slaves in addressing them, and dare not approach them without a ceremonial. Much more reverently ought the Saints to be treated by us, in proportion as heaven is higher than earth — yet I do not think we observe that proportion — our language towards our Lady and the Saints is not so much above that which is used towards great personages

[1] See letter of 27 Aug. to Lavinia Wilson.
[2] The letter has no name, but Edward Berdoe, a London chemist, wrote to Newman on 28 Sept. after having read *Apo.* He had been educated for the Baptist ministry, but had become an Anglican, and said 'I have little doubt that Catholicism is right — but whether Anglo or Roman is the question with me . . . My grand difficulty is the Mariolatry of the Roman Church.' He also was hurt by 'Saint Worship'. He asked for the name of a priest in London, whom he could consult.
[3] On the copy of this letter made by Neville, Newman has written 'not worth keeping.'

on earth, as immortal blessedness is above temporal power. Or take the words used to express human love — they are almost idolatrous — in some cases they are so — i.e. in the *spirit* in which they are uttered — yet I should be very unwilling to allow that the general body of lovers were idolators. Why is it that we are so little jealous of human love, yet suddenly so shocked if we find Catholics transported by affection towards the Saints? Any unconcerned person will feel inclined sometimes to laugh at the terms of endearment used by parties who are attached to each other, and will easily be led to say that they are in very bad taste — such exhibitions are sometimes made when private letters turn up in courts of law, yet no sensible person will doubt on the one hand their reality as confessions of feeling, on the other their exemption from any fair imputation of being idolatrous.

I have not yet touched upon the incommunicable relation of the Blessed Virgin to our Lord, as His Mother — nor again to what is taught us by the primitive Fathers, as St Justin and St Irenaeus, that, as Eve had a share in our fall, so Mary had a share in our redemption.[1]

TO LADY CHATTERTON

The Oratory Bm Octr 2. 1865

My dear Lady Chatterton,

You wished, I believe, to know what the doctrine of the Immaculate Conception is:- it is this, that the Blessed Virgin is exempt from original sin.

By original sin is meant the state of degradation and disadvantage in which the whole world lies in consequence of the fall of Adam. This state is reversed in baptism, when the grace of God is first given to the soul. Then by that grace the soul is brought into the family of God, as Adam belonged to it in the beginning.

In some rare cases, as in St John Baptist's, this grace has been given before birth; so that St John was *not* born in original sin. But, since his soul existed before our Lady's visit to his Mother, up to that time *had* been in original sin; therefore *he was* conceived in original sin, or his conception was *not* immaculate.

By conception is meant the creation of the soul, when at once it is united to the body, and becomes a human being or person. In the first instant then of St John's existing, or on his conception, he was at once, (as being of the lineage of Adam,) brought into the state of degradation to which Adam had reduced himself and his offspring. But, when divine grace was given him at the time of the Visitation, he was taken out, ipso facto, of that fallen state. Had grace

---

[1] Berdoe acknowledged this letter on 5 Oct., and said he would consult Canon Oakeley, whom Newman had recommended. Berdoe wrote again on 28 May 1866, the day of his reception into the Church by Fr Gallwey. He had not continued with Oakeley, 'I was not prepared to submit to the authority of Holy Church,' but had attended St Alban's, Holborn, and 'considered I had the "via media" to perfection but it would not do.'

been given to him, not merely three months before his birth, but from the first moment of his existence as a human being, then it would have been right to say of him, that he was conceived without original sin, or that he had an immaculate conception.

Now this we believe to have been actually the case as regards the Blessed Virgin. At the very time that her soul was created, grace was given to her, so that she never was without grace, never under the power of sin, even original, never otherwise than immaculate.

Next, as to the *antiquity* of the doctrine. In the first ages original sin was not formally spoken of in contrast to actual. In the fourth century, Pelagius denied it, and was refuted and denounced by St Augustine. Not *till* the time of St Augustine could the question be mooted precisely whether our Lady was without original sin or not. Up to his time, and after his time, it was usual to say or to imply that Mary had *nothing to do* with sin, in vague terms. The earliest Fathers, St Justin, St Irenæus etc. contrast her with Eve, while they contrast our Lord with Adam. In doing this — 1. they, sometimes imply, sometimes insist upon, the point that Eve sinned when tried, and Mary did not sin when tried; and 2. they say that, by not sinning, Mary had a real part in the work of redemption, in a way in which no other creature had a share. This does not go so far as actually to pronounce that she had the grace of God from the first moment of her existence, and never was under the power of original sin, but by comparing her with Eve, who *was* created of course without original sin, and by giving her so high an office, it implies it.

Next, shortly after St Augustine, the 3rd General Council was held against Nestorius, and declared Mary to be the Mother of God.

From this time the language of the Fathers is very strong, though vague, about her immaculateness. In the time of Mahomet the precise doctrine seems to have been taught in the East, for I think he mentions it in the Koran.[1]

In the middle ages, when every thing was subjected to rigid examination of a reasoning character, the question was raised whether the doctrine was consistent with the Blessed Virgin's having a human father and mother — and serious objections were felt to it on this score. Men defined the words 'Immaculate Conception' differently from what I have done above, and in consequence denied it. St Bernard and St Thomas, in this way, were opposed to it, and the Dominicans. A long controversy ensued and a hot one — it lasted many centuries. At length, in our time, it has been defined *in that sense* in which I have explained the words above — a sense, which St Bernard, St Thomas, and the Dominicans did *not* deny.

The same controversy about the sense of a word had occurred in the instance of the first General Council at Nicaea. The Nicene Creed uses the word 'Consubstantial' to protect the doctrine of our Lord's divinity against Arius, which the great Council of Antioch some 70 years before had repudiated as a symbol of heresy. In like manner great Saints have repudiated the *words*

[1] Cf. the *Koran*, chapter iii

'Immaculate Conception,' from taking them in a different sense from that which the Church has accepted and sanctioned.

> I am, My dear Lady Chatterton, Sincerely Yours in Xt
> John H Newman of the Oratory

Lady Chatterton

P.S. Dr Ullathorne has written a small work on the Immaculate Conception which you can get at Burns's.[1]

Since writing the above, your letter has come. I wrote to Fr Coleridge of the Month at once — but have not yet heard from him.[2]

Thank Miss Orpen for me for her letter.

TUESDAY 3 OCTOBER 1865   Renouf left   began Terence with the boys and began with Towneley
THURSDAY 5 OCTOBER   Weather broke up about now after a long dry time
SATURDAY 7 OCTOBER   Professor Robertson came

TO JOHN KEBLE

The Oratory Bm Octr 8. 1865

My dearest Keble

I do hope you will not think this letter requires any answer. If I did not rely on your understanding this, I should not write. It would be quite wicked in me to put any thing on you which had the resemblance of a duty or a call to exert yourself — and I write, not for an answer, but merely because I think you will really like to know the impression which Pusey's new book has upon my mind.[3]

Well then — I really marvel that he should have dreamed of calling it an Irenicon — it is said 'If he ask bread, will he give him a stone? or if he ask fish will he give him a serpent? or if he ask an egg, will he give him a scorpion?'[4] I grieve to use such an illustration — But so it is — if Pusey is writing to hinder his own people from joining us, well and good, he has a right to write as he has done — but how can he fancy that to exaggerate, instead of smoothing contrarieties, is the way to make us listen to him? I wish I were not obliged to say that his mode of treating with us is rhetorical and unfair. I will give one instance. The other day, when I was with you, he himself noticed the mistake

---

[1] *The Immaculate Conception of the Mother of God: an Exposition,* London 1855.
[2] Lady Chatterton wished to have a tale she had written published in the *Month.* See letter of 10 Oct.
[3] *An Eirenicon.* It had the form of a letter to Keble. Cf. letter of 5 Sept. to Pusey.
[4] St Luke 11: 11–12

of V. C. Wynter of Intercession for Invocation —[1] yet he seems to me to have fallen into the same. Our received doctrine is, after St Justin and St Irenaeus, as we interpret them, that as Eve had a secondary part in the fall, so had Blessed Mary in the redemption. And interpreting them still, it is our belief, that, whereas all the Saints intercede for us, through the merits and in the grace of Christ, she κατ' ἐξοχὴν, is the Intercessor or Helper ⟨(Advocata, παράκλητος, St Irenaeus)⟩ — that this is her distinct part in the economy of human salvation — so that, knowing the Will of our Lord most intimately, she prays *according* to His will, or thus is the ordained means or channel by which that will is carried out. Therefore 'every thing goes through the hands of Mary —' and this is a great reason for our asking her prayers.[2]

But there is all the difference in the world between saying that 'without her intercession no one is saved —' and 'without her invocation no one is saved —' whereas Pusey at page 102 passes from the one idea to the other, as if authors who said the one must necessarily say, may be taken and understood to say, the other. He quotes Suarez for the power of her Intercession — he quotes St Bernardine (or Eadmer) for the necessity of her Invocation, or of devotion to her — but Suarez is an authority quite in a different line of importance from St Bernardine — ⟨(or rather Eadmer —)⟩ The former is a theologian, laying down doctrine — the latter is a devotional author, — and moreover writes for Italians, for those who already knew and held the doctrine of her Intercession, and were in a country where to neglect devotion to her would have been a rejection of a privilege which they *possessed*. I never can deny my belief that the Blessed Virgin prays efficaciously for the Church, and for individual souls in and out of it. Nor can I deny that to be devout to her is a duty *following* on this doctrine — but I never will say, even though St Bernardine said it, that no one is saved who is not devout to her, and (tho' I don't know St B's writings) I do not think *he* would have said it had he not been in his own Christendom, or had he known the history of the first centuries, or had he seen the religious state of things which we see ourselves. St B. again is not answerable for what *Faber* may have said; but even, if he agreed with him, Pusey has no right to put their doctrine under the sanction of Suarez, unless he produces from Suarez distinct passages, in which he speaks of invocation as well as intercession. As to Faber, I have not read his books — he is no authority — nor did I *ever hear* of the names of Oswald or de Montford, till I saw them in Pusey's book.[3] Now this is a fact much to the point — for it proves that a man (like myself) may be a priest and in ecclesiastical station, may have had a DD degree given him, and set over a new University, without any knowledge whatever of those extreme views which are held by a particular party in the Church, and which they have a right to hold,

[1] The Vice-Chancellor of Oxford University confused the two in 1843. See Liddon's *Pusey*, II, pp. 337–8 and *K.C.*, pp. 229–30.
[2] On this and what follows see *A letter addressed to the Rev. E. B. Pusey, D. D., on occasion of his Eirenicon, Diff.* II, e.g. p. 105.
[3] See third note to letter of 31 Oct. to Pusey.

(so that they don't force me to hold them,) while they keep clear of offending, in their devotional impulses, any doctrine of the Church. As soon as such views approach to such an offence, they are, they have been again and again, censured and beaten back by ecclesiastical authorities. I turned up a letter of mine the other day, (I *think* written to Christie between 1841–1845) in which I speak of the number of books, about our Lady, which Gregory xvi had censured.[1] Of *course* the devotions in question *tend* to superstition — there is no truth that may not be the occasion of error — but usum non tollit abusus — and Pusey's book looks far more like an argumentum ad hominem, because Manning charges *Anglicanism* with running into *infidelity*, than a calm view of the case.[2] Certain I am, that, as an Irenicum, it can only raise a smile — and I wish that were all it would raise. The first duty of charity is to try to enter into the mind and feelings of others. This is what I love so much in you, my dear Keble; but I much desiderate it in this new book of Pusey's — and I deplore the absence of it there — The instance I have given, is but one instance

Ever Yours affectly John H Newman

Revd John Keble.

P.S. Thank you for your account of Mrs Keble — Bournemouth is not such a banishment from home as Penzance must be.
P.S. Oct 19. I have kept this some days — hoping it might not be a duty to send it — but I am obliged unwillingly to say that it *is* a duty — I really think so.[3]

MONDAY 9 OCTOBER 1865 Professor Robertson went. Admitted Joseph Drew to his first probation. Duke of Norfolk came

TO THE EDITOR OF THE BIRMINGHAM DAILY POST

The Oratory, October 9, 1865.

Sir,

I have just seen, for the first time, Lord Lyttelton's address at the opening of the Working Men's Industrial Exhibition, on August 28 last, and I request to be allowed to make an observation in your columns on the portion of it which relates to myself.[4]

---

[1] This letter has not been traced.
[2] H. E. Manning, *The Workings of the Holy Spirit in the Church of England, a Letter to the Rev. E. B. Pusey*, pp. 27–37.
[3] For Keble's reply, see letter of 1 Nov. to him.
[4] Lord Lyttelton at the end of his speech opening this Exhibition at the Bingley Hall, Birmingham, said: 'A man of the highest genius — who may be almost within hearing of what I am saying, and whom I indeed perceive to have been invited on this occasion, though I should think with but the faintest hope that he would accept the invitation — a man of the

I am indebted to his Lordship for the too flattering terms in which he speaks of me; and I know well that, in referring to what I wrote last year, he has no wish at all to say anything but what is considerate to me, and true to the text of my book.

Being sure of this, I read with the greatest astonishment the statement (which he goes out of his way to make), that in my 'Apologia' I have told the world that 'to me the contemplation of the vast material progress about me is a "simple bewilderment." Apol. p. 401.'[1]

I beg leave distinctly to deny that I have said or thought what he here imputes to me. Neither directly nor indirectly have I spoken, in the passage in question, of the 'material progress' of society at all, much less in the language of 'dismay' or 'terror.' I am speaking there of 'secular knowledge,' not of 'material progress;' and when I adopt the word 'bewilderment,' I employ it, not as condemning such knowledge, but as a strong word for 'wonder' which I had used just before. My sentence runs thus:-

'We live in a wonderful age; the enlargement of the circle of secular knowledge just now is simply a bewilderment, and the more so, because it has the promise of continuing, and that with greater rapidity, and more signal results.'

Lord Lyttelton must have spoken from memory. Nor do I suppose, judging by the words in his address which precede his notice of me, that there is any assignable difference between his sentiments and my own as regards 'material progress.' I, too, with him sincerely thank God for the blessings of the 'railway' and the 'telegraph,' and am very glad to have 'commerce unfettered' and 'the press unburdened.' It is only when, instead of using these gifts with thankfulness, men are tempted to think that material progress will stand in the place of religion, that I too consider with him it involves evil; but, according to the old saying, '*Usum non tollit abusus.*' It is hard then to find him contrast me with himself, in a matter too plain, one would think, to afford matter of controversy between us.

I will add that I was so far from disapproving of the Exhibition, to the opening of which I had been courteously invited, that, when I was obliged to decline in my own person, I asked to be allowed to send one of our Oratorian body to it as my substitute.[2]

I am, &c., John H. Newman.

highest genius, but whose views, I must say, have led him to the most dismal and dreary prospect of the condition and the future of his species, has lately told us in his celebrated work, that to him the contemplation of the vast material progress about him is a "simple bewilderment." With these two words he dismisses the subject.'
Lord Lyttlelton's speech, with a reference to *Apo.* in note, was printed as a pamphlet. See also the *Birmingham Daily Post,* (29 Aug. 1865), p. 3.
[1] *Apo.* p. 260.
[2] Lord Lyttelton replied on 11 Oct. to the Editor, that his misunderstanding of Newman's words had been influenced by their context. 'However, all that was my stupidity; and I will only add that when I said Dr. Newman's view seemed to me a dreary one, I was referring, not to a few words, but to the whole of the remarkable chapter in question, in its bearing on this life alone.' The *Birmingham Daily Post,* (13 Oct. 1865), p. 3.

TUESDAY 10 OCTOBER 1865   The Duke went   Miss Meadows called.   Henry went to Rednall for his retreat

TO LADY CHATTERTON

The Oratory Bm Oct 10. 1865

My dear Lady Chatterton,

I have heard from Fr Coleridge. He feels the kindness and advantage of your assistance, but he is hampered by the necessities of his Magazine, and, I suppose also, by the rules prescribed by those whom he has to consult; for he does not say 'I,' but 'we.'

He says in his letter of this morning to me, 1. we want a short story, one which would be complete in six numbers, 16 pages in each number. 2. the love-making, if there must be any at all, understood rather than expressed. 3 as much of character as possible, but this of course is not so easy in a short tale. 4 we should be very glad if she would avail herself of her knowledge of foreign scenes, as Spain. 5. we should like much to have the first instalment sent to us first of all.

He wrote to me some ten days ago without reference to you

'I am almost in despair. I want to find writers who will not be sensational — who will make the love story a subordinate part and depend chiefly upon character. I think we do not require at all any religious element, even so much as in Constance Sherwood.[1] I want a re-action against sensationalism and that perpetual anatomizing of feelings and emotions which has lately been fashionable. And I do not wish the novels to be long. I do not know any much greater benefit that any one could confer on us, than putting us in the way of a good work of this character.'

I am, My dear Lady Chatterton, Very sincerely Yours in Xt
John H Newman of the Oratory

Lady Chatterton

P.S.   Every thing kind from me to Mr Dering and your niece, to whom I had hoped to have written before now.

WEDNESDAY 11 OCTOBER 1865   wrote in the Daily Post about Lord Lyttelton's Address

[1] Lady Georgiana Fullerton's novel, serialised in the *Month*.

TO T. W. ALLIES

Oct. 11. 1865.

My dear Allies,

Thank you for your congratulations, and the beautiful prose you have sent me.[1] No — I assure you I have nothing more to produce of Gerontius. On the 17th of January last it came into my head to write it. I really cannot tell how, and I wrote on till it was finished, on small bits of paper. And I could no more write any thing else by willing it, than I could fly. I am greatly honoured by the good Nuns of Notre Dame having got their children to act it.[2]

Keble has been trying to get me to see him a long time, and after various vain attempts I settled to go to him one day about a month ago. After it was fixed, Pusey wrote me word, not knowing any thing about it, that he was going that very day. It was a trial seeing both at once, but I did not like to put off, and dined tête à tête with them at Hursley (Mrs Keble being ill) — a thing I had never perhaps done in my life before.

His book amazes me.[3] Within the year he professed (unless I quite misunderstood him) that he did now [not] countenance in the Oxford Movement that controversial spirit towards Rome which characterized it when we were together, and he lamented my going to Oxford on this very account that it would make us rivals when we ought to pull together. Moreover he calls his book Irenicon — whereas if any book could irritate, it is such a one as it. I hope it will be answered *well*. The Archbishop is bound to do it himself or by some one else. For myself, I think it rhetorical and unfair, and, were I bound in duty (which happily I am not) to come forward, could do it, I think; but not, except at the expense of theories and doctrines, which the Archbishop thinks of vital importance, and which I cannot receive. Indeed, this will be their difficulty in answering it. They will not like to say out all they hold, yet cannot disown any part of it, so I don't expect any thing bold and straightforward.[4]

I thank you with all my heart for your prayers for me etc etc.

Yours ever affectly in Xt   John H Newman of the Oratory

P.S.   I suppose you have had no news of your boys.[5] I am going to send you my two plays of Terence.[6]

[1] Allies wrote on 10 Oct. to congratulate Newman on the twentieth anniversary of his becoming a Catholic. He sent him an old Latin hymn, a 'prose', asking for a translation.
[2] Allies wrote, 'I saw Gerontius most beautifully acted lately at the Convent of Notre Dame, Liverpool, by the Students of the Training School . . . I feel sure Gerontius does not stand alone: can you not give us some of his brethren.'
[3] Allies wrote of the *Eirenicon*, that in twenty years Pusey had learned nothing of what the Church is.
[4] See end of letter of 17 Nov. to Pusey.
[5] Allies's two sons, Edward and Cyril, had gone sheep farming in Queensland.
[6] *Phormio* and *Pincerna*.

THURSDAY 12 OCTOBER 1865   Dr Maurice of California to dinner
FRIDAY 13 OCTOBER   Mr J. F. Stephen called in evening[1]   Renouf here again
SATURDAY 14 OCTOBER   W. Palmer came.

TO T. F. KNOX

The Oratory Birmingham Octr 15. 1865

My dear Father Supr

I thank you for your news — and trust and am sure that St Philip will support you in your new duties. I said Mass for you with that intention this morning[2]

Yours affectly in Xt   John H Newman of the Oratory

The Very Revd Fr Knox

TO MRS SCONCE

The Oratory, Birmingham. Oct. 15/65.

My dear Mrs. Sconce,

Mr Palmer is here to-day, and tells me that you are still in England. I was away when your letter and present came — and when I returned, I was too late, as I thought from your letter, to write to you in England — so I delayed; but Mr Palmer is to give me your England direction — and I write this in prospect of getting it.

I thought it particularly kind of you to send me so interesting a work.[3] I have been much pleased by what I have read of it — and letters always have the charm of reality. I have before now given this as the reason why I like the early Fathers more than the Medieval Saints viz: because we have the letters of the former. I seem to know St. Chrysostom or St. Jerome in a way in which I never can know St. Thomas Aquinas. — and St. Thomas of Canterbury (himself medieval) on account of his letters as I never can know St. Pius Vth.[4] There is something always to be gained by the sight of a religious man, as he

---

[1] James Fitzjames Stephen wrote on 28 Sept. that he would like to discuss with Newman matters arising out of his review of *Apo.* in *Fraser's Magazine* for Sept. 1864. See letter of 30 Sept. 1864 to William Froude. On 6 Oct. 1865 Stephen wrote that he was the author of the article 'Dr Newman and Liberalism' in the *Saturday Review*. See letter of 2 July to J. Walker.

Stephen had been introduced to Newman by Grant Duff ten years before and now wanted to engage in religious argumentation. Newman regarded such controversies as 'fights in the dark,' as appears from Stephen's letters to him. According to his biographer, Newman told him 'that he could not argue with a man who differed so completely upon first principles.' Leslie Stephen, *The Life of Sir James Fitzjames Stephen*, London 1895, p. 191. For Newman's account of their meeting and his severe criticism of Stephen's article in the *Saturday Review*, see letters of 20 and 26 April 1870 to J. H. Woodward.

[2] Knox wrote on 14 Oct. that he had the previous day been elected Superior of the London Oratory.

[3] A letter of 4 Aug. 1891 from Mrs Sconce to Neville shows that the work was *Life and Letters of Robert Clement Sconce*, by his daughter Sarah Susanna Bunbury, two volumes, London 1861. Robert was Mrs Sconce's father-in-law.

[4] *H. S.* II, pp. 217–24.

is — whether he be in partial error, or on the other hand a Doctor of the Church — and therefore I am very glad to have your present over and above the token of your kindness which I feel it to be.

I hope you are all getting more settled in Italy — and with a greater prospect than hitherto of reconciling Italians to the Holy See.

Mrs. Sconce.

MONDAY 16 OCTOBER 1865   W. Palmer went   letter from Nicholas Darnell

TO MRS THOMAS COMBE

The Oratory Birmingham Octr 16. 1865

My dear Mrs Combe

I much regret that I was away from Birmingham when you and Mr Combe called on me. It was very kind in you both, and I should have written before this, had not so many things come in my way day by day to hinder me.[1]

I left home in order to see Mr Keble who has been desirous of it these two years — but, it is so difficult to get away. I had attempted before in vain, and now, when I was going, Mrs Keble fell ill — and her health continued (and, I fear, continues) so anxious that after all I only saw him for a few hours. As it happened, Dr Pusey was with him — so we three dined tete a tete, a thing, perhaps we had never done before. I should have known Dr Pusey any where, but Mr Keble I did not recognise at all, even in his own house — though, when he spoke familiarly, his old self came out through his eyes and his countenance. Mr Keble did not know me; so, I am altered as much as he — and perhaps *you* would not have known me, even here at my own home.

Had I been at home, I should have liked to have asked you about your own family, of whom I have heard nothing for years.

With kindest regards to Mr Combe, I am, My dear Mrs Combe,
Sincerely Yours John H Newman[2]

Mrs Combe

[1] 'Combe was born in Leicester in 1797, the son of the leading bookseller, and after schooling at Repton he worked in his father's shop, and came to Oxford about 1825 as an assistant in Joseph Parker's bookshop in the Turl; he lived with his sister who kept a stationer's shop and university lodgings in Oriel Street. Pusey, Newman, and Froude were amongst her lodgers and so it was that Combe came strongly under the influence of the Tractarian movement. It was Newman who introduced him to his future wife, Martha Edwards, who had been an active worker in Newman's parish, and he officiated at their marriage at St Ebbe's on 3 September 1840; Mrs Combe was to take a full share, and sometimes the leading part, in her husband's charitable acts. However, before his marriage Combe left Oxford for a time . . . but in 1838, on the recommendation of Henry Parker, he was appointed Superintendent of the Clarendon Press, where he lived for the rest of his life.' A.R.T.R.S. [Dr Robb-Smith], *The Radcliffe Chapel and the Combe Benefactions,* The Radcliffe Infirmary, issued in connection with the centenary of the Chapel of St Luke, Oxford 1965, p. 5. Thomas Combe died in 1872 and left his fortune, £70,000 to his wife, who continued her charitable work until her death in 1894. According to her obituary in the *Guardian,* 'Her friendship with Cardinal Newman remained her greatest interest outside Oxford, and he on his side retained his veneration for her deeply religious character . . .'

[2] Owing to illness, Mrs Combe did not reply until 23 Feb. 1866, when besides giving her family news, she asked Newman to sit for his bust to Woolner. See letter of 15 May 1866 to Rogers.

TO NICHOLAS DARNELL

Oct 16/65

My dear Nicholas

I read with the greatest joy your letter to Fr Edward. It is worthy of you — and I am sure, as far as I am concerned, it has quite set right the past and in saying that, I have said all that need be said.[1]

It interested us to hear that you were making the experiment of taking pupils who had left school — and there will always be parents who wish their sons to be for a while under some regime less strict than school, before going to the University or into the world; but the great difficulty is to get youths to work under such circumstances; and in consequence there will be other parents who prefer to keep them under the stricter system as long as they can. Thynne was just beginning to enter heartily into his work when he left us. C. Murray, I fear, will never work, except at Mathematics; but [Richard] Ward promised to do well. The Balliol entrance examination seems a severe one — but, I suppose there is little to fear at Ch Ch [Christ Church]

Yours affectly J H N

The Revd N. Darnell

TO MRS WILLIAM FROUDE

The Oratory Bm Oct. 16/65

My dear Mrs Froude

I have had so much to do in various ways since I have been back that I have not had time to tell you, as I hoped to do, of my visit to Keble. It was not much of a visit, for first he was obliged to put me off on account of Mrs K's illness. This kept me here and at Rednall, in suspense — Then, when she got better and they returned home, Pusey wrote me word, he too was going to Keble at the very same time — And, to complete the mischance when I got to Hursley, she had just been taken ill again and poor Keble was obliged to be in and out of the room, and out of the room in mind, when he was in it. I did not stop above five hours, and retreated to the Isle of Wight, where, at H Bowden's and Sir J. Simeon's, I waited for her recovery. But when a week had past and Keble wrote me word she was not well enough for me to return, I set off to receive two or three persons of some name and position in Kent — and thence home. But I am too old to travel, and I am only now recovering the fatigue.

[1] In a letter to Caswall of 15 Oct., Darnell made apology for his conduct at the end of 1861, when he resigned the headmastership of the Oratory School and left the Birmingham Oratory. 'I am quite aware that as a member and subject of such a Congregation as that of St Philip, with such a superior, that my conduct was insufferably violent headstrong and conceited generally to the Congregation, and still more insufferably insolent, ungrateful and ungracious to the Father [Newman], and that any thing I have since said by way of acknowledgment of my fault was quite inadequate to the occasion, and could never have been accepted as an apology either by the Father, the Congregation or those externs, alas too many, to whom I must have given scandal . . .'

When I got to Keble's door, he happened to be at it, but we did not know each other, and I was obliged to show him my card. Is not this strange? it is imagination mastering reason. He indeed thought, since Pusey was coming, I should not come that day — but I knew beyond doubt that I was at his house — Yet I dared not presume it was he — but, after he began to talk, the old Keble, that is, the young, came out from his eyes and his features, and I dare say, if I saw him once or twice, I should be unable to see much difference between his present face and his face of past days. As Mrs Keble was ill, we three dined together tête a tête — a thing we never perhaps had done before — there was something awful in three men meeting in old age who had worked together in their best days. Vanity of vanities, in all is vanity, was the sad burden of the whole — once so united, now so broken up, so counter to each other — though neither of them of course would quite allow it — Keble has since written to me, 'When shall we three meet again? . . . . when the hurly burley's done.'[1]

Keble is deaf — but, what is worse, his speech is much impaired — and I think he *thinks* more slowly. Pusey was full of plans, full of meetings. He has since made an important speech at Norwich on the interpretation of Scripture, which will do good, and of this he was full. Then, he was just on publishing his book which he calls an Irenicon, and he was full of it, though he was cautious of letting out all that was in it. Have you seen it? It is anything but an Irenicon — it is likely to make Catholics very angry — and justly angry.

Ever Yrs affectly John H Newman.

TUESDAY 17 OCTOBER 1865   Mr Jones here[2]
WEDNESDAY 18 OCTOBER   Mr Jones received   Profuse rain through October

TO EDWARD HENEAGE DERING

The Oratory Bm Oct 18. 1865

My dear Mr Dering

I am anxious to know something about you all — whether you have made any Catholic acquaintances at St Leonard's, and whether, as I suppose is the case, you have made your first communion.[3]

It was quite natural you should wish to oblige your late clergyman as far as you could — and of course it must be very painful to him, considering

---

[1] *Macbeth*, I, i. 1. Keble wrote on 30 Sept.
[2] This was John Hugh Jones, who went up to Jesus College, Oxford in 1862, and had intended to become an Anglican clergyman. He was ordained in 1872 and was for many years the priest at Carnarvon.
[3] Lady Chatterton and her husband and niece had gone to St Leonards, where they made their first communion as Catholics.

Tenterden is full of dissenters, no longer to be supported by you. I dare say you can in many ways show your wish to be of use to him, still.

I hope Lady Chatterton is better for the change of air. I take it for granted, since I sent on her letter that she has heard from Fr Coleridge

I inclose a note for Miss Orpen, & am Very sincerely Yours in Xt

John H Newman of the Oratory

E H Dering Esqr

TO MRS JOHN MOZLEY

The Oratory Birmingham Octr 18.1865

My dear Jemima

I shall be much pleased to see Frank [Mozley], and will give him dinner; — on Friday the 20th.

It grieves me to think you have bought Corelli's Solos, if so, for me, for there is a copy in the House. Indeed, in a way *I* have a copy — but it is a peculiar edition copyright, and doctored, to make it, I suppose, fit the Piano. I fancied you might have had a copy of mine at Derby, doing nothing.

I should be afraid to play with Charles Mozley — for he is a practised player, and I play no better than a boy[1]

Yours affectly John H Newman

Mrs John Mozley

TO MISS ORPEN

Oct 18/65

My dear Child

I have wished to write to you ever since your letter came — but have so many letters to write, and so many things to do, that I have not found time.

It was kind in you to write about your late clergyman's wish — but I quite understand how the case stood.[2] I suppose *you* must have mentioned it to the Bishop, for *I* did not. All that can be done for the Established Church in Tenterden, ought to be done — for it is far nearer to Catholicism than dissent is.

We will not forget the prayers you ask for. I hope you are all the better for the sea air — and I trust you have found, or will soon find, some Catholics, who will answer the various questions which must occur to you on matters in detail.

[1] Charles Mozley was Jemima's brother-in-law.
[2] Miss Orpen had written to Newman to explain that she and her uncle and aunt had applied to Bishop Grant for permission to attend occasionally the Anglican church at Tenterden, in the hope of giving a good example, not because they shrank from acknowledging their conversion.

Pray let me know at your leisure how you are going on — and don't be angry with me if I am a bad correspondent

Yours most sincerely in Xt   John H Newman of the Oratory

Miss Orpen

TO J. R. BLOXAM

The Oratory Bm Oct 19/65

My dear Bloxam

I have meant to write to you day by day — but cannot find time. Thank you for the letters and the books — I shall value them very much. You must let me delay the photographs — I have them quite at hand, but really I cannot just now command time for any thing. I won't forget Miss Giberne's — but I can't quite tell about it yet.[1]

I have seen Pusey's book — and it has profoundly grieved me. He calls it an Irenicon — but I never read a book more likely to make people angry. It seems to me prodigiously unfair, and unaccountably so. When we were in correspondence in the Spring about my Oxford plan, he said that the times were passed when there was controversy between his party and Catholics as when I was in Oxford — and he regretted my proposed coming as being likely to revive it — and now he goes out of the way to do the very thing — and calls it an Irenicon. It is quite true we think salvation is gained thro' the Blessed Virgin's *intercession* — but not necessarily by her *invocation* — but Pusey confuses Invocation and Intercession just as old Wynter did in the case of Tom Morris.[2] This is only one out of many great unfairnesses. I am very sorry it should be so. But I must cease

Ever Yours affectly John H Newman

FRIDAY 20 OCTOBER 1865   Mr Jones went   Renouf went?

TO HENRY JAMES COLERIDGE

The Oratory Bm Octr 20. 1865

My dear Fr Coleridge

The difference of opinion as to Number 90 between Pusey and myself has ever been this: that I thought such a Catholic interpretation of the 39 Articles a possible interpretation, and he thought it the true, just, natural, normal one. Ward on the other hand professed to hold it, while he called it non-natural. The difference between Pusey and me is brought out in our

---

[1] See letter of 28 Sept. to Bloxam.
[2] See third note to letter of 8 Oct. to Keble.

letters in the Times of the date, I think, of the last week in February 1863.[1]

It also appeared on the publication of the Tract. My view was this — 'the Compilers of the Articles intended the words they used to bear several senses, in order that Semi-Catholics, time servers etc etc might avail themselves of them.' This, in the compilers, was dishonest; but, *since* it was their intention, I considered we might avail ourselves of it. I used to say frankly, 'Either they are dishonest, or I. If I invent the interpretation, then I shuffle — if they meant it, they shuffled.' I thought they meant it — and I said, 'This shuffle told for them in their day, for it kept Catholics in the Anglican Church — and now it tells for us, and shall hinder us going out of it.' This view is brought out in the last paragraph of the Tract — and this paragraph Pusey wished me in the second edition to leave out. 'Why,' I answered 'it is like playing Hamlet, without the Prince of Denmark; that paragraph is the key to the whole Tract; for, if the compilers were not shuffling, I *am* — and I don't intend to allow this.' His answer would be, 'no, there is no shuffling in Compilers or you — for they actually meant the Catholic sense of the Articles, as you give it in the Tract, as the true sense of their words, and not as a mere trap for waverers.'

As to 'General Councils,' I think they meant vaguely collections of Bishops etc from all parts of the world — and this too is what Bellarmine means by them. He says they [are] not true Councils (approbata perhaps is his word) i.e. *may err* unless confirmed by the Pope — and the Article says also 'they may err —' but leaves open the question whether *ever* 'they *can't* err.' Of course if *implies* that they *always* err, but it does *say* that '*all* General Councils may err.'[2]

Ever Yrs John H Newman

TO MISS MUNRO

The Oratory Bm Oct 20. 1865

My dear Miss Munro

You must not be angry with me for my delay in writing to you, as I have been very busy. Gladly would I say any thing to your purpose, but I don't profess to be clever in such matters as you propose to me.

Also, a person who sees you must be a better judge than a person at a distance. *He* may have good reasons for what he says; he may see that, until you have tried and failed, you will not be quiet.

Again, I don't expect that any Religious Superior would keep you against

[1] See letter of 24 Feb. 1863 to the Editor of *The Times*. Coleridge, who proposed to write on Pusey's *Eirenicon*, asked on 19 Oct. 1865, about the meaning of *Tract XC*, 'is it not fair to say that what you contended for was, not that the Catholic meaning [of the 39 Articles] was the meaning of the Anglican Church, but that she meant to tolerate that meaning.' See Coleridge's article, 'Pamphlets on the Eirenicon,' the *Month*, (March 1866), pp. 252-4.
[2] Coleridge asked in reference to Article XXI, 'General Councils ... may err,' whether it was not clear that this meant ecumenical councils.

your feelings, or in any way tyrannise over your own judgment. But it is quite plain, you must go with *faith* in her — it can scarcely be right to put yourself into the hands of any one whom you distrust.

This being said, I will say on the other hand that, speaking of the matter apart from the particular case, I don't comprehend how a person can go into a convent to try, without having a *call* to try. As a vocation is necessary for the religious life, so a call to try a vocation is necessary for trying it. Now you say that your repugnance to a convent is increased. Then I ask, what is it that makes you think that *you* should be a nun any more than that your next door neighbour should be one? I am not denying that you *have* a good reason — but nothing can more clearly show how little fitted I am to give an opinion, than my ignorance of this preliminary point — and nothing is more natural, when you ask me for an opinion, than that I should in turn ask *you*, Why are you going to try? To try without a reason is to tempt. I *suppose* you will say 'I go *in faith on* the opinion of so and so.' Well then, if so, give whole faith, not half faith. But don't have faith enough to go to her, and not faith enough to trust her.

Tell me, if I can say any thing more

Yours affly John H Newman

SATURDAY 21 OCTOBER 1865   Duchess of Argyll here
SUNDAY 22 OCTOBER   Duchess of Argyll all day

TO LADY CHATTERTON

The Oratory Birmingham Octr 22. 1865

My dear Lady Chatterton

It was an extreme pleasure to me to hear so good an account of you all from Mr Dering. As to Dr Coleridge, from his letter, as you quote it, he seems to intend to write to you again soon — and you will be a better judge then, whether you are able to assist him. Of course an Editor has a number of difficulties in the way of acting as he would wish — difficulties which he himself alone can know. And as he has but lately taken to the Month, he is obliged to be cautious — but I am sure he would gladly avail himself of your aid, if he can

Very sincerely Yours in Xt   John H Newman of the Oratory

Lady Chatterton

The Oratory Bm Octr 22. 1865

My dear Mr Monteith

I send you all the information I can give you on the subject of the £100 — not having till now had time to do so.[1]

Any suggestion from you claims my attention, and therefore I have not let pass your proposal without thinking upon it, that I should write on the present anxious crisis at Rome. But I am no politician, ecclesiastical or secular — and to write upon the Holy Father's position is either too easy for me or too difficult.

I never met any one who professed to defend the conduct of the Piedmontese in appropriating Umbria and the Legations. It is universally given up on its own merits, as indefensible; but what men say is, that the Roman administration of those countries was quite *as* indefensible; that there is an excess of bad government possible, such, not as to justify such an injustice, but such as to justify the indifference and inaction of third parties at the sight of it; and that the greatest condemnation of the Roman government of the countries in question, is that the world *was* so unconcerned at the fraud and violence of the Piedmontese.

Moreover, they say, that the Pope originally gained these countries in consequence of the bad government of them by the Byzantine Court, by his own popularity, and by the high violent hand of the Frank Monarchs; and, as he then gained them, so now by parallel causes he loses them.

Now I do not say that all this is true; but I *do* say that I am not historian, or politician, or jurist enough, to say whether it is true or not. It is a task quite alien to my habits; but it would be preposterous in me to publish any protest against the sharp practice of Sardinia, which no one denies, without proving the excellence of the Roman administration of Umbria and the Legations, which I never heard any one maintain

Very sincerely Yours in Xt   John H Newman of the Oratory

R J J Monteith Esqr

P.S.   Fr St John inquires anxiously for any news about Mrs Monteith's friends.

[1] This refers to Monteith's contribution to the Oxford Oratory.

TO JAMES HOPE-SCOTT

The Oratory Bm Octr 23/65

My dear Hope Scott,

Can you do any thing for me in the following matter? i.e. I want a 'situation' for a young man.

I have a penitent, who has been to me from the time she first went to confession. She has fallen in love and engaged herself, without my help, to a Protestant youth, and he has no calling, except that he *has* been in a lawyer's office.

I know nothing of him. It is his *testimonials* must do every thing for him. If *they* are satisfactory, of course I shall rejoice if I can be of use to *her* — but he must stand and fall on his own merits.

Of course I have not said that I am writing to you — but I have thought it just possible you may help me or advise me, in doing something for him, if worthy.[1]

I hope Lady Victoria and the children are all well Some one gave me an excellent account of Ma Mo.[2]

Ever Yrs affly John H Newman

J. R. Hope Scott Esqr

TUESDAY 24 OCTOBER 1865   gave Miss Holmes dinner

TO MRS JOHN MOZLEY

The Oratory Birmingham Oct 24.1865

My dear Jemima

The Corelli came this morning, and I thank you for it. It is an old Edition which I have seen somewhere, I suppose at school. What an odd gift memory is, so long latent, yet so sure.

I was glad to see Frank. He is from top to toe an Oxford man. It is very mysterious, what one means by that. John is as certainly Cambridge.[3] Frank is like his Father, and like you, and like my brother Charles, when he was young. He tells me you keep up your music, which I was surprised and glad to hear.

Ever Yours affectly John H Newman

Mrs John Mozley

---

[1] This letter refers to Eleanor Bretherton and Frank Watt. Hope-Scott replied that he feared he could not help, but that he was about to visit Birmingham, and would discuss the matter.

[2] Mary Monica, Hope-Scott's daughter by his first wife.

[3] Jemima's second son, John Rickards, had been at King's College, Cambridge. Her fourth son, Frank Woodgate, was a Scholar at New College, Oxford.

TO J. O. WOOD

The Oratory Birmingham Oct 24. 1865

sent in substance

J. O. Wood Esqr Deal Cottage New Cut Bristol

My dear Sir[1]

No apology was necessary for your letter. The Church does not require us to believe contradictory facts, and accordingly there is nothing unreasonable in your question, which relates not to facts, but to words.

As to the word 'accidents' it has high authority, but is a scholastic, not a dogmatic word — 'Substance' however is dogmatic, and the simple question is, what it means. The Church gives her own sense to words; and this very word 'substance' which occurs in the Nicene Creed, did not take its place there without fearful controversies and divisions, from the unwillingness of numbers to give up their own sense of the word and to accept the ecclesiastical.

Now as to the Holy Eucharist, the word 'substance' denotes nothing which enters into the idea of *effect*, nothing which appeals to the senses. Intoxication is an effect — poisoning is an effect — they are the effect of a *force* — but force is distinct from substance. What we see, taste, hear etc etc. is no part of the substance of a thing. As an illustration take the doctrine of the Holy Eucharist as held by Anglicans (I do not mean Tractarians). Dr Pusey, for instance, (who, as far as I know, does not go so far as the Tractarian School in its present developments,) holds, or held, with Anglicans that our Lord is present in the Holy Eucharist, in *effect*, not in *fact* — i.e., as we should say, in effect, not in substance; what do these expressions mean? They mean that our Lord is not really present, but such *effects* as *would* follow His presence, if He *were* present, viz. grace, sonship, union with Him, *are* in the Eucharist. And in some what a like way Catholics hold, that, though the bread, that is, the *substance* of bread is not present, yet all those effects upon our senses and upon our bodies, which would follow, were it present, *do* follow though it is not present — viz colour, size, taste, solidity, power of nourishing (for Saints have lived upon the Sacred Host) power of poisoning etc etc. — The change which takes place in Transubstantiation has nothing to do with these effects, — it relates to that *which we know nothing about,* and *can* know nothing about — that substance which is something altogether hidden from us. It is nothing to the purpose then, that, as you say, the species of wine after consecration can intoxicate.

I have not read Fr Dalgairns's book on the Holy Eucharist — but I am told it is a good one[2]

Very truly Yrs John H Newman

[1] Wood's reply on 26 Oct. to this letter shows that he was a Catholic, with a family of six small children.

[2] Wood replied that he was still troubled with difficulties concerning the Eucharist, but would buy J. D. Dalgairns's *The Holy Communion, its Philosophy, Theology, and Practice,* Dublin 1861.

WEDNESDAY 25 OCTOBER 1865   gave Miss Holmes breakfast.   Eleanor B. [Bretherton] brought Mr Watt

TO WILLIAM LOCKHART

The Oratory Bm. Octr 26/65

My dear Fr Lockhart,

As to your painfully interesting letter, you must bear in mind that the Dublin in great measure is but an answer to me.[1] *I have* spoken *already* in my Apologia — there is no reason why I should speak again. Our Bishop as soon as he read my 7th Portion (ch. 5 of second edition) wrote to me, to endorse the doctrine of it. Afterwards an attempt was made at Rome to criticize it — but the Jesuits (I understand) took it up and defended its correctness in all points.[2] Since then, our Bishop has a second time given it his imprimatur. Were I to write something anew, I could not say more than I said last year; why will not that do for the purposes you name? why need I write again? It is not to be supposed that I could bring myself to enter into a personal controversy with Ward.

But further; I could not, if I would. It is impossible for a man to enter into such a controversy without reading up endless theology upon the subject of it — Suarez is but one of a host of divines, whom I must first master; and I have no time, not to say money, even had I strength, for such an occupation — And after all, it [I] could not get up theology in a day — and by the time I was fully furnished for the warfare, the whole scene of things might have been changed — and all my preparation thrown away. Indeed I trust that such a change will come, that what has risen in a night will perish in a night.

[1] Enclosing a letter from H. N. Oxenham, Lockhart wrote on 24 Oct. from the Rosminian church in London, 'I send this letter because it helps to express my mind. Wardian Christianity is in the ascendant with us here, and things have come to this pass, that a book like Oxenhams [*The Catholic Doctrine of the Atonement*] is snubbed dead because it is known to speak a different language. I had the greatest difficulty in getting a fair article on that book into the Register, the Editor saying that he could not go against the view of the Dublin, which was understood to be the Archbishops organ! [*D.R.* had violently denounced Oxenham's book] On Dr Manning's return I mean to go to him on this matter, and I have no doubt he will say that "he is in no way connected with the Dublin etc" but every one knows that Ward would not write as he does if he did not feel sure that he was backed by authority. But it does seem clear that authority with us, is on the side of the extremest Ultramontanism. We feel this, and protestants see it clearly enough. I am told that Ward and his followers taunt any who complain, saying that if their position is not sound why has no one come forward to answer them? It seems as if "judgment would go by default". Can nothing be done? Can you not come forward, and be the expression of "the thoughts of many hearts" We shall have precious souls dropping off from us sooner or later in numbers, even already they have begun to go. As for educated converts we shall have none, unless men who are prepared to go all lengths with the new school . . . As for those amongst us who are in orders and who cannot take up with the dominant views, they must remain in deep silence, or speak out and be branded as "unsound Catholics" . . .'
Lockhart argued that the time had come for Catholics in England, France and Germany to declare clearly 'that they will not accept these new views of Papal infallibility,' which were an obstacle to reunion with Easterns and Anglicans. Lockhart concluded, 'I can not but echo all that Oxenham says in his letter . . . Do see what God may enable you to do . . .'
[2] See first note to letter of 25 Sept. to Whitty. Newman discussed infallibility in *Apo.* Chapter V, 'Position of my Mind since 1845.'

I resign myself to look out, or at least to look forward (for it may not be in my day) to such a termination of our present anxieties; and, if it cannot be expected in any other way, this arises from the circumstances under which the evil has found an outlet and made play and from the advantageous position which it occupies. And perhaps you will bear with me, if, in bringing out what I mean, I am obliged to be roundabout.

I think our great difficulty at present lies in this dilemma:

1. if we do not speak out, we let an exaggerated doctrine be mistaken for Catholic truth to the injury both of Catholics and Protestants; but there again,

2. if we *do* speak, then we create a great scandal, Protestants saying 'So, this is your unity of doctrine! here is the Dublin denying salvation to all Catholics such as yourselves, who will not hold its peculiar dogmas.'

Now how has this scandal originated? it has arisen out of the circumstance that the Dublin is in position and possession — that it has the first say — and that whoever protests against it is the first to break the peace. Thus e.g. it was urged on me last year by a Bishop that, if I said any thing [in] favour of youths going to Oxford, I should be violating the existing harmony among Catholics.

And how is it that the views opposed to the Dublin are not also in existing representative position, and possession; but have to maintain themselves at this disadvantage? It is because their organs, such as the Rambler and the Home and Foreign have been silenced.

And how is it that those organs have been silenced? It is because intemperate writers, such as X Y Z in the Rambler, shocked the Catholic public, and gave a handle to those who would suppress them. X.Y.Z. interfered with the education of the clergy; and now the Dublin etc. succeeds in interfering with the education of the laity.[1]

We have lost our position — we have got our heads under water — we cannot get ourselves into a position in which we might use our arms — and why? because we have been very extravagant, very high and mighty, very dictatorial, very provoking; and now we must patiently suffer the consequences

Patience, submission, faith in God's care of His Church, seem now our one course, our only means of righting ourselves. We do not mend matters by new imprudences, we have sowed the wind, and must reap the whirlwind. This seems to me the long and the short of the matter[2]

J H N

FRIDAY 27 OCTOBER 1865   Mr Everett, American, to dinner[3]

[1] X.Y.Z. was Oxenham himself, writing in the *Rambler*, July 1860. See Volume XIX, Appendix 2.
[2] With his reply to Lockhart, Newman enclosed a kind letter to Oxenham.
[3] Probably William Everett, the American Tractarian, who became a Catholic in 1850 or 1851, and was for many years rector of Nativity Church, New York.

SUNDAY 29 OCTOBER   Hope Scott in Bm[Birmingham] with Lady Victoria — Mr Everett to dinner

TO LADY CHARLES THYNNE

The Oratory, Birmingham. Oct. 29th. 1865.

My dear Lady Charles,

I am much pleased, and half surprised, that you and others should like the Dream of Gerontius. It was written by accident — and it was published by accident. But now that I am encouraged by friends such as yourself, deliberately to commit myself to it, I dare say I shall print it by itself.

I was grieved to hear of the great anxiety which awaited you at Killarney. By this time I trust that Lady Castlerosse has recovered her health and has no remains even of convalescence.[1]

Give my love to Charlie [Thynne] when you write. I am glad that Killarney and Grassmere have done so much for his health and with kindest remembrances to Lord Charles

I am, My dear Lady Charles, Sincerely yours in Christ,
John H. Newman of the Oratory

Lady Charles Thynne.

MONDAY 30 OCTOBER 1865   Oakeley came
TUESDAY 31 OCTOBER   Oakeley went

TO MRS JOHN MOZLEY

The Oratory Bm October 31/65

My dear Jemima

At the end of more years than I can count I have an invitation from you to Derby.[2] About two years ago indeed, when you were so ill, you half suggested, if I went from home, my coming your way, and that was all. Never an invitation from your husband. You have let your children grow up, and I not know them. They have ever been in my prayers. When you came here in 1853, I asked you why you had not brought one of them with you, and you repelled

---

[1] Lady Charles Thynne's daughter was the wife of Lord Castlerosse.
[2] Jemima wrote on 30 Oct., 'Thank you for your letter — it is a great pleasure to me that you have seen another of the boys — it seems next to seeing you myself — This has made me think whether if I made an effort, I might not succeed in accomplishing even that. Now Frank (our brother) has just arrived here, and I do not think there is any thing to take him to London to a day. Now could you come to Derby and see us both together some day this week. I am afraid it may be a wild suggestion — but I thought I would try. We have plenty of room in the house, as all the boys are absent and Janie is going to friends near London tomorrow. Of course I would rather they were here, yet perhaps it will be better in some respects.'

or evaded the question. When you came on that occasion, you pointedly refused to see Mrs Wootten or Mr St John, both of whom you knew. You said as plainly as possible, 'I come to see you, because you are my brother, but I will have none of your belongings.' It was the same when John (your husband) came here — he seemed afraid every minute that I was going to commit him to some recognition of me, as what I am. I turned up last year a copy of a letter of mine to you written (I think) in 1846. There I say to this effect, 'I have wished to write frankly, and tell you every thing about myself leaving the difference of religious sentiment on one side, but I can't, if you don't write naturally, and show interest yourself.'[2] *I did not ignore the Church of England,*

[2] This letter of 16 Aug. 1846 was published by Lieutenant-Colonel E. N. Mozley in the *British Weekly*, (17 Sept. 1936), p. 475. Its existence was overlooked and so it is not to be found in its place. It will be printed in the final volume, with other letters discovered too late, but in view of its importance is inserted here:

'St. Mary's Vale, Perry Bar, August 16, '46.

My Very Dear Jemima,
        I have ever been very ready to give you a full account of myself and my doings, but you have behaved towards me in a way which has been a virtual rejection of my offers.
        It is now going on for three years since you knew of my extreme want of confidence in the English Church; and nearly from that time, or soon after, I said to you something like this: "I do not want to discuss religious points with you — I wish simply, letting you have your opinion and keeping my own, to put you in possession of what I feel, and what I am doing, and to write easily to you, as if (as far as might be) there were no differences between us." One time I recollect, in 1844, thinking you cold, I remonstrated about it to John, saying I really could not tell you more about myself, if you responded so little. You replied by saying it was a mere accident. This I refer to as showing the footing on which I all along wished to stand towards you.
        But now after this what have you done? First of all, John, in spite of the above remonstrance, in answer to my question about his publishing my book, wrote me a letter, not merely declining it, but with such unnecessary harshness that, laden as I was with anxiety and with the effort to that work, so struck down my spirits on receiving it, that I could have gone to bed from very despair and grief. I walked out, instead of working, sick at heart, with hands hanging down and feeble knees. Job's comforter, he grounded his refusal mainly on a rumour (!) that my book was to be severe on the English Church, to which in matter of fact I had been tender even to the prejudice of my argument. It was conscientious in him, doubtless, but it was quitting that neutral ground which I had hoped to preserve between us, and taking a side and putting me on the other. I send [sent?] that letter back to you, and wish never to see it again.
        Then, when my great trial came, my own relations, and they only, were those who could find the heart, or the want of reverence, to write censoriously to me. Others, agreeing with me or not, thought that something was due to my long suffering; it was otherwise with those on whom I had nearer claims. You were their organ; for I will not believe of so gentle and kind a heart that all you said was your own. I will not believe that it was you, though it was your hand, in answer to my own affectionate and confidential letters of many months, that wrote to me in so cruel a way — that wrote, for instance, so prematurely about my remaining at Littlemore, as if it were modest or seemly in you to advise in a matter of detail one from whom you differed so widely in the greatest matters, or as if the World, which had parted company with me, had any claim to know my mind at once on a point of expedience.
        Such letters as these completely swept away that footing which for a year or two past I had been wishing to preserve with you. I could not press you further to what, perhaps, on a feeling of conscience, you rejected. Next, as if to show in a marked way your feeling against that footing, you kept silence about yourself and those about you. You went to the Isle of Wight; for five weeks I knew nothing of your movements. Dear Johnnie was burnt; I heard it first from the people at Littlemore. Then after Frank's birth you kept silence for above two months. Again, at Christmas I mentioned my intention of having called on my aunt in passing through Derby; your answer contained nothing which sounded like an encouragement to do so.
        Now, had my letters been full of controversial matter, there might have been an excuse for this; had I called on you to become a Catholic, you might fairly have retorted on me your protestation. But when I wanted simply to go on with you without controversy, and you on

87

but you persisted in ignoring my religion. Well, you wrote a sort of explanation — and I began to be full in my communications again. I wrote you detailed accounts of my goings on, when I was at Rome. On my return, you expressed interest in the descriptions in Loss and Gain. Accordingly I at once sent you the book. The way you thanked me was to write me word that 'I must not think that it would have any effect on your religious convictions,' as if I had said or thought any thing leading to such a remark. This sort of ignoring what I am, and antagonism to me, you continue down to this day. You never, down to the letter of this morning, direct to me as 'Dr Newman', or as at 'the Oratory.'

This being so, since you have let me alone so many years, since you have let all your family grow up and I not know them, it is not wonderful that I should be surprised at your wishing me to come to you now — surprised in a double way, — because you do so much, and because you don't do more — for who ever heard of an invitation except from the master of the House?

I know how this letter will pain you, but it is impossible I can write any thing else. It would not be honest, if I wrote otherwise. None have so acted towards me as my near relations and connexions. Did I wish to revive the past I could say a great deal — and on some occasions, when I have appealed to you, and tried to get you to make matters better, you have declined to interfere.

Of course it much pleases me to have a change in you, however late — but you cannot bring back past years. I am old now I do not easily move about, never I may say by my will. I have been driven from home by my health. Twice this year I have been obliged to go away for definite reasons; on both occasions I got back quickly, lest I should be taken ill. I am well enough when I keep quiet.

As to the present moment, my duties keep me here — even were there no difficulties about my health. It is impossible I should come — but I am glad to have what I never have had for so long[1]

Yours ever affecty John H Newman

Mrs J. Mozley

your part volunteered so high a tone towards me, and then on the back of it kept silence about yourself — of course, you had a right to do so, you might feel it a duty to do what no one else did, but — you cannot, my dear Jemima, be surprised that I should feel I could not, as I had forewarned you in 1844, go on telling you in an easy and familiar manner what concerned myself, as I could have wished to have done.

And now, my dearest Jemima, before answering me, do me the kindness to read over my letters to you from August, 1844, to Christmas last. It will not satisfy me that you verily wish to try to make matters up with me. I want you to feel that you have not been so kind and considerate as I have been. Better feel pain now than by and by.

Ever yours affectionately, John H. Newman.

P.S. — Your letter came this morning.'

[1] This letter had the desired effect. See letters of 22 Nov. to Woodgate, and 29 Jan. 1866 to M. R. Giberne. Jemima and her husband visited Newman on 18 June 1867, and he stayed with them in May 1871.

TO E. B. PUSEY

The Oratory Bm Octr 31/65

My dear Pusey

Thank you for your interesting account of your visit to Paris, and, if you have occasion to write to the Archbishop, I beg to send him my dutiful respects and to beg his blessing.[1]

It is true, too true, that your book disappointed me. It does seem to me that Irenicon is a misnomer; and that it is calculated to make most Catholics very angry — And that because they will consider it rhetorical and unfair.[2]

How is it fair to throw together Suarez, St Bernardine, Eadmer, and Faber? As to Faber, I never read his books; I never heard of the names of de Montfort and Oswald —[3] Thus a person, like myself, may be in authority and place, and know nothing at all of such extravagances as these writers put out. I venture to say the majority of Catholics in England know nothing of them. They do not colour our body. They are the opinions of a *set* of people — and not of even them permanently. A young man or woman takes them up, and abandons them in a few years. The simple question is, how far they ought to be *censured*. Such extravagances *are* often censured by authority — I recollect hearing more than 20 years ago, instances of books about the B.V.M. which Pope Gregory XVI had censured. I think I am right in saying that very superstition about our Lady's presence in the Holy Eucharist has been censured — I think Rogers told me this in 1841, writing from Rome. Nor is Cornelius à Lapide implicated in it — he says, not that the Blessed Virgin is present in the H. Sacrament, but that, since she was our Lord's mother, what *was once* her flesh, being *now* His, is there. It is no longer hers when he appropriated it. Moreover, he says this commenting verse by verse on a passage of Scripture commonly interpreted of her, and thus (with various success, as all comment-

---

[1] Pusey wrote on 30 Oct. that he had had two interviews with the Archbishop of Paris, Georges Darboy, who replied in the affirmative to Pusey's question 'Would it be a practical thing to work towards reunion, on the basis of the Council of Trent, but *explained*.' Pusey added that Darboy 'seemed to anticipate much change on the decease of the present Pope; said that we too needed reverses; but that if we should make advances, he doubted not that they would be received (of course this is for you alone)' Darboy, who promised to give an opinion on Pusey's *Eirenicon*, sent a respectful and affectionate message to Newman.

[2] Pusey also wrote, 'I never was more at a loss than as to the probable reception of this book. But the idea of a reunion on the basis of the Council of Trent seems to be fairly launched; though, as you will have seen, my own position is, rather not to object than to receive. I mean e.g. that I believe in some purifying dealings of God after death, rather than have any definite belief about purgatory. However the book does seem to be allowed of or received in quarters where I did not expect it . . .

Ward is going, he tells me, to write strongly against it. He calls it an "attack." But unless one states our difficulties, they cannot be met; and I have studied them only historically. Ward tells me "I have heard from undoubted authority that he (you I of course have not named you) is quite earnestly on the same side (as Ward) viz. that your book is not really an Eirenicon, but peculiarly the reverse." I hope this is not so.'

[3] Louis Marie Grignion de Montfort (1673–1716), author of *Treatise on True Devotion to the Blessed Virgin,* published in 1842, was canonised in 1947. Johann Heinrich Oswald (1817–1903), was a German theologian, whose *Dogmatische Mariologie,* published in 1855, was later put on the Index. See *Eirenicon,* pp. 116 and 163, and *A Letter to Pusey, Diff.* II, p. 98.

ators are wont) making something out of each verse, as it comes, to the purpose. He is not propounding a doctrine, but interpreting a chapter.

Then again, I thought no one but V. C. Wynter would confuse Intercession with Invocation — Suarez speaks of Intercession.[1] I have tried to find your passage of him, with doubtful success — but I cannot believe that he enunciates the proposition, without there being some explanation of it, 'No one is saved who is not *devout* to Mary.' But it may be quite true nevertheless, that Mary's *intercession* is a necessary part of the economy of redemption, just as Eve co-operated in Adam's fall. It is in this point of view that St Irenaeus calls her Advocata — whatever the Greek word was in his text. As to Eadmer or St Bernardine, of course, where the religion was *established* throughout a people, and Hail Marys were said every hour, for a man to *reject* such a devotion would be an act so grave, especially if he still kept the *faith*, (which of course such writers supposed, for devotion, not faith, was the need of their day) that I think it would be something like rising up against his own means of salvation. And if you cannot fairly put Suarez, a theologian, in the same boat with Italian preachers and spiritual writers; much less is Faber to be taken as his interpreter. Suarez teaches dogma, and dogma is fixed. St Bernardine is devotional, and devotion is free.

Then as to these excesses, so there are excesses in statements of the doctrine of eternal punishment. I don't suppose either of us would think it fair or sober in a Westminster Reviewer to quote St Ambrose or St Hilary on eternal punishment, add to *their* passages quotations from the Puritans, Westleyans [sic], from Dr Cumming or Mr Spurgeon, ⟨(or say from St Alfonso's or any Italian preacher,)⟩ and to argue from the vulgarities or profanities of such Protestant preachers, against the awful doctrine itself.[2]

An Irenicon smooths difficulties; I am sure people will think that you increase them. And, forgive me if I do not recollect what you have exactly said, but I do not think you have said definitely *what you* ask as a condition of union, in respect to the cultus of the Blessed Virgin. This would be something *practical*. Do you wish us to deny her Intercession? or her Invocation? or the *forms* of devotion? or what? Had this been clearly done, people would have thought you practical — but forgive me if I say that your pages read like a declamation.

If I am not mistaken, you gave this reason last February, why you wished me not to come to Oxford, that it would cause a renewal of the attacks on our doctrines — yet you are doing the very thing yourself — And you said that, since my day, those who agreed with you in Oxford, had *ceased* to attack Rome, and this was a characteristic mark of difference in the Oxford party when *I* belonged to it, and *now*. Yet this is what people are saying against your book, that it is an *attack*. The Guardian of last week says, apropos of what you profess

---

[1] See second note to letter of 8 Oct. to Keble, and *Eirenicon*, p. 102. Pusey later explained that he had taken his Suarez quotation from St Alphonsus.

[2] The Presbyterian John Cumming (1807–81), and the Baptist C. H. Spurgeon (1834–92), were strong Protestants.

to bring out in your pages on the cultus of the B V M 'It is language which, after having often heard it, we still can only hear with *horror*.'[1] Is this the effect which an Irenicon ought to produce on the mind of a reader? What can the Record, or an Exeter Hall Tract do more than excite horror?

I will not go on to other subjects. Bear with me, because you have asked me; and I should have to answer for it, if I did not speak out.[2]

Ever Yours most affectionately John H Newman

WEDNESDAY 1 NOVEMBER 1865   Serjeant Bellasis here and dined

TO JOHN KEBLE

The Oratory Bm Novr 1. 1865

My dear Keble

You may be quite sure, I should not write to Pusey as freely as I have written to you.[3] I *have* written to him, tho' the letter is not gone yet. I don't think I need re-write it, for I never should write sharply to him, tho' it is very difficult to be honest without hurting another. He wrote to me and said he heard I did not like his book — thus to tell him was *necessary*.[4]

I wish an Irenicon as much as you or any one else — but Pusey's book is a great disappointment to me, because I am sure it will have just the opposite effect. It will only make men angry. See what the Guardian said last week — that the passages he brought from Faber etc filled them with 'horror'. Could Dr Cumming say any thing against us which would do *more* than fill a hearer or reader with 'horror?' Is it likely to serve as an Irenicon, to inspire the public with 'horror' of our tenets?

I say of '*our* tenets', for there is nothing to soften the impression he leaves on the reader, of the *universality* of Faber's view. There is no bringing out any other side of the question. There is no reference to such books as the Garden of the Soul, which is a manual *every where*, which are free from such extremes. In spite of his diligent scrutiny and curious investigation of so many points, he

---

[1] The *Guardian*, (25 Oct. 1865), p. 1085.
[2] For Pusey's reply, see letter of 3 Nov. to him.
[3] Keble wrote on 30 Oct. to thank Newman for his letter of 8 Oct., 'too kind to me, but hardly kind enough to Pusey.' Keble argued that Pusey was 'just amplifying and carrying out the idea in Number 90, on which his whole book is grounded — that the English protest and separation were and are resorted to rather as against the practical application and popular construction of certain statements than against the letter of the statements themselves. We have held to this all along, hoping (*inter alia*) that it might prove, so far as it goes, an εἰρηνικόν. God forbid that *you*, my dear N. should be the person to cut away the ground from under our feet, and *that* with such very severe words and thoughts towards one whom you know and love so well. For our Lord's sake let me implore you to reconsider the whole matter: and at any rate (if I may so speak to you) to pause before you give any *public* expression to the feeling which your letter implies.'
[4] On 8 Nov. Keble wrote to Pusey his impressions of Newman's letter of 8 Oct. See Liddon's *Pusey*, IV, pp. 124-5.

has not attempted *this* vein; — it has not struck him whether he should be able to find any censure of any of these extreme opinions at Rome. The whole tone is antagonistic. I am speaking of the matter, in mortification, as a fact, which I may deplore, but and because others will resent.

I have no present (or past) intention of publishing. If in the event I do so, it will be, first, to moderate what others may say — secondly, because so many people wish me to write against the Dublin, — which Pusey has in a way endorsed. Did I write, I hope I should not, with the same peaceful intentions as Pusey, fail as seriously. All I can say is, that, whereas he has taken the line of attack, mine would be that of defence; and defence is in itself *not offensive*.

I am glad indeed you can speak as you do of Mrs Keble

Ever Yours affectly John H Newman

The Revd John Keble

TO HENRY WILBERFORCE

The Oratory Birmingham Novr 2. 1865

My dear H W

I will gladly write to Mme St Maur — if any thing occurs to me to say. Archdeacon Froude used to say that the St Patron in his part of the world, in Devonshire or Cornwall, was 'St Peter on the rocks.' I have not attended to the subject of the English Saints since the time when I drew up the Catalogue which Mme S. Maur refers to — and am little qualified to help her.[1]

Ever Yours affectly John H Newman of the Oratory.

H. W. Wilberforce Esqr

TO MISS HOLMES

The Oy Bm Nov 3/65

My dear Miss Holmes

I am glad to hear that Mr Blount is better. I said Mass for him last Tuesday, as Mrs Blount wished.[2]

Will you let me have a copy WITHOUT NAMES (which I will keep quite secret) of Lady Herbert's letter to you. It will be quite a lesson to friends of mine who are seeking for situations in England

Ever Yrs affly in Xt   John H Newman

Miss Holmes

[1] Madame de Saint Maur, who was translating *Apo.* into French, was evidently concerned with the list of English saints, in Note D, pp. 325–38.
[2] Miss Holmes was still with the family of Michael Henry Blount, Mapledurham, Oxfordshire.

Nov 3/65

My Revd Father

You do not mention the name of the Priest to whom you allude.[1] It is enough for me to say that I have given no priest any authority to go to your Reverence from me on any matter. However, there is a priest who came to me lately without proper introduction or testimonial, and to whom I gave three general letters to friends in London, not pledging myself in any way, because he is a perfect stranger to me, but mentioning who he was. He came from the West of North America. Whether he is the person to whom you refer, I cannot tell. Should any thing bring me to Paris, I will not hesitate to avail myself of your most kind wish that I should make myself known to you. But it is my great misfortune not to speak French

Begging your good prayers for us, I am, My dear Revd Father
Your humble Servt in Xt   J H N

The Very Revd Fr Pététot Superior of the Oratory

TO E. B. PUSEY

The Oy Bm Nov 3/65

My dear Pusey,

I think I quite gathered from your book what you bring out so clearly in your note of this morning.[2]

My great anxiety is, that I fear the substantial framework of it will not be taken in by the mass of readers: but they will go off upon those other portions of it which are so much more easy to understand.

If I am led to publish any thing (of which I have no present intention,) I should treat the book simply as an Irenicon, as you wish[3]

---

[1] Dr Maurice is meant. He had applied to join the French Oratory, of which Pététot was the General, and gave Newman as a reference.

[2] Pusey's letter of 2 Nov. is printed in Liddon's *Pusey*, pp. 121–2, except for the postscript. He maintained that in his Eirenicon he 'had no idea of attacking anything.' He wished the official teaching of the Church alone to be of obligation, and the popular manifestations of devotion to our Lady to be disowned. In the postscript he wrote, 'I thought my line much the same as yours when answering me. I wanted that a quasi-authoritative system should be declared not to be authoritative ⟨not de fide⟩ and that, if we were united, we should not be obliged to receive, what I have put down. I wanted to work for an union, minus certain things, but then I wanted it authoritatively explained that those things are not "de fide".

I fear that I have made a confused mess of this explanation, repeating the same things . . .'

[3] The rest of the page has been cut off, presumably for the signature. Newman's draft shows that his letter ended here.

The Oratory Birmingham Novr 3. 1865

My dear Henry

I shall rejoice to see your friend, Mr Greene — but I fear I cannot promise to take him into our House. Properly this cannot be done, and commonly is not done, without a distinct vote of Congregation in every case — and, as it is, much as we like to see our friends, the so frequent presence of strangers in the House is a distraction to us and a trouble to our servants. And besides, to tell the truth, I have so little time my own that I cannot get even through my letters — and there they lie in heaps, I mean the letters to be answered, like bad dreams or qualms of conscience.

But if he finds it convenient to dine with us the days on which he is in Birmingham, I shall rejoice to make his acquaintance.

Ever Yrs affly John H Newman of the Oratory

H W Wilberforce Esqr

The Oratory, Birmingham Novr. 5. 1865.

My dear Sir

I wish I could return you a more satisfactory answer to your question than this will be.[1]

Many writers, like Mr Allies, rest the argument for Catholicity on the Pope's authority — and your friend joins him on this issue. He says — He says [sic] 'the whole difference between Catholics and Protestants has now come to resolve itself into the question of the Pope's Authority.'

[1] Burnand, who had recently begun to write for *Punch*, of which he was later to be a famous editor, was discussing the Catholic claims, with another member of the *Punch* staff, Percival Leigh (1813–89). Burnand, himself a convert, thought that Percival's conversion would lead to a mitigation of the periodical's anti-Catholic tone.

Burnand wrote on 30 Oct., 'The point is S. Clement's Epistle to the Corinthians. My objector (who is reading Mr Allies' book on the See of Peter) says

"*The Epistle of St Clement* appears to me to negative the Papal claims for these reasons:–

1. It is not written by Clement as from himself. It is written in the name of the Church at Rome to the Church at Corinth.

2. In point of style it does not at all resemble the Bulls, Encyclicals and other letters of Popes, but it does resemble the writings of the Apostles . . . This similarity . . . renders the absence at its commencement, of the Author's announcement of his personal authority the more remarkable . . .

3. It is couched in the language not of dictation but remonstrance.

4. St Clement, to illustrate the doctrine of the Resurrection cites the fable about the Phoenix. Could an infallible Pontiff do that? If I am told the point is not material I answer first that there is no limiting the right to criticise Papal declarations . . . 2ndly that it seems to me inconceivable that Divine Inspiration should permit a Pope to illustrate a truth by an untruth.

St Clement nowhere seems to evince even the slightest idea that he is Pope in the present sense of the word and has inherited the prerogatives of St Peter.

The whole difference between Catholics and protestants has now come to resolve itself into the question of the Pope's Authority . . ."'

I do not at all deny the strength of the argument adducible on this point on the Catholic side — and undoubtedly it is most convenient in argument, from its simplicity in itself, and its decisiveness and summariness in its consequences. But I was not converted by it, and I never use it myself.

What I believe about the Pope, I believe, as I believe any other doctrine, — because the Church teaches it — but, for me, the Church directs me to the Pope not the Pope directs me to the Church. I do not then rest my faith in the Pope on St Clement's Epistle — but *believing* on authority of the Church that the Successor of St Peter *has* such over the whole Church, beginning with this and taking it for granted, I see in St Clement's Epistle a remarkable confirmation of that doctrine.

The doctrine of the Pope's *Infallibility* (Infallibility, as distinct from Supremacy) is not a dogma of the Church — I am not bound to believe that St Clement's Epistle is infallible though I see nothing in it against such infallibility.

Premising thus much, I will say what I think of your friend's remarks on the Epistle, taken in themselves.

1. I have not the Epistle before me, nor do I recollect it in detail, but in answer to the objection 'It is not written by Clement as from himself. It is written in the name of the Church at Rome to the Church at Corinth,' I observe that there are distinct privileges enjoyed by the Church of Rome (the Holy Roman Church) and distinct prerogatives possessed by the Pope. That both authorities, the Holy See and the Roman Church, write to the Church at Corinth, is, so far forth, a spoke in the wheel of the argument *from* the Epistle for the Pope's incommunicable power, but not *inconsistent* with it. It does not prove that the Pope had *not* a power of his own, because the Roman Church had a power too; though at the same time it (in consequence of the two being put together) cannot be adduced to prove that he *had* the power by himself. If I am right the Roman Church (i.e. 'the Presbyters') with [wrote] an authoritative letter to St Cyprian, Romanâ sede vacante; this again (if I am right in my fact, for I have not time to verify my memory) is an instance of the power over other Churches even of the Holy Roman Church, let alone the Pope. And this fact, to my mind, enhances not diminishes, the opinion which is to be held of the then power of the Roman Pontiff; — for even his (local) Church had power. In this primitive phenomenon we have the primitive exhibition and sanction of the present ecclesiastical power of the Cardinals and the Sacred Congregations.

2. 'The Epistle does not resemble in style the Bulls, Encyclicals etc. of Popes.' That is it does not speak in their authoritative tone. This is quite certain — and it is the same kind of difficulty as lies in the absence of Images, clear or public teaching of the Mystery of the Eucharist, of the Trinity etc. etc. in the early Church. One answer is to be given to it in all its shapes. It was impossible in safety to bring out every thing at once. There is abundant evidence in the early Church of the supremacy of the Chair of St Peter, but only slowly could

the portions of the Church be welded together — the local sees of the Apostles etc. St John, St James, St Mark, these had vast authority as being so lately filled by men, who had been immediately commissioned by Our Lord, and who had had extraordinary powers, nay an universal jurisdiction, as wide as St Peter and his successors, and the imprudence of insisting on the rights of Peter, at a time when Councils had not met or doctrines been defined, is seen in the quarrels which took place when first St Victor, and then St Stephen interfered to rule points of discipline in that way in which they *ought* to be ruled, and *were* ruled as they are ruled to this day. It must be recollected that Judah had the supremacy in Israel, as given on Jacob's deathbed, yet Judah was of little note for centuries, nay till David's time. If it be said that all this is an hypothesis to account for a difficulty I allow it — but it is sufficient in order to show that the Pope may have supreme power, *in spite of* St Clement's not positively claiming it. In Chapter xxiii he hints at his possession of it as a last resort to which [mis?] conduct may compel him. But continues the humble language of Divinely Charitable and fraternal remonstrance also in XIX 19. Yet after all it is surely a remarkable fact, that the Bishop of Rome *should* write a letter of exhortation to a distant Church, (just as an Apostle might, who had a universal jurisdiction, e.g. St Paul or St Jude) and more so when we find other marks in Antiquity all pointing in the same direction, viz. of the power of the Roman see and Church. They may not prove the full doctrine but they strikingly confirm it.

3. 'It is couched in the language not of dictation but remonstrance.' I have already answered this.

4. 'The Phoenix.' No one says that the Pope is infallible in *facts*, except they are intimately bound up with doctrine, as that the Blessed Virgin was of the tribe of Judah, no one, even of those who *hold* the Pope's infallibility. Supposing the Pope said that the sun went round the earth by an actual locomotion, this would prove nothing about the fact. And so of the Phoenix. Even the inspired writers might make mistakes in natural history or physics. I do not say they have; but the ends of Inspiration are given by St Paul in the text which speaks of the gift, 'profitable to teach, to reprove, to correct, to instruct in justice, that the man of God may be perfect, furnished to every good work.' Your friend says 'If I am told the point is not material (the Phoenix) I answer first that there is no limiting the right to criticise Papal declarations and distinguish between what is material in them and what is not.' Surely the distinction between secular knowledge and divine knowledge is very real and practical, even though in particular instances it may be difficult to draw the line. 2. it seems to me inconceivable that divine *inspiration* should permit a Pope to illustrate a truth by an untruth. 'What Catholic says the Pope is *inspired*? no one at all. No one says that St Clement's Epistle is inspired — if so, it would be part of Scripture, and might be put into the Canon. The general view of the infallibility of the Pope is this :- viz. not that his *writings* are all gospel, but that when he utters PROPOSITIONS ex cathedrâ whether affirm-

ative or condemnatory (certain conditions being necessary to constitute the idea of 'ex cathedrâ') those propositions i.e. the sense of them as he means them, are true, and true because they are merely a development of what our Lord formally spoke and delivered to the Apostles in the beginning.

No one says that a Pope's brief is inspired. It is no received doctrine that it is infallible

I am, My dear Sir, Faithfully Yours John H. Newman[1]
F. C. Burnand Esqr.

TO EDWARD HENEAGE DERING

The Oratory Bm Novr 5. 1865
My dear Mr Dering

I am very glad your visit to St Leonard's has been so successful — but it is sad to hear from you that Lady Chatterton and Miss Orpen are not better. I hope your building has got on to your satisfaction in your absence.

I sympathise with Lady Chatterton and you in the difficulty you find in making an impression on the current literature, for I have experienced the same myself. For these twenty years I have been obliged to run the risk of publishing on my own account — and, while the printer's bill ran high, the receipts have been only a pound or two year by year. I wish she could have hit it off with Fr Coleridge — but an editor is as much bound by the evils of the day as another, or rather more.

Will you thank Miss Orpen for her letter to me — I have thought seriously of what she says. One obvious step would be to make an engagement with the publishers, such as Burns, Richardson, or Duffy, who often want Catholic Literature, but they too are bound by the popular taste. However, I will not forget the subject.

Very sincerely Yours in Xt   John H Newman of the Oratory
E H Dering Esqr

TO J. R. BLOXAM

The Oratory Birmingham Novr 6. 1865
My dear Bloxam

I am ashamed of my delay. I now return your papers. You will see I have not been able to fill them up entirely. I am puzzled what you mean by Tract Sermons; if you mean Plain, my volume is the fifth.[2]

I have not yet got Miss G's [Giberne] portrait — but, I hope to send you

---

[1] Burnand wrote next day to thank, and the correspondence shows that Newman sent him further letters.
[2] Bloxam was collecting information about the Tractarians. To *Plain Sermons by Contributors to the 'Tracts for the Times'* Newman contributed Volume V, London 1843, now *P.S.* VII and VIII.

meanwhile, if you will excuse the egotism, a set of photographs — there is one that I have not got a specimen of, and have sent to Paris for.

I have been sadly offended by Pusey's book. I think it most unfair.[1] Faber and Ward ought not to be cited as authorities. I don't know Faber's books — and he is sufficiently interesting and lively as a writer to account for the sale of his works, without inferring thence that his extreme views about our Lady are the cause of his popularity at the moment. The extreme views are *not* popular, just the contrary. Then again he confuses invocation with intercession, which I thought no one could do but V. C. Wynter. Suarez speaks of Intercession, not of Invocation or Devotion. This seems to me a deplorable mistake. Of course our Lady's *Intercession* comes into the economy of grace, but this is very different from saying that no one can be saved without *devotion* to her; and, if writers have said this, they so said in a Catholic country, where the devotion was established, and where to cast it off would be a reckless act.

And so again the Dublin Review is no representative of Catholic opinion. All that can be said is that such notions are allowed; but, as to the cultus of the Blessed Virgin, it is a principle with Catholics that, while dogma is one, devotion is multiform — that while faith is fixed, devotion is free. Till writers pass doctrinal bounds, their devotional works are not interfered with — I believe Pope Gregory xvi interfered with various books written on our Lady — and in particular did something about that notion of her being in the Holy Eucharist — at least I had reason for thinking so twenty years ago, though I forget the reasons now

Yours Ever affectly John H Newman

Revd J. R. Bloxam

TUESDAY 7 NOVEMBER 1865   The Bishop called

TO HENRY NUTCOMBE OXENHAM

Sent in substance

The Oratory Birmingham Novr 9. 1865

My dear Mr Oxenham,

By the Schola I mean a generalization, for the decisions of theologians throughout the world.[2] And as in all matters, and not the least in intellectual, there is a natural tendency to collect into centres, the Schola is in fact a general-

---

[1] Bloxam wrote on 21 Oct., 'I am reading over for the second time Pusey's answer to the archbishop —, and I confess it has had a great effect upon me; but I do not profess to be a deep theologian.'

[2] Newman had written to Oxenham, and had agreed to accept the dedication of his translation of Döllinger's *The First Age of Christianity and the Church*. See letter of 17 March 1866 to Oxenham. In the course of a letter of 6 Nov. thanking for this permission, Oxenham wrote, 'I am not quite clear that I understand precisely what you mean by 'the schola,' for you speak of its 'holding the Church together' Do you mean the scholastic theology, or something wider?'

ized name for the bodies of theologians throughout the world, or for the Schools of the Church viewed as a whole. These Schools have for the most part a distinct character of their own, severally — but it may easily happen that a School may contain, and that to its great profit, able men of very different complexions of thought and of doctrine — as the old Universities did.

The first great schools were those of Alexandria, Antioch, and Rome. At present these are nearly all destroyed, in consequence of the Revolutions which ushered in this century. This has been a serious evil, as it throws us back on the Roman School, as nearly the only school in the Church. Nor is it enough to say, as it may be said with much truth, that various schools are represented at Rome — for still it is true also that many are not.

The Schola answers many purposes. It defends the dogma, and articulates it. Further than this, since its teaching is far wider and fuller than the Apostolic dogma which is de fide, it protects it, as forming a large body of doctrine which must be got through before an attack can be made on the dogma. And it studies the opinion of the Church, embodying tradition and hindering frequent changes. And it is the arena on which questions of development and change are argued out. And again, if changes of opinion are to come, and false interpretations of Scripture, or false views of the dogma to be set right, it prepares the way, accustoming the mind of Catholics to the idea of the change, and preventing surprise and scandal.

It is a *recognised* institution with privileges. Without it, the dogma of the Church would be the raw flesh without skin — nay or a tree without leaves — for, as devotional feelings clothe the dogma on the one hand, so does the teaching of the Schola on the other. Moreover, it is the immediate authority for the practical working and course of the Church — e.g. what are mortal sins? what venial? what is the effect of the mass? What about indulgences? etc etc.

Yours very truly John H Newman

TO E. B. PUSEY

The Oy Bm Novr 10/65

My dear Pusey

I wish I had your talent of writing long letters in no time at all — however, I will try to say something on subjects so large that, when once one begins, it is difficult to stop.

I think I quite understood your position and your drift — though I am glad to have my view confirmed by your own account of it.[1]

[1] Pusey wrote on 6 Nov., 'I see that my letter has two aspects. First and originally it was a defence. I know not whether you ever saw Archbishop Mgs [Manning] letter to myself. It denied us every thing, except what in a greater degree Dissenters had too . . .' Pusey then explained that he wrote his Eirenicon, 'to point out or suggest, what we could accept, if it could be made quite clear, that, in accepting this, we did not accept what lay beyond it . . .

I do not say, that this was my only ground for saying what I said. If parts of a family are at variance, the fault must be either wholly on the one side or on the other, or divided. The

It is quite true that I said, and I should say still, that it is a mere doctrinaire view to enter a Church without taking up its practical system — and that, as represented by its popular cathechisms and books of devotion. In this sense I hold by 'the system' of St Alfonso Liguori. But I never meant to say that therefore in all matters of detail I hold by him. I ever use his moral theology, but I do not hold by his doctrine of equivocation, nor is it held here in England; I hold by his numerous spiritual books, but I do not accept and follow views which he expresses about the Blessed Virgin; and, even though I looked upon him as a dogmatic authority, which he is not, I should not therefore feel bound, unless I thought right, to take his anti-Augustinian doctrine of Predestination. The practical 'system' remains, quite distinct from the additions or colour which it receives in this country or that, in this class, in this school, or that.

Nor will any French divine, or German (though *not* a convert), more than myself, criticize or reject the 'practical system' (in the sense in which I have explained it), — nor is there any thing which such a divine is disposed to criticize or abandon, which I should not be ready to do the like with, if I thought fit, myself, *tho'* a convert.

Nor (*excuse me*) do I feel that you were in the dilemma of *not* stating your difficulties, *or of offending* Catholics. When you say or imply that Suarez said what Eadmer said, whereas he only said what St Irenaeus says, you startle

more I smooth down difficulties, the more I should leave our position as unreal, unless there were something behind. A defence, of necessity, involves some fault on the other side. But I hoped that it was no real attack, so long as it did not relate to matters declared to be of faith. At the same time, it is a real practical subject. I have said more than once, that I cannot conceive how any faith could stand, the leaving one system which it had once thought Divine, and criticising any thing in the system to which it had submitted as being alone Divine. I felt that had any thing driven me from the Church of England, I must have and should have submitted myself to the whole practical system, such as it is taught in the book with which we are most familiar, Liguori. A lady to whom I said something of this sort (Miss Ward of Clifton,) appealed, now many years ago to you; she wished to join the Church of Rome, seeing that she could receive the Council of Trent and the Creed of Pius IV. I said that she ought not to join it unless she could receive the practical system as taught by Liguori. She sent me your answer, in which you said, "Dr. P. is quite right; a person ought not" (I forget the exact words, but in whatever way you would express joining the Church of Rome) "unless he can receive the system taught by Liguori." [letter of 12 Oct. 1848] You said to me twenty years ago, "I do not go as a reformer." True; one could only go as a little child, leaving behind every thing which one had thought. While then I approximated, wherein I could, to the Roman system, it seemed to me both honest and the only way not to mislead, to state what to my mind were the real difficulties. Others may dwell on the Supremacy. To me and to all of us the Supremacy, as I said to the Archbishop of Paris[,] would be indifferent but for its consequences. On his asking "What?" I said that the appointment of our Bishops from Rome, involved the appointment of all our teachers, and consequently the authorised teaching of that, which was just our difficulty.

If you could read through what, I wrote, you will have seen another motive in all that which I wrote about the system as to the Blessed Virgin. It seemed to me, that, on the principles and with the object, upon which and with which the Immaculate Conception was made matter of faith, any other popular belief might be made matter of faith. Here was already a fresh difficulty in the way of the reunion of the Eastern Church as well as of our own. Many of your Bishops felt this: I hoped the more that if they thought that it would be a difficulty to the English Church, they might the less decree any thing in the Synod of next year

One more thing must have gleamed through, that the Roman Church had its perils as well as we our's, and that perhaps we might help in averting those perils.

All this, my dearest N. is not mere controversy. If I could have helped the Guardian from saying what it said, of course I would . . .

I am, as you see, in this dilemma; if I do not state difficulties, I seem unreal; if I state them, I seem controversial.'

us, because, instead of stating an existing difficulty, you make one, which you do not show to exist. Suarez's name is authoritative all over the Catholic Church; not so Eadmer or St Bernardine.

I knew the Guardian was no organ of yours — but I wished to point out the effect of your pages on a third person, who is not accustomed to speak strongly against our doctrines.

It seems to me that you should hear all that is said against your book in England, before you translate it into French. You would see perhaps what was likely to give offence in France

Ever Yours affly John H Newman

P.S.   We have a friend here who has lived many years in France (Mr T. Pope) who knows a great deal, and is a friend of various Gallicans — if you want questions answered.

TO E. B. PUSEY

The Oratory Bm Novr 11/65

My dear Pusey,

I meant to have asked a question yesterday, which I now trouble you with — though not as requiring an answer at the moment, but lest I should forget it.

Who is it that says that the English Church is 'the great bulwark against infidelity'? not I. Is it de Maistre?[1]

Ever Yours affectly J H N

P.S.   They say Manning is certainly to answer you.

TO CHARLOTTE WOOD

The Oratory Birmingham Nov 11. 1865

My dear Miss Wood

I had already said Mass for the soul of Mr Telford. It grieved me very much to hear of his death — knowing how you and Mrs Wood would suffer. However he has done a good and great work at Ryde — and you must not grudge him being taken to his reward. He leaves Ryde a very different place, relatively to Catholicism, from what it was when he came.

[1] On page 7 of his *Eirenicon* Pusey quoted 'the statement, "that the Church of England is in God's hands the great bulwark against infidelity in this land."' He then added, 'This saying is not mine, but that of one of the deepest thinkers and observers in the Roman Communion.' This was taken to be a reference to Newman. An anonymous correspondent wrote to Newman. on 8 Dec. attributing the expression to Archbishop Murray of Dublin. See *Diff.* II, pp. 9–11, and letter of 19 Nov. to the Editor of the *Weekly Register*.
Pusey replied on 13 Nov., 'The expression was not taken from a printed book, but from a letter. I put it on purpose so, that no one should identify it. I thought that it might embarrass the writer less, not to mention it; but if you like to know, you shall.'

I pray earnestly that your new Missioner may be as good as the last, and as acceptable to you With kindest remembrances to Mrs Wood I am,

Very sincerely Yours, John H Newman

Miss Wood

TO E. B. PUSEY

The Oratory Bm Novr 14. 1865

My dear Pusey

Most gladly will I do my best to suggest any remarks as to the French translation of your book — but I could not do it at the moment — First because I want to get up your book, next because I could not advise without knowing more than I do now how my people take it — what they dislike, what pains them etc etc. I think too you should see what Manning says in answer. In a word, you should have all the case before you. All this takes time, but in so great a step as you have taken, time must not be grudged. Did I write any thing, it certainly would not be at once, but after I had seen what others said — nor could I write without a great deal of thought and of advice — and the advice at least I could not get in a moment.[1]

For myself then, I could not at the moment be of use to you — and though I rejoice at your proposal of coming here, and thank you very much for it, yet I do not think any thing would come of it at the moment — but I *shall keep you to your intention* to come here, when I am ready for you. Moreover, just now I am very much taken up with our schoolboys, and have not my time my own; and could not satisfactorily receive you.

As to the Month, it is in the hands of the Jesuits, who are far from violent people.[2] But I don't think our people have got hold of the drift of your book, or rather they are shocked at some parts of it, and time must pass before (what I consider, legitimate) susceptibilities calm down. Indeed, did I (e.g.) write and not notice the points which offend them, I should be considered almost disloyal to my professions, and at best very inconsistent.[3]

I feel very much your kindness in respect to Tract 90.[4] Of course the

[1] Pusey wrote on 13 Nov. to ask whether Newman would advise on passages to be omitted in the French translation of the *Eirenicon*, and suggested coming to Birmingham the following week. This letter is printed in full in R.D. Middleton, *Newman and Oxford*, London 1950, pp. 251–2.

[2] Pusey wrote, 'The "Month", I see, has made it a matter of personal attack on me. I am sorry for this because you sometimes write in it. Else it does not matter.' Pusey was referring to 'Dr. Pusey and the Church of England,' the *Month*, (Nov. 1865), pp. 534–50.

[3] Pusey wrote, 'I want also not to let the ends of the Eirenicon sleep. I have been wondering whether you could draw up something which I might put before the English Church, as firm to offer.'

[4] Pusey was bringing out a new edition of *Tract XC*, and wrote, 'The failure of the Eirenicon in your eyes makes me anxious about my preface to Tract 90. I had made it simply defensive of Tract 90 on the historical side. In so doing I have quoted largely from your letter to Jelf, because it was the explanation which the Heads ought to have waited for. I have of course, not cited any expressions which you have since retracted. I have sent it to Copeland, asking him whether there is any thing which he thinks you would not like. I want to rehabilitate Tract 90 . . .

I would ask to send it to you; only I thought that it would leave you freer, that you should not have seen it, and that Copeland's seeing it would be the same.'

historical is its weak side, or rather it does not attempt it — and it is the most important side for it is the question of the matters of fact. I recollect Keble suggesting something to be written on it at the time — but nothing was done — because I had promised to keep silence about the Tract. It is impossible I can dislike any thing you do about it — my own view of it has been expressed so clearly, that, tho' your own differed ever so much, there could be no mistake — but besides, I am far *more* than safe in your hands — and after all, I have nothing to do with the Tract now — whereas in the matter of your recent Volume, it is a matter not of me, but of a multitude of people whom you do not know

Every Yrs affly J H N

P.S. I don't like to put off your coming without naming a time for it. I would try to be better prepared next week or the week after. But I should be sorry if you did not wait to see how you were met by Manning etc.

TO E. B. PUSEY

The Oratory Bm Nov 17. 1865

My dear Pusey

From my position, I take matters more coolly, necessarily.[1] As to the Infallibility of the Pope, I see nothing against it, or to dread in it — for I am confident that it *must* be so limited practically that it will leave things as they are. As to Ward's notions, they are preposterous — nor do I see any thing in the Pope's Encyclical to confirm them. You quote one passage at p 304, but it does not seem to me to be to the purpose. For the Pope, in it, is not speaking in his own person, but condemning a *proposition* which in the Encyclical is quoted off with the usual marks. Now common sense and the rule of the Church requires us to consider this proposition as a whole and not in its separate expressions.[2] Suppose an unbeliever said, 'Matthew, Mark, Luke, and John, Barnabas, Paul, Clement of Rome and Hermas are none of them inspired authorities, — I might say, 'That is a false proposition,' without meaning to imply that the extant works of Barnabas, Clement, or Hermas were inspired. And so to the Pope's condemnation in his Encyclical of the

[1] Pusey wrote on 16 Nov., 'I had your most welcome letter, just as I was going to London yesterday. I will gladly wait . . .
My only ground for hurrying at all, is that I want, if possible, to get a hearing from the Bishops before the Synod of next year, when, perhaps there may be made fresh matters of faith, and that Bishops have been consulted about it, as they were about the doctrine of the Immaculate Conception. Some say, that the personal infallibility of the Pope is to be made matter of faith — and as, on the last occasion, so many Bishops regarded what would be deterring to those not in the Roman Communion, I should like to get a hearing from those who think and feel with me. But the translators can go on with parts which I suppose will stand . . .'
[2] In his *Eirenicon* Pusey quoted from the Encyclical *Quanta cura*, concerning the assent due to 'those judgments and decrees of the Apostolic See' for the general good of the Church, which were beyond the sphere of faith and morals. Pusey then interpreted this by the teaching of W. G. Ward in *D. R.*, (April 1865), 'The Encyclical and Syllabus,' p. 445.

Proposition 'Illis apostolicæ sedis judiciis etc' does not carry with it an affirmation of the word 'assensus,' which is the only strong word to a Gallican. And though he speaks of his 'divine power of feeding the Church,' I don't see that infallibility in him is necessary for the carrying out of that power. And as to what Cardinal Patrizzi says, it is of no authority whatever, however it is to be accounted for.[1]

Then again as to the Syllabus, it has no connexion with the Encyclical, except that of *date*. It does not come from the Pope. There was a great attempt to make it a formal ecclesiastical act, and in the Receuil you have it with the censures annexed to each proposition, as it was originally intended — but the Bishops over the world interfered, and the censures were struck out — and it is not a direct act of the Pope's, but comes to us (the Bishops) from Cardinal Antonelli, with the mere coincidence of time, and as a fact, each condemnation having only the weight which it had in the original papal document (Allocution, Encyclical etc etc) in which each is to be found. If an Allocution is of no special weight, neither is the condemnation of a proposition which it contains. Of course nothing comes from the Pope without having weight, but there is a great difference between weight and infallibility.

Some time ago I got several copies of Cardinal Antonelli's letter taken, and I send you one, lest you should not have seen it. Before sending it, I have compared it with the original, and made some quotations.[2]

But even if the Pope's Infallibility were defined, it is impossible that there would not be the most careful conditions determining what is ex cathedra — and it would add very little to the present received belief

But I don't think there will be any such decree, or about the temporal power. A year or two ago, in 1863 I think, there was a meeting of Bishops at Rome for the Canonization of the Japanese martyrs.[3] Louis Napoleon suspected there was to be something passed of a doctrinal character and he refused to give leave to the Bishops to go, till he had some assurance on the matter from the Holy See. And the Pope accordingly, on the Annunciation preceding, gave an Allocution which was in the Papers at the time, in which he distinctly said that the temporal power was not a dogma of faith, but a necessity of the time. Moreover (in confidence to you) he said to our Bishop here, apropos of a report (not true) that I was adverse to the temporal power, 'You know it is not de fide — he is not obliged to hold it.'

No one seems to know any thing about the meeting next year — the last account I saw was in the Daily News, viz that it was put off till 1867.[4]

Have you seen the advertisement in the Pall Mall Gazette? 'The doctrine

---

[1] On p. 304 Pusey again appealed to *D. R. loc. cit.*, p. 449, in support of his statement that 'Cardinal Patrizi . . . claims for the Encyclical, and, consequently, for every like expression of the Pope's mind, to be *the very word of God*, to be received on pain of forfeiting heaven.'

[2] On Antonelli's letter sending out the *Syllabus of Errors* and the document contained in *Recueil des Allocutions de Pie IX* see *Diff*. II, pp. 267–83.

[3] See diary for 8 June 1862.

[4] The meeting of Catholic bishops in Rome was held in June 1867, at celebrations of the centenary of the martyrdom of St Peter.

and practice of the Catholic Church regarding the worship of the B.V.M. by H. E. Manning'? This surely must be an answer to you in detail.[1]

If you mean 'Oakeley,' I am confident he did not write the Article in the Month upon you.[2] By the bye, he has rather been pained you did not acknowledge the poems he sent you.

Have you thought of Mgr Dupanloup? He (entre nous) was gravely opposed to the issuing of the Syllabus etc and much disconcerted at its appearance. Don't repeat it, but he said 'If we can tide over the next ten years, we are safe.' Perhaps you know him already. You should have seen Père Gratry in Paris — I mean, he was a man to see. I thought Mr Pope could have given you the names of persons who took the same moderate view of ecclesiastical politics.

All my friends think *I* said in my *Apologia* that the Church of England was 'the great bulwark.' You are their authority — they don't look at my book. I have been thought extravagant etc in consequence.

Ever Yours affly John H Newman

SATURDAY 18 NOVEMBER 1865   ended Terence with the boys

TO THE EDITOR OF THE WEEKLY REGISTER

The Oratory Birmingham Nov. 19, 1865.

Sir,

I beg leave to call your attention to a passage in your admirable Review last week of Dr Pusey's recent work. It is there asserted by implication that 'the statement that the Church of England is, in God's hands, the great Bulwark against infidelity in this land,' was 'originally enunciated by Dr Newman'.[3]

I have written in my lifetime a great deal more than I can remember, but I neither know where I have made this particular statement, nor can I conceive I ever made it, whether in print, in private letter, or in conversation. And I am sure I should not have made it deliberately. Certainly it does not express my real judgment concerning the Church of England. Nor have I any reason to think that Dr. Pusey ascribes it to me.

What I said in my *Apologia* was this: 'Doubtless the National Church has hitherto been a serviceable breakwater against doctrinal errors more fundamental than its own.'[4]

---

[1] After Newman's *Letter to Pusey*, which dissociated Catholic devotion to our Lady from the teaching of the extremists, Manning decided not to publish his book.

[2] In his letter of 11 Nov. Pusey wrote of the article in the *Month* for Nov. as 'little more than a personal attack on myself and if I guess the writer aright, he ought to have known my mind better in some things.' H. J. Coleridge was the author.

[3] 'Dr. Pusey's Eirenicon,' the *Weekly Register,* (18 Nov. 1865), p. 329. The review, by Lockhart, was not only sympathetic, but accepted the possibility of a corporate reunion, and welcomed Pusey's efforts towards it.

[4] *Apo.*, p. 342. See letter of 11 Nov. to Pusey, and Liddon's *Pusey*, IV, p. 95, note.

The words 'serviceable', and 'breakwater' both convey the idea of something accidental and *de facto*; whereas a bulwark is an essential part of the thing defended. Moreover in saying 'against doctrinal errors more fundamental than its own,' I imply, that, while it happens to serve Catholic truth in one respect, nevertheless in another it has doctrinal errors, and those fundamental.

I am, Sir, your obedient Servant John H. Newman.

TO G. W. HOGHTON

Nov 19. 1865

Dear Sir

I feel both the consideration in which you hold our School in wishing your son to remain here, and the pain I shall cause you in my inability to comply with your request. But I can do nothing else. At your request I withdrew my first decision upon George's misconduct, that he should leave us, on condition that he was corporally punished. Then, when you changed your wishes, and asked that he should not be corporally punished, I remitted that punishment but returned to my former decision, that he must part from us. And to that resolution of the matter, I am very sorry to say, I must adhere. We have no faults to find with his brother, though of course we must acquiesce in your decision, if you determine to remove him with his brother.[1]

J H N

TO E. B. PUSEY

The Oy Bm Nov 19/65

My dear Pusey

I am much surprised and much rejoiced to see yesterday's article on your book in the Weekly Register. I hope you will like it. I have not a dream who wrote it.[2]

If they rat next week, it will be very provoking — I am not easy about it, for not long ago they would not insert a review of a book *because* it was *not* according to Ward, who *is* according to Manning, who *is* according to the Pope.[3] But this review, tho' not against the mind of the Pope, is certainly contrary against [sic] Ward and Manning.

It has surprised me so much that I said to myself, Is it possible that Manning himself has changed? He is so close, that no one can know.

On the other hand I know some, if not most, of our Bishops are against the

---

[1] The fault of George Hoghton is not specified. In the event, he and his brother Charles remained at the Oratory School until Dec. 1870. Their father wrote from 6 Gambier Terrace, Liverpool.

[2] Pusey wrote in reply, 'I am delighted with the W. R. and I have written a warm letter of thanks to Lockhart, who, I found, sent it me with a note saying that he had written it.'

[3] See letter of 26 Oct. to Lockhart. The *Weekly Register* published a second article by him, see next letter.

Dublin — and it really looks as if they were taking up the matter and that we should have some permanent change in the Register.

I am sure you should not be in a hurry in what you propose to do

Ever Yours affectly John H Newman

The Revd Dr Pusey

MONDAY 20 NOVEMBER 1865   Fr Suffield and his friends to dinner
TUESDAY 21 NOVEMBER   Blennerhassett came

TO WILLIAM LOCKHART

The Oy Bm Novr 21/65

My dear Lockhart

I have read your Article with great interest and pleasure, and, before your letter came, had already sent *one* word in praise of it to the Register. I am glad to find that it is yours, and my sole fear is that there will be some attack on it in next Saturday's Paper; and that the Editor, or Manager, for there does not seem to be an Editor, will veer round.

I am told that you had the Archbishop's leave to insert it, of which I am very glad[1]

Pusey is much pleased at it

Yours affly John H Newman

TO JOHN R. SHORTLAND

The Oratory Bm Novr 21. 1865

My dear Shortland,

It will be a pleasure to me to look over any thing you send me, both because it is your request, and your writing. I wish I could offer to do so in extenso — my time is so occupied, I cannot offer this — but I will look over as much as you think necessary for your purpose of getting my opinion.[2]

Very sincerely Yours in Xt   John H Newman

[1] This Newman learned from Blennerhassett. Lockhart replied on 22 Nov., 'It it true that the Archbishop had heard it read and I offered to burn it or to alter it — he suggested some alterations but assented to its going in as expressing a conciliatory spirit — He told me yesterday that I had not made the Alterations as fully as he could have wished — that it had been attacked to him from several quarters and he had defended me — and he bids me write another article bringing out the incompatibility of the Anglican branch theory with any Catholic basis of reunion. Please let no one consider that the Archbishop has seen the article — I told it only in confidence to the Editor and I think to one more — of course I should have told it to you.' Cf. letter of 8 Dec. to Pusey, for Lockhart's second article.

[2] See letter of 24 Nov.

TO HENRY JAMES COLERIDGE

The Oratory Bm Novr 22. 1865

My dear Fr Coleridge

I am very sorry I cannot send you this month the Saints of the Desert, as I had hoped — I am so busy. I am taking your suggestion, and publishing Gerontius.

The review of Pusey in the Month is ably written and effective. Pusey complains that, instead of meeting his proposition, it is personal[1]

Yours very sincerely John H Newman

TO H. A. WOODGATE

The Oratory Birmingham Novr 22. 1865

My dear Woodgate

⌐I *am* surprised, but not less pleased than surprised, to have your letter.[2]

It is very true that I have felt that you needlessly cut yourself off from me. The only persons, whom I can recollect, as having done as you have done, are Rickards, who is lately gone, and my own relations and connexions at Derby. I am glad to say that my sister has, within this last month, resolved upon a different line. You have now done the same. As to Rickards, he acted on principle,⌐ and in consequence I have no right to complain of him; and he was consistent to the last. Those who change their course, show that they have *not* done as they have done, on principle.

⌐I feel great satisfaction in your letter. It must have cost you something to write it; and you can do no more now. I take it as you offer it.⌐

I thank you for your proposal that I should meet Pusey at your house; but I am obliged to decline it. First, I am not yet prepared to have the conversation

---

[1] See last note to letter of 17 Nov. to Pusey.

[2] Newman's last letter to Woodgate had been that of 8 Oct. 1845, and to it there appears to have been no reply. Woodgate wrote from the Athenaeum on 21 Nov. 1865, 'A letter from me may perhaps surprise you; but I hope it will not be unwelcome.

I have recently been reading your Apologia, and I presume that I am one of the two "Beneficed Clergy" there referred to as able to testify what you were at a certain period of your life — but spoken of as "being no longer your friends." [*Apo.* p. 16. Cf. letter of 26 July 1864 to Lord Lyttelton].

It gives me pain to be thus spoken of by you; though I cannot but feel that, as things present themselves at first sight, I have no reason to complain. I can assure you that at no moment since we last met, have you been out of my most affectionate thoughts, or severed from affectionate and grateful remembrance. — Why we have not met, I feel it difficult to explain. Perhaps Pusey could do that better — at any rate the fault does not in any way rest with you.'

Woodgate then went on to say he had long been anxious to see Newman, and now that Pusey was due to visit him, he wanted the two of them to meet at his house. Woodgate, who was Vicar of Belbroughton, near Rednal, made detailed proposals for a meeting on 28 Nov. He suggested that Newman should write direct to Pusey about the arrangements, 'else, he is such a slippery fish in these matters, that I shall not catch him.'

with him, which he contemplates. And next, I am so busy just now, that I cannot move. Indeed, I never go from home except when simply obliged.[1]

Yours affectly John H Newman

The Revd H. A. Woodgate

P.S. I am much concerned to hear about your eyes.

THURSDAY 23 NOVEMBER 1865   Blennerhassett went

TO E. B. PUSEY

The Oy Bm. Nov 23/65

My dear Pusey

I fear that Lockhart mistakes what I have said — it is *literally* one word about his letter which I introduce into mine.[2] And that, to *support* him, though not fully agreeing with him. I grieve to say I could not have written exactly as he has written. I feel a good deal pained at what you say about our devotions to the Blessed Virgin — and could not write without saying so. But I truly rejoice to find another can write in a less distant way about your book than I could myself — and I abominate the fierce tyranny which would hinder an expression of opinion such as his — and calls to account every one who ventures to keep clear of Ultra-isms.

You may be sure that Manning is under the lash as well as others. There are men who would remonstrate with him, and complain of him at Rome, if he did not go all lengths — and in his position he can't afford to get into hot water, even tho' he was sure to get out of it.

Yrs affectly John H Newman

P.S. It is very kind in you to wish a letter of mine to appear with yours — but there is nothing in mine

TO HENRY JAMES COLERIDGE

The Oratory Bm Novr 24/65

My dear Fr Coleridge

I am sure the series of discussions which you propose will be very season-able. No persons could do them with the exactness and weight which will attach to the writings of the Fathers of the Society.[3]

[1] Woodgate sent this letter to Pusey, who wrote to Newman, 'It was never any want of love in him, that he did not see you, but the difficult circumstances of those times.' For Woodgate's reply, see letter of 16 Dec. to him.
[2] Newman's letter of 19 Nov. to the Editor of the *Weekly Register* would be published in the issue of 25 Nov. Lockhart wanted to publish in the *Weekly Register* the letter of thanks for his review of the *Eirenicon*, written by Pusey on 22 Nov. The latter hoped that his and Newman's letters would appear side by side.
[3] Coleridge wrote on 23 Nov., 'we are trying to get up a set of Essays . . . on subjects *raised* by the Eirenicon, without attacking Dr Pusey where it can be helped. I am going to ask you if you could suggest subjects or give general hints.'

For myself, I would not write even indirectly against Pusey anonymously. If I wrote, if would be in a separate shape with my name. I agree with you that his work is calculated to raise indignation — especially when considered as Irenicon. On its first appearance I wrote to Keble, quoting of it the text 'If anyone ask for a fish, will he give him a stone? etc' *Don't mention this.* He wrote back, begging me not to say so to Pusey, it would hurt him so much. Also, I am sure he and his use the book to keep persons in the Anglican Church, as you say. But he is not inconsistent here, for he says 'Wait, till we *all* can join. I am writing to effect this, and I wish these difficulties which *you* ought to feel, as I do, removed *before* you join.' And again, I verily believe he does mean it as an Irenicon — and though I think he ought to be made to feel how he has wounded Catholics, yet I do not think his book ought to be left there — and I was glad that a reviewer *could* write as the Weekly Register wrote last week, though I could not write so leniently myself, as I have distinctly told Pusey (*don't tell this.*) I think a large body in the Anglican Church are growing towards us, and, while I will not despair even of Pusey, however humanly unlikely, still less do I think it right to do any thing likely to throw back that large body. I cannot help feeling sorrow at the blow struck by the Holy Office at the members of the APUC, or whatever it is called. (I have not got it quite right)[1] And if now they are led to suppose that all Catholics hold with Ward and Faber, I think we shall in a melancholy way be seconding that blow.[2]

Yours very sincerely in Xt   John H Newman of the Oratory
The Revd Fr Coleridge S. J.

TO JOHN R. SHORTLAND

The Oratory Bm Novr 24. 1865.

My dear Shortland

I have received and read your Ms and think it very well composed. I hardly ever read any thing more easy to read, — I mean, so clear, flowing, and natural.

The fault of it is diffuseness — by which I mean that it is more suitable for preaching than for the press. It reads like a Sermon — it is not too *diffuse* for a sermon, and the question is, whether the series of chapters will not be in matter of fact sermons, and will have their true name and place, when so considered.

[1] This was the reply from the Holy Office, of 8 Nov. 1865, to the appeal signed by a number of Anglicans, against the 1864 prohibition of Catholic membership of the Association for the Promotion of the Unity of Christendom. The new letter condemned uncompromisingly the Branch theory. See Butler's *Ullathorne*, II, p. 353, and letter of 23 Dec. 1865 to Ullathorne.
[2] Coleridge replied on 25 Nov. urging Newman to write in answer to Pusey.

Then as to the argument. It is in substance a very good one. No one can doubt that Pius the Ninth is simply supported by faith, — and, if it were God's will would give up his temporal power as cheerfully as retain it. So far you are quite safe — safe too, in saying that the temporal sovereignty is necessary for the present time, because he has said it. But such vast political changes are making, that one does not seem to know what he means 'the present time' to be. It may turn out to be only his time — but any how he cannot mean to prophesy about the future. To be sure, the future is no more our concern than his — but this is just what I mean — if it is wrong to say that the temporal power is *not* necessary for the future, it is at least going beyond him to say that it *is*.

As to the mode of publishing, I rather think octavo size with a thousand copies is £5 a sheet of 16 pages. To this must be added advertising and binding. Advertising perhaps would be £20. A publisher's commission is very high — I fear 40 per cent on the selling price — nearly half. Thus a book of 1000 copies and 400 pages, would cost £125 and with advertisements £145. Let it sell at 10/ and bring in £500; of that take away $\frac{40}{100}$ or £200 for commission, and there remains £300 to meet £145 or £150. This supposes *all copies sold*. If only half were sold, the expenses would hardly be covered. This is a rough account.

I fear the Catholic publishers are very slow to take books on themselves. Could you publish it *in series* in the Lamp?[1]

Yours very sincerely, John H Newman

Very Revd Canon Shortland

SATURDAY 25 NOVEMBER 1865   Miss C Smith and Miss Slinger here

TO EDWARD BELLASIS

The Oratory Bm Novr 26/65

My dear Bellasis,

In the first month of this Term a boy found out that a large sum of money had been taken from his desk. This is only the second case which has occurred here, since the School began, and it was known generally to the boys. About three weeks had elapsed, since the owner had last seen his money, and there was no means of tracing it. And besides, even if the boy who took it, had been discovered, the disgrace would have stuck to him through life, of which there are instances at present in the world.

We had no suspicion who the boy was.

Therefore we took it up as a matter of humiliation for the whole School. We were close upon the time of the day of monthly confession, which is our

---

[1] Shortland's book seems not to have been published.

rule. And we said that the *whole* School, *every boy*, should go to their confessors with this matter especially before them; and that if, after *all* the boys had gone to confession, the money was (secretly) put in a certain spot, we would say nothing about it.

All the boys without any exception did go to confession, and the money made its appearance.

No one of us has any idea who the boy was to this day. His confessor alone knows it.

The boys took it in the best spirit, and the whole School with Fr Ambrose said some Hail Marys for the penitent.

If you want more particulars, we will send them.

Ever Yrs affly John H Newman

TO JAMES HOPE-SCOTT

The Oratory Bm ⌐Novr 26/65⌐

Confidential
My dear Hope Scott

⌐Many persons wish me to write on the subject of Pusey's book [[The Irenicon]], and it has struck me it will be the most inoffensive way of alluding to Faber and Ward, if I can write without hurting Pusey. I am in constant communication with him, and *trust* I should not pain him.⌐ I fear you are going away so soon, that I can't let you see it. So ⌐I will sketch what I mean to do, and you can give me your opinion both of the idea itself and the mode of carrying it out.

1. I hail Pusey's proposals for a basis of negociation for unity —⌐ and say I regret that he should not have laid his conditions, without seeming to *attack* us, as we think generally, though he did not mean it. ⌐I excuse myself for writing,⌐ on the ground that he quotes me all thro' his work, so that I have things to explain where he thinks he *agrees* with me, and to defend where he expresses his *dissent*. I do not accept his apology for my silence on the ground that a convert ought not to write, for (I say) converts younger than me *have* written and with great explicitness, and there was no reason why *I* should not write, if *they* did. And ⌐I expostulate with him⌐ for making so much of men, who, though of great talent and power in writing, could not be called authorities.

⌐Then I say, taking away these, how can you say that, either as to the doctrine about the B.M.V. or the Holy See, English Catholics are extreme?⌐ Who have been, in the passing generation, our chief writers? ⌐Cardinal Wiseman, Dr Lingard, Dr Rock,⌐ Mr Tierney, Dr Husenbeth, which of them is extreme on either doctrine? Look at ⌐the Garden of the Soul,⌐ the Key of heaven, the Golden Manual, etc etc do they contain the expressions etc etc which offend you so much?

2. But he must not suppose that I mean to be lax on either doctrine — So I go into the ⌐Patristical view of the B.M.V. and ask him whether it is not a high one —⌐ and then expostulate with him, for making so much of what is but a slight addition to what the Fathers teach.

3. But ⌐he says, 'I do not think so much of what you hold now, as of what you *will* hold by and bye by the instrument of development of doctrine. We dont know *where* we shall find ourselves, if we commit ourselves to you.⌐ Any thing may be made matter of faith, for what we know.[1]

⌐I answer by quoting a remarkable passage from Cardinal Wiseman's Essays, and commenting upon it, so as to show that *not* everything can be made matter of faith, but only those things which lie within the Apostolic depositum.⌐[2]

4. But he points to the way in which the ⌐Immaculate Conception was defined, viz without an Ecumenical Council —⌐ and I answer this by saying that, even though there was any thing special in the proceedings (which I do not grant) yet that ⌐most General Councils, certainly the Four which Anglicans receive, had severally something special in them —⌐ as e.g. the Third, when St Cyril passed the dogma against Nestorius in one day, before the Bishops of the Antiochene Patriarch had arrived — and I apply my maxim ⌐'Securus judicat orbis terrarum'.⌐

5. Lastly I say that, much as I desire unity, ⌐it is certain that the Holy See will never admit the Anglicans Orders,⌐ on the ground of its having sanctioned conditional baptism in England — ⌐for, if Baptism is given conditionally, so certainly must Orders,⌐ to those who are to continue the Ministerial Office, for Orders never are good in the case of an unbaptized person.[3]

And now, wishing you and Lady Victoria a prosperous time abroad

I am, my dear Hope Scott Yrs affectly in Xt
John H Newman of the Oratory

Jas R HopeScott Esqr

MONDAY 27 NOVEMBER 1865 Miss C. S. [Smith] and Miss S. [Slinger] went

[1] Newman contented himself with the question of our Lady, and did not in his *Letter to Pusey* deal with development of doctrine or Anglican Orders. See *Diff.* II, p. 117, and *A. W.* p. 265. Also letters of 28 Feb. 1866 to H. J. Coleridge and W. Walker, and that of 23 March 1866 to the *Guardian.*

[2] Probably 'The High Church Theory of Dogmatical Authority,' *Essays on Various Subjects,* London 1853, II, p. 155, on how the Church can declare but not create articles of faith.

[3] Hope-Scott replied on 29 Nov. from Boulogne, 'I hope you *will* write — write as you describe in that letter — I feel sure it will do good, both — (so to say —) forward and backward — towards adversaries in front, and friends behind — so do proceed.'

The Oratory Birmingham Novr 27. 1865

Dear Sir

We felt your kindness in proposing to give us from yourself and friends a choir organ. But I felt also, that it scarcely would become me to put myself forward, or let my name be used with a view of obtaining sums towards the purchase of it. For this reason I thought I had better not preach for it.

I have just seen a letter which you have addressed to Miss Farrant, in which you say that you 'have been *requested by Dr Newman to undertake the purchase*' of the organ. This shows that there is an unintentional misunderstanding between the friendly persons who have originated this proposal and myself. I do not at all request you to undertake the purchase of the organ. I should think I was taking a great liberty with you, if I did. And therefore I write these lines, which I send through Fr St John, to say that it will distress me to find my name introduced into the applications made for contributions towards your object.

We have no difficulty in ourselves buying the Organ, thanking you meanwhile for having got it for us. But if it comes from you, it should come as a spontaneous gift, and not as if we asked for it

Very truly Yours John H Newman of the Oratory

— Clarkson Esqr

TO JOHN O'HAGAN

The Oratory Bm Novr 27. 1865

My dear Mr O'Hagan

I feel the extreme friendliness of your writing to me on such an occasion, and I assure you, if you will let me say so, I deserve it so far as this, that there are few persons I have respected and felt drawn to so much as to yourself, from the time I first knew you.[1] You deserve to be happy, and I doubt not God will reward you in your new life for all your devotion to him in your old, which is now passing away. It must be an extreme pleasure and consolation to the Judge, of whose great trials I have heard. Say everything kind and respectful to him from me in the way of congratulations.[2] And, if I may take the liberty, convey my kindest wishes and thoughts to the young lady herself. I hope to say Mass for you on the day of your marriage.

Believe my, My dear Mr O'Hagan, Very affectionately Yours

John H Newman of the Oratory

John O'Hagan Esqr

[1] O'Hagan wrote on 25 Nov. that he was about to marry Mary Frances, youngest daughter of the Irish Judge, Thomas O'Hagan.

[2] O'Hagan wrote that his prospective father-in-law had 'gone through a great deal of family affliction.' Thomas O'Hagan (who became first Lord O'Hagan in 1870) wrote on 30 Nov. to thank Newman for his sympathy.

TUESDAY 28 NOVEMBER 1865   went to Rednall to write my Letter to Pusey
FRIDAY 1 DECEMBER   had some evenings the beginning of my illness

TO W. J. COPELAND

The Oratory Bm Decr 1/65

My dear C

I am at Rednall, which will account for my silence in answer to your sad letter, which has concerned me deeply. Say every thing kind from me to your brother, if he is well enough, and say I hope to say Mass for them.[1]

I am *very* busy now, but some time I will write to you

Ever Yrs affly J H N

P.S.   I quite forget about the 12 and 24.[2] I long to see you, yet can't think of of it just now.

TO WILLIAM NEVILLE

Rednall Dec 1/65

My dear W

You must, please, answer the two inclosed letters, sending Prospectuses. As to *both*, you must consult the Fathers, in *second* recreation today — *Ambrose*, about the age 16, and the Congregatio Deputata about the £35[3]

I don't know what to say — I don't like 16, unless we can ascertain something about the boy, and I suspect from the letter, he needs a merely commercial education. Can Sparrow give any information?

As to the St Leonard's, to *me* the only question is whether the boy will actually cost us any thing —

Ever Yrs affly J H N

P.S.   There is a severe article in the Month against Pusey.[4]
Say in your answers that 'I am away'.

---

[1] Copeland's brother, George, was seriously ill at Cheltenham.

[2] Pusey in his preface to *Tract XC* spoke of Newman asking for 24 hours' grace, for him to explain, before the Heads of Houses condemned the *Tract*. Copeland thought Newman had asked for 12 hours only.

[3] Samuel B. Harper, a convert clergyman, at St Leonards, asked whether his son Thomas, aged 10, could be taken at the Oratory School for £35 a year. The boy was admitted in Jan. 1866.

[4] See letter of 11 Dec. to Coleridge.

Rednall Decr 1/65

My dear Pusey

I shall be much flattered by Mr Earle publishing my verses in his Collection, my 'Lead kindly Light.' Do you know I *can't* recollect him.[1]

I have mislaid your letter in which you asked about the 12 or 24 hours. I do not recollect about it.

Woodgate has not been commonly unkind. But of course nothing is to be said. I am glad he has come round.[2]

Yours affectly John H Newman

TO WILLIAM NEVILLE

Rednall Dec 2/65

My dear W

There are four little books, which I should *like* to have by the first comer, *if he is a safe hand,* for they are valuable. But *I can get on very well without* them, without all or *any*.

1. Bossuet Exposition de la Foi, in French or English. There ought to be a copy in *the Library* — a small unbound book with a blue or lilac cover.[3]

2. Veron's Rule of Faith — it is in Latin bound up with 'the Wallenburghs'; in a *small* volume of Tracts in *the Library* with sealing wax numbering on the back. It is above, in the apse, on the left as you stand looking at the apse — It must be in Marshall's catalogue of Latin Tracts.[4]

3. Holden's Rule of Faith, or work on Faith, a small volume in my room, in Latin — in the bookcase between the fire place and the window.[5]

4. The name has gone out of my head like a shot — the name is Chrisman, or some such name. Ambrose and Henry know the book. Ward has attacked it. It is 'edited by Spindler' and dedicated to Dollinger — the man's name is 'Philip Neri something'. The book is in Latin — in my bookcase which is near my *bed* window.[6]

I am getting on well, but slowly

Ever Yrs J H N

[1] Pusey wrote, 'You must remember Earle of Oriel . . . he asks me . . . to ask you to let him publish "Lead kindly light" in a collection of hymns which he is making.' John Earle (1824–1903), went up to Magdalen Hall, Oxford, in 1841, and took a first in Classics. He was a Fellow of Oriel 1848–58, Anglo-Saxon Professor 1849–54, and a tutor at Oriel until he became Rector of Swanwick, near Bath, in 1857. In 1876 he was re-elected Professor of Anglo-Saxon, defeating Thomas Arnold, and held the Professorship and his Rectory until death.

[2] See letter of 16 Dec. to Woodgate.

[3] *Exposition de la doctrine catholique sur les matières de controverse,* first published in 1671.

[4] Franciscus Veronius, *De Regula Fidei Catholicae,* in the edition of Adrian and Peter de Walenburch, *De Controversiis Tractatus Generales,* Dublin 1796.

[5] Henry Holden, *Divinae Fidei Analysis,* first published in 1652.

[6] Philip Neri Chrismann, *Regula Fidei Catholicae,* new edition revised by P. J. Spindler, Würzburg 1854. See letter placed at 28 April 1865.

The Oratory, Birmingham Decr 4/65

(Confidential)
My dear Dr Russell

I suppose you have seen Pusey's recent book. What do you think of his quotations from de Salazar, de Montford, Oswald etc. about the Blessed Virgin? Are they not startling and unusual?[1]

I will not tell a soul, if you give me a frank opinion, and will burn your letter.

Some one, (was it you?) told me more than 20 years ago, that Pope Gregory had suppressed various books, pictures etc, published in honor of our Lady. Can you throw any light upon this?[2]

Ever Yours affectly in Xt   John H Newman of the Oratory[3]

The Very Revd Dr Russell &c &c

TO JOHN R. SHORTLAND

Rednall Dec 4/65

My dear Shortland

If you asked me what I *wished*, it would be to have your work published. I am sure it would be well done and useful. The enormous difficulty is the expense. There are few educated Catholics, and no books seem to succeed but devotional and story-books. My own books (till the Apologia) have simply lain on the Publishers' shelves. After two or three years I wrote to Burns, who sells about 6 books of mine, as to proceeds — he sent me an account showing he had to give me a pound or two, no more. This was after I had *myself* paid all the expenses of printing.

Here you have the long and short of my opinion

Ever yours most sincerely in Xt   John H Newman of the Oratory

The Very Revd Canon Shortland

---

[1] Russell replied on 6 Dec., 'Frankly I *am* both startled and pained by the expressions and views to which you refer. My instincts and sympathies are all against such views . . . I own I can not accept (unless when most fully explained . . .) those words and phrases which imply *a share in the Redemption* . . . I have never seen any one of the three works which you named.'

[2] Russell could give no information.

[3] Newman evidently wrote at the same time to Edmund O'Reilly S. J., who had been his Professor of Dogmatic Theology at the Catholic University in Dublin. O'Reilly replied on 6 Dec. that he had not yet read Pusey's *Eirenicon*, but would write soon. His answer was not given until 23 Jan. 1866. He thought the quotations about the Blessed Virgin 'would startle some and not others . . . I was startled at the passages, but I doubted whether I ought to be so . . . It is quite possible that some may be true and none heterodox . . .'

Rednall Dec 5/65

My dear William

Miss Giberne is in a sad state of desolation because she has not heard of us so long. Please, send off your letter at once, and say I will write as soon as I am out of the wood of my present business. I hope to finish by the vigil of the Immaculate Conception. But I shall be obliged to have a second letter after Christmas.[1]

Send a *brougham* over for me on Thursday *morning* to be here at 10 o'clock.

Tell Godwin Friday's fish smelt — I had already been going to speak to her about the fish. It was not as it should be, and not well dressed, for two recent Fridays. This is a serious matter now that Advent is come[2]

Ever Yrs affly J H N

THURSDAY 7 DECEMBER 1865 returned from Rednall
FRIDAY 8 DECEMBER Ambrose? Sung High Mass

TO JOHN KEBLE

The Oratory Bm Decr 8. 1865

My dear Keble

I am going to write a Pamphlet on the Irenicon. And I do trust I shall not say any thing to cause pain. It will be my earnest wish to avoid it. Of course I must speak out what I think — else, I shall not carry my friends with me, but I wish to present another view of his book than has been taken. As I anticipated, it has made people very angry.

I hope you are easy about Mrs Keble

Ever Yours affectly John H Newman

[1] See first note to letter of 26 Nov. to Hope-Scott.
[2] Wednesdays and Fridays in Advent were days of fasting, when flesh meat was forbidden.
[3] There are three more undated notes from Newman at Rednal to Neville: 'Monday Don't send out meat this very bad day
I can get on quite well with what I have got
I send the boy to prevent you'
'I have left three letters under a weight on my table. Will you please put them into the Post.'
'Please attend to the inclosed. We must cultivate Lady Ll.
I think you had better by *this* post write her a line to Mrs Herbert (the direction is on her letter) saying you will be very glad to show her ⟨Lady L.⟩ the school, but you regret that I am from Home.
And then tomorrow you must open Lady Ll's letter to me, if one comes, and do the civil thing'.

TO E. B. PUSEY

The Oratory Birmingham In fest. Concept. Immac. 1865

My dear Pusey

You must not be made anxious that I am going to publish a Letter on your Irenicon. I wish to accept it as such, and shall write in that spirit. And I write, if not to hinder, for that is not in my power, but to balance and neutralize other things which may be written upon it. It will not be any great length. If I shall say any thing which is in the way of remonstrance, it will be, because, unless I were perfectly honest, I should not only do no good, but carry no one with me — but I am taking the greatest possible pains not to say a word which I should be sorry for afterwards[1]

I hope you found nothing to annoy you in Lockhart's second article[2]

Ever Yours affectly John H Newman

The Revd E B Pusey D D

TO THE EARL OF DENBIGH

The Oratory Bm Decr 9/65

My dear Lord Denbigh,

I was away as you know, when your letter came. I congratulate you on the opening of your Chapel, and felt the kindness of your wish.[3] I am writing a Pamphlet about Pusey's book. Let me ask your and Lady Denbigh's prayers, for it is an extreme trial and anxiety to me. I inclose a copy of a letter, (I don't think it is a liberty in me to do so,) which I am sending by this Post to Dr Maurice who is at Newnham.

Yours, My dear Lord Denbigh Most Sincerely in Xt
John H. Newman of the Oratory

The Rt. Honble The Earl of Denbigh.

TO R. R. MAURICE

Decr 9/65

Revd Sir,

I would write to our Bishop in your behalf, as you wish me, if you had put me in a position to do so. The letter you gave me from Dr Allemani was so

---

[1] Pusey replied at once, 'As you said of me, "I am safe in your hands." [Letter of 14 Nov.] This discussion is taking too wide a range, for me to wish you to be silent.'
[2] 'Dr. Pusey's Eirenicon and the Difficulties of Reunion,' the *Weekly Register*, (2 Dec. 1865), pp. 363–4. Cf. note to letter of 21 Nov. to Lockhart.
[3] On the death of his father on 25 June 1865, Lord Denbigh inherited Newnham Paddox, and at once had the chapel there re-arranged and consecrated for Catholic use.

damaged — (as you said, I believe) by fire and water, that I could not thoroughly master its contents.[1]

Yours faithfully John H. Newman

The Revd Dr Maurice.

MONDAY 11 DECEMBER 1865   Bishop Willson called?

TO HENRY JAMES COLERIDGE

The Oy Bm Dec 11/65

My dear Fr Coleridge

I have been very busy or I should have written to you before. I have made up my mind to write a pamphlet — it will not be a long one. I dread taking the step very much — as it is not to be expected that I shall make no mistakes. But I felt almost called upon to write.

The Article on Pusey in the present Month is very ably written, and I don't known how he can answer it. But still, I thought it harsh. There is a text about 'smoking flax.'[2]

As to your writing to him, there is a difficulty in keeping up consistently two characters at once — that of a private acquaintance and that of a stranger. He I [sic] may say what business have *you* to write? And yet he is so forbearing and gentle, that it might seem quite a duty to do so. I should wait and see, if I were you.

Excuse a letter written when I am so tired, as to be half asleep, as I write[3]

Ever Yours very sincerely John H Newman

TUESDAY 12 DECEMBER 1865   Mrs Bretherton called?
THURSDAY 14 DECEMBER   Boys examinations   took no part till Saturday

TO E. B. PUSEY

Dec. 14/65.

My dear Pusey,

Thank you very much for your Number 90. I have not yet had time to read it, but I see how kindly you have spoken of me.[4]

---

[1] Maurice wrote on 8 Dec. from Newnham Paddox, where he hoped to be Lord Denbigh's Chaplain. Lord Denbigh complained of the want of formality in his testimonials, 'together with a word erased between the words "censura" and "immunem."'
[2] This was Coleridge's second article, dealing directly with the *Eirenicon*, 'Dr. Pusey as a Controversialist,' the *Month*, (Dec. 1865), pp. 619–38.
[3] Coleridge replied on 12 Dec. that Pusey had kept himself and others back from becoming Catholics. They felt Pusey had 'imposed on and dealt unfairly' with them, and was now doing so with yet others.
[4] *Tract XC. On Certain Passages in the XXXIX Articles* . . . with a historical preface by the Rev. E. B. Pusey . . . Oxford 1865.

I send you some notes Pope has sent me. There is not so much in them as I had hoped.[1]

Don't be persuaded by Lockhart to meddle with the question of the Pope's jurisdiction. He either has it by divine right or has not — and the consequences are serious either way.[2]

Ever Yrs affly John H Newman

SATURDAY 16 DECEMBER 1865   Forty Hours begun

TO EDWARD HENEAGE DERING

The Oratory Birmingham December 16/65

My dear Mr Dering

I have received Grey's Court, and shall make it my recreation, as soon as I am free from my present undertaking — for I am writing a pamphlet on Dr Pusey's recent book, and it makes me anxious how I shall acquit myself. All of you must give me your best prayers.[3]

Very truly yours in Xt   John H Newman of the Oratory

P.S.   I am sorry to hear from Miss Orpen, how inconvenienced you have been about your new buildings etc.

TO H. A. WOODGATE

The Oratory, Bm ⌐Dec 16/65⌐

My dear Woodgate

I have been so busy writing a letter to Pusey, that I have been obliged to put aside all my letters — yours in the number. This will account for my silence.[4]

⌐I can only say, friendships are not put on, put off, put on again, like a glove.

---

[1] See postscript to letter of 10 Nov. to Pusey, who was about to pay another visit to French bishops.

[2] Pusey had said, in his letter to the *Weekly Register* thanking for Lockhart's article on the *Eirenicon*, that he recognized the Primacy of the Bishop of Rome, but not as a matter of Divine Law. On 9 Dec. Pusey wrote to Newman, 'Lockhart presses me not to say that I do not believe the Supremacy to be of Divine right.' See Liddon's *Pusey*, IV, p. 129.

[3] *Grey's Court*. Edited by Lady Chatterton, two volumes, London 1865. She was assisted in writing it by her husband.

[4] Woodgate wrote on 30 Nov. in reply to the letter of 22 Nov., to explain why he had not kept in touch after Newman's conversion. He had been in a state of confusion; at the time of Papal Aggression, when High Churchmen were under attack, Protestants would have been offended; he had a young family that might have been unduly influenced by Newman. Later there was an awkwardness about renewing relations. Woodgate insisted that he had had no ill-feeling towards Newman, and offered to call on him.

It gives me pleasure to accept your offer of calling on me, but I had rather it should be, when I have got my Pamphlet over. At the same time, since I neither have retracted nor mean to retract the Letter to the Newspapers you speak of, perhaps that circumstance may interfere with your coming.[11]

Yours affly John H Newman[2]

TO MRS F. R. WARD

The Oratory Bm Decr 17/65

My dear Mrs Ward

I ought to have answered you before this, but I am over head and ears in a pamphlet on Pusey's book — and it will not come into the right number of pages. In consequence I cut it short ten days ago, and shall only write half my Letter — but, though I am relieved so far, the correcting and passing it through the Press takes up a great deal of time.

Now as to Trinity and Lincoln — I dare say you have found out much more than I am in the way of doing.[3] Ever since I knew Trinity it has been a College of lax discipline. It was so when I was there, and all along up to 1845. Whether it has altered since I do not know. There was a marked difference between the Scholars and the Commoners — the Scholars being superior men, and, as far as I know, as well conducted as any men in the University. It is curious how long the character of a College lasts — When I was entered there, my school-master, who was at Oxford in 1784, on hearing it said 'A very gentlemanlike college —' which I understood to mean that it *was* such, and *also* a rowing College.[4] Did you see in the Times the other day that some Ch Ch [Christ Church] man, in answering Mr Meyrick of Trinity (who had spoken of the Ch Ch bad discipline) said something to the effect of 'Those who live in glass houses etc' Trinity is out and out a pleasanter College than Lincoln. — the garden by itself is enough to make one give it the preference — but I wish you would get some definite information on the point of its discipline. I am glad to hear that Daman has sent his son there — but then Daman himself is close by.[5]

Thank you for your account of the two boys. We shall be glad to see them any time. Any how they must come down, if possible, on St Philip's day, when I suppose we shall have a Latin Play. Thank you for your good news about the

---

[1] Woodgate said he had been 'greatly annoyed' by Newman's letter to the *Globe*, of 28 June 1862, denying that he was about to return to the Church of England.

[2] Woodgate replied on 18 Dec. promising to call. On 23 May 1866 Newman invited him to the Latin Play at the Oratory School.

[3] Mrs Ward wrote on 8 Dec., for advice as to whether to send her son, Richard, to Trinity College, Oxford, which had decided to admit Catholics.

[4] See *A.W.*, p. 30, and for what follows *The Times*, (5 Dec.), p. 9, and (8 Dec.), p. 9.

[5] Mrs Ward wrote that Charles Daman had sent his son there 'and he must know how all the Colleges stand.' Daman went up to Oriel College in 1830, and was a tutor there, 1837–68. His younger son William Charles went up to Trinity in Oct. 1863.

School — which it is pleasant to hear — we hope it is deserved.[1] I will not forget your kind offer, if I come to London but generally my visits are not longer than an hour or two

Yours affly in Xt   John H Newman of the Oratory

Mrs Ward

MONDAY 18 DECEMBER 1865   Forty Hours ended
WEDNESDAY 20 DECEMBER   boys went
THURSDAY 21 DECEMBER   went to London to Lintott
FRIDAY 22 DECEMBER   called on Miss Bathurst — she was out   returned from London. unwell. *very ill*

TO BISHOP ULLATHORNE

The Oratory Dec 23/65

My dear Lord

I thank you for the sight of Mr McCloskey's letter. We will send him a prospectus, so you need not trouble yourself any more on the subject.[2]

I should have written before now to thank your Lordship for your letter of the 17th — had I not been away in London — I feel the kindness which has led you to tell me all you had to say about the Letter of the Holy Office.[3] I am not likely to say much or any thing on the subject of re-union, in what I am writing. I begin with our Blessed Lady — but the subject runs out so that I shall not get further, at least at present. I don't deny I am against treating the Unionists harshly, in spite of their having an article against me in their new number[4]

Begging your blessing on us at this season, I am, My dear Lord,

Your affte & obt Servt in Xt
John H Newman of the Oratory

The Rt Revd Bp Ullathorne

[1] Mrs Ward wrote, 'I hear such excellent news of the School.'
[2] Mr McCloskey of New York had written to Ullathorne inquiring about the terms at the Oratory School.
[3] Ullathorne wrote on 17 Dec. details he had received from Talbot of the rejection of the appeal of 187 Anglicans against the condemnation of the Association for the Promotion of the Unity of Christendom. See end of letter of 24 Nov. to Coleridge. Ullathorne was given to understand that they were watching keenly in Rome how the English Catholics and their bishops were helping the movement towards unity.
[4] 'Musings of a Vert' in the *Union Review*, (Jan. 1866), pp. 49–81. See letter of 18 Jan. 1866 to Rogers.

TO J. SPENCER NORTHCOTE

The Oratory Decr 24/65

My dear President,

We have nothing to say against   ¹except that he is very idle and trouble-some. In consequence *he* accuses us of spiting him, and *we* seriously think he might get on better elsewhere. He has fits of compunction and does better for a time — and relapses. His worst feature is his bullying little boys. There is no reason against your taking him.

We wish you all a happy Christmas. You must not expect much from my pamphlet. Pusey's book is so miscellaneous, that every reader will have his own view of what ought to be said in reply — and thus no given answer will satisfy others.

Yours most sincerely in Xt   John H Newman of the Oratory

The Very Revd Dr Northcote

MONDAY 25 DECEMBER 1865   sung 5 o'clock Mass — preached at 11
THURSDAY 28 DECEMBER   could not say Mass
SATURDAY 30 DECEMBER   could not say Mass
MONDAY 1 January 1866   Ambrose went away

TO EDWARD HAWKINS

The Oratory Birmingham Jany 1. 1866

My dear Mr Provost,

It has been a trouble to me that I have not been able to answer your letter sooner — though it is not worth while to tell you the accidents which have hindered me. Now, however, writing on new year's day, I take the opportunity of offering you and Mrs Hawkins and all who are dear to you my best wishes for your continual welfare and happiness in it.

I will answer your question as exactly as I can.²

When I first saw Pusey's statement, about the 12 hours, it seemed to bring before me an old memory which I had quite forgotten. I *had* quite forgotten it — and yet I seemed to think it true, when I saw it. At the same time, I can-

---

¹ The name has been erased.
² Hawkins wrote on 28 Dec., 'I do not like to trouble you with a question which may recall painful recollections. But you are the only person who can answer it; and several persons, members of the Hebdomadal Board in 1841, are anxious to know what is the exact truth of a story given by Pusey p. xii of his "Historical Preface" to his late republication of Tract 90. He says "an intimate friend, who was daily with Newman tells me that Newman asked for twelve hours to explain himself and was refused them." Pusey makes this a grave charge against the Board, in p. xiii; but not one concerned, who has mentioned it me, can recollect that the application was made; nor can I. And indeed it seems inconsistent with your manly letter to the Vice-Chancellor in p. xv. in which, as it seems for the first time you avowed yourself the Author of the Tract . . .' [*V.M.* II, p. 363]

not at all confirm it on my own authority; and, supposing Pusey were to say that he was wrong and that he found that 12 hours had not been asked, I should have nothing to say to the contrary. If, however, his statement is correct, it is not wonderful that I should have forgotten about it; because, at the time, I thought myself harshly used, and for my own peace and comfort I drove the matter from my mind.

Thus much, however, I recollect clearly — that, together with others, I thought there was a kind of race between the Board and myself, which should get into print first — and that the Postscript to my Pamphlet was an expression of my disappointment that I had been outstripped by a few hours.[1]

I assure you it would give me great pleasure to have an opportunity of meeting you and Mrs Hawkins, though I find it very difficult to leave home — and indeed, now for 20 years, have hardly been into a friend's house, as having duties to my own body. But I will not relinquish the hope, that, if I leave home, I shall come across your own place of abode whether at Oxford or at Rochester, so as to have an apportunity of seeing you again.

I am writing in haste to save the post

Very sincerely Yours John H Newman

The Revd Dr Hawkins

TUESDAY 2 JANUARY 1866   could not say Mass.   really ill
WEDNESDAY 3 JANUARY [also 4 and 5 JANUARY]   hip bath at night   no Mass

TO MRS F. R. WARD

The Orato.y Jan 5/66

My dear Mrs Ward

I know you will excuse a short letter. What you say is quite satisfactory and removes my difficulties about Trinity.[2]

Wayte is a very dry fellow. Once or twice he has written so curtly to us,

---

[1] *V.M.* II, p. 388.

Hawkins replied on 2 April from Oriel:

'It was curious that both you and I should have so entirely forgotten the circumstances connected with the notice taken of the Tract by the Heads of Houses and Proctors in 1841, for on my return to Oxford I was told that I had myself applied for delay.

And so it was. You wrote to me on Sunday March 14, to say that the writer of the Tract had a short defence of it in the press, which he expected would be out on Tuesday or Wednesday. You allowed me to do what I pleased with the note. And I accordingly moved the Board on the 15th that every thing respecting the Tract should be suspended till the promised Defence appeared. My motion was not carried; and I therefore would not vote for the notice, tho' I thought it ought to be issued, if at least we should not be satisfied by the Defence.'

See also Liddon's *Pusey* II, p. 174; Sir J. T. Coleridge in *Memoir of the Rev. John Keble,* Oxford 1869, p. 268; R. W. Church in *Moz.* II, p. 331; and R. D. Middleton, *Newman at Oxford,* London 1950, 'An Echo of Tract Ninety', pp. 244–70.

[2] See letter of 17 Dec. 1865. Mrs Ward's letter is not to be found. Samuel Wayte was a Fellow and tutor of Trinity College, Oxford, and became President at the end of 1866.

that we did not know how to interpret it — so that I am not surprised at what Richard Ward tells you.

Every one will be disappointed at what I am writing — because they don't know what it is about, and therefore will be expecting a great deal.[1]

I return my good wishes for the New Year to you and yours with all my heart.

My work has knocked me up somewhat

Yours ever affectly in Xt   John H Newman

SATURDAY 6 JANUARY 1866   said Mass   Dr Evans every day   crammed Towneley nearly every day through this Vacation.   He came to me in bed.

SUNDAY 7 JANUARY   said Mass

MONDAY 8 JANUARY   *What is the matter with me*

TUESDAY 9 JANUARY   William went away

WEDNESDAY 10 JANUARY   had leeches on

THURSDAY 11 JANUARY [also 12 and 13 JANUARY]   lay in bed all day

SUNDAY 14 JANUARY   said Mass   better

TO MOTHER MARGARET MARY HALLAHAN

The Oratory, Bm Jany 14/66

My dear Mother Margaret

I have been unpleasantly unwell, and this is the first day I have left my bed, after many days of previous indisposition and hard work in passing through the press my Letter to Dr Pusey.

This must account for my silence after your very kind letter on my Feast-day. You must also excuse me on these grounds to Sister Imilda [Poole] — I am lying on a sofa, and write with difficulty.

I am going to ask your acceptance of three copies of my 'Dream of Gerontius' — and wish you would see fit to give one of them to the Sister who painted that St John you sent me.

Beg Sister Imilda to give me her prayers, and you also —

Yours affectly in Xt   John H Newman

MONDAY 15 JANUARY 1866   Ambrose returned

TUESDAY 16 JANUARY   Bowyer called

[1] *A Letter addressed to the Rev. E. B. Pusey, D. D., on occasion of his Eirenicon of 1864.*

The Oratory, Birmm January 16/66

My dear Rogers

I am amused at your consulting me on a point of casuistry, a science for which I have no taste or qualifications, but I suppose it is a way of saying at the beginning of the new year, How d'ye do?

As to the very question, owing to my not having been well this Christmas, all my papers are in confusion, and I must write in answer from my memory of it, as your letter is in a large heap which, alas, has accumulated for some weeks.

You ask, 'If I feel perfectly, absolutely, certain that A.B. wrote a book, from the internal evidence, etc, tho' he never told me, may I, when asked as to the Author, say "I don't know."'

I think the *true and full* answer would be, 'I don't know, but I am perfectly sure.' Then comes the question, 'Are we always bound to tell, not only the truth but the whole truth to a chance questioner?' I think not — yet certainly, since half a truth is next door to an untruth, here is one puzzle, before going further. But I shall assume that we are not bound to say every thing to every body — and only bound, in what we do say, to speak the truth.

Assuming then that if 'I don't know' be true, I may say it, without the addition of 'but I am sure.' I say 'I think it *is* true.' Nay, I think, if I said 'I *do* know,' I should be telling an untruth.

It is unsatisfactory to make the resolution of a question turn upon the definition of a word — but, provided we take the popular received sense, I think we both may, and here must do so. Now by 'know,' it seems to me is ordinarily meant what I gain directly, through the sense or by intuition, and not what I *infer*, however cogently. If I said 'I know A.B. wrote the book,' the inquirer would certainly gather that A.B. or his publisher etc etc had told me. Observe, I account testimony, as coming through the ears, direct information. But, if I had even the fullest conviction that he wrote it from the character of the work, or external circumstances, still I never could say 'I know', without misleading the questioner, for in such case the natural, inseparable expression of my belief is 'I am sure, I am [have] not an atom of doubt, beyond all question etc,' 'If you ask me, I can give you but one answer' — such modes of speech answering to the state of mind in which we stand affected towards a question of fact, on which we can but reason, or come to certainty by indirect processes.

And so much for your puzzle, if I have apprehended it rightly.

I still ie on a sofa — till Sunday last I have been all day in bed. For thirty years I have not had so anxious an illness. And the worst is, it came on so suddenly and without notice, that it makes me dread to leave home ever again, lest I should be seized in a railway carriage, or at a friend's house. The doctor puts it down to the fidget caused by the Letter I have written to Pusey — but, though any application of mind tries me, I cannot credit him. It has been most providential that it did not come on two years ago, when I was in controversy with Kingsley — most merciful again, that I had finished my Letter before the really bad attack came on, and that I have been up and downstairs on Christmas Day, Epiphany, and every Sunday, and now, wishing you and Lady Rogers and all who are dear to you a very happy New Year,

I am, My dear Rogers, Yours ever affly John H Newman

Sir F. Rogers Bart

WEDNESDAY 17 JANUARY 1866 ½ past 2.A.M. got rid of the *unsuspected* causa mali[1] dispatched to London the last revise of my Letter to Pusey

TO JOHN KEBLE

The Oratory Birmingham Jany 17. 1866

My dear Keble

I hear from Copeland what trials you have.[2] For me I am just recovering from an anxious, not to say, serious indisposition, under which I have extreme cause for thankfulness, that my pain has been so very little.

This night I send up my last revises of my Letter to Pusey — and I am sanguine that I shall not pain him or any of you. My sole subject is the Blessed Virgin. I have disowned those extreme statements which he has collected — but, in doing so, I have been obliged in fairness, to speak my *whole* mind, and that of course involves what looks like controversy

Ever Yours most affectionately John H Newman

TO EMILY BOWLES

The Oratory Bm Jany 18/66

My dear Child

I don't wish it mentioned but I have been anxiously indisposed for several weeks, and am still on my sofa — this will account for my not writing in answer to you.

It grieved me to hear you so speak of yourself. You do too much, and your mind works upon your health. You will surely have a great reward for so much trial and suffering.[3]

---

[1] See end of letter of 23 June 1866 to St John.
[2] Keble's wife was dying, and his brother Thomas was ill. For Keble's reply, see letter of 7 Feb. to him.
[3] Emily Bowles, who visited regularly a hospital and a prison in London, wrote on 28 Dec. that she had been unwell.

Don't expect much from my Pamphlet, which is at last through the Press. Pusey's work is on too many subjects, not to allow of a dozen answers — and, since I am only giving one, every reader will be expecting one or other of the eleven which I don't give. Mine is only upon our belief concerning the Blessed Virgin. What I have done, I have tried to do well — but a reader will say '*This* is all! *I* have no difficulties about the Blessed Virgin. Pusey only goes off on the old story, which I heard about years ago.'

You must not speak against Sir G. Bowyer's persistence. He has his own side of the question, and there are two sides; and one side, whether his or the Archbishop's, is not two sides.[1]

Your account of Mr Fullerton is very sorrowful — but I have been prepared for it, ever since I saw him this time four years. He then seemed to me to be so much changed.

As to your wish about Campion, much as I should like to do what you asked me, I am not up to it — and have too many irons in the fire.[2]

You are one of those I have said Mass for this morning

Ever Yrs affly in Xt   John H Newman

TO SIR FREDERIC ROGERS

The Oratory, Birmm January 18. 1866
My dear Rogers

Never fancy I am silent from any such motive as you have half feared. If I did not like a question, I would tell you so at once. As to the case of casuistry, I meant to have said, if I did not, that for myself, did a man ask me whether (e.g.) Ffoulkes of Jesus wrote a certain article in the last January 1st Union Review, (which from internal evidence I think is certainly his) I should have no misgiving in saying 'I really do not know.'[3] If I so treated a friend, I might be unkind etc, but I mean as a question of truth. E.G., supposing a stranger in a railway-carriage, to whom I had no call to open.

I have sent for the Ecce Homo.[4] I see very few books — indeed I have not time — and much thinking, and still more composing, tries me. Did you ever hear me say, what I am ever saying, that with me the composition of a book is a child-birth? — It is so indeed. It takes a vast deal out of me, and I dread it. I have hardly ever written except from necessity — the consequence is I have nothing in writing which has not been published. People say, 'You could so easily look into your portfolio and give us something for this or that use' — but I have no portfolio.

[1] See letter of 27 Nov. 1864 to Bowyer.
[2] Emily Bowles wanted Newman to write 'an introduction — say of 40 or 50 pages' to a life of Edmund Campion, which seems not to have been published.
[3] E. S. Ffoulkes's article was 'Musings of a Vert', the *Union Review*, (Jan. 1866), pp. 49–81.
[4] Sir John Seeley's *Ecce Homo* was published anonymously at the end of 1865. Newman reviewed it in the *Month*, (June 1866) pp. 551–73; *D.A.*, pp. 363–98. The book, which caused a sensation, described our Lord simply in His human character.

And so again I have a great laziness about reading books. A man gave me one some time back, — I have not (alas) read it yet — if I had, I might say at once that it did *not* answer to your account of what the author of Ecce Homo would write — Yet I never should be surprised if he is the author of such a book. We are in a strange time. I have not a shadow of a misgiving that the Catholic Church and its doctrine are directly from God — but then I know well that there is in particular quarters a narrowness which is not of God. And I believe great changes before now have taken place in the direction of the Church's course, and that new aspects of her aboriginal doctrines have suddenly come forth, and all this coincidently with changes in the world's history, such as are now in progress; so that I never should shut up, when new views are set before me, though I might not take them as a whole. And further, I know your own great desire to grasp a fuller and exacter truth than you have — and your praise therefore of a book is not a slight matter.

For these reasons, I wish to read the Ecce Homo — but on the other hand I cannot promise to read it, when it comes, or to write to you, if I read it. I am not strong, and anything like excitement of intellect has a bodily effect on me, a local effect — and then again my Letter to Pusey only goes through a portion of my subject — and the second part, which I have not begun, will require the most delicate and cautious writing — and at this moment I am wearied out with the small publication I am just finishing.[1] It has been done indeed since the beginning of December — but the passing thro' the Press has been trying.

The thing I am most anxious about in your account of Ecce Homo, is your saying that it is Anti-monophysite — lest it should mean that it is Nestorian, which in fact would be a disguised Unitarianism.

I cannot understand its being a *known* writer. There are various new writers now a days, who seem to make their maiden effort cap-a-pie. As to the author of Ecce Homo, you must not expect, putting aside the question of congeniality, it will affect every one as strongly as it does you. Your feelings perhaps have been pent up — those of others may have already found their object and poured themselves out upon it.

Ever yrs very affly John H Newman

P.S. I am getting well, but weak and low

Sir F. Rogers Bart

---

[1] The second part of his *Letter*, dealing with Infallibility, Newman never published. He decided that he had done sufficient to check the extremists, and did not wish to risk the success already achieved. Ignatius Ryder later took the subject up in his controversy with W. G. Ward. Cf. *Ward* II, p. 107. Newman's notes for the second part of his *Letter* will be published among his theological papers.

TO J. WALKER OF SCARBOROUGH

The Oratory Bm Jany 18/66

My dear Canon Walker,

My last revise went from me last night. My pamphlet, such as it is, was finished in the beginning of December — but the passing through the Press, Christmas interfering, is a long business. You will be amused to find that I have only got through one of Pusey's many subjects, and you will say 'Is *this* all!' in much disappointment. 'All that could be said about the Blessed Virgin has been said long ago'.

I have been ill (*don't tell*) anxiously so — and am still on my sofa — but, thank God, am now convalescent. This is why I have not written to you before.

Very sincerely Yours in Xt   John H Newman

TO T. W. ALLIES

The Oratory Bm Jan. 19./66

My dear Allies,

I am just recovering from some anxious indisposition, but quite recovering from it, thank God. It has spoilt my holidays, and left on my hands a pile of letters to answer. My doctor has left me today for good, I hope, — and this must be my excuse for not answering you more speedily.

You will find my Pamphlet is but a fragment of what it should be — and that most likely I shall have to pursue my subject. This, I much regret, hinders me from reading your fresh lectures.[1] My doctor makes a great fuss of my not doing too much, and till I get off my hands whatever I have to say to Pusey, I must think of nothing else.

I have not more hopes of Pusey than I had, though he has certainly changed his view of things in contemplating the possibility of his leaving the Church of England, but there are a number of men, for whom he speaks, and whose difficulties it would be a great thing to succeed in removing.

I cannot understand how the Archbishop manages to get through so much work. I see, besides his work on the Blessed Virgin, he is publishing on the reunion of Christendom.[2]

Ever yours affly John H Newman

[1] i.e. those for subsequent volumes of Allies's *The Formation of Christendom*.
[2] Archbishop Manning, *The Reunion of Christendom, A Pastoral Letter to the Clergy*, London 1866.

The Oratory Bm Jany 19/66

My dear Church

Connecting you with St Wolstan, whose day this is, I had been saying Mass for you and others this morning — and now comes your affectionate letter which I answer at once.[1]

(Private)

Yes, I have been anxiously ill, but my Doctor has just taken leave of me, and put me in good spirits. Since I wrote to Rogers, and *thought* I was convalescent, the real cause has appeared and been got rid of, — and so wonderfully that I feel like the man, who, when he saw next morning the chasm he had galloped over the night before, fainted away. I might have had months of extreme pain, such as would perhaps have killed me, but, as if miraculously, suddenly the cause passed away, and by passing disclosed itself, where there had been no suspicion of it before. My Doctor, who is a person of considerable name, thinks that, now that the evil is known, it need never return again. All this has quite unsettled me, the surprise and thankfulness, and I have been both joyful and dejected.

You may send this to Rogers. You may understand that it is painful to me to talk about myself.

I shall rejoice to see you as the days lengthen,

Ever yrs affly John H. Newman.

The Oratory Bm Jany 19/66

My dear Monsell

You must not be angry with me for not answering you. I have been anxiously unwell, and confined to my bed — but now, please God, I am all right again, and my Doctor has today taken leave of me.

I am glad to think we shall see you soon. Every one will be disappointed at my Letter to Pusey, because it is only a fragment — but it is 159 pages, and I had no room for any thing else. My own experience, as Dr Moriarty's, is, that he quotes very much at random.

I am very much pleased at the French Apologia, and feel how much I owe to those who have taken so much pains with it, and such successful pains.[2] The accounts I have from Dublin about the University agree with your own. I see de Vere has a letter today in the Times about the Irish Priesthood. It was very satisfactory that he was allowed to write on the subject of their recognition by

---

[1] In the *Lives of the English Saints,* London 1844, Church wrote that of St Wulstan, whose feast was on 19 Jan.
[2] See letter of 7 Aug. 1865 to La Serre.

the State — but would not both Exeter Hall and the clergy themselves set themselves against the Endowment or Stipend which he seems to be aiming at ?[1]

Ever Yours affectly in Xt   John H Newman of the Oratory
The Rt Honble Wm Monsell M P

TO E. B. PUSEY.

The Oratory Bm Jany 19, 1866

My dear Pusey

Had I known you were returned, I should have written to you.[2] The last revise goes out of my hands with this letter, and I have told Rivington to send you the sheets as they are struck off. I wrote to Keble last night, to say that I trusted I had guarded myself from saying any thing which would pain him or you.

I have only got through the subject of the Blessed Virgin, though I run to 159 pages. There is an introduction of (say) 32 — and notes of about 32 — therefore nearly 100 are on that main subject.

As to your question, I never heard any one maintain that the activa conceptio was immaculate. The 'first moment' is the first moment of the passive. What they said in the middle ages I don't know. The 'first moment' is not contrasted to 'second moment' but to all subsequent moments. If I can find the slip or page I will enclose Suarez — as a specimen of what is held.[3]

I have been anxiously ill for a month past, and have had a sad Christmas, many days in bed. My doctor has left me only today, and I have been out for half an hour. I have had a most merciful escape from suffering which might have killed me, but they say I am all right now; but of course I am weak, and anxiety of any kind throws me back. If I write more, I shall take my time about it.

Ever Yours affectly John H Newman

---

[1] This was a long letter, headed 'Fenianism,' *The Times*, (19 Jan.), p. 10, and was followed by another, 'The Ecclesiastical Settlement in Ireland,' (26 Jan.), p. 7. De Vere showed how loyal the Irish had been, in spite of the grossest injustices, and in his second letter maintained that religious equality was necessary if there was to be a settlement in Ireland.

[2] Pusey returned to Oxford on 18 Jan., after spending a month in France visiting bishops there.

[3] Pusey asked a question concerning the Immaculate Conception which he had raised in his *Eirenicon*, p. 147. It was defined in 1854 that the Blessed Virgin was preserved from original sin 'in primo instanti conceptionis suae.' Pusey remarked that 'S. Thomas uses the self-same phrase as to the conception of our Blessed Lord's Body,' and asked whether this implied that the active as well as the passive conception of our Lady was immaculate. See letter of 22 Jan. to Pusey.

Jany 20/66

Dear Mrs Seager

Thank you for your letter. I should have answered it sooner, had I not been unwell — with kindest remembrances to Mr Seager, I am &c[1]

J H N

TO CHARLOTTE WOOD

The Oratory Birmingham Jany 20. 1866

My dear Miss Wood

I thank you very much for your deeply interesting account of Mr Telford's last days. I will not forget one who was so kind in his thoughts to me. I should have written sooner, except that I have been unwell myself — and though, thank God, I am well again, such occurrences are warnings that at length there will be an illness which has no recovery.

I am glad to hear of Mr Maclaurin.[2] What became of his daughter about whom you were so sollicitous? or else, it was the daughter wrote to me, and from circumstances I had no opportunity of answering her.

I will not forget your wishes about him — and with kindest remembrances to Mrs Wood, I am,

My dear Miss Wood, Sincerely yours in Xt
John H Newman of the Oratory

Miss Wood

TO CATHERINE ANNE BATHURST

The Oratory Bm Jany 21/66

My dear Child

Though I do not wish it mentioned, I have been anxiously unwell since that 22nd when I was in London. I went back in considerable pain, and, though I am convalescent, I am not yet well — and am to be under a strict regime for at least a year — perhaps always.

I should have liked much to have a talk with you — and I was not well when I came to your dwelling.[3]

As to Pusey, I don't *see* any chance, but then he is changing his *basis*, and he has contemplated the *possibility* of his joining the Church; he allows that in

---

[1] Mrs Seager, in a letter of 1 Jan 1866, excused herself rather than apologized for her readiness to believe that Newman had been, four years earlier, on the point of returning to the Church of England. See letter of 4 June 1862 to her.

[2] This was W.C.A. Maclaurin, Dean of Moray and Ross, who became a Catholic in 1850, and was then reduced to great poverty.

[3] See diary for 22 Dec. 1865.

his book. But, if even he is in that condition, others must be so still more; and I fear I must say, in what I am now on the point of publishing, I am writing for these more than for him — I run to 159 pages, but do not get further than the Blessed Virgin.

We have two novices, one an Oxford convert, the other an Ushaw youth.[1] They seem to promise, John Stokes is in the House, wishing to be a novice, but we are keeping him back and employing him in the school. There is another convert too, an elderly parson, who is not unlikely to join us.[2] The school flourishes, except in numbers — we are nearly 70. if we had 80, both ends would meet, and this is all I desire. We are all getting some what older, I certainly.

Our boys who have left us, are doing us credit, Some are going to Oxford. We have them all under our roof now, having given up the whole of our upper story to them.

I wish I heard a better account of your health and of your prospects — one report was that you were going to Stroud to the noviciate, which I was glad of — another that you were quite uncertain of your future. I have been saying Mass for you lately

Pray for me Ever Yrs affly J H N

TO HENRY BEDFORD

The Oratory, Birmingham. Jan. 21st. 1866.

My dear Mr. Bedford,

I was very much pleased to have your letter and pamphlet, which I read with great interest. It gives a lively account, and is a valuable record, of the Christmas Festival at Rome. I should have thanked you for it before this, but that I have been especially busy in what will, I fear, be much ado about nothing — in passing a Letter to Pusey through the Press.

Pray present my best remembrances to those of your party, if there are any now, whom I had the pleasure of knowing at All-hallows, when I was in Ireland, and believe me to be

Most truly yours in Christ   John H. Newman.

TO MISS MUNRO

The Oratory, Birmm Jany 21. 1866

My dear Miss Munro,

You must not be angry with me for not writing. It is a month, I think, during which I wrote no letters. I had to write a Pamphlet, to pass it through

[1] Joseph Drew and John Norris.
[2] Thomas Alder Pope.

the Press, and then to fall ill. I am now getting well. As your letter is not dated, I can't tell how long I have let it lie.

I hope you mean to let Stone alone.¹ But perhaps you have already been at it. You have done all that you need to — and it seems to me Divine Providence has made His will clear to you. I hope you will let us see you some day

Yours affly in Xt   John H. Newman of the Oratory

MONDAY 22 JANUARY 1866   in bed again.   Dr Evans came.

TO ROBERT ORNSBY

The Oratory Bm ⌐Jany 22/66⌐

My dear Ornsby

I have long wished to write to you, and had intended to do so this very day, when comes your letter.²

⌐You have done so very much for the University, that no one can complain of your now leaving it — yet my sense of it makes me feel sad at your retirement, rather than thankful⌐ to Providence and to you ⌐for having continued there amid so much discouragement so long. I rejoice in the thought that you have done a work there, and the knowledge that I persuaded you to enter upon it is a consolation to me amid my many shortcomings. You as much as any one, and more than most, have tided over the University's most difficult years, and you leave it, when your reward ought to be beginning. Sic vos non vobis.³ I do not know how I shall be able to think of the University, with such various friends away, who belonged to it. I went first [[indeed]] — but I could not stop without ruining this Oratory. My presence here was imperative.⌐

I congratulate you on what I hope is an otium cum dignitate for you, and I hope the sea breezes will be of service to Mrs Ornsby, to whom say every thing kind from me

Ever Yours affectly in Xt   John H Newman of the Oratory

R. Ornsby Esqr

¹ i.e. Mother Margaret Hallahan's convent at Stone. See letter of 20 Oct. 1865 to Miss Munro.
² Ornsby wrote on 21 Jan. from Arundel to say he had resigned his professorship at the Catholic University in Dublin, on his appointment by the Duchess of Norfolk as librarian at Arundel Castle and keeper of the records at Norfolk House.
³ 'Sic vos non vobis mellificatis apes,' attributed to Virgil when certain of his lines were claimed by Bathyllus.

TO E. B. PUSEY

The Oratory Birmingham Jany 22/66

My dear Pusey

I hope others will be as kind to my Pamphlet, as you are.[1] I have intended it sincerely to meet your challenge that members of the Church of Rome should come forward and say they did not accept the extreme statements about the Blessed Virgin which you call attention to. But I could not do this without bringing out my whole mind — if I had not, my co-religionists would have said it was unfair — and I should have had no right to disclaim what was objectionable. It was no good writing at all, if I did not carry them with me — so I was obliged to say, however temperately I said it, that there were things in your Volume which I agreed with them in feeling I could not accept.

As to the question which I answered hastily in my last, the 'in primo momento' in our Lord's case is both body *and* soul, because, the Divine Person being with them from the first they were made contemporaneously — whereas the first moment of the Blessed Virgin only relates to her soul, which is herself. Whatever may be said in the middle ages, such has long been the recognised language of divines — thus Suarez (e.g.) speaks both of the Blessed Virgin being procreata ex viri et feminæ conmixtione carnali, and also of her being preserved from original sin in primo suae conceptionis instanti, the activa conceptio not coming into the question at all. The Pope, in his Bull, used the received language of the theologians.

Ever Yours affly John H. Newman

FROM FELIX DUPANLOUP, BISHOP OF ORLEANS

Paris le 20 Janvier 1866

Mon Révérend Père

Je viens de recevoir à Orléans la visite de M. le docteur Pusey.[2] J' ai été très touché de sa droiture, de sa candeur, de sa sincérité. Il m'a paru très occupé de l' idée de la Pacification, et très désireux d'y arriver. Il m'a même exposé les points sur lesquels il aurait encore besoin de quelques explications et éclaircissements. Je regarderais pour ma part le retour à l'Eglise Catholique d'un tel homme comme un grand bonheur pour l'Eglise et un grand exemple pour votre pays. Mais avant d'entrer en correspondence sérieuse avec lui sur une affaire de cette importance, voulez-vous me permettre de vous demander, *très confidentiellement*, à vous qui connaissez beaucoup le Docteur Pusey, et êtes, je crois, un de ses plus anciens amis, quels conseils de prudence et de charité vous croiriez pouvoir m' offrir relativement à une question pratique si délicate, et qu'il vaudrait peut être mieux ne pas entamer, s'il n'y avait des chances sérieuses de la mener à bonne fin. Je pense, mon Révérend Père, que vous ne trouverez pas trop indiscrète une demande que je ne vous adresse que par une entière confiance en vos lumières et en votre zèle, et dans l'unique vue du bien.

Agréez, mon Réverénd Père, tous mes plus respectueux et dévoués hommages.

Félix, Evêque d'Orleans

[1] After reading Newman's *Letter to Pusey*, the latter wrote, 'Thank you for all your love. I have just finished your letter to me which I hope will be a harbinger of good . . .
    I will add that in nothing which I wrote had I any reference to yourself, except when I quote you . . .'
[2] Pusey visited Dupanloup at Orleans on 21 Dec. 1865.

Permettez moi de vous remercier de votre dernier ouvrage, dont vous m'avez fait l'honneur de m'adresser un exemplaire. — Je suis charmé que ce soit un de mes diocésains, M. de St Maur qui l'ait traduit en français.[1]

TO FELIX DUPANLOUP, BISHOP OF ORLEANS

The Oratory, Birmingham die Januar 25. 1866

Praesuli Revmo et Colmo Felici Episcop. Aurelian.

Utinam Amplitudini Tuae, Praesul illustrissime, possim responsum dare, et tuis par meritis et voluntati meae! Sed ita comparatus est amicissimus vir ille, de quo me rogas, ut, licet omnium quotquot vivunt candidissimi sit et sincerissimi animi, tamen nec seipsum nôrit bene, neque ab altero, quamvis sibi conjunctissimo, facile perspici possit et intelligi. Neque sane ego confidenter dixerim, utrum hoc tempore revera progressum aliquem faciat versus Ecclesiam catholicam, an ea contra, quae nunc agit, reditura sint ad nihilum.

Hoc tamen sedulo considerandum est, illum, hominem in sua sententia prope immobilem, nunc tandem, post tot annos disputantem cum catholicis, subito in novam operationum basim (ut aiunt) transmigrasse, ita ut canones Sacrosancti Concilii Tridentini (quos hactenus repudiaverat) lubenti animo accepturum se esse profiteatur, — id est, dummodo prodeat aliqua declaratio a nobis, gravi quadam auctoritate sancita, quae sibi confirmet nullam esse catholicis fidelibus obligationem, immodicis laudibus Beatam Virginem colendi, neque Sanctae Sedis infallibilitatem confitendi.

Hoc quoque notatu dignum est, quod amicus meus in hac re non est solus. Grandiorem hominum circulum repraesentat. Orator est ad Te, Praesul Reverendissime, et specimen ipse, multarum animarum, quae, tamquam vulnere affectae, lugent perpetuo infortunium suum, nempe se a Christianorum plenitudine avulsos esse, et solitarie Deum et Christum colere. Oculos vertunt, nunc ad catholicam Ecclesiam, nunc ad Graecos, sperantes tandem aliquando aditum fore, quo sibi intercommunio vel cum his vel, quod melius putent, cum illa restauretur.

Et huc usque illos laudaverim; sed progrediuntur ultra et maiora quaedam audent et infeliciora, — edocti, ut credunt, a de Maistre, qui in opere quodam suo, magnificum sane munus Ecclesiae Anglicanae adjudicavit, illius nempe ministerio divulsas partes Christianitatis in orbe terrarum (graecam, latinam, anglicanam) inter se progressu temporis rursum nectendas esse et uniendas.[2] Quae quidem opinio vanissima est; tum quia Ecclesia anglicana non eam veritatis et sanctitatis habet vim, neque apostolicam eam agendi libertatem, quâ rem tantam possit efficere, tum quia non vult tali officio fungi; namque

---

[1] i.e. the French translation of *Apo*.
[2] Joseph de Maistre, in the conclusion of *Du Pape*.

amicus meus et sui, quamquam magna pars communionis Anglicanae, sunt solummodo una pars ex tribus in illa partibus seu factionibus, inter se jugiter decertantibus, scilicet catholicismi, Puritanismi, liberalismi fautoribus.

Praeterea Anglicana haec factio, quae unionem cum Ecclesia catholica hoc tempore expetit, forsitan a scopo sibi proposito vel in melius vel in pejus mox deflexura est.

Enimvero aliqua subest spes, dum fratrum tam diu inter se discordantium reconciliationem meditantur hi et affectant, illud passuros esse optimos homines, quod fieri solet fluvii alveum ingredientibus, nempe vi fluminis amissis pedibus abripi; atque adeo, immemores incepti sui, felici et fausto cursu in catholicitatis portum deferri.

At contra locus est metuendi quoque, ne iidem, si a praesulibus Galliae nimio favore excipiuntur, elatiores fiant, credentes se jam paratum habere refugium in Ecclesiâ catholica quo uti poterint quandocumque lubet, si quando res suae male sibi habent domi, et proinde hujus refrigerii professione minitari posse et terrere Episcopos suos, et factiones duas sibi oppositas, quasi dis-cessuri sint protinus ab Anglicanismo ad Ecclesiam catholicam, nisi sibi concedatur plena libertas catholica dogmata praedicandi, catholicos ritus celebrandi in communione sua anglicana. Quod quidem si evenerit, nullum prorsus fructum percepturi sunt ex charitate sua Praesules catholici, quos minime decet, in peregrinorum et acatholicorum rixis, huius vel illius factionis utilitati, nullo catholicorum emolumento servire.

Accedit quod Galliae episcopos adeunt, quia Praesules catholici in Anglia aurem illis praebere nolunt.

Quamobrem, in re difficili et dubia, hoc Amplitudini Tuae consilium humillime offerre ausim, scilicet ut ne pedem moveas ipse, donec ii qui ad Te confugiunt, ultro rem aliquam actu praestiterint, quo comprobetur palam et aperte illorum animus simplex non nugandi, non causandi, non cessandi, sed strenue agendi, exempli gratia: quamquam adhuc morantur in Ecclesia anglicana saltem edant professionem distinctam aliquam Fidei, plurimorum nominibus subscriptis.

Accipias haec qualiacunque solita benevolentia Tua, Praesul insignissime, Tui observantissimus Joannes H. Newman[1]

The Oratory Bm Jany 26/66

My dear Monsell

I hope you won't be here on the 30th — for Myles O'Reilly is coming for that day — and I should like you to be here by yourself. Thank you for your

---

[1] The copy of this letter was carelessly made and contains minor inaccuracies which have been corrected from Newman's draft.

Athenaeum Speech. I said to myself 'He should go to Sullivan for information' and I found you had been.[1]

It is true that you are to move in the Commons the Address? I am struck at A de Vere's Letters in the Times as a sign of the Times[2]

Ever Yours affly John H Newman

The Rt Honble Wm Monsell M P

SUNDAY 28 JANUARY 1866   Dr Russell here for a few hours   not so well again

TO THOMAS ARNOLD

The Oratory, Birmingham, January 28. 66.

My dear Arnold,

I ought to have thanked you for your interesting letter long before this — which gave me a great deal of news about Oxford;[3] but many things prevented me, I had for a long while to put aside all correspondence, being engaged in writing and printing a Pamphlet and at nearly the same time falling ill — and, when I came at last to my correspondence, it had become such a heap that it seemed as if it never would be got through, I have heard of you once or twice through our own people here.

The caricature you sent me was capital.[4] Though I have not seen Lightfoot for 20 or 30 years, I recognized the likeness — and Vulcan fell more naturally than I could have fancied he could have been drawn falling. However, in the event, he has not fallen upon the land, but into the waters, if what the papers say of Crigley [Cripley] Meadow (or whatever it is to be called) is true. It may be a right or wrong thing to bring the Great Western Works to Oxford, but it has seemed most wonderful to me to place them near Port Meadow, so notorious for its floodings.

I wish very much that the Oxford arrangements allowed of the ambulatory Examiners to examine *us*. We *could* get an examiner from Cambridge — but I cannot make out that Oxford will do anything for our School, unless we chose to go to the Town Hall for the Middle School Examinations — which of course we don't like to do. A hint was thrown out to me that perhaps the

[1] This concerned the proposed charters for the Catholic University and the new Royal University, of which it was to form a part.

[2] See letter of 19 Jan. to Monsell. Monsell moved the election of the Speaker of the House of Commons on 1 Feb.

[3] Arnold wrote on 29 Nov. 1865.

[4] This was a photograph of 'one of a separate series of Oxford caricatures made by Sydney Hall of Pembroke College (now a well known artist), and issued in Oxford in photographic reproductions. It represented Lightfoot, then vice-chancellor of the University (which had just refused to allow the railway company to establish their carriage works at Oxford), as Jupiter confronting Vulcan, and hurling him down from heaven.' Arnold, *Passages in a Wandering Life*, London 1900, pp. 203–04.

Ambulatory system would be extended to take in the public Schools etc. — but I fear this is far in the future.[1]

What you said of Hawkins made me muse.[2] I suspect he is just what he was, it is not defect of temper, unless he has altered with age, but a determination to reduce the tutor's work to the mechanical carrying out of a paper system of his own, allowing no free judgment or action to those who have the real work, this it is which has ruined the prospects of the College; — and that for more than 30 years

I am, my dear Arnold, Very sincerely yours, John H. Newman

TO WILLIAM PHILIP GORDON

The Oratory Birmingham Jany 28/66

My dear Fr Philip

I am glad to have done a thing pleasing to you and to your Mother — I was prompted to it by that never-sleeping remembrance which I have of your dear Brother[3]

Yours affly in Xt   John H Newman of the Oratory.

The Revd Fr Gordon

TO BARTHOLOMEW WOODLOCK

The Oratory Bm Jany 28/66

My dear Dr Woodlock

I thank you very much for your Pamphlet.[4] It is wonderful to me, living at a distance, that Sir D. C. should have gone out of his way to interfere with the Catholic University. I rejoice to hear your negociations are going on so well;

---

[1] Arnold replied from Oxford on 9 June: 'I have made various inquiries respecting the means by which the school could be supplied with an examiner from here. I am told that the cases in which such examiners are appointed by public academical authority are quite exceptional; Rugby of course is an instance, and perhaps there may be one or two more; but the general practice is for the school authorities to make private inquiries among their friends here or at Cambridge, and so arrange the whole matter for themselves . . .'

[2] Arnold had written on 29 Nov. 1865: 'Dr Hawkins is still at Oriel, as of course you know, and is far from having lost his vigour. I hear that some defect of temper prevents him, as a general rule, from getting on well with the tutors of the college, and that a decline in its popularity and academical reputation has been the result . . . He has become more and more conservative . . .'

[3] Newman dedicated the first edition of *The Dream of Gerontius*, after its publication in the *Month*, to John Joseph Gordon.

[4] In his letter of 26 Jan. enclosing this pamphlet, Woodlock wrote: 'For reasons you will easily see, I did not put my name to it.' It was evidently *Notes on University Education in Ireland addressed to D. J. Corrigan, Esq. M. D.*, Dublin 1865, by 'R.U.', the reply to a pamphlet by Sir Dominic Corrigan, (he had just been made a baronet), *University Education in Ireland*, Dublin 1865. Corrigan was opposed to giving the Catholic University the benefits of State recognition. Woodlock was his brother-in-law.

and cannot doubt that they will be successfully carried forward to the end. And your news about the University Church is very good.[1]

All who know Ireland well, speak very seriously about Fenianism. The obvious evil is the unsettlement it must cause, when, whether for religion, education, or trade and manufacturers, repose is the one condition needed for a happy progress.

I have been unwell, but am now well again — thank you

Ever Yours very sincerely in Xt John H Newman of the Oratory

The Very Revd Mgr Woodlock

TO MARIANNE BOWDEN

The Oratory Bm In fest. S. Franc. 1866

My dear Child

I have been saying Mass for you this morning, as I always do on this day. I wish you spoke of yourself as stronger — but you are in the hands of that dear Lord to whom you have dedicated yourself, and He will never forsake you. You know, I recollect you from a child; and know how He who made you, has from the first, and before you knew it yourself, drawn you to Him as His own. I remember how your dear Father, when you were quite a little thing, always said that you would be a Nun. Your God and Saviour has loved you from everlasting, and He will love you and you will love Him to everlasting and through ages everlasting. I am never long without saying Mass for you.

You must pray for me, for I was very unwell, when your letter came — and I am not quite right now, though almost recovered. I am old; and this is the reflexion which is left on my mind by illness, even though I get well again. There will be at length an illness, from which I shall not get well.

I have not been able to say Mass lately for many days. I hope to say Mass soon for the Holy Soul who has just been taken from you[2]

Ever Yours affectly in Xt John H Newman of the Oratory

Sister M. Dominica

TO MISS M. R. GIBERNE

St Francis. Jany 29. 1866 Oy Bm

My dear Sister M. Pia,

It is very long since I have written; but I have been very busy, and had a host of letters to write. Then came the writing and printing of my Letter to

---

[1] Woodlock reported 'We have just succeeded in securing a lease for 999 years of the University Church.'

[2] Marianne Bowden wrote on 10 Jan. to ask prayers for Sister Mary Sales Weld, who had recently died.

Pusey (which will be published in a few days) — then I fell ill, anxiously so, — and, when I got well, I had a host of letters to answer, which takes a great deal of time. I have been well again about a fortnight. Just when I was at the worst, came a letter from my poor Brother, saying that his wife was dying — water in the lungs — at Hastings. I wrote to him the next hour; but I have not heard again. This was near three weeks ago. He said recovery was impossible. I have been expecting to hear daily, and have not liked to write to ask, so I am still in suspense. Poor fellow, I thought it might be a time when he would soften, especially if she made a Christian end, and exhorted him. But he is so very touchy on that point, that no one but she could say a word. He wrote quite wildly and incoherently — said he never would ask for sympathy and condolment from others — but that he would engage his mind by working hard, and would live on her memory.[1]

My sister in October at length asked me to Derby, after 18 years excommunicating me. I wrote to say I was glad to have the invitation, but who ever heard of an invitation not coming from the Master of the House? I suspect I hit the right nail on the head; for John Mozley kept silence, when I thus asked for a line from him. She wrote back to say that she wrote hastily, but that her husband *did* join with her in asking me. I *could* not have gone then; indeed I am too old to move about without discomfort, though very well when I keep quiet. I could not at any time go to her without an effort. But I think I may ask for a letter from John Mozley as the price of it.[2] Poor Mr G. Copeland is lying under a stroke of paralysis, and thinks he shall die. His brother is a great deal with him; he is *very* near the Church, I think — I wish George would convert him.[3]

Pusey's move is remarkable — he is at once trying to get into communion with the Greeks and with us. He has been in France lately as low down as Bordeaux, calling on the Bishops. He has changed his basis, and says that, provided *he* is not obliged to use the Italian devotions to our Lady, he will let what he calls popular corruptions take their course in Italy etc, and is willing to unite the Anglican to the Catholic Church on the basis of the Council of Trent. You recollect that at the beginning of the Tracts for the Times the Council of Trent was considered to be the act of apostasy; — so that it is a very great move on his part. Your good Nuns must pray for him.

I hope the Catholic University is to be put on a firm basis. Government is taking it up — and is making great concessions to it; perhaps will endow it with £25.000 a year. The general state of Ireland is very anxious. This Fenianism is a wide spreading conspiracy against British Rule — backed up by the United States, especially the Irish there. Considering our treatment of Ireland, it is not at all wonderful. Most people in England hoped that the States would break up in this terrible war — but the North have conquered

[1] F. W. Newman's wife, Mary Kennaway, who was a Plymouth Sister, did not die until July 1876.
[2] See letter of 31 Oct. 1865 to Jemima Mozley.
[3] This refers to W. J. Copeland.

the South, and they are all one country again. In consequence they are full of resentment against England — and would like much, if their finances let them, to go to war with us. They have taken up the Fenians instead — and may do us a great deal of mischief without going to war. But, if war *did* arise, then we should have also this domestic enemy to contend with. There has lately been a fear lest the Custom House in London, Somerset House etc., should be burned down by the Fenians. The London Docks *have* been set alight. I don't know with how much damage.[1]

Ever Yrs affly in Xt   John H Newman

P.S.   William and I said Mass for you and Miss Bowden today

TUESDAY 30 JANUARY 1866   Major O'Reilly came

TO FRANCIS RICHARD WEGG-PROSSER

The Oratory Bm Jany 30/66

My dear Mr Wegg Prosser

We will attend to your boy's music, as you wish: — at the same time, it is our rule to introduce music and drawing into our course of education, and judge ourselves, when, and if, a boy should be put to them. Of course we never can resist the expressed wish to parents — but, if this does not coincide with our own, then music and drawing become extras.

I will put your boy under another music master, since you say he has fallen back.

No one is a greater advocate for music than I am — but also all my experience goes to make me think that it is a mistake to begin too young. It is difficult to devote any portion of a boy's time to music without the loss of important elementary lessons in other things — He commonly gets discontented, if his music lesson is in play time — and is still more put out when he is set to practise, and that in play time too — and without regular practice, what is the use of his music lesson? Then again, who is to see that he practises? Masters and Tutors like their play time as well as the boys and do not relish having to superintend practice. When boys are older, if they have an ear, they take to music readily, and are only tempted to give too much time to it. This is my experience. For myself, I began the violin when I was 10 or 11. I see boys in our school, who have begun at 13 or 14, playing as well in two years, as I did at the end of 6 or 7. I used to find practice very dull work.

However, your boy is so attentive to all his duties, that I dare say he will find time for music without neglecting either his studies or his necessary exercise

Very truly Yours in Xt   John H Newman of the Oratory

F. R. Wegg Prosser Esqr

[1] There was a great fire on 1 Jan.

WEDNESDAY 31 JANUARY 1866   Major O'Reilly went.   my Letter to Pusey published

TO T. W. ALLIES

The Oratory Bm Jan. 31./66

My dear Allies,

Thank you for your volume. I have read enough of it to see that Pusey owes you an apology, and, in saying that, I imply a good deal.[1] When my own pamphlet will be out, I cannot conceive. It has been all printed off nearly a fortnight. The clean sheets went to Pusey ten days ago. I thought Longman was waiting till the 1st of the month, but I have not had my copies yet, and I see no advertizement fixing the day in the paper. It is going on for eight weeks since it went to press, and is no more than 160 pages. Of course Christmas was a great interruption. It is only on the subject of Our Lady, and, as that is so trite, and other subjects in the Irenicon are more exciting at the moment, I anticipate that it will disappoint the general reader.

Yours affecly in Xt   John H Newman of the Oratory

TO MOTHER MARGARET MARY HALLAHAN

The Oratory, Bm Jany 31. 1866

My dear Mother Margaret

I grieve to hear you have been ill. If all is well I propose to say Mass for you once a week between this and Easter, for your soul, body, mission, and work.

This day is the anniversary of my being had up for sentence in the Queen's Bench, before Judge Coleridge.[2]

Ever yrs affectly in Xt   John H Newman

SATURDAY 3 FEBRUARY 1866   Monsell and Judge O'Hagan came

[1] The volume was the third edition of *The See of Peter,* London 1866, which Allies sent to Newman on 30 Jan. Allies inserted a long preface to this edition, 'A letter to Dr. Pusey,' in which he rebutted a criticism of himself in the latter's *Eirenicon,* p. 237.

[2] Imelda Poole replied on 1 Feb., 'Our dear Mother is deeply grateful to you for your most kind letter and still kinder promise of prayers. She cannot express all she feels in words — all she can say is, and she bids me tell you so — that she always was *fond of you* and now shall be *fonder of you* than ever, and she is afraid she shall live and die with an *irregular affection* for you — These are her own words . . .'

TO MALCOLM MACCOLL

The Oratory, Birmingham, February 4th 1866.

My Dear Sir,

Your letter is far too kind and friendly, but I gladly welcome and accept it, as showing the feelings you entertain towards me, and testifying to those of others. Of course I desire the good opinion of such persons as you represent, and I only have to pray, that God will keep me from desiring it or taking pleasure in it inordinately.[1]

I will beg your acceptance of my remarks on Dr Pusey's 'Eirenicon,' and, while I do so, I am going to ask you to let me leave your question without any answer, at least for the present. I have been much indisposed, and am only just recovering, — and have so much writing, that I do not know how to get through it — and am very tired.[2]

I had seen portions of your vindication of Gladstone already, and am glad to have it and your other pamphlets.[3]

You must not suppose I have not read your and Mr Oxenham's correspondence with interest, because I do not remark upon it, but it is impossible to say what has to be said in few words.

I ought to have stated above that, as I wrote my letter to Pusey with the set view of lessening the difficulties which Anglicans feel in our cultus of the Blessed Virgin, what you say about my Letter is especially gratifying to me.

I am, My Dear Sir, Very truly yours John H. Newman.

The Rev. M. MacColl.

MONDAY 5 FEBRUARY 1866   Monsell and Judge O'Hagan went

TO AMBROSE PHILLIPPS DE LISLE

The Oratory Bm Feb. 7. 1866.

My dear Mr de Lisle

I thank you most sincerely for your letter It is a great encouragement to me. I have been full of anxiety about my Pamphlet, there being so many various parties and persons whom I had to keep in view, and to avoid hurting or

[1] MacColl wrote on 3 Feb., 'to thank you for your letter to Dr Pusey, which I have just read with unbounded pleasure. Your luminous explanation of the doctrine in dispute seems to me to remove all difficulties from the minds of English Churchmen; it *must*, I should think, satisfy the minds of the Catholic party among us.' MacColl added, 'Of course you know that your *Apologia* has turned the tide of English feeling completely in your favour . . .'
[2] MacColl asked Newman's opinion on a friendly controversy in which he was engaged with H. N. Oxenham in the *Ecclesiastic,* on the Catholic doctrine of the Atonement.
[3] MacColl ended his letter, 'May I venture to send you two pamphlets of mine, not because I deem them worthy of your perusal, but by way of showing you how impossible I find it to think or write on any subject without having you in my mind?' One of the pamphlets was evidently *Mr. Gladstone and Oxford* by Scrutator, written at the time of the General Election in July 1865, when Gladstone lost his University seat. See Malcolm MacColl, *Memoirs and Correspondence,* edited by G. W. E. Russell, London 1914, p. 24.

offending. I have an especial desire to act considerately towards the Catholic movement in the Anglican Church because they have been severely handled, and because kindness seems a better way of dealing with them.[1]

As to the letters in my Apologia of which you speak, I should have written to you for your permission to use them, had I known for certain that they were written to you — I knew that I had written some letters to you but I was not sure which they were — There were some too which were written and did not go. I have been struck to find in Mr Bloxam's possession some in my writing, addressed to you, which either never went to you, from the shifting circumstances of the time, or else are copies of those which went.[2] Let me say, while speaking of Mr Bloxam, that I was at his house in the Autumn, and he spoke with the utmost respect and warmth of feeling of you.

I am now getting old and tired — and have difficulty in laying out work for myself in prospect. You must not forget me in your good prayers.

Most sincerely Yours in Xt   John H. Newman of the Oratory

A. P. de Lisle Esqre

TO JOHN KEBLE

The Oratory Bm Febry 7. 1866

My dearest Keble

What am I to say to your most touching letter? I can do no more than think of you and her. I cannot write except to tell you that I am so thinking.[3]

---

[1] De Lisle wrote on 3 Feb., 'Your work on Pusey's Eirenicon will give an immense impulse to the Reunion Movement . . . The Secretary of the A.P.U.C. [F. G. Lee] was with me when your Book arrived, and it would have gratified you, if you had heard the intense satisfaction he expressed at every part of it from beginning to end.'

[2] De Lisle was delighted to see some of Newman's letters to himself quoted in *Apo.*, pp. 138–9 and 187–92. Cf. R. D. Middleton, *Newman and Bloxam*, London 1947, pp. 101–62.

[3] Keble wrote on 3 Feb., referring to Newman's *Letter to Pusey*, 'My dearest Newman, I received your kind present this morning, and the more ashamed was I, because I have two little notes or three, was it? — already to acknowledge — little in size, but great as tokens of kindly love — They are precious as signs beyond doubt that you daily remember me: and Oh how much I need those remembrances! For that which I have daily and almost hourly feared for so many years is now, humanly speaking without doubt coming upon me. We came here [Bournemouth] for the second time after I saw you at Hursley; my wife had begun to look up a little and so she has once or twice for a day or two at a time since then: but on the whole it has been what G. Herbert calls a steady "undressing" — something or other which seemed to be a part of her laid by day after day — chess, the piano, drawing, writing, accounts — and now even reading a few verses is almost too much for her. She keeps her bed entirely, and almost half her time seems to me to be spent in faintings. Yet her mind, when not so employed, is clear, strong, and bright as ever: and she looks on what is coming with a calm awe which I cannot describe and only wish to learn something of. You never saw much of her dear Newman, so I ought not to run on about her: but you can understand how at such a time [Two lines are missing here, where the page has been torn away at the bottom] come over ones heart, and make one seem to know a little — a very little of what it must be when we shall be face to face with Him in whom is all love and purity, and shall have to feel as a sinful creature may, what we and our doings appear in His sight. This is why I say no more to you at present than to desire the continuance of your earnest prayers both for myself and for this beloved one. I have not opened your book [Again two lines are missing on the reverse side]
Ever believe me, dear old friend, very affly

yours J K

I trust you are really recovered — Do take care of yourself.'

You are under the severest trial which man can suffer; and I earnestly pray that you and she may be supplied in all your need, day by day, and have every grace necessary to bring you both to heaven. When I think how ill you have been lately, I am full of anxiety.

I can do no more than think of you and love you. I wish I could do more — but there is only One who is powerful, One who can will and do

Ever Yours affly John H Newman

TO J. SPENCER NORTHCOTE

The Oratory Birmingham Febr 8. 1866

My dear President

I congratulate you on your anxiety being brought to an end, and on your gaining a verdict which is virtually a triumph.

I am not the only one here, who has said Mass for you during the trial[1]

Very sincerely Yours in Xt   John H Newman of the Oratory

The Very Revd Dr Northcote

TO J. P. TAYLOR

The Oratory Bm Febry 8/66

Dear Mr Taylor,

I thank you for your letters.[2] I have ordered the book you speak of — and, even though it be written by a Catholic, I shall be glad to have it; for though it will not contain the testimony of a stranger to a Catholic Truth, it will be the learned illustration by a Catholic of matters especially interesting at this time

Very truly Yours, John H Newman

TO ARCHBISHOP MANNING

The Oratory Bm Feby 9/66

My dear Archbishop

I was going to write to thank you for your Pastoral — and now I have to thank you also for your remarks on my Pamphlet in the letter which has just

[1] In March 1865, David, son of J. D. Fitzgerald, an Irish judge, was expelled from Oscott College by Northcote, the President, for breaches of discipline. Judge Fitzgerald brought an action, which was decided in his favour by a Special Jury in the Court of Queen's Bench, on 7 Feb., but with the award of only £5 for damages.
[2] Taylor recommended to Newman Henry F. A. Pratt's *The Genealogy of Creation, newly translated from the unpointed Hebrew text of the Book of Genesis,* London 1861, which bore testimony to the doctrine of the Immaculate Conception, thinking the author to be a Protestant, and then wrote to correct this.

come.[1] My notice of St Justin, St Irenaeus and Tertullian, as a basis of argument, is taken from my Essay on Development of Doctrine, as indeed is the greater part of my Pamphlet. I have done little more than throw it into a more popular form[2]

Yours affectionately John H. Newman of the Oratory
The Archbishop of Westminster

TO DANIEL NOBLE

The Oratory, Birmingham. Feb. 10th. 1866.
Dear Sir,

I thank you for your Lecture on Statistics, which you have been so good as to send me. I have read it with much interest, and a sense of the soundness and perspicuity of the remarks it contains.

Very faithfully yours, John H. Newman.
D. Noble Esq. M. D.

TO WILLIAM WALKER

The Oratory Birmingham Febry 10. 1866
My dear Mr Walker

Your letter was a great gratification to me.[3] I wrote my Pamphlet with much anxiety, how it would answer the purposes I had in view, and, if it has at all succeeded in that respect, I have gained what I desired and have reason for being very thankful.

I wonder what the other subjects are on which you thought I might have been writing. Are you alluding to the question of science and Scripture, when you speak of 'subjects which are at present agitating the religious mind of

---

[1] Manning's pastoral was that on *The Reunion of Christendom,* which came out at the beginning of Feb. On 8 Feb. he wrote to Newman, 'I asked Canon Morris to express to you the pleasure with which I had read your treatment of the Patristic proof of the dignity and Sanctity of our Lady. I should have written myself but I was not well: having an influenza . . .

Your proof of the devotion of the "undivided Church" is complete: and I thank you for doing, so much more fully, that, which I was going to attempt. I had especially marked the passages from S. Irenaeus, S Justin and Tertullian which seem to me the basis, abundantly wide enough.

It seems to me also that you have very justly, and very kindly shown how completely absent from Dr Pusey's book is any recognition of what he would profess to be due to our Blessed Mother either of veneration or of love.

All this cannot fail to do much good, and I trust your treatment of it will have a wide effect.

Believe me always Affecly yours ✠ Henry E. Manning.'
[2] See *Butler*, I, p. 362, and first Memorandum of 26 March 1866.
[3] Walker, who was one of the old Catholic priests, wrote from Preston on 5 Feb. of the 'unmixed satisfaction and admiration' with which he had read *A Letter to Pusey*. He only wished Newman had covered more topics. See also letter of 28 Feb. to W. Walker.

England?' If so, they hardly come into the range of questions, large as it is, which Dr Pusey touches upon. And besides, one should like, before writing, to have some sort of notion what is the line of argument which would be satisfactory to authorities at Rome. It would not do much good to propose palliatives, which were of the wrong sort. Moreover, the facts of the case, if difficulty there really is, are so far from being certain as yet. It is poor comfort to tell men to be patient, but I don't see that much more can be said just now.

The other main question, which Pusey's Volume opens, is that of doctrinal development and the Church's, or rather the Pope's, infallibility. It would be easy to show how he exaggerates and distorts the subject (though not intentionally); and it is quite a fact that he has made (some) Catholics uncomfortable. But the perplexing problem is, how to set him right without offending (other) Catholics.

I wish you would be so good as to send me your thoughts, if you are so disposed — of course they would not go beyond myself

Very truly yours in Xt   John H Newman of the Oratory

The Rev Wm Walker

TO RICHARD GELL MACMULLEN

The Oratory, Birmingham, February 11. 1866.

My dear McMullen

I have not answered your letter till now, because I hoped that I might fall upon some remarks or some authorities, which would be worth while sending you. But, in spite of my rummaging a number of books, I have found next to nothing.

Kenrick, in his Moral Theology says something to the point. He proposes the question whether a Priest is bound by his ordination engagement to obey his Bishop who forbids him a certain society — and he decides that he *is*: I suppose, on the ground that the Bishop enjoins him *not* to have to do with it, and he himself is under no contrary obligation on the other hand to *have* to do with it. If what happens in Ireland is a precedent, the obligation of obedience goes further still; for the Bishop determines absolutely who are to be the M.P's, and orders his clergy to advocate their cause from the pulpit.

It is about the Pulpit, I suppose, and other means of publicly expressing an opinion, to which your question refers — for in the Confessional it seems to me you are supreme and subject to nothing but the rules of moral theology and your own best judgment. If anyone came to you there, and asked you what he ought to do with his son, you are responsible to no one but your own best judgment in his particular case.

But, out of the Confessional, though you cannot of course take the Bishop's words into your mouth and pretend to have an opinion which you have not, still, as far as I see, you *are* bound to say that the Bishop precludes you from exercising your own judgment in the matter, because he has exercised his own; that he has stopped your mouth, and that your friend, knowing the Bishop's opinion, must judge for himself.

I am sorry to say I cannot think of anything more or better to send you by way of answer than this. In case you have not at hand Kenrick's Works, I transcribe one or two of his sentences, which after all, do not determine much.

Very sincerely yours, John H. Newman[1]

TO THE EARL OF DENBIGH

The Oratory, Birmingham Febry 12. 1866.

My dear Lord Denbigh,

Thank you for your kind remarks upon my Letter to Pusey. As you imply, I have had great difficulty in reconciling my duty towards our Lady with my wish not to hurt one who loves me, and whom I love, so much.

You can guess whom the inclosed refers to. His Bishop has sent it to me — I have sent a copy to our Bishop.[2]

Most sincerely Yrs in Xt   John H. Newman of the Oratory

The Earl of Denbigh.

TO THOMAS HARPER, S.J.

The Oratory Birmingham Feby 12. 1866

My dear Fr Harper

I wish I could convey to you the gratification which your letter, just received, has given me.[3] How indeed could it not give me the highest? I must beg you to convey to your Father Rector and your Professors my best thanks, both for the honour they have done me, and the encouragement which I gain from their message. I have written and published with much anxious thought, having to steer my course clear of opposite difficulties, and, though I cannot hope to have succeeded in this perfectly, yet I am truly pleased to find from you that I have done so in such satisfactory measure.

Moreover, I have to express my deep gratitude to you and your community for your prayers. It is quite true that my bodily strength is not what it was —

---

[1] The postscript, quoting from Francis Patrick Kenrick, *Theologia Moralis,* was omitted by the copyist.

[2] This was a letter about Dr Maurice from Archbishop Alemany of San Francisco. Cf. letter of 9 Dec. 1865 to Lord Denbigh.

[3] Harper wrote on 11 Feb. to thank Newman, in the name of the professors at the Jesuit Theological College, St Beuno's, North Wales, for his *Letter to Pusey*.

and, though I am quite well for ordinary purposes, yet thinking, composing, and printing for publication take a great deal out of me.

> I am, my dear Fr Harper, Affectionately Yours in Xt,
> John H Newman of the Oratory

The Revd Fr Harper S.J.

P.S. I am looking forward with great interest to the Essays which we are to have from St Beuno's.[1]

TO E. B. PUSEY

> The Oratory Birmingham Febry 12. 1866

My dear Pusey

I don't doubt for a moment that you hold the Catholic doctrine of original sin — I have spoken of the *Protestant* doctrine, as different from the Catholic.[2] As St Paul calls concupiscence sin, therefore I suppose the Council of Trent uses the words that it is not *'vere* and *proprie* peccatum,' not to seem to oppose what in his mouth it considers to be a metonymy; (as, repentance leading to penal acts, those penal acts are called a penance.) I think it is taught that concupiscence is nothing else than a *disorder* of faculties and powers; and therefore cannot be in itself of the *nature* of sin; though that disorder cannot go on for long, without issuing in sin. The grace of the first man kept him from this disorder — but, when that grace was forfeited, the disorder at once ensued, and sin in consequence of it.

As to the 'læsus in naturalibus,' this was the *consequence* of deprivation. My words are 'deprivation and its consequences.' A nature is in a very different state which has never had grace, and which has forfeited it, as a dethroned and beggared prince is worse off than one who never was rich or great. If I wanted to use an image, I should say that grace, once given, clung to us, like a robe; and that the robe could not be torn off without skin and flesh coming off with it; thus man, by the deprivation of grace was læsus in naturalibus, and had a number of wounds, as Hercules, when he tried to tear off the fatal garment.

I am grieved to hear what Father Galwey says. I had not heard of it. But

---

[1] Harper wrote, 'We are occupied here with a set of Essays, but they are intended rather as theological answers to difficulties suggested by Dr Pusey.' This project was not fulfilled, and instead Harper published *Peace through the Truth; or Essays on Subjects connected with Dr. Pusey's Eirenicon,* first series, London 1866.

[2] Acknowledging the copy of *A Letter to Pusey,* which Newman had sent, Pusey wrote, 'Thank you for your kind words on the top of your "letter" I believe it will be best for me to write "A few words of explanation *to*" you.'

Pusey disputed Newman's statement that Catholics thought of original sin as negative, Protestants as positive. *Diff.* II, p. 48. Pusey wrote, 'I never could make out any differences between the Roman and Anglican doctrine of Original Sin. In that the Council of Trent denies that concupiscence is *"vere et proprie peccatum"* it surely implies that it has something of the nature of this sin . . .

Then you too, hold that man was "laesus in naturalibus." . . . There is something then transmitted ordinarily, more than mere privation of supernatural grace . . .'

I know many people are, I grieve to say, very angry — I have wished to be the means of carrying it off, and hindering others writing.[1]

Ever Yrs affly J H N

P.S. I cannot foresee the chance of my saying one word more in consequence of the remarks which you are proposing to write. (Except it should be in the way of agreement.)

I am very glad to have your Norwich paper, which has just come.[2]

TO BISHOP ULLATHORNE

The Oratory Febry 12. 1866

My dear Lord

After all, in spite of our wishes and efforts to continue our responsible duties at the Workhouse, I am sorry to say we have at last unanimously decided that they are too much for us, much as we regret to say so. Some of us are older than we were in point of health and strength — we are fewer in number — and we have works in another direction. All this indeed is an old story — and is only what we could have urged several years ago; but we have been very loth to admit its force, and we have struggled on, in spite of it, as long as we could. Now, however, we can no longer deceive ourselves, that, in attempting to serve the Workhouse, we are going beyond our powers.

When I mentioned our difficulties on the subject several years ago, you told me, if we had any thing formally to say to you about it, we had better put it in writing. That I now am doing, with the hope that your Lordship, without much inconvenience to yourself or the Diocese, will be able to relieve us of the charge which now for fourteen years we have held. That you should have allowed us to hold it so long, is a consideration, which has made us very unwilling to give it up — it is like spoiling a good work. But on the other hand, the length of our service is a sort of plea for asking leave to resign it[3]

Begging your Lordship's blessing I am, My dear Lord, Your dutiful & affte Servt in Xt

John H Newman of the Oratory

The Bishop of Birmingham

P.S. The accompanying letter is from the Bishop of the Priest to whom it relates.[4]

Fr St John forgot to take this to day.

[1] Pusey wrote 'How fierce F. Gallwey is! He calls me by Satan's name, "the Accuser;" directly applies the description of Satan Rev. xxii 10, to me, besides putting many things in my mouth, which I have never said.' This was in Gallwey's sermon, The Lady Chapel and Dr. Pusey's Peacemaker, London n d (1866), preached at Oakeley's church in Islington on 26 Nov. 1865. See pages 11 and 55.
[2] The Spirit in which the Researches of Learning and Science should be applied to the Study of the Bible, a paper read at the Norwich Church Congress in 1865.
[3] On moving to Edgbaston in 1852 the Oratorians undertook the charge of the Birmingham workhouse, the prison and the asylum. For Ullathorne's reply see letter of 20 March.
[4] This was a letter about R. R. Maurice, from Archbishop Alemany of San Francisco.

TUESDAY 13 FEBRUARY 1866   Dr Evans came about now for the last time

TO CHARLES RIDDELL

The Oratory Birmingham Febry 13. 1866

My dear Mr Riddell

We are sorry to lose your son, but we will do all we can for him in the way you mention during the weeks in which he still remains with us. Indeed, we had already put him into classes which have, for their special object, the preparation of boys for such professions as that of civil engineer.

Very truly Yours John H. Newman of the Oratory

Charles Riddell Esq

TO BISHOP ULLATHORNE

The Oratory Birmingham Febry 13. 1866

My dear Lord

I feel very grateful to your Lordship for your valuable and discriminating letter.[1] In proportion to the anxiety which my Pamphlet has caused me, is the relief, and the gratification I feel, in finding that you think it may be useful. I have had to steer amid opposite difficulties and dangers, and to say what I had to say in such a way as not to do harm in one quarter, while I was striving not to give offence in another, and not to compromise truth and honesty, while I was consulting the feelings and the claims of particular persons.

Thank you especially for your remarks on my passage about Original Sin. I am sending up corrections to the Printers by tonight's post — that is, I am leaving out both 'imputation' and 'propagated.'[2]

I am, My dear Lord, Your affecte Servt in Xt

John H Newman of the Oratory

The Rt Revd The Bp of Birmingham

[1] Ullathorne wrote on 12 Feb. to thank Newman 'for your most beautiful Reply to Dr Pusey's Irenicon.

You have thrown a fresh light upon the doctrine of the Immaculate Conception, and have rendered a great service to the Church in this country, by securing the understanding of what that doctrine is, and is not, to many souls'.

Referring to *Diff*. II, pp. 98–9, Ullathorne said, 'I always regretted that Dr Faber published the translation of De Montfort's book, advocating as it does, an unsound devotion.'

[2] Ullathorne had found that some priests, while admiring *A Letter to Pusey*, were uneasy about Newman's exposition of original sin. 'It strikes me,' Ullathorne said, that it is probably this. "Protestants hold that it is [a disease, a change of nature] a poison internally corrupting the soul, and propagated from father to son [after the manner of a bad constitution] . . . We hold nothing of the kind." Of course it is not a poison, that is, a positive something in the soul, propagated etc. But most readers do not stop to weigh words accurately, and the impression that the propagation of original sin is somehow denied gets imprinted on their minds.

Then just before you have said it denotes "the *imputation* of Adam's sin, or the state to which Adam's sin reduces his children." Bellarmine has also used the phrase "imputation of Adam's sin," but it is unusual, and in this country, the unorthodox doctrine conveyed in the phrase "imputation of righteousness" . . . may convey to readers the notion that original sin is not inherent . . .'

In the second edition Newman altered the first passage to, 'Protestants hold that it is a disease, a radical change of nature, an active poison internally corrupting the soul, infecting

WEDNESDAY 14 FEBRUARY 1866   Ash Wednesday.   I gave ashes.

TO W. J. COPELAND

The Oratory Bm. Febry 14/66 Ash wednesday

My very dear Copeland

What must you think of my not having written to you all this time? It is too long a time for me to be able now to tell you how it came about. One thing is, that I thought you would be coming here — another, that I have been variously busy, as with my letter to Pusey — and then I have been ill.

But you must not suppose that I have not thought of you and your brother. Nor have I neglected to say Mass for you both. I hope your anxiety and constant journeying to him will not be too much for your own health. Surely you could get some one to take your duty for several months, so as to be able to remain at Cheltenham without the wearing passing to and fro.

Your Christmas turkey was wonderful — but, time passes so quick, it is now a matter of history. We are steaming on to Easter, and it will be upon us before we know where we are. The pace, at which time seems to me now to go, is something portentous — it is like the rapids before the cataract. Crabbe says that, to the old, days are long and years are short — but to me days and years are short alike.[1]

I had a most touching letter from Keble about his wife. He seemed to have given up all hope, and could only watch her steady calm decline.

Ever Yours most affectionately John H Newman

THURSDAY 15 FEBRUARY 1866   2000 copies of my Letter sold — corrected it for 2nd Edition

its primary elements, and disorganizing it . . . We hold nothing of the kind.' *Diff*. II, p. 48. And the second to, ' "Original sin," with us, cannot be called sin, in the ordinary sense of the word "sin;" it is a term denoting Adam's sin as transferred to us, or the state to which Adam's sin reduces his children . . .' *Diff*. II, pp. 47–8. First and second editions, pp. 50–1.

[1] 'This age's riddle, when each day appears So very long, so very short the years . . .' George Crabbe, *Tales of the Hall*, Book X, 'The Old Bachelor,' near the end.

TO AN UNKNOWN CORRESPONDENT

The Oratory Bm Feby 17. 1866

My dear Child

In answer to your letter of this morning, I have only to say that I think you should accept Revd Mother's offer of paying a visit to her Convent for a retreat; and I pray God to bless you and to be with you

Yours affectly in Xt   John H Newman

TO J. WALKER OF SCARBOROUGH

The Oratory Bm Febry 17/66

My dear Canon Walker

You have acted the part of a very good friend.[1] As to the passage about a people's corruption, I have added in the 2nd Edition, to 'A people's religion is a corrupt religion', the words 'in spite of the provisions of Holy Church', which, I hope, will make it unmistakeable that I am not covertly insinuating that Holy Church herself can ever be corrupt.[2]

As to writing a second Pamphlet, it is no good writing, unless you have a fair chance of success. I hoped to undeceive Anglicans on the subject of our Lady — and hitherto I have had various testimonies from quarters, at once distinct, and some of them not favorable to us, that I have succeeded. But I have no such anticipation I can make them see the unsoundness of the 'Union' hypothesis.[3] For years and years every thing has been said that can be said — and for myself I have said all I have to say, and in vain. In the case of our Lady, it was different. I had not spoken except in my Essay on Doctr. Development, which nobody read — and in my recent Pamphlet I have but cogged out of that unread work. On the other hand my Anglican Difficulties, Loss and Gain, and many of my Sermons are expressly on the question of the Unity of the Church, of Branch Churches etc etc. Therefore absolutely I have nothing to say more.

Very sincerely Yours John H Newman of the Oratory

The Very Revd John Canon Walker

[1] Walker wrote on 15 Feb. of the warm welcome given to *A Letter to Pusey* among priests in the north of England. 'I was reading your letter to Dr Gillow who was charmed with it all through and specially delighted with your accurate (excuse that compliment) and beautiful exposition of original sin. Then came in a certain Episcop*ulus* who objected to the religion of the vulgus being called vulgar and corrupt always and Dr G. was about to give in to it. "Now now, I said, you are not going to segregate that from its context. Is it not plain — passing by ourselves — is not this of the Irish vulgar and corrupt, that of the Neapolitans aye and all over the world. The Bishop went away about now and Gillow gave in saying you meant not that the doctrine taught was such but that the vulgus made it such. Why of course said I. We are all taught to wear coat waistcoat and breeches but compare those of the Vulgus with Canon Searle's for example!'
[2] *Diff.* II, p. 81. First and second editions, p. 86.
[3] Walker wrote, 'Wont you come out on the topic of union? I wish you would tho' I confess I dont understand it.'

TO W. G. WARD

The Oratory Bm Febry 18.1866

My dear Ward,

I thank you very much for the present of your volume, and for your kind letter — but far more of course for your prayers.[1] I do not feel our differences to be such a trouble, as you do; for such differences always have been, always will be, in the Church, and Christians would have ceased to have spiritual and intellectual life, if such differences did not exist. It is part of their militant state. No human power can hinder it; nor, if it attempted it, could do more than make a solitude and call it peace. And, thus thinking that man cannot hinder it, however much he try, I have no great anxiety or trouble. Man cannot, and God will not. He means such differences to be an exercise of charity. Of course I wish as much as possible to agree with all my friends; but, if, in spite of my utmost efforts, they go beyond me or come short of me, I can't help it, and take it easy.

As to writing a volume on the Pope's infallibility, it never so much as entered into my thoughts. I am a controversialist, not a theologian. And I should have nothing to say about it. I have ever thought it likely to be true, never thought it certain. I think too, its definition inexpedient and unlikely; but I should have no difficulty in accepting it, were it made. And I don't think my reason will ever go forward or backward in the matter.

If I wrote another pamphlet about Pusey, I should be obliged to have a few sentences to the effect that the Pope's infallibility was not a point of faith — that would be all[2]

Ever Yours affectly in Xt   John H Newman of the Oratory[3]

W G Ward Esqr

[1] W. G. Ward wrote on 17 Feb., 'You speak *personally* with so much kindness of me in your pamphlet [*Diff.* II, pp. 22–3] (for which I am most grateful) that I take the liberty of sending you my new (or rather cooked up) volume . . . [*The Authority of Doctrinal Decisions, which are not Definitions of Faith,* essays reprinted from *D R*, London 1866]

All the world says you are writing on the infallibility of the Pope: and though my volume is rather on the extent of the *Church's* infallibility, it might be convenient for your purpose of reference.

I need not say how keen a grief it is to me that we are thrown more and more into the position of opponents. The chief point of agreement must be, that we both regard the point at issue as inappreciably important.

You will well have known beforehand what parts of your new book I thoroughly like; what parts less thoroughly; and what parts not at all. I may express however a humble opinion that those parts which I like thoroughly (far the larger part of the pamphlet) are to my mind among the very ablest things you have ever done.

I hope you will pray for me, as I do habitually for you, that whatever the truth is we may be drawn to it.'

In a postscript Ward asked to be told when Newman's supposed second volume was likely to be published.

[2] See letter of 23 March to the *Guardian*, and those of 28 Feb.

[3] Ward passed this letter on to Manning, according to *Purcell* II, p. 321.

The Oratory Bm Feb. 19. /66

My dear Allies,

Your letter was a great gratification to me. Thank you for reminding me of the passages of the Epistle and [to] Diognetus, which I certainly ought not to have omitted. It has come just too late for the second Edition, but I shall send it up to the Printer.[1]

As to Pusey, it is harsh to call any mistakes of his, untruthfulness.[2] I think they arise from the same slovenly habit which some people would recognise in his dress, his beard, etc. He never answers letters, I believe, which do not lie in the line of the direct *work* which he has on hand. And so, in composing a book, he takes uncommon pains about some points, as in his analysis of the Episcopal Replies in re Immaculate Conception;[3] but he will combine this with extreme carelessness in respect to other statements. Then, from that radical peculiarity of mind which interferes with his being a Catholic, he goes by books, not by persons. Thus he is tempted to trust to what he gathers himself from the text of the Bull Ineffabilis, more than to the testimony of its meaning borne by a score of Bishops.[4] I say 'tempted,' not that he would carry it out. Then again, (speaking antecedently, for it is 20 years since I actually knew him) surely a habit of carelessness in stating and ruling points must be generated from the fact of his position, as being testis, judex et magister to so many people. He goes into print with the same heedless readiness and decisiveness with which he would say words in conversation. All this I can imagine, as an hypothesis, and it does not involve more than humanum quid, but it is a strong thing to speak of untruthfulness.

Yours affectly in Xt   John H Newman of the Oratory

The Oratory Birmingham Febry 19. 1866

My dear Ellacombe

I would gladly do any thing in my power in solving the mystery which is

---

[1] On 15 Feb. Allies called Newman's attention to a passage at the end of *The Epistle to Diognetus,* which could be added to the testimonies of the Fathers that Mary was the second Eve, in the first note at the end of *A Letter to Pusey.* In the third edition, p. 128, Newman added a Postscript to this note: 'A friend reminds me that I have omitted, among the instances of the comparison of Eve with Mary, the passage at the end of the Epistle to Diognetus, a testimony most important from the great antiquity of that work, from the religious beauty of its composition, and the stress laid upon it by Protestants.'
Newman later became more doubtful. See *Diff.* II, p. 124.
[2] Allies wrote, 'I admire particularly your courtesy, for I have heard many remark, how intolerably offensive P's book is to them; and for myself his *untruthfulness* is so revolting, that I am obliged to shut the book: and can only look at it at intervals with the greatest pain: and I find it difficult not to shew one's sense of this untruthfulness.'
[3] *An Eirenicon,* pp. 127–37.
[4] *An Eirenicon,* pp. 146–8, on the Bull defining the doctrine of the Immaculate Conception.

the subject of your letter — but you imagine I know much more of Catholic families than I do.[1]

I never heard of any of the names you mention — Pearsal — Hughes — or the others you mention. Nor do I think, I regret to say, I should be able to do any thing, even if you could tell me more than you seem able to do. For instance, in what part of Germany was Mr R. L. Pearsal buried? in what kingdom or state? and what town or parish? Till this is known, the search in registers etc would be interminable.

I suppose you have inquired of Mrs Hughes.

It seems to me very improbable that the Carlton family would allow a second marriage, unless there was unmistakeable evidence of Mr. R. L. P's death.

By their unwillingness to state particulars, I should fancy that there were circumstances attending it which they did not like to mention.

It has given me great pleasure to hear from you — and I thank you for what you say of my Apologia. I had not heard of the additional bereavements which you have sustained.

Believe me, My dear Ellacombe Very sincerely Yours John H Newman

The Revd H T Ellacombe

TO JULES GONDON

Febr 19. 1866

answered that money could not be raised — that I should feel the compliment of his translating my Letter to Pusey — that I will send him a copy — that I would gladly offer him £25 towards the expenses — that I should like to see the translation before publication, in order to revision, and he may keep the £25, though he does not translate etc[2]

J H N

[1] Ellacombe wrote on 17 Feb. about the son of Robert Lucas Pearsall (1795–1856), the musical composer, who became a Catholic with all his family. Pearsall's daughter, Philippa, married a Mr Hughes, and his son Robert made an unhappy match with a granddaughter of Dr Lee, Canon of Bristol. Ellacombe first heard of Robert's death, some time in 1865 in Germany, through seeing in *The Times* of 6 Feb. 1866 the announcement of his widow's marriage to a Mr Carlton, eldest son of the Coroner of Kent. Ellacombe made inquiries and was told that Robert 'was unfortunately accidentally drowned.' Carlton refused to answer his further inquiries and so he turned to Newman.

[2] Gondon wrote on 15 Feb. to explain how he had been prevented for years from continuing his interest in the Catholic Church in England. His attempts to set up a periodical had been thwarted by the press laws of the French Empire, and the consequent lawsuits had left him heavily in debt. His friends were trying to collect money for him, and proposed to appeal in England and Ireland, but had been discouraged when their letter to Archbishop Cullen had received no answer. Gondon hoped now to continue his former interest with an edition of Newman's works in French. He also asked permission to translate *A Letter to Pusey*.

This was published later in the year, *Du culte de la sainte Vierge dans l'Eglise catholique*, in a translation by Georges du Pré de Saint-Maur, authorised by Newman.

TO ROBERT CHARLES JENKINS

The Oratory, Birmingham. Feb 19, 1866.

Dear Sir,

I thank you for your courteous and kind letter — and I am sure you will not think it an uncourteous return on my part to it, if I say that my engagements do not permit me to enter into controversy with you on the subject of it.

My recent letter to Dr. Pusey does not undertake a history of the doctrine of the Immaculate Conception of the Blessed Virgin, but an argument from the Fathers in behalf of the Catholic Doctrine and devotion concerning her.

As to Cardinal Dominic's judgment and that of the many other Divines you speak of, I do not feel it is to the purpose, because they all meant something different from what we mean now in speaking of the 'Immaculate Conception'.[1] There is a sense doubtless in which the words may be taken, which would be, if not heretical, very like heresy. The history of the word Homoüsion is a parallel. The Great Council of Antioch, 70 years before Nicaea, rejected it *in the sense* in which Paul of Samosata and the Manichees understood it. And even long after the Council of Nicaea, orthodox Catholics had a difficulty in taking the word in what to them was a new sense, but the Infallible Church put its own sense upon the word and introduced it into the Creed — and in like manner, after a far longer controversy and probation, the Infallible Church has rejected certain old notions attached to the words 'Immaculate Conception' and has used the phrase to express that old truth conveyed in the doctrine of the 'Second Eve'.

If I understand your sentence, you ask if any Fathers taught a 'profectus fidei' from 'a germ'[.] Vincent of Lerins says 'Crescat oportet,' and multum vehementerque proficiat . . . tam unius hominis quam totius *Ecclesiae*, aetatum et saeculorum gradibus, intelligentia, scientia, sapientia — in eodem scilicet dogmate, eodem sensu, eademque sententiâ' . . . And 'Cum aliquid ex illis seminum primordiis *accessu temporis evolvatur* (developed), et nunc laetetur and excolatur; nihil tamen de *germinis* proprietate mutetur' etc.[2]

I do not feel Epiphanius's words which you quote are to the point in the argument I pursue in my Pamphlet, for I neither think Mary a god, nor that she has the worship due to God.[3] When, in my 'development of doctrine' I use the phrase 'deification of the Saints,' and therefore of the Blessed Virgin, I am

---

[1] In a long letter of 17 Feb. Jenkins, who was a high churchman, criticised parts of the *Letter to Pusey*. He quoted from the *Tractatus de Conceptione* of the Dominican Cardinal, Blessed John Dominici (1357–1419), in denial of the Immaculate Conception. For what follows see *Ari.* pp. 184–8.

[2] Vincent of Lerins, *Commonitorium*, XXIII, 28 and 30. Jenkins questioned Newman's statement in *Diff.* II, p. 26 that the doctrine concerning the blessed Virgin had been 'in substance one and the same from the beginning.'

[3] Jenkins quoted from St Epiphanius against the Collyridians, *Adversus Hæreses*, III, ii.

only using the language of St Athanasius on which I am, if I remember right, commenting.[1]

I cannot follow you in your prophecies about new definitions of faith. It has taken many hundred years to effect the one in question. And it is 300 years since the last definition was made on any subject.

Let me repeat my sincere thanks for the very kind way in which you speak of my past life,[2] and believe me to be,

with much respect, Sincerely Yours, John H. Newman.

TUESDAY 20 FEBRUARY 1866   began shower bath again about now — after several months cessation

TO ELEANOR BRETHERTON

The Oratory, Birmingham. February 21. 66.

My dear Child,

Thanks for your affectionate letter. May all the kind thoughts, which you have for me, return upon your own head and into your own heart abundantly — and be a sort of stock of blessing for you all through life, in all trials and troubles, which you cannot now anticipate, and I shall never see.

I grieve to hear what you say of Mamma's health — certainly she ought not to abstain at present. Tell her so.

I might have been very seriously ill — but, thank God, I am well now — though I don't like to boast.

Remember me kindly to Mr. Watt and believe me, my dear child,

Yours affectionately in Christ, John H. Newman of the Oratory.

From William Ewart Gladstone

11 Carlton House Terrace S.W. Feb. 18.1866[3]

My dear Dr Newman,

To those who have once known you or your writings, any work from your pen must be a matter of interest; and to receive the Letter you have just published from yourself, with words of kindness upon it, has been to me that and something more. It lets in a rush of memories of what was, and what might have been; but with these it stirs up sentiments of admiration and of thankfulness, on which it is more seemly and more suitable to dwell. Your style, as you must well know loses none of its clearness with the gathering in of years; but what I have a better right to thank you for is the frank, kindly, tender spirit which possesses you, and which breathes in every line. I am sure that this is widely felt and appreciated, and that in that recognition you will think you have your reward.

---

[1] Jenkins thought the deification of our Lady would come to be defined. See first edition of *Dev.* pp. 403–4, where 'Deification' is used in the heading of the pages. Newman later substituted 'Dignity,' *Dev.* pp. 135–47.

[2] Jenkins spoke of reading 'Your triumphant defence of your life with the deepest interest and sympathy.' He explained that he had only once spoken to Newman, 'when I joined in a discussion in a bookseller's shop on the Editions of Aquinas.'

[3] Gladstone's last letter before this present one, appears to be that of 15 June 1845, to which Newman replied on 17 June 1845.

I hope you will allow me to claim a common interest with you in works such as this and that which preceded it. The internal condition of the great and ancient Church, which has for its own one half of Christendom, cannot be matter of indifference to Christians beyond its borders. Ignorantly perhaps, I contemplate with pain and alarm what appears to be the ruling course of influences and events within them. It seems hardly too much to say that we see before us an ever growing actual necessity, in the world of thought, for a new reconciliation of Christianity and mankind. Any who have the feeling, that these words very concisely and crudely express, must earnestly wish God speed to those distinguished persons in the Roman Church who like yourself, or like Dr Dollinger, seem to labour in the great and sacred cause.

Forgive my having said so much, in reliance on your generous indulgence, and in the haste to which I am a slave. May I hope, let me rather say I *will* hope, to see you if you come to town. Believe me with respect and regard

Very sincerely yours W. E. Gladstone[1]

TO WILLIAM EWART GLADSTONE

The Oratory Birmingham Febry 21. 1866

My dear Mr Gladstone,

I will not encroach upon your time further than to thank you, as I do very heartily, for your most kind letter. You may be sure that, if I come to London, I will avail myself of your permission to call on you — but I very seldom leave home[2]

Very sincerely Yours John H Newman

TO MRS JOHN MOZLEY

The Oratory Birmingham February 21.1866

My dear Jemima,

I thank you for the remembrance of this day, which now comes more quickly round than ever. It seems only yesterday that Frank wrote to me to observe with a note of admiration that I was *60* — and five years are gone like lightning, now that they are over, though many great events, great in themselves and to me, have happened in the course of them. And they bring home to me their presence, though they be past, in the effects which they leave behind them — for though they fall as softly as snow, they are so weighty too — and year by year I have less physical strength and resisting force, though I am just now quite well. My mind is as much my own as ever it was, but it fatigues me more and more, that is, my nerves, my limbs, my heart, in other words my physical life, to use it.

Within the last six weeks I have had an escape from a most serious and painful illness — an escape so wonderful as quite to frighten me. I was in my

---

[1] This letter is preserved at the Birmingham Oratory. It is printed in *Correspondence on Church and Religion of William Ewart Gladstone*, edited by D. C. Lathbury, London 1912, II, pp. 88–9. Gladstone kept a verbatim copy or draft. B. M. *Add. Ms* 44409. No 198.
[2] See diary for 20 June 1866.

bed or in my room for many days. However, I had no pain or headache — and managed, even in bed, to pass the sheets of my Letter to Pusey through the Press; nay, when I could get up from time to time, I was able to read for and write parts of it. I don't wish all this known, for many reasons.

Frank tells me this morning pretty much what you do, about Maria,[1] a long illness, with an almost certain issue — though he dreads its uncertainties and ups and downs. I think it must, for all its sadness, be soothing to him too.

I was very sorry to hear of Mrs Mozley's illness — pray say so to her and believe me to be

Ever Yours affectionately John H Newman

Mrs John Mozley

P.S.   I am glad you saw Mrs R. [Rickards] It must have been a great comfort to you and to her. It is 40 years this summer since I knew her.

TO THOMAS JOSEPH BROWN, BISHOP OF NEWPORT

The Oratory, Birmingham Feb 22. 1866

My dear Lord,

I feel great gratification in the approval which your Lordship has sent me of my recent letter to Dr Pusey. I assure you I shall keep it, as one of the most important expressions in my behalf, which I have received from any quarter.[2]

Allow me also to thank you for the very kind notice which you take now a second time, of my little 'Dream.'[3]

Begging your Lordship's blessing, on myself and all of us here, I am

My dear Lord, Your faithful Servt in Xt
John H. Newman of the Oratory[4]

The Rt Rev The Bp of Menevia and Newport.

[1] The wife of F. W. Newman.
[2] Brown wrote on 21 Feb. to thank Newman for his 'admirable letter to Dr Pusey. The reasoning is irresistible, and I am specially gratified by your rejection of the ill-advised terms whereby some writers have sought to exalt our Blessed Lady.'
[3] Brown wrote of *The Dream of Gerontius,* 'With me it replaces a meditation Book.' See also letter of 28 Aug. 1865.
[4] Brown added in a postscript, 'I wish you could be induced to go on with the translation of Scripture.'

SUNDAY 25 FEBRUARY 1866   The first sharp weather this season snow ice.

TO ROBERT CHARLES JENKINS

The Oratory, Birmingham February 26. 1866.

My dear Sir

I thank you for your additional instance of a comparison between Mary and Eve — but there are many others short of his age.[1] The comparison is given in the Epistle to Diognetus, one of the earliest relics of antiquity, and in St Ambrose, and elsewhere.

As to my citation from St Epiphanius I cannot follow you in your criticisms, which seem to me to be quite irrelevant.[2]

1. As to μήτηρ ζώντων I *do* expressly translate his words 'It was a wonder that *after* the fall etc;' and at page 34[3] I distinctly contrast this general title given after the fall, and belonging to her as mother of the race, with her special office in the trial which resulted in the fall. She could not have had more honour after the fall than she would have had, if she had not fallen.

2. Of course the comparison between Eve and Mary is in all the Fathers 'mystical throughout,' not literal. Our Lord is Adam mystically — and Mary is Eve. Unless there is a likeness, there would be no mystical relation. The Lamb of *God*, the King of Israel, the Elias that was to come, the New Jerusalem are all mystical; but we interpret the *new* by the *old*. We say that our Lord was a sacrifice, *because* he was mystically a Lamb — and Mary sinless because she was mystically Eve. And I put in δι' αἰνίγματος.

3. My translation of ζῶντα 'living things' seems to me better than yours, especially as ζώντων follows immediately.[4]

4. I *do* omit the passage ζωὴ ἐγεννήθη *because* I have inserted a parallel clause, αὐτὴ ἡ ζωὴ γεγέννηται — and I *mark* its meaning in the translation by printing 'Life' with a capital initial.

5. How 'fall' and 'transgression' differ in sense, I do not see; but, if more copies are printed off, I will alter 'fall' into 'transgression.'

6. As to πρόφασις 'causa' is not an uncommon sense of it; but at page 39 I imply that in the Greek of Irenaeus 'causa' might be πρόφασις or '*occasion*.' 'Pretext' does not make sense.

As to St Justin, *if* I denied that our Lord was the one Saviour and Deliverer, there would be a fault in omitting to go on to the next sentence — but I have all through *insisted* on this in the strongest way — and St Justin says nothing more. And I begin with Ὑιὸν θεοῦ etc, if I do not *end* with it.[5]

As to Tertullian, I thought and think his words so vague as regards the

[1] Jenkins in his letter of 24 Feb. mentioned a sermon of Pope Innocent II in 1130.
[2] Newman replies in six points to criticism Jenkins raised in his letter, to the translation, in *Diff*. II, p. 40, of the text from St Epiphanius, quoted on p. 122.
[3] *Diff*. II, p. 31.
[4] Jenkins thought that ζῶντα referred only to our Lord.
[5] *Diff*. II, pp. 33 and 119.

Blessed Virgin, as not to be in point, as a witness against her sinlessness — He speaks of our Lord's brethren.[1]

I find in the last lines of St Irenaeus, some MSS. read solvatur, for salvatur. I shall notice it in my next edition — but the various reading does not alter the general sense.[2]

No apology was needed for your letter, so kindly worded.

Very truly Yours John H. Newman

TUESDAY 27 FEBRUARY 1866   Wenham came

TO AMBROSE PHILLIPPS DE LISLE

The Oratory. Bm Febry 27. 1866.

My dear Mr de Lisle

It is a shame that I have not acknowledged your kind present before this — but it has not been from any neglect — for I have daily been writing to you, though I have never written.[3]

I was very glad to hear it from *you* — but it was not new to me, and I had intended, but forgot, in a former letter, before it came, to have stated the gratification which I had felt in finding how very much I had in my own pamphlet run along the same line as you. But it was not merely this personal gratification that I felt in reading it, for every one equally with Dr Clifford must admire the spirit and the tone of the whole composition.[4]

I am truly glad to hear you have such encouraging news from Rome.[5] But, besides this, I do not think it right to judge of such publications as the Archbishop's Pastoral, as if they were merely private and personal compositions. An Archbishop has great duties to perform — he has to defend the faith — he must beware of betraying it — and he must emphatically put truth in the first place, and charity in the second. He cannot, by virtue of his office, indulge his feelings; and he seems to be stern, when really he is but faithful to his trust.

[1] Jenkins referred to *De Carne Christi,* 7.
[2] *Letter to Pusey,* third edition, p. 128; *Diff.* II, p 121.
[3] On 14 Feb. de Lisle sent Newman a copy of the *Union Review,* (Jan. 1866), to which he had contributed 'Mr. de Lisle on Reunion,' pp. 82–99.
[4] De Lisle wrote on 26 Feb. that Bishop Clifford of Clifton had 'bestowed *unqualified* Praise' on his article. The markings in Newman's own copy of the *Union Review* for Jan. show how much he found to approve in it.
[5] De Lisle wrote on 26 Feb., 'I have received a most satisfactory letter from Monsignor Talbot, containing a strong approval from the Pope Himself of a Letter I wrote to Monsignor Talbot on the proper Line of conduct in regard to the Reunion Movement in the Anglican Church. A more conciliatory Policy is beginning to be inaugurated at Rome, and if I mistake not, eer [sic] long our Chief Hierarch will find it prudent to modify the harsh course which he has hitherto been taking.' On 14 Feb. de Lisle had complained of Manning's 'harsh and repulsive Line,' and said how much his pastoral letter *The Reunion of Christendom* was regretted by Lockhart.

I am glad to hear what you say of L'Union Chrétienne, and the Church Times and Church Review — The Times is the only one at present which I ever see.[1]

Fr Lockhart is coming down here to give our boys a Retreat in a few weeks. It is pleasant to see how much better he is.

Ever Yrs My dear Mr de Lisle Most sincerely in Xt
John H. Newman of the Oratory

A. L. P. de Lisle Esqr

WEDNESDAY 28 FEBRUARY 1866   Wenham went

TO HENRY JAMES COLERIDGE

The Oratory Birmingham Febry 28. 1866

My dear Fr Coleridge,

I thank you very much for your critique on my Pamphlet in the Month.[2] It will do me a great deal of good. I am sensible I have been bold, perhaps venturesome, in some things I have said — but I have said them nevertheless deliberately and as a matter of duty — and trusting that my good intention, and my confidence that on the whole and in substance I am right, will be allowed to compensate for those imperfections which humana parum cavet natura. And many of your remarks shelter me. I have not observed any thing which I should have wished otherwise, except that in one place you seem to imply that I charge Pusey with not really believing in our Lord's Divinity — but perhaps you don't imply this — and that somewhere you quote me as saying Anglicans, when I have said Protestants.[3]

I have not yet had time to read the Number — but, as I cut open the leaves, the Articles seemed to me to maintain that steady advance in merit which has characterized the magazine for some time past.

I have *almost* entirely given up the thought of finishing my subject in a second Letter. My prima faciê reason for this decision is that time has gone on — and, since I am not strong enough to write quick, perhaps months in addition would elapse before a Second Pamphlet was through the Press. I

[1] On 14 Feb. de Lisle asked if Newman saw the 'Russo-Greek Periodical published at Paris under the title of *L'Union Chrétienne*? There is much in it to grieve a Latin reader, but there is much in it to make him think and look about him. It is a fact that there is a Party both amongst the Gallican Clergy and the German Catholic Clergy, who are now looking to a Union with the Eastern Churches *against Rome* tired out with the excesses of Ultramontanism — I see no way of meeting such a movement as this but in a well combined effort to overthrow Ultramontanism . . .'
On 26 Feb. de Lisle wrote of the *Church Times* and the *Church Review,* 'You should take in both these Papers to judge well of the immense Revolution in the English Church.'
[2] 'Pamphlets on the Eirenicon,' the *Month*, (March 1866), p. 249–70. *A Letter to Pusey* was discussed in the second half of the article.
[3] Coleridge made Newman describe Anglicans as ignorant of the Catholic doctrine of original sin. *Loc. cit.*, p. 264.

always see revises — sometimes I have two — and then I have to send slips here or there for revision to friends, as you know — Hence the Press moves on very slowly. By the time then I get a second Letter published, the state of the controversy would have changed perhaps.

Then again, I had this advantage in the doctrine of the Immaculate Conception etc etc. that there is no difference among Catholics as to what is de fide-received-authoritative etc — such differences as exists lying in particular meditations, devotions, etc etc about our Lady: whereas, if I went to the question of the Church and Holy See, even though I were ever so successful in keeping within allowable limits, (and that is not very easy to compass,) yet I could not carry with me the sympathy of *all* Catholics, *whichever* line of theological opinion I took, and, even though I should *only* attempt (which would be the case,) to keep 'libertas in dubiis,' yet, in doing that very thing I should be doing the most offensive thing of all to some influential people. Yet I may be challenged to write, till I am obliged to write[1]

Very sincerely Yours John H Newman

TO WILLIAM WALKER

The Oratory Bm Febry 28/66

My dear Mr Walker

I am much obliged to you for your letter, and certainly shall not put it out of my thoughts.[2]

However, to write a treatise is beyond me. I never did such a thing in my life. I don't know theology enough, and I have not physical strength for the sustained study.

Then, I know nothing of cotton manufacturers, and could not in

[1] In the bundle of 'Notes in preparation of my proposed Second Pamphlet to Pusey on the Pope's Powers, which was superseded by Ignatius's [Ryder] Pamphlets to Ward,' Newman wrote on 26 Feb. 1866, 'My doubts about a second Pamphlet in continuation of my letter to Pusey are such as these. ⟨arising from my feeling more and more the *extent, difficulty*, and *variety of* views taken, of the Treatise de Ecclesiâ and de Summo Pontifice.⟩

I have not enough to say, nor would it be tanti, to write simply against *him*, unless I did something to establish a moderate view about the Pope and the Church, as against Ward, as in my first Pamphlet I had established a moderate view about the Blessed Virgin as against other extreme writers.

Now the case is very different of the former undertaking, from that of this new one.' Newman then drew out these differences.

[2] Walker wrote on 18 Feb., 'The authority of the church is the one question on which above all others I have long wished for a treatise at your hands . . . I should like this authority brought out in a dogmatic treatise written in English and keeping as clear of controversy as the nature of the case will allow . . . You have a great audience now . . . I am not thinking of mere theologians like Dr Pusey but . . . thoughtful Protestants whose confidence in the established church is going or already gone. When cotton manufacturers become accessible to a different order of religious ideas and begin to suspect that after all the Catholic church may have paramount claims on their submission, it is not unreasonable to expect an abundant harvest elsewhere . . . I am persuaded a work by you on the authority or infallibility of the church . . . would produce most wonderful results.' Newman cut out the name and address on this letter, evidently in order to send it to a third party. The author is clearly identified by the handwriting and by Newman's replies of 28 Feb. and 6 March.

consequence write for them. To address men, you must know their principles, what they will grant, and you may safely assume — what on the contrary you must prove. I know the so-called Anglo-catholics, but none else.

The only opening which Dr Pusey's letter gives me is to remove his alarm about any incroachment on the part of the Holy See on the rights of the Church — and to state what the Catholics hold, and what they do not hold here. This entered into my original plan, and at this moment various critiques on my letter are challenging me, if I dare, to com[1]

much trouble on a Pamphlet.

Then again there is far more difference among Catholics on questions connected with the Church than on those rising out of our doctrine about the Blessed Virgin — and I should not be doing any good service as against Dr Pusey, if I introduced an apple of discord into our own camp.[2]

P.S.   We shall be truly grateful for your present to our Library. It would be a real accession — but why should you rob yourself of them?[3]

2 MARCH 1866   put on full winter clothing for first time

TO CATHERINE ANNE BATHURST

The Oratory Birmingham March 2/66

My dear Child

I fancy Miss Wilson was at the Convent de Nazareth, but I don't know.

I am well aware I have reason to be grateful to the Dominicans, as you say, and I am quite able to believe all you say of them. Apropos of my last Pamphlet, I have received a most encouraging letter from one of their communities.[4] As to my going to see them, much gain as it would be to me, I am too old for moving about, unless I am obliged to do so. I am well at home — but, if I go elsewhere, my health gets put out — and I return here indisposed.

At present it *seems* as if I should not write more in answer to Pusey. It takes me a long time to compose, and, whereas a long interval has already

---

[1] Five lines are missing where the top part of a page was cut out for the sake of the signature on the reverse side.
[2] The conclusion has been cut out.
[3] Walker asked if he might present the Oratory with the works of Edward Hawarden (1662–1735), the Catholic controversialist. Walker sent *The True Church of Christ* and *Charity and Truth*. Of the former work Newman already had a copy at Littlemore.
[4] Mother Margaret Hallahan's convent at Stone.

passed since his book came out, a long one would also pass before I could get a second pamphlet written and through the press. By that time, the interest of the public may have passed to other subjects, and I might have my trouble for nothing.

I fear you suffer from this cold weather

Ever Yrs affly John H Newman

TO ISAAC THOMAS HECKER

The Oratory Bm March 2. 1866

Dear Very Revd Father

I ought to have answered your Reverence's letter before this — and hope you will be so kind as to forgive what looks like negligence. However, I hope I may say that it was not such; but the circumstance, that every day brought its own work, — and that a duty on the other hand which is not fixed to a particular hour is like to be put off and with difficulty gains a time for its fulfilment.[1]

Of course I cannot but be much flattered at your proposal — and I know well the great field which your country presents for exertion in the Catholic cause, and how rich an harvest is there to be expected. But, in truth, the same impediments which have kept me from answering your letter before this, much more exerted a continual influence upon both my time and my strength. I am not as strong as I was — I cannot compose so quickly, from the physical exhaustion it is to me — and I have so much work of various kinds, that I dare not engage in any thing additional. Accordingly, I have not been able to do any thing for two publications, one in England, the other in Ireland, which have a sort of claim upon me already, and to which I must contribute, before I can contribute to any other work.[2] Under these circumstances I am obliged to decline the offer which you so kindly make me; for there is nothing else left for me to do.

I received some time since the third New York Edition of my Apologia. I do not know from whom it came — if from you, I take this opportunity of thanking you for it. It is beautifully printed — and brings my whole book, together with the preceding correspondence, into a very compact shape.

I am, Dear Very Revd Father, Sincerely Yours in Xt
John H Newman of the Oratory

The Very Revd Fr Hecker

[1] Hecker wrote on 22 Jan. requesting articles for the *Catholic World*, which he hoped 'to elevate to the position of a periodical of the first class.'
[2] i.e. the *Month* and the *Atlantis*.

TO AMBROSE PHILLIPPS DE LISLE

The Oratory Bm March 3. 1866

My dear Mr de Lisle

You seem in your letter to imply a wish that I should regard your Article in the Union in concurrence with its *object*, viz. the corporate re-union of the Anglican Church with the Catholic Body. When I read it, I was naturally attracted in the first place to what is after all the real *subject* of it, viz. the doctrine of the Immaculate Conception — and that the more, because I had just been myself writing on the same subject, and, to my very great pleasure, found that I had been running, in my remarks, almost in the very groove which I found laid down in your Paper.[1]

Now, however, I will say all that I have to say about Corporate Union. I say 'all I have to say' because I find it very difficult to realize such an idea as a fact. As a Protestant, I never could get myself to entertain it as such, nor have I been able as a Catholic. Nothing is impossible to God — and the more we ask of Him, the more we gain — but still, His indications in Providence are often our guide, what to ask and what not to ask. We ask what is probable; we do not ask definitely that England should be converted in a day; — (unless under the authority of a particular inspiration,) such a prayer would be presumptuous, as being a prayer for a miracle. Now to me, the question is whether the conversion of that corporate body, which we call the Anglican Church, would not be in the same general sense a miracle, — in the same sense in which it would be miracle for the Thames to change its course, and run into the sea at the Wash instead of the Nore. Of course in the course of ages such a change of direction might take place without miracle — by the stopping up of a gorge or the alteration of a level. But I should not pray for it; and, if I wished to divert the stream from London, I should cut a canal at Eton or Twickenham — I should carry the innumerable drops of water my own way by forming a new bed by my own labour — and for the success of this project I *might* reasonably pray. Now the Anglican Church is sui generis — it is not a collection of individuals — but it is a bed, a river bed, formed in the course of ages, depending on external facts, such as political, civil, and social arrangements. Viewed in its structure it has never been more than partially Catholic. If its ritual has been mainly such, yet its Articles are the historical offspring of Luther and Calvin. And its ecclesiastical organisation has ever been, in its fundamental principle, Erastian. To make that actual, visible, tangible body Catholic, would be simply to make a new creature — it would be to turn a panther into a hind. There are very great similarities between a panther and a hind. Still they are possessed of separate natures, and a change from one to the

[1] See letter of 27 Feb. to de Lisle, who explained on 28 Feb. that his article in the *Union Review* was written with the express purpose of diminishing difficulties in the way of corporate reunion, and that he was about to contribute an article on the subject to *Essays on Reunion*, London 1866, edited by F. G. Lee, with a preface by Pusey.

other would be a destruction and reproduction, not a process. It could be done without a miracle in a succession of ages, but in any assignable period, no.

See what would be needed to bring the Anglican Church into a condition capable of union with the Catholic body. There have ever been three great parties in it. The rod of Aaron (so to call it) must swallow up the serpents of the magicians. That rod has grown of late years — doubtless — but the history of opinion, and of Anglican opinion, has ever been a course of re-actions. Look at ourselves, truths de fide are unchangeable and indefectible, but you yourself were lately predicting, and with reason, a re-action among us from Ultra-montanism. The chance is, humanly speaking, that the Catholic movement in the Anglican Church, being itself a reaction, will meet with a reaction — but suppose it does not. Then, it has to absorb into itself the Evangelical and the Liberal parties. When it has done this, the Erastian party, which embraces all three, and against which there is no re-action at present, which ever *has* been, which is the *foundation* of Anglicanism, must begin to change itself. I say, all parties ever have been Erastian — Archbishop Whitgift, a Calvinist, was as Erastian, as much opposed to the Puritans, as Laud was. And Hoadley, the representative of the Liberals, was of course emphatically an Erastian. But let us keep to the Catholic party. They were Erastian in Laud, they are Erastian in their most advanced phase now. What is the rejection of Gladstone at Oxford, what is the glorification of that Angel Disraeli, but an Erastian policy? and who are specially the promoters of it but the Union Review and the party it represents?

When then I come to consider the possibility of the Established Church becoming capable of Catholicism, I must suppose its Evangelical party adding to its tenets the Puritanism of Cartwright as well as disowning at the same time its own and Cartwright's Protestantism;- I must suppose the Catholic party recalling the poor Nonjurors and accepting their anti-Erastianism, while preserving and perfecting its own orthodoxy — and the liberal party denying that Royal Supremacy which is the boast of members of it, as different from each other in opinion as Tillotson, Arnold, and Colenso. I must anticipate the Catholic party, first beating two foes, each as strong as itself, and then taking the new step, never yet dreamed of except by the Nonjurors, who in consequence left it, and by the first authors of the Tracts of Times, the new step of throwing off the Supremacy of the State.

Then comes a question, involved indeed, but not brought out clearly, in what I have been saying. Who are meant by the *members* of each party, the clergy only or the laity also? It is a miracle, if the 'Catholic' *clergy* in the Establishment manage to swallow up the Evangelical and Liberal — but how much more difficult an idea is it to contemplate, that they should absorb the whole laity of their communion, of whom, but a fraction is with them, a great portion evangelical, a greater liberal, and a still greater, alas, without any faith at all. I do not see, moreover, how it is possible to forget that the Established

Church is the Church of *England* — that dissenters are, both in their own estimation and in that of its own members, in some sense a portion of it — and that, even were its whole *proper* laity Catholic in opinions, the whole population of England, of which Dissenters are nearly half, would, as represented by Parliament, claim it as their own.

And of course, when it came to the point, they would have fact and power on their side. It is indeed hard to conceive that the constitution of the Church of England, as settled by Act of Parliament, can be made fit for re-union with the Catholic Church, till political parties, as such, till the great interests of the nation, the country party, the manufacturing, the trade, become Catholic, as parties. Before that takes place, and sooner than it will, as it seems to me, the Establishment will cease to be, in consequence of the Free Church and Voluntary principle and movement. So that from my point of view, I cannot conceive, to end as I began, the Establishment running into Catholicism, more than I can conceive the Thames running into the Wash

And now excuse me, if I have been at all free; but, since you seemed to wish to know what I think on so momentous a subject, and it seems to be a time when we shall all arrive best at what is true and expedient, and at unanimity and unity, by speaking out, I have thought I might throw myself on your indulgence, even in such respects as I fear will not commend themselves to your judgment[1]

I am, My dear Mr de Lisle Very sincerely Yours in Xt
John H Newman of the Oratory

Ambrose L. M. Phillipps de Lisle Esqre

TO ROBERT CHARLES JENKINS

4 March 1866

Dear Sir

My second edition has been out several weeks — but, though it were not, I should not alter a word in my Pamphlet in consequence of your letter of this morning. I differ from you in your opinion that I have published '*a complete misrepresentation* of the doctrine of the Roman Church on original sin.'[2]

2. I differ from you in your opinion that I have published 'a complete misrepresentation of the doctrine of your own Church.'

3. I differ from you in your opinion that I have assumed that the controversy on the Immaculate Conception originated as you say in a misunderstanding between Catholics and Protestants on the doctrine of original sin. I beg you

---

[1] De Lisle's reply of 6 March is printed in *de Lisle* II, pp. 267–271.
[2] Newman's quotations are from Jenkins's letter of 3 March.

will excuse me if I do not write again to you, since you talk of 'appearing in public in the controversy.'[1]

J H N

5 MARCH 1866   many very fine days still

TO THE EDITOR OF THE TABLET

The Oratory March 5. 1866[2]

Sir,

Your review of my recent letter to Dr. Pusey is written with such extreme consideration, not to say indulgence, towards that portion of it which may be unpleasing to many excellent and devoted Catholics, that I hope you will let me show my grateful sense of it by pointing out to you that I had already, in a passage of my pamphlet which you quote, at least evidenced my anxiety to soften their criticism by anticipating and deprecating it.[3]

In allusion to the judgment which I was about to express on the devotions of which they feel tender, I have said, at p. 85, 'Holy minds readily adopt and become familiar with language which they would never have originated themselves, when it proceeds from a writer who has the same objects of devotion which they have; and, if they find a stranger ridicule or reprobate supplication or praise, which has come to them so recommended, they feel it as keenly as if a direct insult were offered to those to whom that homage is addressed.'[4]

Such persons will, I am sure, bear in mind that there are others, like myself, who are as zealous in their own way of devotion as they are in theirs; and who feel the 'supplication or praise' in question to be an actual dishonour to the object of it, however little intended to be so; and who have to bear at least as much, when they meet with instances of it, as they themselves, on the contrary, when they encountered such animadversions upon it as my own.

Nor do I think I was bound towards the authors of such devotions to do more than to state that their words would bear a good sense, and that in that good sense doubtless they wrote them, and moreover, to give specimens of that good sense which Dr. Pusey had failed to discover. So much I did; but[5] to have gone through all his instances one by one, would have been to compose a second distinct pamphlet.

And then, too, I considered that I had the precedent of Gother, Challoner,

---

[1] Jenkins replied on 7 March that he had 'as little intention to come before the public' as to say anything to 'provoke such a chain of denials' as Newman's letter contained. He added, 'Those into whose hands your Letter [to Pusey] has fallen will as easily discover its discrepancies with Roman doctrine as I have done.'

On 14 March Jenkins wrote to thank Newman for sending him a copy of *The Dream of Gerontius*.

[2] The address and date are from Newman's holograph.

[3] The *Tablet* review of *A Letter to Pusey* was spread over the numbers of 17 and 24 Feb. and ended on 3 March, when at p. 138 the subject to which Newman refers, was treated. See also letter of 12 March to Walker.

[4] *Diff.* II, p. 80.   [5] The *Tablet* misprinted 'not.'

173

and Milner, to shelter me in the course I was pursuing. They, instead of explaining such strong passages about the Saints as occur in Catholic authors, from St. Athanasius downwards, simply enter their protest against them when viewed according to a Protestant interpretation. 'The Papist misrepresented and represented;' (says Dr. Milner in his End of Controversy) 'a work of great authority among Catholics, first published by our eminent divine Gother, and republished by our venerable Bishop Challoner, pronounces the following anathema against that idolatrous phantom of Catholicity, which Protestant controvertists have held up for the identical Catholic Church: 'Cursed is he that believeth the saints in Heaven to be his redeemers; that prays to them as such; or that gives God's honour to them, or to any creature whatsoever. Amen. Cursed be every goddess-worshipper; that believes the Blessed Virgin Mary to be any more than a creature; that worships her, or puts his trust in her more than in God; that believes her above her son, or that she can in anything command him. Amen.'"[1]

Your obedient servant, John H. Newman.

TO WILLIAM WALKER

The Oy Bm March 6/66

My dear Mr Walker

Your kind present is come — and a very handsome copy of Hawarden it is. We are very glad to have it. — and I trust you will some time come and be so good as to write your and our name in it[2]

Very sincerely yours John H Newman of the Oratory

The Rev Wm Walker

TO WILLIAM MONSELL

The Oy Bm March 7/66

My dear Monsell,

The inclosed letter has been waiting some time for a young convert, of whom you spoke to me, but who has never come here, nor, as far as I know, was likely to come. I have kept it thus long, on the chance of his coming — but at length send it to you, who know, I think, where to find him.

Supposing, amid the cares of the nation, it comes into your head to do so, please, tell Mr Moore, that his £100, if not used for its intended object, towards which I have bought fresh land at Oxford, will come back to him[3]

Ever Yours affectly John H Newman of the Oratory

P.S. I meant to have asked you, when you were here, what you were to be, and then in a few days I saw it in the Papers.[4]

[1] John Milner, *End of Religions Controversy*, Letter XXXIII.
[2] See letter of 28 Feb. to W. Walker, who did inscribe his name.
[3] See letter of 26 Oct. 1864 to Monsell.
[4] Monsell had been made Vice-President of the Board of Trade in Earl Russell's government.

The Oratory Bm Mar. 9. 1866

My dear Allies,

I would gladly engage in a task so interesting as that of looking over your Lectures, but I really have not the time.[1] I am deep in arrears. At this minute I have those Essays, truly so called, works they were meant to be, begun, one say four years ago, one autumn year, one last autumn,[2] each in turn intermitted by the stress of little work or odd jobs coming upon me, by school work, by Oratory accounts, by correspondence, by greater matters such as my Apologia and the present controversy. I am suspending, perhaps ending, my correspondence with Pusey, mainly because time has gone on, and nothing done towards continuing it from the press of other work. This very week and day I am attempting to get through what I have aimed at doing since the beginning of January, viz. merely looking over, sorting, burning, and storing in pigeon holes, my letters as received since December last. Then on the other hand to look over Lectures with so much thought as yours and on such important subjects cannot be done off hand or without really making leisure for them.

I can't at the moment put my hand upon Oxenham's letter, but I think I may say for certain that the book of Dollinger's he is translating is a continuation of the work which is translated already by Darnell — a new Church History taking up the subject with an account how Christianity grew up out of Paganism. It will be in a certain way your own subject, except that, in his way, he will be bristling with facts rather than drawing out views. Every one is biassed in his view of facts by controversy, as you say, but you yourself have leant a good deal on his former work. Thank you, however, for mentioning the matter.[3]

Yrs affectly John H Newman

The Oratory Bm March 9/66

My dear Mr de Lisle

I cannot help sending you a line to thank you for your truly interesting letter.[4] You must not suppose, because I do not fully go along with it, that I

[1] These were lectures Allies thought of publishing in the *Atlantis*.
[2] These essays, more or less preparatory to *G. A.*, will be included among Newman's philosophical and theological papers.
[3] Allies wrote on 8 March, 'I hear also that Oxenham is going to publish a translation of Döllinger's medieval Papal Fables dedicated by permission to you. If that be true, I hope you will know exactly the contents of the book, before you appear as patron of it.' See letter of 13 March to Allies.
[4] That of 6 March, in the last paragraph of which he spoke as though the alternative to his own view involved overthrowing the Anglican Church.

have any wish to 'overthrow the Established Church —' You know I have in print distinctly said the contrary.[1] I have only given my *reasons* for thinking it will never rise above the level of its source (Henry viii, *I* say) or stretch beyond its measure — but that it is a providential instrument of great good to England, and all along has been, I fully grant. I never should wish it destroyed till England got *something better*. So far we are quite agreed.

Very sincerely Yours in Xt John H Newman of the Oratory.

Ambrose de Lisle Esq.

SATURDAY 10 MARCH 1866   thaw
SUNDAY 11 MARCH   frost

TO WILLIAM MONSELL

The Oratory Bm March 11/66

My dear Monsell

I want to send you an immediate answer, as far as I can do so, to your question — but I ought to have more time, and am somewhat wearied. But I send you whatever I can.

Speaking then, according to my best knowledge, I conceive that a higher law may suspend a lower one — Thus, to take an instance which occurred some years back, the Governor General of India interfered in the army dispositions of the Commander of the Indian forces. Here was the will of a superior authority superseding the command and decision of an inferior.

And thus, medicine has its laws — and a physician might tell a paterfamilias that he must go to the sea side for a year — and the same paterfamilias might say, 'My duty to my wife and family forces me to keep to my business.' And then the medical man would say, 'That is your matter — but I speak, and of course only speak, as a physician.'

And so, if *moral theology* led me to be sure that early marriages were sometimes expedient, I could not take part in passing a law which enacted (on the most undeniable truths (if so) of *political economy*) that no one should marry till he was 25.

Therefore, if the Church says that it is a mortal sin to alienate Church property in which individuals have only a life interest, I do not see how I can pass a law subjecting Church property simply to a code of laws which does not acknowledge this fact.

A Judge indeed is bound to decide according to that law which is the rule of his court — but he did not make the law, and he is always at liberty to retire from his office. No one forces him to be a judge. Thus I have heard it debated whether a Catholic *could* at this time consent to be put upon the bench, on the

[1] *Apo.*, pp. 339–42.

ground that all judges are bound to take the place of the Judge of the Divorce case, should the proper judge be unable to act. Judges *find* a particular state of law; they do not originate it.

And so again, as to Act of Succession, I may find a certain state of things *existing*, and acquiesce in it — or not. Any how I do not make it. But an Act of Parliament makes the law, be it good or bad.

But in the particular case two questions arise — 1. do *you* make the law adverse to the Church? 2. or does *any one* make a law adverse to it?

Now here I do not know the facts exactly perhaps — but it seems to me that, 1. last summer you did *make* a law in a sense in which you do not make it now, because you *brought in a bill*, whereas now you do but acquiesce in what others do.[1]

2. I conceive the new bill, even with its amendments, is an improvement on the old one, and you take it as such — not denying that it might be better still, but accepting it for what it concedes over and above what was given before.

On these grounds, it seems to me, that, *granting* you *could* not *bring a bill in* enacting the two points in question, yet you can (1) *take part* in a measure which (2) on the whole *improves on the* existing state of things.

The question of scandal remains — but I don't feel that there would be any scandal in the case.

And now excuse me, if I have missed the point — for I am very puzzle headed at this minute

Ever Yours affly John H Newman of the Oratory

The Rt Honble Wm Monsell M P

MONDAY 12 MARCH 1866   snow

TO JOHN THOMAS WALFORD

The Oratory Bm March 12/66

My dear Mr Walford

I praise and bless God with all my heart for your good news — and I thank you very much for your detailed and deeply interesting account of yourself.[2]

---

[1] In 1865 Monsell introduced a Roman Catholic Oaths Bill which passed the House of Commons on 15 June, but was thrown out by the Lords. A Parliamentary Oaths Amendment Bill, introduced by Sir George Grey, passed its second reading on 8 March.

[2] Walford, who had visited Newman on 22 April 1865, and later corresponded, wrote on 6 March from Milltown Park, Dublin, that he was about to be received into the Church. He thanked Newman for his help and also for his writings, 'especially your Apologia and Loss and Gain, in which you often seem to be reading my soul, and expressing my thoughts, and relating events which occurred to me, or conversations in which I have taken part.'

Of course I shall be truly glad to make the acquaintance of any friend of yours, as you propose — and would do all I could for him.[1]

It astonished me to hear there was a chance of one of the Mozleys. I have been sedulously kept from them — and know nothing about them. There is a good nun praying for all of them in France very hard. She told me lately that she was doubling her prayers for them. I shall write to her the news — but it would not do to let it be known. Things must take their course, or rather God must guide them.[2]

I hope you will make a point of coming here, when you leave Ireland.

Very sincerely Yours in Xt   John H Newman of the Oratory

J. D. Walford Esqr

TO JOHN WALKER OF SCARBOROUGH

The Oy Bm March 12/66

My dear Canon Walker

Thank you for your friendly anxiety about me. I should not dream of answering Mr Martin. I hope you do not think I was wrong in writing to the Tablet, as I did.[3] It struck me that it is my interest to soften opposition as much as ever I can. For this, among other reasons, I have put off, or rather changed, my purpose of a second Letter to Pusey to complete my subject. That letter would be about the Pope's Infallibility in *some* measure, and about the subject matter of the Church's Infallibility. Don't mention this. Any how, it would be a very delicate subject, and I should not do it without the greatest deliberation and the most anxious efforts to say nothing fairly open to dispute or animadversion. But of course I should displease some extreme people. Well, I want them to cool down first, before I go on — and I put that letter in the Tablet to assist the process. It is the only sequel that can be required to my Pamphlet, and a natural one. I could not say 'I am sorry if my Pamphlet has

---

[1] Walford, who had earlier resigned his assistant mastership at Eton which he held from 1861 to 1865, wrote, 'There is another master there, who has been quite satisfied by your letter about the cultus of the Blessed Virgin Mary, and over whom you have through your works great influence — He would join too, could he brace his will to such an effort: but he shrinks back on the "liberal" ground of the sacredness of doubt.' This was probably William Cory, later Johnson, a master at Eton from 1845 to 1872.

[2] In a postscript Walford wrote, 'I have great hopes that your own nephew my late colleague and brother at Eton, H. W. Mozley will before very long follow my example.' He was a master at Eton from 1864 to 1897. The nun in France is Miss Giberne.

[3] In the *Tablet*, (10 March 1866), p. 149, on the same page as Newman's letter of 5 March, appeared a long letter from E. R. Martin in Rome, attacking him violently. 'He has put up our Mother in a public place, and taken her prerogatives to pieces, not reverently, not lovingly, not devotionally, but coldly, dogmatically and drily . . . One might hazard the remark that there are statements in the book which would ensure for them the condemnation of the Holy Index, were it formally submitted to that congregation.' The Editor of the Tablet justified the insertion of the letter, which occupied three and a half columns, in the name of free expression of opinion. Walker wrote to Newman on 11 March, strongly urging him to take no notice of Martin.

hurt you,' till it actually was published and in operation. But now it is natural to say 'Did I tread on your toes? I really beg your pardon; but I am so pushed about in this crowd of opinions, that I really could not help it.'

Thank you for your interesting account of the Lingard Controversy. I have two volumes of the Catholic Miscellany — none, unluckily of the Magazine[1]

Very sincerely Yours John H Newman of the Oratory

The Very Revd Canon Walker

P.S. I have already told you my difficulty of attempting a direct argument against the Anglican Claims — viz that I have already done so on various occasions, and only made the claimants angry. If I did it now, perhaps they would refuse to read me altogether.

TUESDAY 13 MARCH 1866   sleet

TO T. W. ALLIES

The Oratory. Bm March 13. 1866.

My dear Allies,

I am glad to hear from you that the report, that I was giving currency to some statement about 'Papal Fables,' rests on no better foundation than you now assign to it. It has brought before me vividly, as never before, in what way false reports grow and take shape; and how they are proof against antecedent probability.[2]

Thank you for now stating your real objection to the leave I have given to Oxenham, — which lies, it seems, not against the work dedicated, but against the person dedicating.[3] However, I have had many friends before now kind

---

[1] Walker wrote, 'I am happy to think that the grumblers are not found among the old Catholics,' and referred to a controversy in the *Catholic Magazine* of 1832 about the Litany of Loreto, in which Lingard was the protagonist of moderation, and to whose rescue Walker came. See Martin Haile and Edwin Bonney, *Life and Letters of John Lingard, 1771–1851,* London n.d., [1914], p. 245.

[2] In answer to Newman's letter of 9 March, Allies wrote next day, 'From what you say the work of Döllinger must be the first volume of his history, "Christianity and Church at the period of the foundation." I know it well, and have no objection to make to it . . . My inform- ant could not tell which work it was, and when I mentioned the "medieval fables on the Popes" said he was almost sure that was it . . . I have not read "the fables" yet . . . No doubt your appearing as the Patron of the former book is very different from your appearing as Patron of the latter.' *Fables respecting the Popes of the Middle Ages* was translated by Alfred Plummer, London 1871. The book Oxenham translated, dedicated to Newman, was *The First Age of Christianity and the Church,* two volumes, London 1866.

[3] Allies wrote, 'It is possible you do not know to what degree Acton and Simpson and Company claim you as on their side: how they say, Fr Newman never speaks more than half his mind: we speak out what he *means*. And how again persons the most opposed to Acton and Simpson are inclined to say what they say in this matter. Of course it would help both sides to see a book of Döllinger's translated by Oxenham and dedicated to you. You probably mean it as a mark that you sympathise with what some think hard treatment received by Oxenham. But it will carry a much larger meaning to both these classes. Few things in this world would grieve me more than not to feel that there was a deep gulph between you and Acton and Simpson . . . Just then when it seems as if two parties were likely to grow . . . I mean a party taking you for their watchword, and a party taking the Archbishop, comes an act slight in itself, but associating you much in appearance with the most extreme and heterodox. And then, again, Döllinger is understood to be writing against the Temporal Power.'

enough to dedicate books to me, and, in accepting their compliment, I never considered I was pledging myself to any thing more than a general agreement with their opinions. Nor do I feel that Döllinger and Oxenham are so substantially unsound, so radically bad, as to oblige me, in the case of an unexceptionable book, to deprive myself of what in itself is a harmless and natural gratification. Did I act otherwise than I am doing, I should justly incur the blame of being a party man.

It has to be shown that the 'understanding' that Dollinger is writing against the Temporal Power, of which you speak, has better foundation than the report about the 'Papal Fables.' I only know this, that he has lately written a book in which he has spoken for it. But antecedent probability goes for nothing against 'understandings.'[1]

Nor am I bound to accept the 'watchwords' which other people may create out of particular names or opinions, nor to contribute to form parties by proclaiming their existence. And, if any man associates my name with party, I shall think he is taking a liberty with me.

As to certain friends of mine, whom you mention, who are reported to say that I only half speak out my mind, perhaps this report also rests on no satisfactory ground. All I can say myself is this, that I have before now spoken out my mind to you with a freedom which I have not used towards them, and have before now written to you in confidence, which I have never, I think, gone so far as to do to either of them. This will enable you to judge of the value of this report.

On the subject of reports in general I have written a good deal in my 'Catholicism in England.' I have outlived them as spread against me by Protestants; I do not dread them as now spread by Catholics.[2]

And, as to theological opinions, in which Catholics differ, of course there are many of them which I do not follow, and that, in various directions; but, provided they are not condemned by authority, certainly I will not presume to forbid them, nor do I feel any sort of sympathy with those who do.

Yours affectly in Xt   John H Newman of the Oratory

[1] Döllinger defended the temporal power of the Pope in *The Church and the Churches; or the Papacy and the Temporal Power,* translated by B. MacCabe, London 1862. Allies, in his reply on 14 March, said, 'As to the "understanding" about Döllinger, I will also tell you exactly my ground. About three weeks ago the Archbishop, at one of his receptions, came up to me, and said "Do you know what is coming upon you" — his tone was so emphatic, that I thought immediately of some personal calamity, and I answered with some trepidation, "No, what is it." "Döllinger is writing against the Temporal Power." I did not ask him what his grounds for believing it were; but this was my information . . .'

[2] *Prepos,* Lectures III, IV and VIII. Allies replied that he had not mentioned to anyone the report about the dedication, which he had heard from Edward Dean, and that Newman's letter would be an additional motive 'to avoid anything which can lead to any report of any kind.'

TO AN UNKNOWN CORRESPONDENT

March 13, 1866

. . . . I have felt it as a most anxious task to have to write on the subjects which have engaged me lately — no one can write without making mistakes — I don't doubt have made some, though I hope not great ones. If a man waited till he could write without any mistakes, he would not write at all. There is in every man's work matter which may be taken up for hostile criticism, if readers are so minded. But I have done my best, and have all along trusted I should be judged by my good intention and the substance of what I have written, and not by what comes of human infirmity and imperfection. . . So I rejoice very much to have your letter — and take it also as an earnest that you do not forget sometimes to think of me in your good prayers . . .

THURSDAY 15 MARCH 1866   fine days now and then

TO HENRY JAMES COLERIDGE

The Oratory Bm March 15/66

My dear Fr Coleridge

What would you say to a Paper on the Life and Times of Sully, for the Month? I have been making (hitherto) unsuccessful attempts at such a result. I *could* not promise them — 1. Because I cannot reckon on time. 2. nor on capacity — but I will at least try, if you encourage me. But don't think of it, if you really would not risk it. If you did wish it, tell me how many pages each number should be[1]

Yours very sincerely in Xt   John H Newman of the Oratory
The Revd Fr Coleridge S. J.

TO MICHAEL KELLY

The Oratory Bm March 15. 1866.

My dear Revd Father

I thank you for the compliment you pay me in wishing me to preach on the happy occasion you mention.[2] I am sure, however, that you will allow me to decline it, sorry as I am not to acquiesce in such a request, when I tell you I

---

[1] Newman never found time to write on this subject.
[2] Michael Kelly had been in charge of the Augustinian mission in Hoxton since 1862, and had just finished building the church of St Monica there, for the opening of which on 4 May 1866 Newman was evidently invited to preach.

have not preached in London since the year 1849 — and do not preach any where but in my own Church

Very truly yours in Xt John H Newman of the Oratory

The Revd Fr Kelly

TO WILLIAM CLIFFORD, BISHOP OF CLIFTON

The Oratory Bm 17 March 1866

My dear Lord,

I have just read your Lordship's letter in the Tablet about me, and with extreme gratification.[1] You may easily understand with what anxious thought and care I wrote my letter to Dr Pusey; and, while I knew I should be offending various excellent persons any how, in things which I felt it a duty to say, I was very conscious also, that, whatever pains I took with my language and sentiments, I should come short of that exactness in statement and that tenderness for others, which was possible and desirable.

No one can do more than his best. I tried to do my best; and, having done so, felt myself willing to submit myself to whatever just criticism came on me for not doing better. When then I read a public expression of opinion, so favourable to me as that in today's Tablet, from a person such as your Lordship, a Bishop and a theologian, and so well acquainted both with Rome and with England, it is as great a relief and encouragement to me as could be granted to me.

This I say in the first place; but secondly, my special gratitude is due to your personal kindness to myself, in going out of your way so generously to defend me, when there was no direct call on you to put yourself to that inconvenience.[2]

Begging your Lordship's blessing, I am, My dear Lord, Your affecte
servt in Xt John H Newman of the Oratory

The Rt Revd The Bp of Clifton

[1] Clifford's defence of Newman against Martin's attack appeared in the *Tablet*, (17 March 1866), p. 165.

In particular Clifford denounced 'the practice which some people have of peremptorily setting down as un-Catholic, and anti-Roman, and contrary to this spirit of the Church, every practice and every teaching which does not coincide with their own views. Father Newman expresses himself unwilling to accept as oracles every opinion which is advocated by F. Faber or "The Dublin Review," and forthwith Mr. Martin denounces him as anti-Roman and as a Jansenist. Such tyrannical dogmatism is not to be tolerated.'

[2] Clifford replied on 19 March that Ullathorne had written his entire approval of the letter in the Tablet. Ullathorne's letter to Clifford of 18 March is preserved in the Clifton diocesan archives: 'I write a line to thank you for your judicious defence of Dr Newman, it is, if you will let me say so, judicious in point of time as well as matter. You have anticipated, perhaps prevented an injudicious criticism of Dr N. in the next Dublin.' See first Memorandum of 26 March.

TO HENRY NUTCOMBE OXENHAM

March 17/66

My dear Mr Oxenham

I am very sorry to say that your letter of this morning rather adds to my perplexity than removes it.[1]

When you were so kind as to propose to dedicate Dr Dollinger's Church History to me, I fancied I knew his sentiments about Christianity and its propagation well enough to be sure that it would be nothing else than an honour that you were intending for me in connecting my name with such a work. But I did not mean to assent to more than this; nor can I make up my mind to do so now.

And, though I am sure there is nothing but what in your intention is considerate and friendly in the matter of your dedication to me, yet I cannot agree with you in considering that it is uncommon under particular circumstances to let dedications be seen by those who are the subjects of them — on the contrary, unless they are simply formal expressions of kindly sentiment, I think it is both natural and usual, as a matter of caution, not to put any thing into them without the certainty that it will not cause embarassment where it was intended to be a compliment.

As to Fr Lockhart, I cannot but feel that he has done both you and me a service, by obviating the chance of what would be painful to both of us.

Certainly, I must still press you to let your dedication be nothing beyond a few words of course.[2]

JHN

SUNDAY 18 MARCH 1866 dark, foggy, thawy

[1] In consequence of Allies's letter of 9 March, Newman wrote to Lockhart who was in touch with Oxenham, to find out which translated book of Döllinger was to be dedicated to him. Lockhart confirmed on 12 March that it was *The First Age of Christianity and the Church*, and added that in the dedication Oxenham described Döllinger as 'the first divine of the continent.' This Lockhart described to Newman as 'a regular slap at the Roman divines.' Newman made a summary of his reply to Lockhart: 'I could not let my meaning be mistaken. E.g. I thought Döllinger the first ecclesiastical historian of the continent, and the first in philosophy of ecclesiastical history, *not* the first divine, and that it was a dangerous confusion to say so.'

Newman then wrote to Oxenham, who replied on 16 March that Lockhart had been guilty of a breach of confidence, and that in fact Döllinger had been called 'the great Catholic divine of the Continent.' Oxenham also maintained that the form of a dedication was never submitted beforehand to the person concerned.

[2] Oxenham sent Newman a copy of his proposed dedication.

TO JAMES GUBBINS

March 19/66

My dear Revd Father

I thank you for your letter just received.

I quite follow you in your view of the word 'contained' etc as used by Catholic theologians'.[1] But then Dr Pusey and Anglican divines are not such; and I do not follow you in what I understand you to imply, that they use the words in the same sense as Catholics. I do not think they do; and accordingly it is my hope that they will not be unwilling to accept the Catholic sense of them when it is explained to them.

I have attempted in the Letter to press this upon them in the passage of my Letter to which you refer; and, though I do not yet know what they will say to it, I shall be disappointed if they do not accept it.

You know how frequently Catholic controversialists use the word 'distinguo.' Thus I mean to distinguish – and say that proprie and in the sense of theologians not all revealed doctrines are contained in Scripture — but improprie and in a possible sense, i.e. the Anglican, they may be said to be so

Hoping this will be satisfactory to you   I am

J H N[2]

TO HENRY NUTCOMBE OXENHAM

March 20/66

My dear Mr Oxenham,

I really am very sorry so to annoy you, and feel how very ungracious it is in me to do so.

Nor would I dream of doing so, or of interfering, so strangely as you may think, with a kind act of yours towards me, unless I really had cause for fearing that important interests might be depending, just now, on the use of words. It requires great circumspection not to be answerable for results, in which I wish to have no part.

You must not suppose I quoted any exact words of Fr Lockhart's about your dedication. What he said arose out of my questions to him a propos of the false report; and I wrote to him, not to you, as not at the moment knowing (as I told him) your address.

It is now for nearly eight years that it has been considered in high quarters that I am in league with Dr Döllinger to make a party in the Catholic Body,[3]

[1] Gubbins, an Oblate of Mary Immaculate, wrote from Dublin on 17 March that Newman had made an erroneous statement in his *Letter to Pusey*: 'Thus *you* [Pusey] do not deny, that the whole is not in Scripture in such sense that pure unaided logic can draw it from the sacred text; nor do *we* deny, that the faith is in Scripture, in an improper sense, in the sense that *Tradition* is able to recognize and determine it there.' First edition, p. 14; cf. *Diff*. II, p. 12.

[2] For Gubbins's reply see letter of 7 April to him.

[3] See letter of 18 Oct. 1858 to Allies. Letters in the Manning archives at Bayswater show him writing in March 1866 to Ullathorne, 'I am very sorry that he [Oxenham] and others hover about Dr Newman: and that Döllinger's name should be linked to his . . .' Ullathorne wrote on 9 May to Manning, 'I am sorry that Dr Newman accepted Oxenham's dedication of Döllinger's History. I don't like this particular association of names.'

of course it is in itself a simple honour to me for any (as you have done) to associate my name with his; but it will be a great disservice to Catholic truths and principles, which I feel (and I am sure he feels) to be very important, and which there is an attempt to obscure, if it is thought, and much more if it is implied, which is not the fact, that we are acting together in any way. Your words in a dedication, to which I am a party, though I am not a party to the wording, will in fact be taken as my words.

I hope I shall not displease you, if I ask that the idea of 'fitly introduced' should not be found in it. What I should *like* would be something of this sort (I am not of course dictating the wording) 'To J H N This translation of the work of the great Catholic divine of the continent is by his permission dedicated.'[1]

J H N

TO BISHOP ULLATHORNE

The Oratory Bm March 20/66

(*Private*)

My dear Lord

I thank you very much, as we all do, for your great consideration in making so great an effort to relieve us from the Workhouse at once. Since Fr Ryder was at the Bishop's House yesterday, Mr Ivers has wished us to keep it in our hands over next Sunday — which we have willingly consented to do.[2]

I should like to know your Lordship's wish (at your convenience) about the *furniture* etc of the workhouse chapel. Fr Flanagan collected money for that express purpose, which he laid out in Altar, Altar picture, vestments etc etc. In addition we have lent from our own Church benches etc. We have got an inventory of the whole.

I do not know what your rule is. We shall *like* to make it over to you, as Bishop — as a sort of trustee — but, if this is giving you trouble or otherwise does not approve itself to you, we are quite willing to become trustees ourselves. The meaning of this would not be more than this — viz that the Workhouse furniture would be secured against the chance at some future time, i.e. while a Chapel remains there, of being transferred to Green's Village etc.[3]

I am, My dear Lord, Your affte & obt Servt in Xt
John H Newman

The Rt Revd The Bp of Birmingham

[1] Oxenham agreed to modify his dedication which eventually read as follows: 'To the very reverend John Henry Newman, D. D., whose illustrious name is alone a passport to the hearts and a secure claim on the intellectual respect of his countrymen both within and without the Church, this translation of a work by the great Catholic divine of the continent, is by his permission, dedicated.'

[2] With reference to Newman's letter of 12 Feb., Ullathorne wrote on 19 March that Bernard Ivers, priest at St Peter's, Birmingham, would henceforth take charge of the workhouse. The Oratorians continued to be chaplains of the prison.

[3] Newman did not want the chapel furniture taken from the workhouse, and used for a chapel elsewhere. Green's Village was in St Peter's district, near the present New Street Station.

The Oratory, Birmingham March 21. 1866

My dear Child,

17th, 18th, or 19th of April will be the same to me. I earnestly pray God, it may be the beginning of much happiness to you, and a long happiness. I shall say Mass for you once a week till the day . . .[1]

I want you to be so kind as to accept the inclosed from me, to lay out upon yourself in any way you please.

Ever yours affly John H. Newman of the Oratory

THURSDAY 22 MARCH 1866   Mr Walford called and went.   Mr Neligan came   snow again but melting

TO THE EDITOR OF THE GUARDIAN

The Oratory, March 23. 1866

Sir,

I beg you to allow me to contradict at once a report, of which I was not aware before the appearance of Mr. Williams's letter in your paper of last Wednesday.[2] He will be glad to know that there is no foundation at all for his statement that I have been 'prevented by superior authority from publishing a second letter to Dr. Pusey on the subject of Papal Infallibility,' or on any other subject whatever. I wish absolutely to deny that any expression of opinion, or any advice, or any wish of any kind, has been conveyed to me directly or indirectly by any one whether in authority or not, of the nature of either a prohibition or a dissuasive. On the other hand, various persons in ecclesiastical station and of high consideration have urged me to proceed with the subjects of discussion to which Dr. Pusey's volume might be considered to invite me.

Nor, in fact, did I ever myself intend to include formally among those subjects that of the Pope's infallibility. What I proposed to do, when I began my Letter, besides what I have actually done, is stated p. 18 — viz., to treat of the question of Doctrinal Development.[3] In considering it, I certainly should have been led to devote a few pages to the former subject; but not so much to the fact of the Pope's infallibility, as to the doctrine and the probability of its

[1] Newman officiated at Eleanor Bretherton's wedding at St Chad's Cathedral on 17 April. See diary.

[2] George Williams, a high churchman and Fellow of King's College, Cambridge, wrote to the *Guardian* (21 March 1866), p. 300, in defence of Pusey's *Eirenicon*. He thought that Newman's explanation had 'softened down' the dogma of the Immaculate Conception. Williams continued, 'And who knows whether, if Dr. Newman had not been prevented by superior authority, as I am told, from publishing a second letter to Dr. Pusey on the subject of Papal Infallibility, that acute mind might not have "softened down" another stumbling-stone in the path towards an united Christendom.'

[3] *Diff.* II, p. 16.

definition as a Catholic dogma. I did not intend to do more than this; that in the event I did not do so much is to be attributed to reasons of literary expedience, if I may use the term, which it is not worth while here to recount. First, I merely postponed what I had proposed to myself, *vid*. p. 123;[1] and then, by the time that I had written the Notes and passed the whole through the press, I found myself so tired that I willingly acquiesced in the belief that I had said enough on the subject of Dr. Pusey's book for the moment.[2]

John H. Newman.

TO DAVID MORIARTY, BISHOP OF KERRY

The Oratory Bm March 23. 1866

My dear Lord,

When I was writing my Pamphlet, one of the persons whom I first thought of, in my anxiety, and whose approbation I felt would be a support to me, was your Lordship. It is in consequence a very great gratification to me, and a reward for my trouble, to have received it — and I feel great gratitude to you for having given it.[3]

I had intended to pursue the other topics Dr Pusey introduces into his Volume — but I found myself so fatigued when I came to the end of it, that I easily acquiesced in the belief that I had said enough for the moment. And so I think I have. As you have noticed, some strong feeling has been excited, though not in very important quarters. On the other hand, I have had expressions of opinion to the same effect as your own, from quarters whence I had no right to expect them, as well as from various persons in authority. Dr Clifford's letter has been a great encouragement to me.

I am not so strong in health that I can reckon on writing more on the subjects which Dr Pusey's volume opens — but I will not forget your Lordship's suggestions.

Begging your blessing, I am, My dear Lord, Yours most sincerely in Xt

John H Newman of the Oratory

The Rt Revd The Bp of Kerry

P.S.   I am told there is to be a mild animadversion on me in the Dublin Review.[4]

---

[1] *Diff*. II, p. 117.

[2] On 7 April Williams wrote to thank for an unsolicited letter of forgiveness, which Newman had sent him, and added, 'I have this morning received from my "authority"! an explanation remarkably coincident with your own, virtually giving up the whole thing as a fabrication.'

[3] Moriarty wrote on 19 March that he had not intended to trouble Newman with his congratulations on the *Letter to Pusey*, 'When I saw however some adverse and ignorant criticism which astounded me it seemed to me a duty to say that nothing better, safer, or sounder was, as far as my knowledge goes ever written by theologian on the cultus Deiparae.'

Moriarty added, 'How I wish you would answer that part of Dr Pusey's book which relates to the Holy See. It puzzled me quite and I said to our friend Monsell that no one could answer him but you, there is such a jumble of history to be unravelled.'

[4] See Memorandum of 26 March.

SATURDAY 24 MARCH 1866   Fr Lockhart came for the boys Retreat
SUNDAY 25 MARCH   Palm Sunday I took function   The Bishop called, offering us Oxford again   Ambrose went to Rednall

TO RICHARD SIMPSON

The Oratory Bm March 25/66

My dear Simpson

I am sorry I have not answered your letter earlier — but at this season I am pulled about in various directions.

There is very good matter in Fr de Buck's Paper, as one would expect — and it ought not to be lost.[1] At the same time, I am against translations primâ facie. It is difficult to make them read well. Then again the cast of thought, the sequence of ideas, is different in different countries; and a good work in consequence falls flat when it is transplanted. Then, there are further difficulties in a controversial work — its object, I suppose, is to persuade opponents, or at least to make opponents feel that they have been beaten, or that third parties are very likely to think so. Now I think you may as well fight the Yankees, with the Atlantic between you and them, as fight Pusey from Belgium. It is impossible to bring your guns to bear, or to cover your object. Or to take another illustration; a theologian who begins a controversy with a stranger, is like a tailor who makes you a coat without measuring, and without fitting it on you — it is seen to bag, or be too tight, when it comes home.

Therefore I don't think it would answer to translate Fr de B. All the same, it is a pity so valuable a composition should be lost. Of course Pusey will see it any how. If I wrote more about his book, I certainly should take the liberty of referring to it. I am struck at his use of Gregory xiv [xvi]. I had meant to have made use of it myself[2]

Yours affly in Xt   John H Newman of the Oratory

R. Simpson Esqr

MONDAY 26 MARCH 1866   boys' retreat [until 28 March inclusive]

[1] This was evidently Victor de Buck's review of Pusey's *Eirenicon* in the French Jesuit review *Études*, (March and April 1866), pp. 132–44, and pp. 259–86.
[2] De Buck quoted on pp. 281–5 from the work of Gregory XVI, *Trionfo della Santa Sede*, as to the limits of papal infallibility, and also on p. 271 as to indifferentism in religion.

TO EDWARD HENEAGE DERING

The Oratory Birmingham March 26. 1866

My dear Mr Dering,

You have anticipated me in your kind letter just received. As soon as Easter came, I meant to have sent you all my congratulations on the season. Now then I will do so by anticipation. I wish you were not at such a distance from Catholic centres, and grieve to hear of your being all invalids. Is not the beautiful Weald of Kent somewhat possessed with influenza influences? The wind has a fair field for its keenest operations.

Mr Martin is simply unknown. As far as I can make out, he was received into the Church about two years ago, and is a young man in a family. I don't know whether you observed that the answer to him in the Saturday in which your first letter appeared was by the Bishop of Clifton — and to be understood to be intended as settling the matter.

I thought both your letters particularly good, and so did others — and I am very glad to learn that they are yours.[1] With my kindest regards to Lady Chatterton and her niece,

I am, My dear Mr Dering, Sincerely Yours in Xt
John H Newman of the Oratory

E. H. Dering Esqr

P.S. When I say that your letters were 'particularly good,' I seem to be praising myself, since they were so full of kindness towards me. I know this, and I felt very grateful to you for what is so personally favorable to me — but what I mean by 'very good' is that you took a line which was likely to be *effective* with my critics, and calculated to make them leave me alone.

MEMORANDUM I W. G. WARD AND A LETTER TO PUSEY

March 26. 1866

Yesterday, Palm Sunday, the Bishop called on me.

He asked whether I knew that the Article about or against me in the Dublin was not to appear.

He hoped I liked Dr Clifford's letter in the Tablet — he said that he had expressed to him his own approval of it, and that there was in it *more than seemed*: viz.

Archbishop Manning had proposed, or Ward had proposed through Manning or Ward had proposed by himself, (I forget which) to the Bishop ⟨Ullathorne⟩, to *revise* the forthcoming Article ⟨of Ward's⟩.

The Bishop said he answered, that, if he *did* pronounce any thing unfav-

[1] One of Dering's letters was presumably that defending *A Letter to Pusey*, in the *Tablet*, (24 March 1866), pp. 187–8, signed 'One of the Multitude whose conversion may be distinctly traced to Dr. Newman.'

ourable about me, he would do it directly, as he was my Bishop — not in any indirect way. And he declined.

Then, Ward sent the Article to Dr Clifford to revise. But Dr Clifford sent back word, that he thought my pamphlet a very good one, and he would have nothing to do with criticising it.[1]

Then, the Archbishop wrote to our Bishop to say that Ward had, in a most Catholic spirit, consented to withdraw the Article, though he felt of course its truth. Also, it had been revised already by a theologian, whom our Bishop would pronounce to be prudent.[2]

This last fact is much to the point. Ward sent the Article to our Bishop, *not* for revision, it seems, but simply to gain his sanction, and preoccupy the ground against me — that my natural or ordinary judge should already be committed before I opened my mouth.

The Bishop gave as his reason for wishing Ward's article withdrawn, that on many points there were opinions to adjust, and it might be all very well to do so among ourselves — but that it was not well to wash our dirty linen in the sight of a Protestant public.

In connexion with this correspondence, Dr Clifford wrote his letter to the Tablet.

A short notice of my Pamphlet is to appear in the Dublin, revised by the aforesaid prudent theologian.[3]

The above account brings to my mind what occurred last October and on St Charles's day after the Archbishop had returned from Rome. Our Bishop

[1] W. G. Ward had printed for *D R* an article critical of parts of *A Letter to Pusey*, and Manning wished it to be read and passed for publication, by Ullathorne and Bishop Grant of Southwark. Ullathorne refused on the ground that he was Newman's ecclesiastical judge, and would not commit himself by any extra-judicial opinion. Ward replied to Ullathorne on 8 March, 'the Archbishop says he thoroughly understands your feeling on the matter; and I have asked the Bishop of Clifton to do me the service in question. I am extremely anxious to act rightly in the matter and to do nothing which can possibly lead to any breach of charity. Yet several religious and others have written to me about it; and I think some mention should be made of the objections which they entertain.'

Bishop Clifford described, in a letter of 19 March to Ullathorne, his reply to Ward: 'When I received a request to look over an article in the *Dublin* written, I was told, because it was necessary not to pass over in silence the slur Dr Newman had cast on foreign Catholics, and to correct several anti-Catholic statements in his Letter, which was, moreover, stigmatized as Protestant, I felt it was time to speak out. I wrote back to say that I was not a fit person to be censor to the article in question, inasmuch as I greatly admired Dr Newman's *Letter*, and had failed to discover in it either Protestantism or anti-Catholic sentiments, or any attempt to cast a slur on foreign Catholics.' *Butler*, I, p. 363; see also letter of 3 Jan. 1867 to Emily Bowles.

St John made notes of a conversation he had with Ullathorne on 29 March. Ullathorne said, 'That he had an eye on what the Dublin might say about the Father's [Newman] teaching[;] that had not Ward withdrawn his article . . . he should have advised F. N [Newman] to call on the Archbishop to call Ward to account for censuring the teaching of a Priest, and that the Archbishop would have been obliged to silence him — that if he attempted any thing more he the Bishop should feel it his duty to oppose him most resolutely . . .' Ullathorne went on to approve of Newman's views both as to our Lady and to as papal infallibility.

[2] This letter of 24 March from Manning to Ullathorne is in *Butler* I, p. 363, and in *DR*, (April 1920), p. 211.

[3] *D R*, (April 1866), pp. 544–6. This notice disapproved of Newman's contrast between English and foreign devotions, his reference to a people's religion as corrupt, and his refusal to defend extreme Catholic writing about our Lady. It also maintained that the infallibility claimed for the Pope by *D R* was that claimed by Pius IX himself.

remonstrated with him about Ward's articles in the Dublin about the Pope's etc Infallibility. He answered 'he *really* had not *read* them' — and then he went and let them be dedicated to him in a volume.[1]

The other day he asked Lockhart '*Whether* I was *pained* at Mr Martin's letter in the Tablet.' He'll do *any* thing he *can*, *every* thing he *can*, to check us. The Bishop went on to renew to me his offer of the Oxford Mission.[2]

J H N

MEMORANDUM II   PRIVATE MEMORANDUM

March 26/66

As to our taking the Oxford mission, as our Bishop has now again, (that is, the second time since I formally declined it in February 1865)[3] offered [it to] us, I think as follows:

We cannot retain it, if we take it, beyond my life — therefore both the Oratory and myself are undergoing the risk of expending time and labour, and money, with very little ultimate advantage.

Especially, to undertake to build a Mission Church, and previously to buy the ground, would be a great responsibility; and it is included in the Bishop's purpose. And he is the more desirous of this, because of the increase of Catholics at Oxford which seems probable, from the establishment of the Great Western Railway works there.

I certainly *cannot* undertake to build a mission Church and this perhaps may put an end to the negociation at once.

But what I would consent to is this:- to nurse up the mission towards the accomplishment of the project for a Church — to look out for ground, according as opportunities occur, and to supply the Mission with a more central place for service in the meantime.

The Bishop does not like our ground opposite Ch Ch [Christ Church] for a Church — but it might do for an Oratory chapel — and we might lend that Chapel for the mission services.

Then, if ground were ultimately purchased and a Church built, or when the time came for us to go, it would not be difficult (if the then Bishop did not

---

[1] W. G. Ward, *The Authority of Doctrinal Decisions which are not Definitions of Faith, considered in a short series of Essays reprinted from the Dublin Review*, London 1866. Ward, in his dedication, spoke of Manning's permission to dedicate as giving the work his blessing. See also the end of Memorandum of 17 May 1866.

[2] Newman wrote at the beginning of a collection labelled '1866 Correspondence consequent upon my Letter of [to] Pusey,' 'It is clear Archbishop Manning wished it so censured as to hinder my going to Oxford.

On occasion of the Apologia two years before — he published a pamphlet against it, accusing it 1. of calling the Church of England a bulwark of the Catholic Church, which it *did not do*. 2. of denying that natural reason was sufficient for the proof of a God which it did not deny. 3. of implying that *faith* was only the acknowledgment of a probability. On the face of it, it was written against me, but also I think he distinctly told Canon Walker that it was.' See letters of 24 Oct., 17 Nov. and 28 Nov. 1864 to Walker.

[3] The first time was on 26 Aug. 1865. See letter of 27 Aug. to St John.

like a second Catholic centre in Oxford) to sell so small an establishment as ours would be for some University purpose — for a Hall, etc etc. The situation is very good for some such purpose.

This Oratory Chapel I should build with my own friends' money, not from contributions from the parishioners — and they should collect a yearly sum among them as rent to *the Oratory* (not to me) for the use of it at certain hours.

I should place a resident curate there — who would give the mission, errors excepted, a Mass every morning. Then in term time the Fathers of the Oratory would come, and the Oratory services would be given in addition. The curate would be on the look out for ground for a mission Church, and would report to the Bishop, whenever an eligible site came into the market.

TUESDAY 27 MARCH 1866   in retreat
WEDNESDAY 28 MARCH   Ambrose returned from Rednall

TO AMBROSE PHILLIPPS DE LISLE

The Oratory, Bm March 28/66

My dear Mr de Lisle

I wish I deserved one hundredth part of the praise you give me. I should think myself very well off.[1] I can but act for the day, and leave the morrow to take care of itself. Because I am able to do a thing today, it does not follow that tomorrow I shall be able to do another. God has no need of men; He uses His instruments, and suddenly breaks them and takes others at His Supreme and Most Blessed Will.

No one has directly or indirectly put any spoke in my wheel as regards any projected Essay on the Pope's Infallibility — nor indeed have I had a design of attempting such a work. I had intended to write more to Pusey — but I found myself unwell, when my (published) Pamphlet came to an end — and then again, when after a few weeks I returned to the thought of saying more, I found my second letter would run into the question of the Pope's Infallibility more than I liked, and that such a subject could not be undertaken in a hurry — and then again I thought I had already said enough for the present so I have left the matter.

Dr Clifford has done me immense service by his letter — and has laid me under a great obligation.

I have no great love for the Conservatives, as being Erastians of a type which I do not think you can admire — but I speak of them as a *party* — as to individuals, I know what excellent, estimable men there are among them. —

[1] DeLisle, who wrote on 23 March, from Belvoir Castle, described the appreciation of Newman's work shown by a large house party there.

and I shall rejoice at their coming into power, if, without upsetting the State Coach, they can keep it from running off the high road, the King's highway.[1]

Begging a share of your good prayers at this Sacred Season, I am,

My dear Mr de Lisle Most sincerely Yours in Xt
John H Newman of the Oratory.

A. L. M P de Lisle Esq.

TO R. F. WILSON

The Oratory Bm March 28/66

My dear Wilson

It is with extreme distress I have read your letter — yet who can be surprised at its contents? I have had dear Keble and his wife before me day after day — that is my only comfort — only last Saturday I made him the intention of my Mass. Fervently do I pray that he may have a 'finem perfectum' when it is God's will to take him Alas! he may be gone even now. He is, and ever has been, pars animæ meæ in so special a sense, though I have but once seen him in twenty years and more, that I can't tell how I shall feel when he is taken away.

It has been very kind in you to write. Of course one can't help thinking of the 6th after Trinity 'Think on the minstrel, as ye kneel' — which I recollect applying to Walter Scott in 1832.[2]

Rogers said I was near seeing you in London last summer — I should have been very glad had it been, not almost but altogether.

Yours affectly John H Newman

The Revd R. F. Wilson

THURSDAY 29 MARCH 1866   Fr Lockhart went.   Holy Thursday I took the functions [i.e. also on Friday and Saturday]

TO LADY CHATTERTON

The Oratory Bm Holy Thursday 1866

My dear Lady Chatterton,

It grieves me deeply that you should be suffering so much, knowing as I do how much you desire to do God's will, and knowing too how much it must distress you to differ from Mr Dering and your niece, and how it must distress them to differ from you.

---

[1] De Lisle hoped that the Conservatives would come into power, which they did in June.
[2] 'If ever, floating from faint earthly lyre,
Was wafted to your soul one high desire,
By all the trembling hope ye feel,
Think on the minstrel as ye kneel.'
The Christian Year, Sixth Sunday after Trinity, penultimate stanza.

These are trials, which God puts upon us; and we cannot at our will put them aside. You have been so kind as to state fully your difficulties, and to say that you do not wish for an answer. Nor could I, without writing a volume, go through them all. Nor do I think, any more than you do, that it would fulfil any good purpose to attempt an elaborate answer to them. To make you happy, as a Catholic, is the work of God alone; if you put yourself into His hands, and ask for His grace perseveringly, He will gradually remove all your doubts and perplexities; of this I am most confident.

To me it is wonderful that you should speak as you do. Why, what exercise of devotion is there, which equals that of going before the Blessed Sacrament, before our Lord Jesus really present, though unseen? To kneel before Him, to put oneself into His hands, to ask His grace, and to rejoice in the hope of seeing Him in heaven! In the Catholic Church alone is the great gift to be found. You may go through the length and breadth of England, and see beautiful prospects enough, such as you speak of, the work of the God of nature, but there is no benediction from earth or sky which falls upon us like that which comes to us from the Blessed Sacrament, which is Himself.

And so far from the teaching of the Church concerning the Blessed Virgin being a burden, it seems to me the greatest of privileges and honours to be admitted into the very family of God. So we think on earth, when great people ask us into their most intimate circle. This it is, and nothing short of it, to be allowed to hold intercourse with Mary and Joseph; and, so far from its hindering our communion with out Lord, and our faith in Him, it is all that we should have had without it, and so much more over and above. As He comes near us in His Sacrament of love, so does He bring us near to Him by giving us an introduction (as I may say) to His Mother. In speaking to her, we are honouring Him; as He likes to be petitioned by His chosen ones, so does He especially love the petitions which she offers Him; and in asking her to intercede for us, we are pleasing both her and Him.

Every society has its own ways; it is not wonderful then, that the Catholic Church has its own way of praying, its own ceremonies, and the like. These are strange and perhaps at first unwelcome to those who come to them from elsewhere, just as foreign manners are unpleasant to those who never travelled. We all like home best, because we understand the ways of home. Abraham doubtless found his life in Canaan not so pleasant to him, as his native Mesopotamia. We ever must sacrifice something, to gain great blessings. If the Catholic Church is from God, to belong to her is a make-up for many losses. We must beg of God to change our tastes and habits, and to make us love for His sake what by nature we do not love.

You speak as if what is pleasant to the feelings must be true; and that what is true must be pleasant. But this is not so. The idea of Purgatory, as you say, is not pleasant, but that does not prove it is not true; and, if it be true, as the Catholic Church teaches, it will not save us from it hereafter, that we felt it painful to think upon here. And so of other doctrines.

At this sacred season then, my dear Lady Chatterton, I appeal to you by the love of Christ, and beg of you, to resolve to take on you His easy yoke. Do not attempt to live without any yoke at all; take on you the yoke of Christ. Submit your reason and your will to Him, as He speaks to you in His Church. In addressing you, I feel I am not addressing a common person, but one who can distinguish great things from little, and who will not, on seriously weighing the matter, put details and minutiae before the great matters of the law. St Paul says that the Church is the pillar and ground of the Truth. He says that there is *One* Body as there is *One* Faith. Our Lord has built His Church on Peter. These are great facts — they keep their ground against small objections, however many the latter may be. I cannot call your objections great ones; nor would you, if you saw them from the proper stand-point.

May God bless you, and give you grace, and lead you on, and may you bear patiently this time of darkness, till the True Light shines upon you[1]

Very truly Yours in Xt   John H Newman of the Oratory

Lady Chatterton

FRIDAY 30 MARCH 1866   Mr Neligan went
SATURDAY 31 MARCH   news of Keble's death   Mr Rymer came

TO H. P. LIDDON

The Oratory Bm March 31. 1866

My dear Mr Liddon

You must not write to me as a stranger, which you cannot really be, when you have shown so much consideration towards me as your letter and its inclosure imply.

Mr Wilson wrote me word of what was coming a day or two ago — and since then I have in fact considered him as gone from us, as he is.

Mr Young, whose letter I return, says that Mrs Keble reminded him of the last verses of J. K's Hymn on Good Friday. For these thirty years and more ⟨(ever since 1832)⟩, I have thought that, did I out live him, I should have in my mind the concluding stanzas of that for the sixth Sunday after Trinity.[2]

Very truly Yours John H Newman

The Revd H P Liddon

[1] Lady Chatterton did not overcome her doubts and difficulties until Aug. 1875.
[2] See letter of 28 March to R. F. Wilson. The final stanza of the hymn for Good Friday in *The Christian Year* runs:

'Wash me, and dry these bitter tears,
    O let my heart no further roam,
Tis Thine by vows and hopes and fears
    Long since — O call Thy wanderer home;
To that dear home, safe in Thy wounded side,
Where only broken hearts their sin and shame may hide.'

Peter Young was Keble's curate at Hursley from 1841 to 1857.

TO CHARLES CRAWLEY

The Oratory Birmingham Easter Day [1 April] 1866

My dear Crawley

It is very kind in you to write to me to give me the news[1] — Other friends have shown the same kind anxiety — and I put their letters together in one place, as a memorial for which I am very grateful. I had given him up for some days — indeed who could expect, for months past, that he would be able, in his state of health, to bear up against such wearing suspense and exertion as his wife's illness caused him. He wrote me word several months ago, using Herbert's word, that she was gradually 'undressing' for the grave. She had laid aside her music, then her drawing — then her books — and at length had taken to her bed. Yet he has gone first. Accept for yourself and Mrs Crawley my best Easter greetings and wishes and believe me to be,

My dear Crawley,[2]

C. Crawley Esqr

TO THE EARL OF DENBIGH

The Oratory Bm Easter Day 1866

My dear Lord Denbigh

I return you and Lady Denbigh my warmest congratulations on this great Day, and pray God that its best blessings may descend on you and on all who are dear to you.

As to your two questions about my recent Pamphlet, I gladly answer them.

1. 'Habits of belief and devotion.'[3] 'Habits of belief' seem to me different from 'the faith.' 'The faith' is immutable — but habits of belief vary with the age and country. For instance, there was an early belief that our Lord was to come again without any delay. This St Paul alludes to — St Gregory at the end of the 6th century believed it — At the end of the first 1000 years it filled Christendom so as even to affect (I think) the business and routine of secular life. There was a belief among the Fathers of the Ante-nicene Church, that the passage in Genesis about the 'Sons of God' etc was to be understood of Angels — and a belief that, whenever the Roman Empire fell, Anti-christ would come. I almost think Bellarmine, in the 16th century, still believed this, interpreting the Roman Empire to be the revived Germania, which remained till Napoleon's day. And people may fairly hold this still, or they may not. So also, *before* the Church decides, there may be two opposite *beliefs*, while, when she *has* decided, there is one *faith* — thus in early times, half the members of

---

[1] Crawley wrote on 31 March to announce Keble's death, lest Newman should first hear of it through the newspapers.
[2] Conclusion and signature have been cut out.
[3] Lord Denbigh wrote on 31 March that, having spent much time abroad, he could appreciate Newman's distinction between English and foreign habits of devotion, but could not understand his preference for English habits of belief. *Diff.* II, p. 20.

[the] Church believed, and the other half disbelieved, that the Apocalypse was canonical. 2. As to your second question about 'a people's religion being ever a corrupt religion,' I am speaking of the subjective religion, not the objective.[1] The Catholic religion is ever one and the same in itself, and as the Church teaches it; but not one and the same in this or that portion of it, viewed as received by the people. I have already complied by anticipation with your suggestion to make my meaning clearer in my second addition [sic], and have written 'a people's religion is ever a corrupt religion, *in spite of the provisions of Holy Church.*' As instances of what I mean, though they abound in every age and place, consider the practice in the early African Church, of administering the Holy Sacrament to the dead, which, I think, the 3rd Council of Carthage forbade. Also, at this day the notion of the poor Irish, (of which I have heard of instances both here and in the United States), that a suspended Priest has the gift of healing. Hoping this will satisfy you, I am,

My dear Lord Denbigh, Very sincerely Yours John H. Newman.[2]

[1] *Diff.* II, p. 81. See letter of 17 Feb. to Walker.

[2] There is a Memorandum of 11 May 1866 in Newman's hand:

'The difference between the passages in Dr Newman's Anglican Difficulties and Letter to Dr Pusey is not greater than that which strikes a stranger between photographs of the full face and the side face of the same person. They are different aspects of the same object.

The grace of God is good without mixture of evil; but it operates upon an imperfect and corrupt subject matter, the human heart; and, while its manifestations are one and the same in every people, at the same time those manifestations are not simply good, but good and bad mixed, good viewed as coming from divine grace, not simply good, but partly extravagant and perverse as being distorted and, as it were refracted, by the human medium, in which that grace is received.

This is Dr Newman's doctrine in both his works.

In his Anglican Difficulties he says "Such is the very phenonemon which must necessarily result, from a revelation of divine truth falling upon the human mind in its existing state of ignorance and moral feebleness." Lecture 9, p. 222. [*Diff.* I, p. 268] In his Letter to Dr Pusey he says, "A people's religion is ever a corrupt religion, in spite of the provisions of Holy Church." p. 86 second edition. [*Diff.* II, p. 81]

In his Anglican Difficulties he analyses the phenomenon in one way, and says it consists in the excess of faith beyond love which will ever take place in a popular religion.

"It is the spectacle of supernatural faith acting upon the multitudinous mind of a nation; of a divine principle dwelling in the myriad of characters, good, bad, and intermediate, into which the old stock of Adam grafted into Christ has developed." p. 229. [*Diff.* I, p. 277] "Faith and love are separable." p. 239 [*Diff.* I, p. 290]

In his letter to Dr Pusey he analyses it in another way; and imputes it (1) to the natural ardour of human affections, which is not sinful, pp. 84, 85; (2) to false logic, p. 86 (3) to human perverseness. p 86 [*Diff.* II, pp. 79–81]

The instances he gives of it in his Anglican Difficulties, are superstitions, false miracles, affronts offered to saints, the Carnival, devotion of brigands in the midst of crimes with an idea of being blessed in mortal sin, sacred pictures in bad houses etc.

The instance he specially gives in his letter to Dr Pusey, is the belief that Mary is present in the Blessed Sacrament in the sense in which our Lord is present.

In saying, in his Anglican Difficulties, that extravagances would be found in England, were the population Catholic like Naples, he does not deny that those about the Blessed Virgin would still be kept in cheque, as they are not kept in cheque at Naples, by the sobriety of the English natural temperament.

In saying, in his letter of Dr Pusey, that English good sense would prevent certain particular extravagances, as those about the Blessed Virgin, from becoming general, he does not imply that in many other ways English Catholics would be as extreme as Neapolitans, or that after all there would not be a broad general likeness between England and Italy.

Such general likeness, constituting a specific difference between Catholicism (considered as a manifestation) and other religions, is quite consistent with differences between nation and nation. And in like manner, if England itself were Catholic now, doubtless it would differ somewhat from itself as it was in the middle ages, because it has grown in sobriety.'

TO ARCHBISHOP MANNING

The Oratory Bm Easter Day 1866

My dear Archbishop

I thank you for your Easter greetings and return them with all my heart.[1]

I don't know how far your know the particulars of Keble's death. His wife had apparently only a few hours to live, so said the doctors, about a fortnight ago. He had nursed her till then; but then he was seized with fainting fits, which turned to erysipelas in the head, and he died in the early morning of Holy Thursday. His wife is still alive, but her death is constantly expected. He is to be buried at Hursley next Thursday. His brother and brother's wife are with them, viz. at Bournemouth. I heard some months ago, that his brother too was in bad health.

Yours affectionately in Xt   John H Newman of the Oratory

The Most Revd The Archbp of Westminster

TO BISHOP ULLATHORNE

The Oratory Easter Day 1866

My dear Lord

I enclose the Inventory.[2] A duplicate will go to Mr Ivers.

Both when I saw you, and when I wrote, I have been on the point of thanking you for your Lecture, which you were so good as to thank [send] me — but have not done so. It interested me exceedingly — both from the historical notices it contains, in which your Lordship is so intimately connected — and also for the broad view it gives of the subject of which it treats, and of the relation of the rules of penal discipline to the monastic system.[3]

[1] Manning wrote on 31 March: 'I have just heard of dear Keble's death: and I feel as if it had put me back half my life to the days when we used to look to him and his Christian Year as the service of our happiest thoughts. Nobody can understand this as you, and I write to you almost instinctively.

I shall never forget the Long Vacation in 1830 when Saml Wood and I were together in Oxford before the term began and I dined with you after the Service at St. Mary's one Sunday. Memory is very sweet, but the hope before us is sweeter.

I hope you are well.

With Gaudia Paschalia believe me, always Affecly yours, ✠ H. E. Manning.'

Newman's diary for 12 Sept. 1830 has the entry:
'Wood dined with me — H. W. [Wilberforce], Manning and Acland with R. W. [Wilberforce]'

[2] Of the Workhouse chapel furniture.

[3] On the Management of Criminals, London 1866, a paper read at the Academia of the Catholic Religion. Ullathorne had ministered to the convicts in Australia.

Begging your Easter blessing, I am, My dear Lord Your obt and affte Servt in Xt

> John Newman of the Oratory

The Rt Revd The Bp of Birmingham

P.S. Fr St John tells me he is writing to your Lordship about me. I will add to what he may say, that, on my reception, I took the name of Mary at Confirmation, and that only — that, on coming from Rome with our Brief, I set up the English Oratory on the Purification, and next year the Birmingham Oratory also on the Purification; that I in like manner set up our House and Church here under the Invocation of the Immaculate Conception and placed an Altarino and Image of our Lady in our entrance Hall; that, when I went to Ireland, I at once placed the new University under Mary, as 'Sedes Sapientiae' and the University Church, which I built, under Saints Peter and Paul. Since I have mentioned the special Patrons of the Holy See, I will add that Fr St John reminds me (what I had forgotten) that on leaving the Roman territory, on my way home with our Brief, I knelt down and kissed the earth in token of obedience, and that, when the Holy Father's troubles began recently, I sent him as much as £50.[1]

MONDAY 2 APRIL 1866   Mr Rymer went.   Ambrose went away.   Mr Hardy? came

TO ELEANOR BRETHERTON

> The Oratory, Birmingham. April 2. 66.

My dear Child,

The Vicar General has been up here today — he says the 17th. is the Chapter day — so that we must all be cleared out of the Cathedral by 10 o'clock.[2] I told him I would lose no time in letting you know. I am rather anxious that Mr. Watt should come regularly to Father Edward and at once — Reception is too serious a matter to be put in the second place — and I know that Father Edward would wish him thoroughly instructed.

My best Easter greetings to Mamma, you and him, and to all of you,

Ever yours affectionately in Christ, John H. Newman of the Oratory.

[1] Ullathorne was collecting material for his public letter in defence of Newman's devotion to our Lady. See letter of 7 April to him, and Appendix 1.
[2] For the wedding of Eleanor Bretherton to F. J. Watt.

TO SISTER MARY IMELDA POOLE

The Oratory B^m April 2/66

My dear Sister Imilda

Thank you for your welcome letter, and for your Revd Mother's message. And I am much rejoiced to hear so good an account of her.[1]

One can't do better than one's best. I have done my very best in my Pamphlet — but bad is the best I dare say — certainly we may say of Our Lady, as we say of the mystery of the Holy Eucharist, 'quia major omni laude, nec laudare sufficit.'[2] It is still more difficult at once to praise her, and to dispraise some of her imprudent votaries. On the other hand it is very easy to criticize, what we should not do a bit better if we ourselves tried our hand at it Therefore I am not surprised that I am open to criticism, and have been criticized, and in spite of that, not at all dissatisfied on the whole with what I have done, for I have had a number of letters from important quarters, all in my favour. One, which is the most gratifying is from our own Bishop.

With my best Easter greetings to your Revd Mother and all your Community I am

My dear Sister Imilda most sincerely Yrs in Xt

John H. Newman of the Oratory

P.S. You have heard of dear Mr Keble's death. His wife has been failing since September, when he could not take me in at Hursley in consequence. A fortnight back the doctors told him she could not live many hours — he had long been nursing her. He was seized with fainting fits which ended with erysipelas in the head. He died in the early morning of Holy Thursday. She is still alive, and knows that he is gone. She can't live many days. He is to be buried next Thursday.

TO E. B. PUSEY

The Oratory Bm April 2/66

My dear Pusey

Thank you for your announcement, though, as you expected, it was not news. Of course every one must have been prepared for it, cutting as the event is, when it comes.[3]

---

[1] Imelda Poole, when sending, on 1 April, the congratulations of the nuns at Stone on *A Letter to Pusey*, wrote that Mother Margaret Hallahan 'was exceedingly struck with the way in which you have brought out the title "Mother of God". She says it has given her a fresh devotion to our dear Lady beyond what she had before, and you know she has been fighting our Lady's battles all her life.'

Mother Margaret Hallahan 'intensely admired Dr Newman's celebrated "Letter", and was only deterred by timidity from writing him her thanks; but when, as it was read aloud to her, the reader came to that page in which he enumerates, in order to condemn, certain exaggerated and preposterous expressions . . . she stopped her ears, and desired that they might be passed over in silence.' *Life of Mother Margaret Mary Hallahan*, London 1869, p. 320.

[2] From the Sequence for the Feast of Corpus Christi.

[3] Pusey wrote on 31 March about Keble's death, of which he had only just heard. He added, 'In the last conversation I had with him he spoke of the comfort of the thought of purgatory.'

Thank you for your sympathy about the attacks on me — but you have enough upon yourself to be able to understand that they have no tendency to annoy one — and on the other hand are a proof that one is doing a work.[1] I hail the Article in the Times with great satisfaction as being the widest possible advertisement of me.[2] I never should be surprised at the comments being sent by some people to Rome, as authoritative explanations of my meaning, whenever they are favorable to me. The truth is, that certain views have been suffered without a word, till their maintainers have begun to fancy that they are de fide — and they are astonished and angry beyond measure, when they find that silence on the part of others was not acquiescence, indifference, or timidity, but patience. My own Bishop and Dr Clifford, and I believe most of the other Bishops are with me. And I have had letters from the most important centres of theology and of education through the country, taking part with me. London, however, has for years been oppressed with various incubi; though I cannot forget, with great gratitude, that two years ago as many as a hundred and ten priests of the Westminster Diocese, including all the Canons, the Vicars General, the Jesuits, and other orders, went out of their way (and were the first to do so,) to take my part, before the Apologia appeared.[3]

I am very sorry the Jesuits are so fierce against you — They have a notion that you are not exact in your facts, and it has put their backs up; but we are not so exact ourselves, as to be able safely to throw stones.[4]

As to union in prayer, it is not allowed.[5] Not that it is positively unlawful, but any application to Rome is answered in the negative. The Jesuits used to allow converts to go to family prayers in Anglican houses — Whether they do so now, I do not know — but I have heard those, who had received leave, express their regret afterwards that they had availed themselves of it, under the feeling that the practice had put them in a false position, as regards their family, out of which they could not get without inflicting pain. And most people feel, that it is honestest and most straightforward, not to smooth over differences which really exist.

What is prayer but communion? to pray together is to be in the same communion. If the two bodies form one communion, all controversy ceases — differences become little more than pious opinions, or incidental defects; and

[1] Pusey wrote, 'I have been very sorry to see the attack which your letter to me has brought on you. But the noble defence of the Bishop of Clifton must more than have compensated to you for Mr Martin's attack.'

[2] *The Times*, (31 March 1866), devoted a page to a review of Newman's *Letter to Pusey*. Its author was R. W. Church, and it was reprinted in his *Occasional Papers*, London 1897, II, pp. 398–440.

[3] See letter of 16 March 1864 to Badeley. Among the London incubi were Archbishop Manning and those surrounding him, the London Oratory, and perhaps the Redemptorists at Clapham.

[4] See letter of 12 Feb. to Pusey, and those of 3 April (postscript) and 13 April to H. J. Coleridge.

[5] Pusey, who wished to see established an association of prayer for reunion, wrote, 'Archbishop Manning seems to object to all praying with us. Mgr Dupanloup, on the other hand, told me that if I would send him the prayers which were used, he would have them used in his Diocese.'

for three hundred years the whole world has been under an enormous hallucin-ation. This few people will grant; they will think it not common sense. And at Rome, as in Cardinal Patrizzi's letter, they call it 'indifference'[1]

> Ever Yours affectionately With best Easter greetings,
>> John H Newman

P.S. As I have mentioned Cardinal Patrizzi's name, I am led (as in the story of the German flute) to his brother. *When* you have quite done, (but not *till* then,) with Patrizzi on the Canon, and the other volume of the Abbé Migne, will you let me have them back.[2]

I was *obliged* to Mr G. Williams for giving me an opportunity of writing to the Newspaper. There is all sorts of gossip going on about me in London — and I am not sorry to have come down upon it.[3]

TUESDAY 3 APRIL 1866   Mr Hardy? went   Fr Sisk came

TO HENRY JAMES COLERIDGE

The Oy Bm April 3/66

My dear Fr Coleridge

I have heard various things of Keble, and knew he was dying. He wrote me word about two months ago, that his life was slowly leaving him, but surely. About a fortnight ago he was told by the doctors he could not live many hours. He was seized with fainting fits — then with erysipelas in the head — which took him off. She is still alive. The funeral is on Friday.

The report you speak of is a simple thing-that-is-not. What I have ever said is this — 'that Keble had from a youth a great drawing to Catholicism, and that Pusey had never had, as far as I can see, any such drawing.' People may have (if they please) their *own* sentiments, and *infer* from this, that Keble was not in good faith, and that *I* think so — but I repudiate and spit out the idea with great indignation — I never said or thought any such thing. I don't think I should dare to say of any one that he was not in good faith — or should presume to compare one man with another in the balance of responsibility. And whoever has so interpreted me, has coloured my words, with a meaning which I shrink from. If this is not the origin of the report, I can't tell what is. Any how, it is simply untrue.

I have *begun* my article on Ecce Homo, but I never can reckon against

---

[1] i.e. the letter of 8 Nov. 1865 from Cardinal Constantine Patrizi of the Holy Office. See end of letter of 24 Nov. 1865 to H. J. Coleridge. The story of the German flute is probably that preserved by Grimm among others, — a bone, from the skeleton of a man murdered by his brother, is found and carved into a flute. It sings a song that makes known the murderer.

[2] See letter of 28 Sept. 1865 to Pusey.

[3] See letter of 23 March 1866 to the Editor of the *Guardian*.

interruptions — and then I fall back, and have to get the steam up again. So that I cannot promise it by a particular time — all I can say is, that I will do my best.[1]

> Very sincerely Yours in Xt   John H Newman of the Oratory

The Revd Fr Coleridge S J.

P.S. If I had time, I should take you to task, not for *proving* things against Pusey, but for calling him names, imputing to him motives etc. etc. This is as unlawful as using poisoned weapons in war.[2]

TO HENRY WILBERFORCE

> The Oratory Bm ⌜April 3/66⌝

My dear H W

A happy feast to you and all yours. I grieve to hear that you have been ill — we have heard nothing of it. Have you not got into a new house? was it dry?

⌜It is impossible I should write upon Keble — if you saw my Table, you would understand this. I have one stratum of work upon another, deposited and unfinished. The lowest is a treatise on certainty (tho' there were others below that, which have been put away in despair —) certainty, one chapter alone being written, was laid aside last September — on it has been deposited the Pusey Controversy, that too unfinished, but not given over in intention [[viz. on the Pope's Infallibility]]. Upon it comes a series of papers historical, which I have promised for a purpose, if possible. This too is suspended for the moment by a critique which I promised [[on 'Ecce homo']], if possible, two or three pages alone written. All these are further held over by a host of letters, some [[of them to be]] long ones — and by school exercises, and house accounts. Added to this, my strength does not allow me to write on for a long time together — So your proposition is an impossible one.

You know I saw Keble last September, for an hour or two. His wife had been taken ill that morning, and he could not keep me. I hung about in the neighbourhood, hoping she would mend, but she did not. Then he went to Bournemouth, and I have heard from him several times. She was dying about a fortnight ago. The doctors told him she could not live many hours. He had borne up till then — but he was seized with fainting fits — then with erysipelas in the head, which carried him off. When last he saw Pusey, he said to him, that the thought of purgatory was a great comfort to him. The funeral is on Friday at 11. She is still alive.⌝

I am in *earnest* about the names I quoted. 1. they are *witnesses*, and it does not require to be great authors in order to witness well. Ward and Faber, as well as myself, never had a course of theology. I at least have been a year at

---

[1] See letter of 18 Jan. 1866 to Rogers.
[2] See also letter of 13 April to Coleridge.

Rome. Other writers, such as Allies, also are not theologians. The ecclesiastics I named have been in seminaries. 2. Their *literary* merit may not be high, but Lingard, Rock, Wiseman, Tierney, Oliver, are the *first* in their lines. I might say more[1]

Ever Yrs affly J H N

WEDNESDAY 4 APRIL 1866 Fr Sisk went
THURSDAY 5 APRIL called on the Bishop and half agreed to take the Oxford Mission

TO LADY CHATTERTON

The Oratory Birmingham April 5. 1866
My dear Lady Chatterton

Gladly would I answer your remarks at length, if I had time — but I grieve to say I have more work to get through in the day, than I can properly do — and I could not, if I tried, do many things which I should like to do.

You must recollect that I am not young — and really have not strength for much writing. Medical men tell me to do less than I do — but it is very difficult to lessen work — but if I attempted more, I should do less.

I am sure you will understand this, and not think it any want of respect in me, or any want of sympathy, if I do not enter into the details of the difficulties about which you write to me. Really I think that in a while you will be able to solve them by yourself, from the force of your own mind — and I think too that many of them are difficulties which you will be able to satisfy yourself about by the vigour of your own thought *better* than any one for you.

Thank Miss Orpen for her letter, and with my kindest regards to her and to Mr Dering, I am, My dear Lady Chatterton,

Sincerely Yours in Xt   John H Newman
Lady Chatterton

P.S. Will you let me recommend to you, my dear Lady Chatterton, the *Clifton Tracts*. They can be got at Burns's 17 Portman Street, and I think they meet all the difficulties contained in your Letter. They were written about 10 years since, and are intended to explain points on which questions may be asked.[2]

[1] Wilberforce was referring to *A Letter to Pusey*, 'But the plain fact is this, — they [F. W. Faber and W. G. Ward] came to the Church, and have thereby saved their souls; but they are in no sense spokesmen for English Catholics, and they must not stand in the place of those who have a real title to such an office. The chief authors of the passing generation, some of them still alive, others gone to their reward, are Cardinal Wiseman, Dr. Ullathorne, Dr. Lingard, Mr. Tierney, Dr. Oliver, Dr. Rock, Dr. Waterworth, Dr. Husenbeth, and Mr. Flanagan; which of these ecclesiastics has said anything extreme about the prerogatives of the Blessed Virgin or the infallibility of the Pope?' *Diff*. II, p. 23.
[2] These tracts answering objections against Catholicism, sponsored by the converts living at Clifton, were published from 1851 onwards. See letter of 4 Dec. 1850 to Northcote.

The Oratory Bm April 5/66

My dear Miss Orpen

Don't think I do not keenly feel the force of your letter and the affection for Lady C. which dictated it — but I *could* not, unless I had two heads and four hands do what she would wish, and I could wish too

Do get the Clifton Tracts. They are very good.

God bless you
Ever Yours sincerely in Xt   John H Newman

TO J. WALKER OF SCARBOROUGH

The Oratory Bm April 5. 1866

My dear Canon Walker

I intend to be here next week — and shall be glad to see you, as you propose

Very sincerely Yours John H Newman

The Very Revd John Canon Walker

TO JAMES GUBBINS

April 7. 1866

Dear Revd Sir

I am sorry my silence upon receipt of your second letter has been open to an interpretation which has been far indeed from my meaning, and I beg your forgiveness for causing you anxiety in consequence.[1]

Your letter contained nothing but what was kind and frank.

It is my usual way, if possible, not to have the last word. I felt obliged by your remarks, but I did not agree with them. They were not new to me. In the letter I wrote to you, I set before you my own judgment, and hoped that it would have approved itself to you. I am very sorry that it did not; I still hope you will see cause to modify your own conclusions, but if you knew how many letters I have to write, and how much work of various kinds I have on my hands, you would quite understand that it is simply impossible for me, unless I broke into my necessary night's rest, to avail myself of the various opportunities of controversy which are offered to me.

With my best Easter greetings & begging your good prayers

I am &c J H N

---

[1] To Newman's letter of 19 March Gubbins replied on 20 March, denying that all revealed doctrines were contained in Scripture in the way Newman had explained, and added, 'on this point you are not quite orthodox.' When there was no answer, Gubbins wrote again on 5 April, fearing that he might have annoyed Newman. Gubbins added that 'a very eminent theologian' he had consulted, shared his own view of the matter.

TO BISHOP ULLATHORNE

The Oratory Bm April 7. 1866

My dear Lord,

In spite of all you told me and read to me of your Lordship's letter, I was not prepared for such extreme kindness and tender considerateness for me as it displays.[1]

We hope you will allow us, without seeming officious, to return to you our best thanks for the signal honour you have done us, in what you say of our Church and its services.

It is a letter which must ever act as a great encouragement to us, as leading us humbly to trust, that, in receiving the approbation of our earthly Superior, we have received the blessing of Him whom he represents, and to whom, amid all our infirmities and sins, we have wished to dedicate our lives

I am, My dear Lord, begging your Lordship's blessing, Your obedient & affecte Servt in Xt

John H Newman of the Oratory

The Right Revd The Bishop of Birmingham

SUNDAY 8 APRIL 1866   Canon Walker came in the night of 8th–9th

TO EDWARD HAWKINS

The Oratory Birmingham April 8. 1866

My dear Mr Provost

I thank you for the considerateness of your letter, and for your Pamphlets.[2] Of course you had a right, nay a call to publish after Pusey's pamphlet — and, as I gave leave for the re-publication of Tract 90, (because it was published originally after the deliberation of a year, and because, in spite of its many

---

[1] This was Ullathorne's letter of 4 April, defending Newman's *A Letter to Pusey*, and giving proofs of his devotion and that of his Oratory to our Lady. It was published in the *Tablet*, (7 April), p. 219. See Appendix 1.

[2] Hawkins wrote, on 2 April, (a letter partially quoted in note to that of 1 Jan. 1866 to him), about Pusey's republication of *Tract XC*. Hawkins explained to Newman, 'I had written a Pamphlet in 1864 upon "Subscription, Clerical, and Academical", and I thought of writing some "Additional Notes" on the subject in consequence of what had occurred in 1865 with respect to both our Clerical and Academical Subscriptions. But Pusey's republication of the Tract was sadly in my way; for I felt that according to my view of the subject (and you will not be affronted at my saying so) I could not hope to maintain our Subscriptions if they could be made on the principles of the Tract. Hence I was tempted to advert to the Tract; much against my will I may say; and I think I have hitherto almost always avoided writing anything directly against, or quoting, Pusey, or Keble, as yourself . . .

I have given you the history and occasion of my touching on the Tract; and of course you cannot like what I say. Yet I think it better to send the Pamphlet at once to you (and the former "Notes" with it), lest if you only heard of it, or saw it advertised, you might think I had treated you worse than I have. — I considered indeed that I was not so much attacking you or your Tract, as Pusey and his republication of it. But it grieves me that I should have had any occasion to write against either of you.' This letter is printed in full in R. D. Middleton, *Newman at Oxford*, pp. 268–9.

imperfections and faults in detail, I still hold to its principle,) so I cannot wonder at your feeling that no delicacy need be observed in criticising it. I could not have put an obstacle in the way of Pusey's republication of it without implying I was ashamed of it; but, while I maintain it myself, I can quite understand others being strongly opposed [to] it. How far it is faulty, and how far not, the next generation will be better judges than we are.

It was certainly very singular that neither you nor I should have recollected my application to you on the Sunday before the Hebdomadal Meeting.[1]

I suppose you were prepared, as I was, for dear Keble's death. I saw him for an hour or two last September at Hursley. His wife was so ill that he could not keep me — and, though I remained in the neighbourhood some time, he was obliged to give up the chance of seeing me again.

You will be sorry to hear (what I have not told any one yet, and wish kept secret) that there is much probability now of my bringing the Oratory to Oxford. This is the third time I have been pressed to do so — and, though I am very unwilling, I do not know how I can refuse[2]

Very sincerely Yours John H Newman

TO MRS JOHN MOZLEY

The Oratory Bm April 8/66

My dear Jemima

I shall be rejoiced to see Frank [Mozley], tell him. Next Friday, you say, the 13th. He can have a bed, if his arrangements admit of it — and he need not determine till he comes. Any how, I will have a room ready for him.

I was quite prepared for the loss of Keble. When I saw him in September last, I saw how very frail he was. I had made several attempts to fix a day, and his wife's illness disconcerted them. When they had returned from Bournemouth, I named a day again. He was, I found accidentally, going to receive Pusey that very day. Then I put it off; I told him I could not bear to meet two — one was trial enough — so I determined to go to the Isle of Wight, to the H. Bowdens, till Pusey was gone. Then, when I got into the train here, I said to myself, 'This is cowardice' — so I stopped at Southampton and went over to him next morning, the 12th. He was at his door, when I got there — and not expecting me, did not know me. I had to show him my card. What was stranger, I did not know him, and, though there he was at his own door, I could not address him as Keble. He told me that his wife had that morning had a bad attack — in consequence I could not stay — I dined with him and Pusey. Unless I had gone that day, I should not have seen him at all. For I was to have come back when his wife got better, but she never got better, and he

---

[1] See letter of 1 Jan. to Hawkins.
[2] Ullathorne asked Newman to undertake the Oxford Mission on 23 Aug. 1864, 26 Aug. 1865 and 25 March 1866.

was obliged to give up the idea. The wonder is how he could ever bear so long the suffering which his wife has undergone. Spasmodic asthma is a fearful complaint to see. Mr St John has for years suffered from it, though he is better now — it is like seeing a person in a chronic condition of hanging or drowning. I don't suppose men suffer so much in either death. And it must have been enough to drive Keble wild. I heard of his faintings on the Wednesday. The news of his death came on Saturday the 31st. Thank you for the sight of Miss Yonge's letter. I have taken the liberty of copying it — omitting the signature.[1]

Strange that I should have heard of the prospect of his death a week before you heard of his death. I met Miss Yonge at Otterbourne in (I think) July 1839.[2]

As to the Times, it is so minutely accurate, that I thought it written by T. Mozley.[3]

Yrs affly John H Newman

TO CHARLOTTE WOOD

The Oratory Bm April 8/66

My dear Miss Wood

I was prepared for dear Mr Keble's death, from knowing how frail he was and how his wife's illness tried him. I last heard from him about two months ago — He then said she was slowly (using a word of George Herbert's) 'undressing—' she had been obliged to give up first her music, then her drawing, then her books — and so, she was stripping herself of every thing but her body — which God would take off from her in His own time. It was a sort of race between them which should die first. I think you will like to see the inclosed — it is a copy of a letter written to my sister. Please, let me have it back.

The one doctrine dear Keble did not receive was that communion with the Holy See was necessary for being in the Church. The few hours that I saw him in September, it astonished me how far he seemed to go. I suppose he looked forward to Purgatory with real comfort, as a mode of honouring God. Had I not seen him for that brief space, I should not have seen him at all. I waited at Swainston, hoping he would be able to see me — but in vain — his wife was still so ill; and she has been ill ever since.

I gladly inclose what you ask for Mrs Wood.

I consider I have been very much prospered in my recent Pamphlet. The

[1] Jemima had received a letter of 5 April from Charlotte Yonge about Keble's death, in which she wrote, 'I believe your Brother's visit to Hursley was a great peace to him.'
[2] This was on the occasion of the consecration of Keble's church at Otterbourne on 30 July 1839.
[3] i.e. the obituary of Keble in *The Times*, (6 April 1866), p. 5.

Times paid me a great compliment in giving me so much space, and will puff it for me well — and I agree with you in thinking the tone kind, and the intention too. On the other hand do you see what an overpowering by [but] gratifying letter our Bishop has put into yesterday's Tablet?

I am now very well, thank you.

Most sincerely Yours in Xt   John H Newman

MONDAY 9 APRIL 1866   Mr Morell here — Canon Walker went — Lady Simeon here — and Mr Wegg Prosser

TO HENRY JAMES COLERIDGE

The Oratory Bm April 9/66

My dear Fr Coleridge

I am much concerned to hear of your indisposition — but who can wonder, when Lent, the Confessional, and the Month were all upon you at once? You, Jesuits, live fast — I am glad you are going away.

However, this has altered an intention of mine. I was going by this post to send you a sample of my article (little enough) but I thought you would like to see it — but, since I am quite uncertain whether I shall get through it in time for this May Month, I don't know why I should needlessly torment you with it — and have therefore stayed my hand.[1]

You are quite right in calling me to account for the 'masterly —' would 'elaborate' have done? I am sorry to hear you say that Pusey's book is doing harm; I had hoped it would only tell, where readers already wished it to tell on them.

I have no intention, thank you, of writing on dear Keble. How strange it is! he seems to have received all doctrine, except the necessity of being in communion with the Holy See. His wife, as far as I can make out, is still alive. She kept back the funeral a day, hoping to be buried with him. Her grave is made. To continue what I said the other day, it seems to me no difficulty to suppose a person in good faith on such a point as the necessity of communion with Rome. Till he saw that, (or that he was not in the Church) he was bound to remain as he was. And it was in this way that he always put it. Of course it would be a great kindness, if you negatived the report about me, should you hear it.[2]

1. Pusey and Dornford, I think, persuaded me to vote for Hawkins — but, besides this, I knew Hawkins and he had taken me up, while Keble had fought shy of me.[3] But it is a sort of College secret, and you must say nothing in your article which you learn from *me*. I thought Hawkins would make the better

[1] Newman was preparing his article for the *Month* on Seeley's *Ecce Homo*.
[2] The report was that denounced forcefully by Newman in his letter of 3 April to Coleridge.
[3] Coleridge asked for information about the election of the Provost of Oriel in 1828, in connexion with his article for the *Month* on Keble. See letter of 20 April.

Provost. I said 'If we were electing an Angel, we ought to take Keble, but we are only electing a Provost.' Others voted for him on seeing us three, Dornford, Pusey and me, for him — for the doubt was whether he would get on with the Fellows — and there could not be a greater proof that he would, than to find that three residents voted for him — For some time I wavered between Keble and Hawkins, but felt drawn to Hawkins by his past kindnesses.

2. I have seen that beautiful poem, though I don't recollect it accurately. Certainly I think you might describe it[1]

Very sincerely Yours in Xt   John H Newman of the Oratory

The Revd Fr Coleridge S.J.

TO LADY CHATTERTON

The Oratory Bm April 12. 1866

My dear Lady Chatterton

I have delayed sending you the MSS, which I now forward, hoping to have made some annotations on them, or at least to have made references in places to passages in the Clifton Tracts — in which an answer is found to the questions contained in them. I much regret to say that my intention, on account of the various matters I have on hand has not been fulfilled. I do not like to retain them longer

Very sincerely Yours in Xt   John H Newman of the Oratory

Lady Chatterton

TO HENRY JAMES COLERIDGE

The Oy Bm April 13/66.

My dear Fr Coleridge

You say nothing of your health, and your movements.

1. As to my review, I am at it every day — but the interruptions are many, and, when I come back to it, I am so tired, that I cannot get on. And I have not yet read the book through. I could send you, as I said, a portion to hasten the printing, but I could not promise the day on which it is to be finished — nor do I know your latest day.

I should send you a portion, if I did, for *revision*. It will need carefully

---

[1] This was Keble's 'Mother out of Sight,' about devotion to our Lady, who appeared to be 'out of sight' in the Anglican Church. Coleridge described the poem in the *Month*, (May 1866), pp. 455–6. It was intended for inclusion in Keble's *Lyra Innocentium* in 1846, but was omitted at the request of Coleridge's father, Sir John Taylor Coleridge, and the Dyson family. Keble was much annoyed at this opposition. See the *Month*, (Feb. 1903), p. 116. Sir John Taylor Coleridge published it in *A Memoir of the Rev. John Keble*, Oxford 1869, pp. 305–9, and it was included in Keble's *Miscellaneous Poems*, Oxford 1869, pp. 254–9. It is also printed as an appendix, at the end of Walter Lock's edition of *Lyra Innocentium*, London 1903.

looking through, and I will attend to any remarks you make. This consideration seems to show that it *cannot* comfortably be ready for this month.

2. Church is just the man, if he will undertake it.[1] My own notion of
writing a life is the notion of Hurrell Froude's, viz. *to do it by letters* and to
bring in as little letter press of one's own as possible.

Froude has so done his Becket. It is far more real, and therefore interesting
than any other way. Stanley has so done Arnold's.[2]

3. As to Pusey, I *fully* think that whatever is misrepresented in facts should
be brought out, as well as what is wrong in theology. But, as I should say to
Church, put in original letters with as little comment of your own as possible,
so I say in this other matter, Show that Pusey's facts are wrong, but don't
abuse him. Abuse is as great a mistake in controversy, as panegyric in biography. Of course a man must state strongly his opinion, but that is not personal
vituperation. Now I am not taking the liberty of accusing you of vituperation,
but I think an Anglican would say 'The writer is fierce', and would put you
aside in consequence as a partizan. He would shrink into his prejudices, instead
of imbibing confidence.

Now mind, I am not accusing you of all this maladdresse, but bringing out
what I *mean*. But I will tell you, if you will bear with me, what does seem to
me an approach to it in what you have written. E.g.

1 'the great name of Bossuet has been *foolishly* invoked by Dr Pusey. p 384

2 there can be no more mistake about the fact . . . than about [the] *impression which Dr Pusey has meant to produce* on his readers. p 387 note

3 how does this . . . differ *from the artifice* of an *unscrupulous advocate?* p 389

4 great confusion of thought. p 388

5 in happy unconsciousness of the absurdity of his language. p 389

6 This language shows as much *confusion* or *ignorance* etc p 389

7 He does not understand that . . . p 389

8 He *talks* of a continual flow etc 389

9 this is very *childish* p 389

10 Dr Pusey then must have deliberately ignored the distinct etc p. 389[3]

It must be recollected that your object is to convince those who respect
and love Dr Pusey, that he has written hastily and rashly and gone beyond his
measure. Now, if even *I* feel pained to read such things said of him, what do
you suppose is the feeling of those who look up to him as their guide? They
are as indignant at finding him thus treated as you are for his treatment of
Catholic doctrine. They close their ears and hearts. Yet these are the very
people you write for. You don't write to convert the good Fathers at Number

---

[1] i.e. the biography of Keble. At Mrs Keble's request, it was undertaken by Coleridge's
father.

[2] Cf. Letter of 18 May 1863 to Mrs John Mozley. A. P. Stanley's *The Life and Correspondence of Thomas Arnold* was published in 1844.

[3] Newman is criticizing Coleridge's 'Archbishop Manning and the Reunion of Christendom,' the *Month*, (April 1866), pp. 379–91.

9,[1] but to say a word in season to *his* followers and to *his* friends — to dispose them to look kindly on Catholics and Catholic doctrine — to entertain the possibility that they have misjudged us, and that they are needlessly, as well as dangerously keeping away from us — but to mix up your irrefutable matter with a personal attack on Pusey, is as if you were to load your gun carefully, and then as deliberately to administer some drops of water at the touch hole.

Now excuse me for all this, but you have put me on my defence by making the point of issue whether or not the 'Papers should be suffered all to assume that his statements are founded on real theological knowledge —' which is *not* the issue[2]

Very sincerely Yours, John H Newman

TO T. W. ALLIES

The Oratory Bm April 15./66

My dear Allies

Thank you for your book. You seem to have done your work very thoroughly. I wonder whether any one will attempt to answer you. Our Bishop goes over a portion of your ground. Thank you for quoting a passage from me at p. 67. It will do me service in this season of lies.[3]

Yours affly in Xt   John H Newman of the Oratory

TO MISS BRISTOWE

The Oratory, Birm — Ap. 15. 1866.

My dear Madam

I can quite understand the painful perplexity you are in — be sure God will be with you, if you, unreservedly throw yourself upon him. If you simply beg of Him to lead you into the truth and ask His grace to enable you to follow Him, He will not fail you, I know.

As to your question, 'whether I should have left the Anglican Church, if it had been twenty years ago what it is now —' it seems to me to admit of an easy answer. I left it because I was sure that it was not a portion of that Catholic Church which our Lord and His Apostles established, as the source of teaching and the channel of grace till the end of the world. We are saved by

---

[1] 9 Hill Street, Berkeley Square, was the Jesuit house in London.
[2] Coleridge later commented: 'The latter part of this letter shows his extreme kindness, and I quite acknowledge that the faults he pointed out were such. I lived in an atmosphere where Pusey's name was a bugbear. We heard constantly of his unfair dealings in controversy.... Still, Newman was right in his criticism of me, and I hope I told him so.' The *Month*, (Feb. 1903), p. 118.
[3] *Dr. Pusey and the Ancient Church,* London 1866. On p. 67 Allies quoted Newman's list of the ante-Nicene testimonies for the Papacy in *Dev.*, pp. 157–8; first edition, pp. 22–3.

grace, and grace is ordinarily supplied to us through the sacraments, and, excepting baptism, no sacrament exists outside the Church. If the Church of England is not part of the Catholic Church, it does not possess the sacraments of confirmation, penance, Eucharist, or extreme unction, to give to its people — and these are the ordinary means of grace. It cannot give them even though it professed to give them. Then, even as to its baptism, this is very doubtful. I joyfully believe that the rite is administered much more carefully, than it was thirty years ago by many clergymen, but I much doubt whether the majority administer it safely even now.

And this brings me to the next point. I have said what my convictions about the Anglican Church were twenty years ago. Now how does it differ now, from what it was then? Not in itself at all — but in this, viz. that the Catholicizing party in it has *grown* — it is much larger and bolder than it was; — this is all. Does that party tend to grow and grow, till it embraces the *whole* Anglican body? Supposing it did so, still it would not be part of the Catholic Church, till it actually submitted itself, confessed its past rebelliousness, and re-entered into communion with her. Much less is it part of the Catholic Church now. But this is not all — I have said 'supposing the high Church party *tends to* embrace the whole Anglican body' — yes — but supposing it *does not*.

Now, let it be recollected, that, if in the last 20 years, the high Church party has spread, so also has the Liberalizing party. I think *it* has spread far more, and is quite as likely to eat out the Catholicizing party, as the Catholicizing party to eat out it. However, all this belongs to the future — we belong to the present. The question is, what is *our* duty *to day*? is the Church of England *now* Catholic in its doctrine? no. Is it a part of the one Catholic Church? no. That I said twenty years ago when I was an Anglican — that I say now, when I am a Catholic — that I *should* say now, I believe, were I an Anglican now.

As to your age, and whether you ought to wait any time before deciding, I cannot answer the question, as I do not know you. Your best adviser would be some judicious Catholic Lady, who could talk with you. There are Catholic ladies in Ryde, and prudent and kind ones. Do you know any such? They would help you best.

They have good Priests at the London Oratory — but that Oratory has no more connexion with me and the Oratory here than with any other religious body. Your best advisers in London would be the Jesuit Fathers at 9 Hill Street, Berkeley Square — their Church is in Farm Street, close by.

Very truly Yours John H. Newman

Miss Bristow

April 15/66

My dear Dr Doyle

Thank you for your kind and generous letter to the Tablet about my recent Pamphlet, but tell me, when did I ever write a letter to the late Editor (Lucas) which he, instead of publishing, consigned to his waste paper basket? I have no recollection of it.[1]

Don't suppose I am going to write about it to the present Editor. I have no wish for his basket any more than for Lucas's. For me, your statement shall stand just as it is for posterity; I owe you too much for your present bottle holding, to grudge you the satisfaction of this incidental slap[2]

J H N

TO ROBERT ORNSBY

The Oratory Bm April 15/66

My dear Ornsby

I owe you several letters. I hope this will catch you — if not, it can't be helped.

I was prepared for Keble's death as knowing the cruel sufferings of his wife, which were enough to kill an old person so weakened already. The doctors said she could not last many hours — soon after he was seized with fainting fits. They took him out of his wife's room. When he got to his own, he thought he was in Church — he knelt down and said the Lord's prayer, and then went off to a Latin Hymn, which they could not make out — they were his last words.

[1] Doyle wrote in defence of Newman to the *Tablet*, (14 April 1866), a letter headed 'St George's and Rev. Dr Newman.'
'What has the Rev. Dr Newman to do with St George's? He has much to do with it, because he preached his first sermon after his conversion in St George's. I read a part of his last publication in our pulpit, viz., as much as I could, the Sunday after I received it. It is not for me to say more as to my poor judgment on this wonderful work. I say nothing but think much, and give thanks that so great and good a man is one of us. What the *Tablet* ought to have done on receiving that vexatious attack on this gifted man, was what Mr Lucas did with the Rev. Dr Newman's attack on me many years since, viz. to have thrown it into the waste basket.
The Rev. Dr Newman has all the faith and feeling as to the Blessed Mother of God that the best of us have, with twenty times our sense and discretion. The night is coming on when no man can work, and we wait with impatience for his clear, masculine, and accurate view, on the question of the Popes. May I presume to say that his pen must not rest until his fingers fail, and may that be long away. God bless dear Dr Newman and I forgive him, although he made a desperate thrust at me. However, it made me laugh almost as much as did his simple avowal that he put *Callista* aside because he could not find a new character to make up the story.'
[2] Doyle replied on 16 April, '"*Deuced* hard teeth" was the rousing point that made you hit at me. Don't you recollect it now? I trembled in my shoes when you shewed fight because I knew that I must come in for the worst of it.'
In *The Great Link, A History of St George's Southwark*, London N.D. (1948), p. 261, Bernard Bogan quotes Doyle's letter to the *Tablet*, and says that 'No reference of any kind can be traced as to the occasion or substance of Newman's attack on Doyle.' See, however, remarks on a sermon of Doyle's, Volume XIV, p. 119.

I hope you will have a pleasant trip. It will be hot, won't it? I am glad you give so good an account of Mrs Ornsby

Ever Yours affectly in Xt   John H Newman

TO BISHOP ULLATHORNE

The Oratory April 15/66

My dear Lord

I have to acknowledge, as we all have, the receipt of your Lordship's important Letter, which I trust will do a great deal of good.[1]

I don't know whether it is worth while to add, that, since such publications are expensive matters, we are quite ready, as your clergy, to contribute towards the cost, when you think fit to call on us.

Your Lordship's obt & Afft Servt in Xt
John H Newman of the Oratory

The Rt Revd The Bp of Birmingham

P.S. May I take the liberty of inclosing a note to the Vicar General?

TO EMILY BOWLES

The Oratory Bm April 16. 1866

My dear Child

You don't say how you are. I am afraid not well.

As to myself, you don't consider that I am an old man and must husband my strength. When I passed my Letter through the Press and wrote my notes, I was confined to my bed, or barely sitting up. I had a most serious attack — it might have been far worse. I did not know how much worse till (through God's mercy) it was all over. It would have been very imprudent to have done more. Nor *would* I write more, hastily. I should have much to read for it. Recollect, to write theology is like dancing on the tight rope some hundred feet above the ground. It is hard to keep from falling, and the fall is great. Ladies can't be in the position to try. The questions are so subtle, the distinctions so fine, and critical jealous eyes so many. Such critics would be worth nothing, if they had not the power of writing to Rome, now that communication is made so easy — and you may get into hot water, before you know where you are. The necessity of defending myself at Rome would almost kill me with the fidget. You don't know me, when you suppose I 'take heed of the motley flock of fools.'[2] No — it is *authority* that I fear. Di me terrent, et

---

[1] *The Anglican Theory of Union as maintained in the Appeal to Rome and Dr. Pusey's 'Eirenicon,'* London N.D. (1866).
[2] *As You Like It*, II, vii.

Jupiter hostis.[1] I have had great work to write even what I have written — and I ought to be most deeply thankful that I have so wonderfully succeeded Two Bishops, one my own, have spontaneously, and generously, come forward. Why cannot you believe that letter of mine, in which I said I did not write more because I was 'tired'? This was the real reason, then others came in. The subject I had to write upon opened, and I found I had a great deal to read, before I could write. Next, I felt I had irritated many good people, and I wished the waves to subside, before I began to play the Æolus a second time.[2] Moreover, I was intending to make a great change. I thought at length my time had come. I had introduced the narrow end of the wedge — and made a split — I feared it would split fiercely and irregularly — and I thought by withdrawing the wedge, — the split might to left at present more naturally to increase *itself*. Every thing I see confirms me in my view. I have various letters from all parts of the country approving of what I have already done. There are just two or three cliques in London who are the other way. The less I do myself, the more others will do. It is not well to put oneself too forward. Englishmen don't like to be driven. I am sure it is good policy to be quiet just now.

I have long said 'the night cometh etc,'[3] but that does not make it right to act in a hurry. Better not do a thing than do it badly. I must be patient and wait on God. If it is His will I should do more, He will give me time. I am not serving Him, by blundering.

You will be glad to know, (*what (at present) is a great secret*) that we are likely to have a house at Oxford after all. Be patient, and all will be well.

As to dear Keble, I have lent a letter about him, or I would send it you. It is grievous that people are so hard. In converts it is inexcusable; it is a miserable spirit in them. Keble was told his wife could not live many hours. He had borne up, in spite of his great infirmities, longer than I had supposed possible. He was seized with fainting fits. His friends took him from her room. When he got into his own, he fancied it a Church. He knelt down, and said the Lord's Prayer. Then he began a Latin Hymn — they could not make out what. Those were his last words. Thus he ended with the prayer which he first said on his knees as a little child.

Ever Yours affly in Xt   John H Newman of the Oratory

Miss Bowles.

TUESDAY 17 APRIL 1866   married Eleanor Bretherton to Mr Watt — went to the breakfast

WEDNESDAY 18 APRIL   decided in General Congregation to take the Oxford mission, if the Bishop grants us our conditions.[4]

[1] *Aeneid*, XII, 895.
[2] *Aeneid*, I, 50–156.
[3] *St John*, 9:4.
[4] See letter of 23 April.

TO HENRY JAMES COLERIDGE

April 18/66

My dear Fr Coleridge

In great haste. The article on Keble in the Times was so very accurate in its Oriel facts, that I think it must have been written by T. Mozley.

I voted for Hawkins. I wrote to Keble to say why I did so etc ending by saying 'however it was unnecessary — for I knew he did *not wish* to be Head.' He wrote me back a kind letter, but said I had no right to take for granted he did not wish to be head — I recollect being very much surprised. I must have his letter somewhere. I think he meant partly to snub me, as if I had no right to conjecture in so serious a matter what I knew nothing about — and had no right, writing to him, to put him aside in a cavalier way — but I am half inclined to think he *did* wish to be head[1]

Ever Yrs sincerely John H Newman

P.S. There was no formal *standing* for the headship — but Keble's friends put him forward.

FRIDAY 20 APRIL 1866   Frank Mozley here for some hours

TO HENRY JAMES COLERIDGE

The Oratory Bm April 20/66

My dear Fr Coleridge

The article on Keble is very able and very beautiful. It must do a great deal of good, in this respect, if in no other, in interesting Anglicans in the Month, and again in interesting Catholics in a very remarkable adherent to Anglicanism. It is a mode of bringing two sets of men together more powerful than any other, and one which involves no violation of principle. And it tends to show that a rigidly Catholic publication, such as the Month is, is able to recognise facts as facts, and is not afraid for the Catholic religion, if moral goodness is to be found in bodies not Catholic.

p. 442. 'shedding a dew etc'[2] This is very happy; it is Keble all over. Whately used to spit into the fire, between two friends sitting opposite to him at table. Such is the character of some men's minds. Even if they bring out

---

[1] See Newman's letter of 16 Dec. 1827 to Keble. For the article in *The Times* see letter of 8 April to Mrs John Mozley.

[2] Newman is criticising the proof of Coleridge's article, 'John Keble,' the *Month*, (May 1866). Coleridge wrote, 'His bright, fresh, joyous and affectionate nature was like an ever-flowing spring, always at play, always shedding a gentle, imperceptible, and recreating dew upon those who come within its reach.'

what is true and good, still they spit; but Keble was like the dew from a fountain, as you say.

p. 444 for 'newborn isle,' read 'rill.'[1]

ibid Fairford was not his father's living. I forget the name of it (was it Combe?) very small and without a parsonage — so they lived at Fairford, in a house with a largish paddock, which was a great gain to his invalid sister, who could not move except in a chair.[2]

p 445. It is *quite* true that for the Provostship 'he neither put himself formally forward, nor exerted himself to obtain it.' When he said to me what I told you, I think he meant 'you must not shelter yourself behind any imagination of that kind, when your duty is to take the best man, whether he likes it or no.'

p 446 Had not Hawkins been Provost, we should (humanly speaking) Wilberforce, Froude, and I have worked on as tutors under Keble for years — we had given ourselves to Tuition — we had greatly reformed the College under Hawkins — we had kept up, perhaps increased the number of first classes — we insisted on making the office *pastoral* — at least I did, — and that was the acknowledged issue between Hawkins and me.[3] I would not act as any thing short of pastor to my pupils. I would not *resign*, saying my office was by the University Statutes, a University not a College office — the dispute ended in his cutting off the supplies — he gave me no new pupils — Sir F. Rogers was about my last, in 1832. He took two first[s]. The succession of honours has ceased from that time to this. My heart was wrapped up in that kind of life — and, though I liked ecclesiastical history, and had begun reading it systematically in 1828, (so that my pupils on my ceasing to be Tutor, made me a present of many of the Fathers, not of plate,) yet I doubt whether I should have *written* on such subjects. Thus the movement would not have begun, I think but for the act of Hawkins. As I, on leaving the Tuition took to the Arians, so Hurrell Froude took to St Thomas à Beckett.

p 448 'impertinent and preposterous —' rather it would be 'simply untrue' — Unless you say something equivalent to this, will you not seem unkind to *Mrs* Keble? You only say it would be *impertinent* to call her a Xantippe.[4]

p 449 'admirable commentary on the Gospels —' *I* don't want you to alter it —but I am thinking what would people say if you spoke of Nicolas's or Quesnell's 'admirable etc' — Of course the latter authors are actually condemned by the church — not I.W.[5]

---

[1] This misprint in a note, which quoted the first line of the poem for Easter Monday in the *Christian Year,* was corrected.

[2] Coleridge changed 'living' to 'residence,' John Keble senior was Vicar of Coln St Aldwyn, near Fairford.

[3] See A. Dwight Culler, *The Imperial Intellect,* New Haven 1955, pp. 72–4. Newman and his friends greatly increased the first classes at Oriel.

[4] Coleridge spoke of how the country parson with his family failed to produce intellectual work, and referred to 'the Xantippe of the good Hooker.' He then went on to say, 'It would be impertinent and preposterous to suppose that these remarks can be applied in their full sense to the case of John Keble.' This was altered to 'It would be altogether untrue to suppose . . .'

[5] Coleridge omitted the word 'admirable' when referring to Isaac Williams's *Commentary on the Gospels.*

p 449. note — Was he 'twice Vicar?' or first curate, and then Vicar? Certainly he was not Vicar in 1828 — I think not in 1829, or till 1835.[1] As to Keble's theological works, are you sure he has not left a commentary on the Gospels behind him?[2]

p 451. 'We need hardly ask to be forgiven —' . . . *'indulgent'* and 'fall' — people will say you apologize too much, and are tame, on alluding to a great insult to the Bride of Christ.[3]

ibid. towards the end — *'almost* undue *extent —'* I should have thought 'he certainly allowed their influence to an unlawful extent etc'[4]

p 454 'nineteenth' I suppose is right? no, surely ninetieth — for you say 'this year.'[5]

p 457 — Your ending about Penelope is extremely beautiful — (and I am so glad you like the Odyssey. It has always been a puzzle to me why it is postponed to the Iliad, which is so very bloody and barbarous.) And I think your words 'The dream of a student etc' embody a great truth[6]

Yours most sincerely John H Newman

[1] Coleridge corrected this note. Keble was curate at Hursley in 1825, for a year, and did not return as Vicar until 1835.

[2] Fragments of a commentary on St John's Gospel were published in 1877 in a volume called *Studia Sacra*, prefaced by Canon J. P. Norris.

[3] This passage, evidently referring to the Catholic Church, has disappeared from the article. Coleridge wrote on the same page, that Keble 'could even venture to be serenely indulgent and compassionate towards Catholics; to bid his readers "speak but gently of our sister's fall."'

[4] This change was made as follows: 'Again, it was characteristic of Mr. Keble to vindicate the right of dutiful feelings and religious sentiments to control practical action, as indeed he certainly allowed their influence to an unlawful extent as grounds for faith itself.'

[5] Coleridge wrote of *The Christian Year*, 'The ninetieth edition, printed this year, lies before us.' According to *DNB* there were ninety-five editions before Keble's death.

[6] 'Homer ends his Odyssey with a touching but very natural scene, which has always seemed to us to be full of the deepest significance. Penelope has been faithful all those long years to the image of her husband; it has been the food of her thoughts and her dreams, and she has proved her constancy in the way which has made her so famous. At last Ulysses returns; the suitors are slain — all fear and peril are over; but she shrinks back from his embrace, and doubts her own happiness. She has the image in her heart of the hero of twenty years ago; and the careworn, tempest-beaten, half-aged stranger that stands before her is so unlike that image, that she does not know him. The parable is repeated, almost certainly, whenever something which we have long dreamt of, and around which our fondest affections and fancies have clung, is presented to us in the reality which it wears in the world of truth and life. Mr. Keble had been baptised, as every one of us is baptised, into the Catholic Church; but he was brought up unconsciously outside her pale, and he had been taught and had accustomed himself to give his duty and his allegiance to a system alien to her. But his regenerate nature yearned for its true Mother; and he had gathered from the ancient sources and the records of Scripture the details of her features and her character, and woven them into an ideal on which he had lavished all the love of his heart. It was certainly not so beautiful, so majestic, so tender, so divine, as the reality; rather, as was inevitable it fell far short of it, in every element of grace and dignity, as the creature of human imagination compared with heavenly verities. But it was a poetic Church, a church for the refined scholar in his cabinet — a personification of abstract qualities and special attributes, rather than the "pilgrim of eternity," the Church of conflict and action, which has been beaten by the storms of eighteen centuries . . . which has made itself common because its mission is to the whole world . . . The dream of a student can never be like the reality of the work of God.'

TO ROBERT EDMUND FROUDE

[20 April 1866][1]

. . . .

Then, as to your doubts, it is wonderful if they never had come upon you. I have expected you would have them all along. It is impossible that a young and opening mind, such as yours, should not have them sooner or later. There are large questions which cannot be taken in all at once — and they must come as questions before they admit of answers. They are like plus and minus quantities, equal to each other severally, in an equation. The plus come first, I mean, objections — then come the minus, the answers; and the equation is left at the end, as it began. This subject is beautifully treated, poetically not algebraically, in the Hymn in the Christian year on the Epiphany.[2]

God is not a hard master — nor is the Church severe — you have an honest heart, and desire to do what is right. Sacraments are not snares — privliges are not burdens. Put off your trouble as much as you can, put yourself into God's hands and be patient. I shall be glad to see you at any time.

Every yrs affly John H. Newman.

TO E. B. PUSEY

The Oy Bm April 20. 1866

My dear Pusey

I have just seen your kind letter about me in the Churchman.[3]

I sent up a note to be added to my third Edition about 'solvatur' two months ago — and I have no doubt it is inserted — though I have not seen this copy.

I am not at all sure which reading is right — though the MSS of St Augustine give solvatur.

---

[1] Date given in *Harper*, p. 183.
[2] 'Too soon the glare of earthly day
　　Buries, to us, Thy brightness keen,
And we are left to find our way
　　By faith and hope in Thee unseen.

What matter? if the waymarks sure
　　On every side are round us set,
Soon overleaped, but not obscure?
　　'Tis ours to mark them or forget.'
[3] Pusey wrote in the *Churchman*, (19 April 1866), about Newman's quotation from St Irenaeus. See *Diff.* II, p. 121, and *Letter to Pusey*, third edition, p. 128. F. Meyrick blamed Newman for reading with the Benedictine edition 'salvatur' rather than solvatur.' Pusey deprecated this attack, and wrote: 'The Benedictines mostly did their work in so masterly a manner that I should myself have reposed unhesitatingly upon them, and have translated as Dr. Newman did. The reading *salvatur* was adopted by the Anglican Grabe . . . Nor do I see that the reading makes any doctrinal difference . . .'

But it seems to me of little consequence, which reading is taken, since St Irenaeus also says 'causa facta est salutis.' 'Causa' is as strong as 'per'.

Besides, solvatur as the antithesis to 'adstrictum *morti*,' is equivalent to 'solvatur' in *vitam*. Besides it must be '*obedire Deo* uti . . . solvatur;' which makes the solutio more pointedly depend on the obedientia.

Do you see that our Bishop speaks against de Montfort's book as *a book*, and condemns the object (I think) with which it is written.[1]

You will be distressed to know (what is not decided, and, *please, don't mention it*) that it is very likely after all that I shall go to Oxford. I have been urged now for the third time. We have made conditions — but the chance is that they will be accepted. It is a great trial to me. I had quite given up the idea.

Ever Yours affectionately John H Newman

TO BISHOP ULLATHORNE

The Oratory. ⌐St George's day. 1866. [[April 23]

My dear Lord,

I hope you will not think us insensible to the great kindness and confidence shown us by your Lordship, in now renewing to the Oratory the offer of the Oxford Mission, if we venture to set before you several primâ facie difficult-ies,⌐ which stand in the way of our giving you an answer. It is the very import-ance of that offer, and our sense of our own insufficiency, which oblige us to do so.

1. We know that Catholics in Oxford are very eager to build a Church on a new site; and your Lordship has shared in their wish. With a view to it they have collected the sum of £187 which at present is in my hands; £300, I believe, is in your own, the contribution of a lady in Holywell Street; and Messrs Smith and Hanley have promised £200; that is, altogether £687. But this will go a very little way towards the expenses of ground and building, and these expenses would come upon us. Now, by the rule of the Oratory, one house cannot retain or govern another; each house must be distinct; as soon then as the Oxford Oratory is strong enough to go alone, the Birmingham Oratory must let it go. When that time comes, it will be found, that we have laid out time, trouble, and money at Oxford, which has been just so much loss to Birmingham, or nearly so; and the Oxford Mission Church, which we should have built, would be the measure and the monument of our injustice to our own successors here. How is the Oxford Mission, small moreover as it is, ever to repay us? Then, I have a difficulty of my own in undertaking a new Mission Church. I have, in my time, built three, or rather four, Churches;[2] and

---

[1] Towards the end of Bishop Ullathorne's letter in the *Tablet*, (7 April 1866). See Appendix.
[2] i.e. at Littlemore, at Alcester Street in Birmingham, the University church in Dublin, and at Edgbaston.

221

I know the toil and anxiety which such a work involves. It would be too much for my strength, and would hinder me giving my attention to the proper interests of the Oxford Oratory, and to the state of religious parties in the University.

This is the difficulty, — but we do not say it cannot be overcome; and we propose the following method of doing so to your Lordship's consideration. We have, as you know, a piece of ground of our own, opposite Christ Church. I gave you the other day its dimensions. It is probable, if we had the means, we could increase it on three sides, with a frontage on two streets. If we could not, we should have ultimately to place ourselves elsewhere; and if so, from its situation, and from the building movement now going on in the University and likely to continue, we do not anticipate any difficulty in parting with it advantageously, even though buildings were upon it. Under these circumstances we should feel no difficulty in undertaking at once to build an Oratory Church upon it. This Church would be used by us for the strict purposes of an Oratory, for sermons and lectures, for popular services, according as there was an opening for them, for confessions, and for Catholic young men at the Colleges, the charge of whom is an especially Oratorian work. But we would also lend it to our Missioner (that is, to one of the Fathers,[1]),) and to the Mission for the purposes of the Mission; that is, we would assign a certain number of sittings, and then charge the Mission a certain annual rent for the use of them. The Catholics of Oxford have already a sum in hand towards meeting this rent, viz. the £687 which I have mentioned above. They might put it out to interest for that purpose, and, if at length, years hence they thought it prudent in conjunction with the Oratory to build a new Church on a new site, it would be ready as a part of their contribution towards it. In the meanwhile, they would have the use of a Church without paying any thing for its erection; for the Oratory would build it from its own means and those of its friends. What rent the Oxford Catholics should pay to the Birmingham Oratory will be a future consideration.[2]

2. We are told that the Oxford Mission does not support a priest; this seems to me very unlikely. Your Lordship will be able to inform us on this point without trouble.[3]

3. A third and an obvious difficulty lies in the question, how we are to serve the Mission? We shall do so ourselves certainly, if it is possible; but our

---

[1] In the draft Newman wrote here in pencil 'of the Oratory'.

[2] Ullathorne, who acknowledged this letter on 28 April, replied on 22 May, saying as to this first point, 'certainly the Catholics of Oxford have long been anxious to have a Church in place of the poor contracted room in which the Catholic Religion has been so long concealed in that City. And were such a work commenced, I could not think but that external aid would be obtained to increase the very limited resources at present available . . .

Yet I believe that your building an Oratorian Church on the site contemplated would satisfy the desires of the Congregation, especially as it would bring the zeal of the Oratorian fathers to bear on that City.' Ullathorne expressed gratitude for the proposal to build the church exclusively from means provided by the Birmingham Oratory.

[3] Ullathorne thought that the increasing number of Catholics in Oxford would enable a priest to be supported.

Fathers are so few, that we must at least contemplate the chance of having to obtain the services of a resident Curate. But if so, what would be his relations to your Lordship? would you look to me, as directly responsible to you for the Mission, and not recognise him except as our assistant and subordinate? or would you think it right to put him (to the exclusion of us) in direct and immediate relations with yourself, as Fr Flanagan was at Smethwick? We feel, if the latter was the case, that he would practically be the head authority, and not we. *We* should go there (say) once a week, and we should find *him* at home there. And in consequence there might be collisions between him and us.[1]

4 We have a scruple arising from the course which Propaganda took in relation to Catholic youths at Oxford a year and a half ago. We did not expect it; and the Sacred Congregation may now again take some step which we do not anticipate, and thus accidentally derange our plans. Twice before that, Cardinal Barnabò had acted towards us with great abruptness, and on the latter of the two occasions had brought upon us much anxiety and considerable expense.[2] It would be imprudent in us not to guard ourselves now against a fourth mishap. Accordingly, we hope it is not too much to ask your Lordship to gain for us from the Sacred Congregation the necessary permission, that our House and Church at Oxford shall be considered an integral part of the Birmingham Oratory during my life time and for three years after it. We know Propaganda has great affairs to manage, and Cardinal Barnabò told me on one occasion with his own lips that the Oratory was of too little importance for me to have a right to petition (as I was doing) for a certain privilege in behalf of the London Oratory. This makes me feel so anxious on this point, that I do not see my way to incur any expense at Oxford in building or the like, till his Eminence makes the ground sure for us.

⌐5. This leads me to mention to your Lordship a last anxiety. My object in connecting myself with the Oxford Mission, is to be of such real and substantial service to the Catholic cause in Oxford, as God may permit. What shape that service may take, it is impossible to anticipate beforehand; but so far is clear, that the presence of Catholic young men in Oxford, be they many or few, will be of great use to us, as taking off the edge of the offence and irritation, which our going is likely to create there in many quarters, by suggesting an intelligible and reasonable motive for our taking that step. It is but natural and right, as all Protestants will feel, that the Catholic Bishop of the Diocese should protect the young members of his own communion; but it will be thought a simple aggression, if men who once belonged to the University, as ourselves, return thither as Catholics for no other assignable purpose than that

---

[1] See Memorandum of 17 May. Ullathorne approved of Newman's proposals and explained that 'the relations of the Oxford House and mission to the Bishop can be settled upon the principles and rules in operation with respect to Churches served by regulars.'

[2] The meeting of the English bishops at the request of Propaganda on 13 Dec. 1864 led to the collapse of the first plan for an Oratory at Oxford. For the other episodes see letters of 24 and 25 Nov. 1849, and the correspondence in the autumn of 1855 and Jan. 1856.

of preaching Catholic doctrine in a Protestant place of education. Now we are quite content that things should remain as they are; that Catholics should be discouraged going to Oxford without being forbidden; for our purpose ten Catholics are as good as a hundred; nor do we wish, as we did wish a year and a half ago, before the Bishops had spoken, to start by publishing any advertisement to the effect that we were going there avowedly for the sake of Catholic students. So far we have no difficulty; but we have heard with great concern, that a præceptum has been promulgated in the Diocesan Synod of Westminster, making it necessary for all priests within its jurisdiction to preach, argue, and bring about by all means and to the best of their power, the eschewing of Oxford by all Catholics. This step seems to us much in advance of what was done by the Bishops last March year; and, if it were taken in other dioceses, would indirectly affect our position at Oxford seriously. Shall we then be going too far, if we ask your Lordship, whether there is any chance of other Bishops following the example of the Archbishop? or again, of his decision in his own diocese becoming a rule for English Catholics by some act of Provincial Synod.[1]

I hope you will excuse the anxiety which has dictated these inquiries; and, let me beg your Lordship's blessing especially at this moment, when we have such a momentous question under consideration.

Your Lordship's obedient & affte Servant in Xt
⌐John H Newman⌐ of the Oratory

The Right Revd The Bishop of Birmingham

TUESDAY 24 APRIL 1866   Boys went to Rednall.   Mr Walker of Preston called
WEDNESDAY 25 APRIL   went to Town — saw Lintott and Clutton — returned

TO M. J. RHODES

The Oratory, Birmingham April 25. 1866
My dear Mr Rhodes,

If you knew how many engagements I have, and how tired my hand is with writing, I am sure you would not have let me correspond with you on any point of theology which was not of special importance.

[1] Ullathorne replied, 'With respect to the education of Catholics at the University, I can only refer to the decision of the Bishops already promulgated, to the effect that they hold it their duty to discourage Protestant university education for Catholics, a decision which the Holy See approves as in conformity with its own views; and which was published for the guidance of the clergy. What future steps the Bishops might think it their duty to adopt it is impossible for me to say from my present information; but should the practice of sending Catholics to the University grow much more frequent than at present, it would of necessity force on a reconsideration of the whole subject, and that in the direction of discouragement, and of finding, as far as possible, a practical remedy against this frequentation.' See also Memorandum of 17 May 1866, *Purcell* II, p. 300, and letter of 16 April 1867 to Ullathorne.

What I have said in my Letter was but a matter of fact, viz. that the Decree of 1854 did not deny that our Lady was under the debitum — that no Catholic was called to deny it — that I did not deny it — that Suarez, the greatest theological authority of these latter times, affirmed it.[1]

I did not say that every Catholic was obliged to affirm it — or that there was not a certain particular sense of the word in which divines, such as Viva and your own Jesuit author, considered that they were at liberty to deny it.

For myself, such subtleties, touch neither my heart nor my reason. They don't seem to me to add one atom of honour to our Lady — they do but deprive her Son of subjects. I do but associate them with the loss of souls. It would not lead me to say with a clearer conscience 'Per te, Virgo, sim defensus, in die judicii,' to have the misgiving within me, that by my officious zeal for her honour, I had prevented my brethren from submitting to the Catholic Church, and enjoying the blessings of Catholic communion.

I had rather be silent on the subject — but it would be rude in me not to write, considering you have showed your anxiety by four or five letters on it — and, if I do write, I can only write plainly what I feel.

I am, My dear Mr Rhodes, Sincerely yours in Christ
John H. Newman of the Oratory

M. J. Rhodes Esqr

April 26. Thank you for your kind letter of this morning.

TO G. D. BOYLE

The Oratory, April 28. 1866.

My dear Mr Boyle

You are quite right in thinking your most flattering proposal would astonish me. It has certainly done so — but, as is natural, it has gratified me quite as much, and made me feel grateful towards those persons, yourself especially, who have done me so great, and, as I cannot but be conscious, so little deserved an honor. But in a matter of this kind I must submit, rather than oppose myself, to their indulgent judgment of me, whatever may be my own feelings about it.

However, will it be ungracious in me, if I ask some short delay, before I

---

[1] In *A Letter to Pusey* Newman suggested that the doctrine of the Immaculate Conception was not universally accepted because 'to many it seemed to imply that the Blessed Virgin did not die in Adam, that she did not come under the penalty of the fall, that she was not redeemed,' whereas 'the doctrine meant nothing else than that in fact in her case the general sentence on mankind was not carried out, and that, by means of the indwelling in her of divine grace from the first moment of her being (and this is all the decree of 1854 has declared) . . .' Some theologians wished to argue that the Blessed Virgin was preserved not only from original sin, but from the obligation (debitum) of incurring it.

definitely answer you? Had it not been uncertain when you would reach home, I should have called on you today, instead of writing.[1]

I am, My dear Mr Boyle, Very sincerely Yours John H. Newman
The Revd G. D. Boyle

TO W. A. WEGUELIN

The Oratory, Birmingham April 28th. 1866
My dear Mr Weguelin,

I have not been neglectful of your wishes about your son's going to Oxford. I heard you were returning, and waited to write to you till I heard you had got back. This I did [not] hear till just now.

I should have written to you at Rome, but, to tell the truth, I have not been satisfied with your boy's progress since Christmas — but he certainly must exert himself more, if he is to go through this University respectably. I don't think he has been idle — but he has been giving his time to English verses — for writing which he has a turn. This, as you will agree with me, is very well in its way — but I hope he will really work hard this term.

This is what has kept me from getting his name put on the books of any of the Colleges — and then, as time went on, I thought I had better wait, as I have said, till your return.

The two Colleges I am led to recommend are Christ Church and Trinity. R. Ward is to be at the latter — several Edgbaston boys are, or are to be at the former. I made particular inquiries about Trinity, because it used to be a fast College — but I am told it is really changed in character now. The great recommendation of Ch. Ch. is that there are so many Catholics there, and that in a large College it is easier to choose the set in which one should like to live, than in a smaller. I suspect the entrance examination is more difficult at Trinity. Towneley is going to Ch. Ch. As Trinity was my own College, I have a liking for it, which makes *me* recommend it. I know some of the authorities — I know nothing of Ch. Ch. Father St. John, however, is of Ch. Ch. and recommends it instead of Trinity.

You will see that it does not seem to matter a great deal, which College he goes to. Perhaps *you* will have a choice — if not, I will make up my mind, and, in your name, write to the proper person.[2]

Very sincerely yours, John H. Newman of the Oratory.

W. A. Weguelin Esqre

[1] Boyle wanted Newman to have his portrait painted for the Midland Institute, in Birmingham. Newman, after twice refusing, eventually accepted. See letters of 7 May 1866 and 3 Sept. and 8 Dec. 1867. The portrait, painted in 1874 by W. T. Roden, eventually went to Manchester.
[2] But see letter of 29 July to Weguelin.

The Oratory April 29/66

My dear Child

I congratulate you with all my heart.[1] May all the best blessings descend upon you, and be with you. I will say a Mass for you to morrow morning, St Philip and St James.

Yours most sincerely in Xt   John H Newman of the Oratory

Miss Orpen

TO E. B. PUSEY

The Oratory, Birmingham April 29/66

My dear Pusey

I am grieved to think it vexes you so much to hear of the chance of our going to Oxford.[2] You may be sure we should not go to put ourselves in opposition to you, or to come in collision with the theological views which you represent. Of course we never could conceal our convictions, nor is it possible to control the action of great principles when they are thrown on the face of society — but it would be a real advantage to the cause of truth, if our opinions were known more accurately than they are generally known by Anglicans. For instance, what surprise has been expressed at what I have said in my Letter to you about our doctrine of original sin and the Immaculate Conception! even now most men think that I have not stated them fairly. And so with many other doctrines. I should come to Oxford for the sake of the Catholic youth there, who are likely to be, in the future, more numerous than they are now — and my first object *after* that would be to soften prejudice against Catholicism by shewing how much exaggeration is used by Anglicans in speaking of it. I do trust you will take a more hopeful view of my coming, if I do come, which is not certain. Personally, it would be as painful a step as I could be called to make. Oxford never can be to me what it was. It and I are severed, it would be like the dead visiting the dead. I should be a stranger in my dearest home. I look forward to do it with great distress — and certainly would not contemplate it except under the imperative call of duty. But I trust that God will strengthen me, when the time comes, if it is to come — and I trust He will strengthen you.

[1] On her engagement to Marmion Ferrers of Baddesley Clinton, whom she married on 18 July 1867. See also letter of 30 April 1866 to E. H. Dering.

[2] In reply to Newman's letter of 20 April, Pusey wrote, 'Thank you for the information which you have given me. The one thing which I have desired is not to be in collision with you. Perhaps before you come, I shall be gone. A little more than 4 years will complete the threescore and ten.

The memorial of dearest J. K. [Keble] seems likely to take the shape of a College for diligent students living simply (100 of them) I took a part in promoting it. Had I known the intention of your authorities, I don't think I could have done it i.e. had the heart to do it.'

I wish I could do more than lament over the misunderstandings which you suffer at the hands of Catholics — but it is the necessary penalty of controversialists. I do all I can against it, but can do very little. I can't be sorry that you are about de Bandelis — for it is well to have all the facts out in the light of day.[1] So far you *must* be doing a service. When you really take a thing up, you do it thoroughly — the complaint which our people made of you was, that there are many points which you had *not* really taken up. God bless you, my dear Pusey, and comfort you in your present bereavement

Ever Yours affectly John H Newman

MONDAY 30 APRIL 1866   Dr Case came   bitter wet weather

TO EDWARD HENEAGE DERING

The Oratory Bm April 30/66

My dear Mr Dering

Thank you for the very pleasant news which you have sent me this morning. It is very kind of you, to have done so. It must be a great satisfaction to you and Lady Chatterton. I inclose a few lines for Miss Orpen.

By a strange mishap, just as I am beginning to write to you, I have mislaid your letter — and cannot recollect what else I had to say to you.

I wish you had some real literary work to do. The volumes you were kind enough to give me, showed me that you could undertake some serious matter, if you would. But it should be a real work — and should be an occupation.

I am glad to say that Leonore is reviewed in the Month[2]

Very sincerely yours in Xt   John H Newman of the Oratory

TUESDAY 1 MAY 1866   Dr Case went   my first cold these two years   snow, sleet

TO HENRY JAMES COLERIDGE

The Oratory Bm May 1/66

My dear Fr Coleridge

My hand is so tired I can hardly make strokes. I intend tonight to send up 18 pages of my Article to you — one of my pages makes one of the Month's I think. About 5 or 6 more are to come; they are all but finished.[3]

---

[1] Pusey was pursuing the controversy over the Immaculate Conception, which was denied by Vincent Bandellus (1435–1506), who claimed, unwarrantedly, to have two hundred theologians on his side.
[2] *Leonore, a Tale,* by Lady Chatterton, was reviewed in the *Month,* (May 1866), pp. 531–3.
[3] The article on Seeley's *Ecce Homo.*

If you think it well to send the 18 which I send you to the press, bidding the printer to send the proof to *me*, and allow me to send the rest straight to the printer with a like message, it will be all ready for your literary and theological animadversions by the time you are out of retreat. Is it your way to have copy put in *slips* instead of pages? *If* so, mine had better be in slips. I have been at it today for eight hours, and shall require at least one more, before I get tonights parcel off

    Very sincerely Yours in Xt John H Newman of the Oratory
The Revd Fr Coleridge

P.S. Post time has come and the 18 pages are not throughout corrected — so I must send them up tomorrow (Wednesday) night.

WEDNESDAY 2 MAY 1866 dark
THURSDAY 3 MAY very dark, almost needing candles at 11 ⟨candles quite necessary. I have lit them.⟩ Dr Moriarty came
SATURDAY 5 MAY Dr Moriarty went

TO JOHN THOMAS WALFORD

        The Oratory Bm May 6. 1866
My dear Mr Walford,

  Thank you much for your very pleasant and kind letter. Though we do not pretend to give a high remuneration, we could never think of accepting your services without acknowledging them — but your kindness would remain the same, whatever was our ultimate determination.

  I shall be disappointed if you don't come soon — for time is going on, we cannot hope you can give much time to us, and we wish to make the most of you while we have you. We have a youth preparing for his entrance and little go at Oxford — and you could be of much use to him, especially in Latin composition

    Very sincerely Yours in Xt John H Newman of the Oratory
J. Walford Esqr

TO G. D. BOYLE

              May 7/66
My dear Mr Boyle

  I called on you last week with the hope of explaining better than can be done on paper some of the reasons which made me hesitate in at once availing myself of an honour which for the very reason it was so high I should not be duly appreciating if I lightly accepted it from the gentlemen you represent.[1]

---

[1] See letter of 28 April to Boyle.

I am deeply conscious that I have been of no use whatever to this great Town. I have in no way forwarded its various interests. I have almost been a stranger amid its large population — nor have I had any share in the establishment of the great institution which you propose to make the place of record of the honour you think of doing me.

This consideration causes me much perplexity how to answer you. It has led me to take advice of friends, and their feeling about it has sanctioned [?] my own.

I hope you will not consider it ungracious in me thus to scruple to accept so rare a kindness as you have been the medium of offering me. Any how, even though it is not carried out in the event according to your intention, I shall still have the satisfaction of possessing in your letter on the subject, the memorial of my good fortune in having excited so warm an interest in my behalf in the minds of persons whom I have not the pleasure of knowing

JHN

WEDNESDAY 9 MAY 1866   engaged this month in finishing Article on the Ecce Homo — and in teaching the boys for the Play.[1]   cold wind all thro' the month.

TO MRS JOHN MOZLEY

The Oratory Bm May 12. 1866

My dear Jemima

I have been made rather uneasy by seeing that the Derby Banks have been affected by this London panic. I hope it has not been a trouble to any of you.[2]

I have not forgotten the Characters[3]

Yours affly John H Newman

Mrs J. Mozley

TO SIR FREDERIC ROGERS

The Oratory, Birmingham. May 13th. 1866

My dear Rogers,

I hope you have not thought I have been neglectful on the subject of your last letter, because I did not write to you.[4] The chief cause of my silence has been the fear I did not do justice to the book you spoke so highly of, and a

[1] *Pincerna,* 'The Cup-Bearer,' Newman's adaption of Terence's *Eunuchus.*

[2] The failure of the firm of Overend Gurney and Co. was followed by many others, on 'Black Friday' 11 May, and the Bank of England Charter had to be suspended.

[3] Jemima had asked to see the characters which Samuel Rickards told from handwriting, of some of Newman's Oriel friends in 1827. See *Moz.* I, p. 168. On one of these Newman has written, 'June 4/66 J C M [Mozley] has just told me by letter that this character is Isaac Williams — and that it was given by Mr R. in his drawing room September 27. 1836'

[4] See letter of 18 Jan. 1866 to Rogers, concerning Seeley's *Ecce Homo.*

wish to be more enthusiastic about it than I felt I was. But, to speak honestly, I can't be. And I wish to agree with you too earnestly, to like to be obliged to say so.

What curious tests such differences of feeling and judgment are of some latent difference of mental position! Let me be honest, and say that I had the greatest difficulty to get on with the book; and, having other things to do, broke down, and put it aside. This process has been repeated more than once — and now, though I suppose I have got through it, yet whatever probability there is of my judgment being unfair about it, lies in the extreme want of interest which has attended my perusal of it.

There seemed to me little new in it, but what was questionable, or fanciful. And it seemed to me that the author treated things as discoveries, when they were only new to him.

At the same time the book, I grant, is full of interest as a sign of the times — and as likely to influence the course of thought, as it is now running in the religious world.

I am sorry to say all this, and do pay me off, by saying you have attempted to get through (a very different composition) the Newcomes — and the more you read, the less you like it.

So, Mrs. Keble is gone at last — What a strange time of suffering she has had; and how touching that two brothers should marry two sisters, and then that the one pair in their old age should nurse and bury the other.[1]

I may be in London in June for a day or two, and shall try to find you out. I don't know my movements yet.

Ever yrs affly John H. Newman.

TO THOMAS HARPER, S.J.

The Oratory Birmingham May 14. 1866

My dear Fr Harper

I hope I shall not be encroaching on your or your Father Superior's kindness in the request I am about to make. Our Fathers here have urged me to do so.

It is to ask you to preach in our Church here on St Philip's Day, which we keep on the 30th instant, next Wednesday fortnight.

Of course we should be very sorry if you put yourself out of the way, or if you felt a difficulty in saying 'No.' We are not asking you to more than a sort of family meeting. We are not a great place as London is. A few parents of our boys will be here — It is no great compliment in the way of external recommendations — but we ask you, at least I do, from gratitude which I personally

---

[1] i.e. Thomas Keble and his wife Elizabeth Clarke, sister of John Keble's wife Charlotte, who died on 11 May, six weeks after her husband.

feel to you and your community for the letter I lately had from you, which leads me to wish that, by doing a favour to St Philip, you will gain a return which I cannot give you.[1]

Don't suppose you need make any extraordinary preparation — if so, I shall have to apologise for the shortness of notice. But a few words, spoken in honour of the Saint to those who come together for his sake, will come home to our hearts, without exertion on the part of the preacher.

After the Vespers on Tuesday we act a Latin Play — and after High Mass on Wednesday, we have (if the weather is fine) a dejeuner at our Cottage a few miles out of Birmingham.

Hoping you will be able to come, but not at all wondering if you can't[2]

I am My dear Fr Harper, Sincerely Yours in Xt

John H Newman of the Oratory

The Revd Fr Harper S.J.

TO W. J. COPELAND

The Oratory. Bm May 15. 1866

My dear Copeland

I am very glad to hear from you — I am always thinking of you and your brother. Your account of him might be better: and I grieve to hear of your news from Cornwall.

It would be very pleasant, if you thought of coming here from Cheltenham. My only reluctance is, that we are very busy just now, and I could not give you as much time as I could wish. St Philip's feast day is at hand — After first Vespers we have a play of Terence. *I* have given it a new name and cut out what is objectionable — and Ambrose and I are hard at it, teaching the boys.

In June, early I think, I shall be in Town — and I thought of running down for a night at Farnham, if it was convenient to you.

T. Keble was kind enough to write me a line on the day his sister-in-law died. It is most touching that he should bury two. £50,000 is an immense undertaking. I suppose you would not have begun it, unless it was to succeed.[3]

Do you know (though nothing is settled, and I don't want it mentioned) there is still a notion of my going to Oxford? Our Bishop has now spoken to me about it, for the third time. I have made conditions, and am not sure they will be granted.

Ever Yours affly John H Newman

The Rev W. J. Copeland

[1] See letter of 12 Feb. 1866 to Harper.
[2] See letter of 20 May to Harper.
[3] i.e. for the college at Oxford in memory of Keble. See note to letter of 29 April to Pusey.

TO SIR FREDERIC ROGERS

The Oratory, Birmingham. May 15th. 1866.

My dear Rogers,

I am quite ashamed at receiving from you so touching an answer to a letter which I wrote with great diffidence, yet wishing to be honest. I feel every word you say and, I think, heartily concur in it — but I am far from sure that you do not see into the book in other respects more truly and more deeply than I do. I know of old, whether I may happen in the particular case to agree with you or not, how much there is always in your judgments, and therefore I am quite sad to think that you should speak, as you do in the first sentence of your letter, of the first effect on you of reading what I said. Now don't smile at this, nor think I am writing too seriously, for, I think I love you too well not to wish you to agree with me, yet it annoys me to think that you should take me, or my words, at more than they are worth.

I see and feel quite what you say about the difficulty of introducing Catholic thoughts into liberal minds, and about the necessity of a liberal calculus, and you, who must see more of liberals than I do, are better able than I to understand how skilfully the work does this — Were I sure, or did I suspect, that it was done by the author designedly, I should feel great interest in him — As it is, I do not go further than to welcome him heartily, though he 'followeth not us',[1] and look with great hope on the effect of his work on the religious world. What on earth, or rather below the earth can Lord Shaftesbury really intend by his Exeter Hall judgment upon the book?[2]

If I am in London, it will be to sit for my bust to Woolner.[3] I don't know whether I stop a day or a week. I don't think I could come to you, thank you. If I stay anywhere, I suppose Bellasis will kindly take me in. But I hope to find you out.

Ever yours affectionately, John H. Newman.

TO HENRY WILBERFORCE

The Oratory Bm ⌜May 15. 1866⌝

My dear H W

We shall be much pleased to have Wilfrid, if you really think it is for his good. I mean, if you do not feel it will be a disadvantage to him to come back,

[1] *Mark* 9:38.
[2] At a meeting of the Church Pastoral Aid Society on 12 May, Lord Shaftesbury denounced *Ecce Homo* as 'the most pestilential book ever vomited from the jaws of hell.' See Edwin Hodder, *The life and work of the Seventh Earl of Shaftesbury*, London 1886, III, p. 164.
[3] Mrs Combe wrote on 23 Feb. 1866 asking Newman to sit for his bust, which, after her death and that of her husband, was to pass to Oxford University. She asked if she might put Thomas Woolner in touch with him, and Newman arranged with him to go to London in June. The bust is now in the National Portrait Gallery. The first cast was in 1916 presented to Cherwell Edge Convent, Oxford, by the Misses Woolner.

when those boys he knew are either gone, or have got into a higher form than perhaps his illness has admitted of his taking.

Come not later than the first days of June, if possible — as I expect to have an engagement in London which I shall be obliged to keep soon after June begins. I hope you have quite got over your illness, though this is not very good weather for recruiting. ⌐I suppose you have seen in the Papers that Mrs Keble is gone. She suffered a great deal at last; so, Keble was spared a great deal. When I found she was surviving, it struck me (I trust it is a really charitable thought) that she was to be kept awhile to do penance for having kept Keble from being a Catholic. I hope they are now both in that blessed state, where no one can ever sin again.⌐

With my affectionate remembrance of your wife, and your daughters, (unless they are in London) and Wilfrid

Ever Yours John H Newman of the Oratory

P.S. Our Secretary has thought you would wish to see the state of our account — so I inclose it.

TO AUGUSTINE FRANCIS HEWIT

The Oratory Bm May 16. 1866

My dear Fr Hewit,

I have had your Volume on my table and in my mind ever since I received it. Though I did not acknowledge it, I felt very much the kindness of the gift, and also of the words you had written in it. And now after all, before I have done such justice, as I could wish, to its most interesting contents, I write to you, lest you should think me very ungrateful and give me up.[1]

It does not need me to tell you how touching your Memoir of your dear friend is, for every one must have told you that already, who has looked into it. But to me it has a special interest, over and above its own, from the circumstance that I have for so many years followed the history of the religious school in the United States, of which you tell us so much, as far as I have had the opportunity of doing so. My first interest in your ecclesiastical affairs was raised by Bishop Chase, not a very high Churchman certainly, who dined with us at Oriel on the day I received the Anglican diaconate.[2] About the same time I saw Bishop Hobart in Oxford; and at a later time I made the acquaintance of Bishop Doane, when the Anglican movement was far advanced.[3] Perhaps it was from the likeness to Hurrell Froude, which you

---

[1] This was evidently the *Life of Rev. Francis A. Baker,* New York 1865.
[2] 13 June 1824. Philander Chase (1775–1852), a Low Churchman, was Bishop of Ohio, 1819–31, and then of Illinois (1835–52). He was in England in 1824 on a begging tour.
[3] Bishop Hobart of New York was at Oxford in March 1824. See *Moz.* I, p. 83, and 'The Anglo-American Church' in *Ess.* I, pp. 309–86. Bishop Doane of New Jersey visited England in 1841 and defended *Tract XC.* See also R. D. Middleton, *Newman at Oxford,* pp. 50–1.

suggest, but for some reason or other I was much moved by what I heard of Arthur Carey. On his death I put down his name in my Obituary under date of April 4, 1844; and daily, every since I have been a priest, up to this very morning, I have, before I began my Mass, mentioned his name with that of Hurrell Froude and of other Anglican friends, in my Preparation, recommending them to the mercy of God.[1]

I wish there was a chance of your visiting this country, that I might learn from you more of the things among you which have so long and so deeply interested me, and might have an opportunity of showing you the gratitude which I feel for the warmth with which you have so perseveringly thought, and now have written about me.

Mr Searle, who has been lately here, tells me that Fr Tillotson is better. It gave me great pleasure to hear it.

I am, My dear Fr Hewit, Most sincerely Yours in Xt
John H. Newman of the Oratory

The Revd Fr Hewit

TO MARIANNE FRANCES BOWDEN

The Oratory Bm May 17. 1866

My dear Child,

I hope you and your sisters will come to our Play. It is Latin certainly — but I send by this post an English Libretto. which I address to Fanny [Frances Jane Bowden], lest she should think I bear a grudge against her for her many acts of tyranny

Ever Yours affectly John H Newman of the Oratory

Miss Bowden

TO JAMES HOPE-SCOTT

The Oy Bm ⌐May 17. 1866

My dear Hope Scott

I have just had a long talk with our Bishop about the Oxford scheme. He has left me a good deal down-hearted. If there was a chance of your coming here, it would be most opportune, for it is a perplexing matter. I think I shall be in London for a day or two in June, and then at least shall try to see you⌐

Yours affly John H Newman[2]

[1] On Arthur Carey (1822–44), see letter of 23 Feb. 1863 to Copeland.
[2] Newman also sent the following:

'Oratory School
St Philip's Day 1866.
On Tuesday Evening May 29, after first Vespers will be performed

MEMORANDUM. INTERVIEW WITH BISHOP ULLATHORNE

May 17th 1866.

4.35 p m.   The Bishop is just gone. He has left a depressing effect on my mind — he has almost put me in a fix what to do about Oxford. Yet it is most difficult to back out.

He began by saying in reference to my letter which he had in his hand that there was one point on which he was clear that there must be no divided responsibility — he had put my letter on the question to the Vicar General and to Mr Estcourt separately and they came to the same conclusion that he had done.[1] During some minutes conversation I had not a dream what he meant, and fancied he was approving and assenting to our wish that the Curate should be entirely under us — but at length it turned out that he did not approve of our lending our church to the Mission and after considerable beating about he pitched on the phrase in my letter, 'the Missioner will pay the Oratory so much a year for the use of the Church' when I explained to him that it was only a logical distinction for the sake of clearness for the Missioner would be one of ourselves and it would be only a mode of expressing, our way of repaying ourselves by the Mission, parallel to the Oratory paying its Missioner who is one of themselves for his trouble (e.g. for his cabs etc) he said his objection was instantly taken away. In our previous conversation on the point, while we were beating about the bush, he had said the building of the Mission Church could not be delayed. I answered 'then I feared that would put an end to the whole negotiation.' I then urged that I thought our site a very bad one for a mission Church, though good for an Oratory — that it ought to be in St Giles's, in order to command both the railway quarter and the New Park Town — that I hoped that the mission would so increase in time that it need not be dependant on the Oratory — on

The Pincerna
commencing at half past Eight p.m.

——:——

Characters

Phaedria	. . . .	Pope	Chremes	. . . .	Charlton
Parmene	. . . .	Sparrow	Dorias	. . . .	Wheble
Thais	. . . .	Gaisford	Dorus	. . . .	Bellasis
Gnatho	. . . .	Weguelin	Sanga	. . . .	Preston
Chaerea	. . . .	Simeon	Sophrona	. . . .	Wingfield
Thraso	. . . .	Shiel	Laches	. . . .	Wild
Pythias	. . . .	Gould			

The Fathers of the Oratory hope to be honoured with the presence of Mr Hope-Scott at the performance.

May 17 1866.

My dear Hope Scott.
                    It would be too good tidings to be realized, to find you can come — but I send this for the chance. We can give you a bed.

Yrs affly J.H.N.

[1] Letter of 23 April.

236

consideration he seemed to allow all this and to withdraw his difficulty. Returning to his real hitch of the double responsibility I clenched my explanation by inserting in my letter after the word Missioner in the passage above referred to, the words 'That is one of the Father's of the Oratory.'[1] In this I feel I have gone somewhat too far — for I have in my letter, taking my words in their letter pledged myself, that one of our Fathers should be the Missioner.

All he could say on the question about the Mission supporting itself was, that somehow the Priest had always got on there. Then came the question of the prohibition of the Catholic youths going to Oxford. He conceived that the Archbishop's præceptum was not stronger than the act of the Bishops of March 24. 1865, which of course may be taken in two ways, and he seemed to take it in the sense of raising the force of the prohibition on the part of the Episcopal meeting of last year. He allowed that it could not be called improbable that in a provincial Synod the subject of a prohibition would be mooted, that the Archbishop was very decided on the point. That for himself speaking of his view of the matter at this moment he thought it imprudent to run the chance of the Bishops setting themselves against the laity, in a matter not of faith or morals. It would be decided by the majority in the Synod. On my happening to say that I had dissuaded Lady Wolseley from sending her son there, he said 'that he was struck at my saying so, for that she had every-where said the reverse.' I said I thought that young men would go whether the Bishops wished it or no. He said 'What he should like would be to pick the men who were to go, that there were two men there who were doing the Catholic body great credit. That Weld Blundell had got into disgrace.'

I asked 'What would he say, if we proposed to return our Church on the Bishop's hands and retire from the Mission in case the Synod moved in the matter.' He answered, 1st that it would be open to us to ask his interpretation of the act (of the Synod), and he should give it. For the Bishops need not take precisely the same view of it. Next he said 'That of course we were at liberty to retire.' I said 'That it would be so very painful to us to be brought into direct collision with the authorities at Oxford as we should be if there were no Catholic young men there and it would be so great a disadvantage to have the University in open opposition to us that I doubted whether we should not do more good at a little distance from Oxford as e.g. at Birmingham than to be in possession of the Oxford Mission' He said 'I perfectly feel what you say — of course you must have considered it well, if you (meaning me personally) appeared at Oxford yourself once or twice you might excite the University against you and its power is so great that it even might get a law passed to cripple your operations and so as regards your success in the mission also.' (I am not sure that I understood him here.)

He treated very lightly the application to Propaganda, and said he would make it at once.

---

[1] The last three words were only inserted in Newman's draft, not in the letter sent.

In conclusion, digressing to other topics, he expressed 'his regret which was shared by others that I had allowed Oxenham to dedicate to me a work of Dollinger's.' I answered 'that I could not refuse his application without acting as if from party spirit, that I did not see what reason I could give for such a course and that I felt, as doubtless the Archbishop did when he allowed Ward to dedicate his recent volume to him.' He said something of Oxenham's 'forwardness in writing on theology though a layman, without position' and I answered 'that he shared that disadvantage with Ward.' He seemed to be not at all indisposed to stop Ward and Oxenham too.[1]

Soon after this he went away.

My impression is, from this conversation, that on going we shall come into collision both with the (people of the) Mission and the University. With the people of the Mission because we will not build them a church and take of them a rent for the use of ours, and with the University from the great probability that after all only a few Catholic youths will be in residence to form an apology for our going there. Our missionary efforts will be simply stifled, both as to the University and the town, and we shall be left to waste our time on the meagre remnant of Catholics who at present constitute the Mission,

On reflection, it seems to me we have certainly brought out very clearly, what perhaps we were not aware we had in view, that the Oratory's connexion with the Oxford mission would be only temporary — so long, that is, as the mission could not support itself by itself, with an independent Oratory at its elbow and no longer. Above I have spoken of a prospective Mission Church on a different site from our own present ground — and I have implied that it would depend on the converts in Park Town or Villas and on the Irish in the New Great Western works; while the Oratory would find its own work in the University. I think this is a just view, but it may have frightened the Bishop.

TO THOMAS HARPER S.J.

The Oratory Bm May 20. 1866

Mr dear Fr Harper

I know too well the misery of being in a Printers hands not at once to pity you and to understand, loss as it is to us, why we cannot have you on our Feast day.

It is good news to find that we are soon to have a book from you — and a pleasant thought that your labours are so near their termination[2]

Very sincerely Yrs John H Newman

[1] See letters of 16 and 20 March to Oxenham, and First Memorandum of 26 March.
[2] *Peace through the Truth; or Essays on subjects connected with Dr. Pusey's Eirenicon,* First Series.

TO HENRY JAMES COLERIDGE

The Oratory Bm May 22/66

My dear Fr Coleridge

Thank you for making the correction. If there were no other good in it, there is this which is a great relief to me, — it is a sensible proof that careful eyes have been at my Article. My ambiguity arose from the circumstance, that in English 'tradition' is both the act and the thing, the modus tradendi and the res tradita. I was speaking of the res tradita which is one — but there are two channels of information, Scripture and Tradition. You could not have put a better word than 'account,' as you have done.[1]

I am very sorry that your Article on Keble has been attacked; and cannot conceive why? is it for what you leave out? that you have not said that he died without hope? or that he rejected grace? You have not done so certainly — but it is very hard if you may not state the facts of a man's history and character, and there leave the matter. If you have any means of knowing, I shall be very glad, if at some time you tell me what the definite charge is that is brought against the Article.

Most sincerely Yours in Xt   John H Newman of the Oratory

The Revd Fr Coleridge S.J.

TO EMILY BOWLES

The Oratory Bm May 23. 1866

My dear Child

I was deeply concerned to learn from the Papers Lady G. F's new sorrow, and I said Mass for her intention upon it.[2]

I should have written to you before this to say so, but I have hoped day by day to tell you something of this Oxford scheme, but I have nothing to tell. It is just a month today since we sent in our remarks on the Bishop's offer, and he has not yet replied. He called, and asked the meaning of some parts of the letter, and no answer has come. I do not think his hesitation arises so much from any thing we have said, as from a vague misgiving when it comes to the point, and perhaps from what people say to him. Two years ago there was a bold assertion that I was just the last man whom Oxford men would bear to be in Oxford, and from something the Bishop said it would appear that this idea is not altogether without effect upon him. I wish it were decided one way or the other — for it keeps us in various ways in suspense. It must now be

---

[1] 'In that first age they [the books of the New Testament] were the only account of the mode in which Christianity was introduced to the world.' 'Ecce Homo,' The *Month* (June 1866), p. 554; *D.A.*, p. 368.
[2] Lady Georgiana Fullerton's only sister, the wife of the fourth Baron Rivers, died on 30 April, two days after Lord Rivers. They left one delicate son, who died in 1867, and seven daughters.

decided for good and all — for my age neither promises a future, nor is consistent with this work-impeding uncertainty.

We are going to have a Latin Play next week in honour of St Philip — I wish you were with us

Every Yours affectly in Xt   John H Newman of the Oratory

Miss Bowles

TO H. A. WOODGATE

⌐May 23. 1866

I fear it is no compliment to ask you to our Play . . . We have asked several neighbouring clergymen, among them Dr Oldknow. I inclose a play bill⌐

TO MARIANNE FRANCES BOWDEN

The Oratory Bm May 24. 1866

My dear Child,

I know well how hard it is to bear trouble which we must keep to ourselves — and am very glad, and think it very kind, that you have said what you have said to me. I can only give you what I can — but that is what every one cannot give. I will please God, give you a Mass for your intention once a week for some time to come.[1]

Tell Fanny [Frances Jane Bowden] I am very glad she is coming, though it would be better if it were all of you. Now, my fear is about the weather. Rain is wanted to bring out the May — but, when it comes at all, it may come as a deluge, and we shall not get to Rednall at all.

Ever Yours affectly in Xt   John H Newman of the Oratory

Miss Bowden

TO MALCOLM MACCOLL

The Oratory, Birmingham. May 25. 1866

Dear Mr MacColl,

I am not the person to consult, when you want an opinion on so difficult a book as the Ecce Homo. I have not had time to do it justice; not did I find the book carry me on, as I had expected, and then, I was perplexed at the hypothesis started, (which your information seems to confirm) that the writer was a man of orthodox belief, simulating liberalism. And it seemed to me there was a spirit in the book, for which I had no sympathy, and its fancifulness indisposed me to take much interest in it on its own account.

I tell you just what I have felt about it, because you ask me, but not as at all depreciating it, or thinking lightly of the ability of the writer, (though there seemed to me a haziness about his fundamental position) or being insensible

---

[1] Miss Bowden perhaps thought of becoming a nun. See letter of 5 June to her. She was the eldest girl in a motherless family.

to its importance, as a sign of the times. The sensation it has made is certainly very remarkable, and means something or other.

If you wish to see more definitely what I think of it, I must refer you to an article in the forthcoming Number of the Month (for June), which expresses what I should say about it, if called on to bring out my meaning fully. At the same time I by no means consider the article a complete or adequate review of it.

Excuse a hasty note, and believe me,
Very truly yours, John H. Newman.

The Rev. M. MacColl.

P.S. I know from what Mr Gladstone wrote to me how kindly he thinks of me

TO W. J. COPELAND

The Oratory Birmingham May 27. 1866

My very dear Copeland

What a deal of trouble our merciful Lord brings upon you. I fear you must be very much pulled down. You may meet one of our boys on June 5 at Trinity — Richard Ward, the son of that lawyer who is brother to Richard Ward late demy of Magdalen (I think), a friend of Daman.[1] The boy left us a year ago, fairly prepared — and through the year has been at Darnell's on Grassmere. Whether he had got on well there, I don't know — but, unless he has a great deal of innate energy, he would have done more by remaining with us. I should think he is full young to pass the Trinity examination, which they tell me is severe.

You can't tell how very much down I am at the thought of going to Oxford, which is now very probable. I should not go there with any intention of catching at converts — though of course I wish to bring out clearly and fully what I feel to be the Truth — but the notion of getting into hot water, is most distasteful to me, now when I wish to be a little quiet. I cannot be in a happier position than I am. But were I ever so sure of incurring no collisions with persons I love, still the mere publicity is a great trial to me. And even putting that aside, the very seeing Oxford again, since I am not one with it, would be a cruel thing — it is like the dead coming to the dead. O dear, dear, how I dread it — but it seems to be the will of God, and I do not know how to draw back.

Keble's friends could hardly be pleased at movers, seconders, Bishops of Winton, £50,000, etc etc.[2] I so want to talk to you about half a hundred things

Ever Yours affly John H Newman

[1] Richard Ward went to Oriel College in 1830, but seems never to have been a Demy at Magdalen.

[2] At a meeting at Lambeth Palace on 12 May to arrange a memorial for Keble, the resolution that £50,000 should be raised for a college at Oxford was proposed by the Evangelical C. R. Sumner, Bishop of Winchester. As Keble's bishop he had long opposed him. The seconder of another motion was Robert Eden, Bishop of Moray and Ross, an opponent of the high church friend of Keble, A. P. Forbes, Bishop of Brechin.

TO SISTER MARY IMELDA POOLE

The Oratory, Bm May 27/66

My dear Sister Imilda

We all thank you for your Communions — St Philip has been very good to us, but we want him to be better still — for there is again a chance of the Oratory making its appearance in Oxford, and the prospect is a load which requires a great deal of faith and love to bear without wincing. I am so old, have so little strength, and so little heart for anything. It is pleasant to think that we have anticipated the Holy Father in joining together St Catharine and St Philip by saying Mass for you on her day, as you go to Communion for us on his. I wish they were joint protectors of Oxford, which might be a little Rome, if it were on the right side.[1]

You must not speak as if I had anything to bear in what has passed about my late Pamphlet. Nearly every one has been kind to it. Two bishops (one my own) have actually written to the public Papers in my behalf, and at great length. And in private (though I don't tell people this) a Benedictine Bishop has written to me about it in high terms of commendation[2] — so have a Community of Dominican Fathers — so has a Jesuit College — not to speak of other Jesuit Communities in England and Ireland; a prominent Irish Bishop, a friend at Maynooth[3] — a number of secular priests scattered about the Country[4] — and some of these persons with special reference to that particular portion of my Pamphlet, with which some persons are dissatisfied — So I have everything to be grateful for, and no draw backs —

Ever yours most sincerely in Christ   John H. Newman of the Oratory

TO MRS F. J. WATT (ELEANOR BRETHERTON)

The Oratory, Birmingham May 28/66

My dear Child

Thanks for your congratulations on the day. We do not forget though the Bride cake is gone. Fr Ambrose is afraid that Brenda will be too great a charge, and with many thanks declines it. I am glad to hear so good an account of you. As to the photographs, I have called, others have called, in vain, none have yet been sent to me.

All kind regards to Mr Watt and believe me ever yours affecty
John H Newman of the Oratory

P.S.   I wish indeed we could take so beautiful a dog — and am very loth to

---

[1] On 8 April Pius IX declared St Catherine of Siena Patron of Rome, in addition to St Philip.

[2] See the letters of 7 April, 17 March and 22 Feb., to Bishops Ullathorne, Clifford and Brown, who was a Benedictine.

[3] The Jesuit College was St Beuno's, the Irish bishop Moriarty, and from Maynooth Dr Russell.

[4] These included Husenbeth, Logan, Tate, John and William Walker, and Waterworth.

decline her. And it would be a nice remembrance of you — but we think we had better not. I hope the sale will go off well. Is Mama with you? my affectionate remembrances to her, if she is.

TUESDAY 29 MAY 1866   Walford came   first Vespers   2nd performance of Play, for boys' friends

WEDNESDAY 30 MAY   Kept St Philip's day.   Mass (Dr Case celebrant) coram Pontifice no Sermon, but account of St Philip's death.   party at Rednal.[1]

THURSDAY 31 MAY   Corpus Christi — I celebrant — Procession inside Church, etc.

TO E. B. PUSEY

The Oratory Bm May 31/66

My dear Pusey

It is absurd your asking me a question, which you cannot solve yourself. If I were asked to give the sense of 're' in the passage you quote, if that is your question, I should construe it by 'in return,' or the like, in opposition to Adam. Thus

'From the bond of the old sin the Mother of our Redeemer herself is not exempt; He alone, who nevertheless out of that debt in return (or by retaliation, alluding to the first Adam who incurred the debt,) is born, by the law of that ancient debt is not held.' This is the sense of 're' in repromissio, I suppose, which is a patristical word; and in other words, I think.

The papers say, you are going to America. I am afraid our clergy would be more severed from you there than they are in Europe. Father Hecker of New York is the only one I happen to know of, who would understand you[2]

Ever Yours affly John H Newman

The Revd E. B. Pusey D D

SUNDAY 3 JUNE 1866   Procession.   Ambrose celebrant.

[1] 'St Philip's Feast was kept first, by a High Mass with stringed instruments played chiefly by the boys, — then by a large party of guests and schoolboys being conveyed about seven miles in omnibuses and other carriages to spend the afternoon at Rednall, the Oratory country-house, where we had luncheon in a large covered pavilion. Everything was bright, gay with flowers, and festive with delightful conversation; the Father [Newman] himself attending to the guests and providing for their accommodation and comfort until absolutely forced by Father Ambrose with playful violence to keep his seat and take his own food. After the luncheon, or dinner, the boys chiefly resolved themselves into croquet and cricket parties, or quiet strolls with their own people among the guests, while a party was organised to walk over the famous bilberry hill so as to get an extensive view over many counties. ... To my infinite joy, for I had thought important guests would have claimed him, the Father came to say he was going to walk over the hill with me ...' Emily Bowles's account in her 'Memorials of John Henry Newman.'
[2] Pusey replied that he had not 'the slightest thought' of going to America.

MONDAY 4 JUNE   F Denny and Mr Morgan (American) to dinner[1]

TO MRS JOHN MOZLEY

The Oratory Bm June 4/66

My dear Jemima

I had just been saying Mass for the soul of Mary Kay, when your letter came about her.[2] Frank had told me of her death. I have ever thought of her with great tenderness, though I can't have seen her at least since 1812 — and therefore I am pleased to find she did not forget me.

I am sorry that you find Mrs Richards not so well as you had hoped. Say every thing kind from me to her and believe me

Ever Yours affly John H Newman

TO BISHOP ULLATHORNE

The Oratory, Bm June 4. 1866

My dear Lord,

I hope your Lordship will excuse the delay which has occurred in answering your letter of May 22, against our will.[3]

We thank you for the careful consideration which you have given to our difficulties in undertaking the Oxford Mission, and for the sight of your proposed letter to Propaganda, which I now return, and which fully expresses all that we could wish — which moreover, I take for granted, from what your Lordship said to me, will be as perfectly understood and accepted by Propaganda, as it is in itself exact and perspicuous.[4] On two occasions Cardinal

[1] They came with an introduction from James O'Connor, who had known Newman at Propaganda, 1846–7. O'Connor wrote on 21 May from the Seminary of St Charles at Philadelphia:

'The bearer, Rev. P. McC. Morgan, is on his way to England, to see what he can see there, and, perhaps, to apply for admission among the Oblates of St. Charles. He is accompanied by his old friend and college mate, Rev. H. Denny, already a member of that Congregation.'

Harmar Charles Denny, third son of Harmar Denny of Pittsburgh, Pennsylvania, was matriculated at St Mary's Hall, Oxford, on 1 Dec. 1853, aged twenty. He became a Catholic and was now an Oblate of St Charles, at St Mary's, Westbourne Grove, London. He later joined the New York Jesuits.

[2] Newman noted in his book of Anniversaries that Mary Kay died on 30 May 1866 at Midnight.

She was a relative of the Newman family and Jemima wrote to Newman on 14 June 1872 about the family's genealogy, 'now dear Mary Kay is gone there seems no one left who can tell us anything.'

[3] See notes to letter of 23 April to Ullathorne.

[4] Ullathorne's proposed letter of 23 May ran:

'Gulielmus Bernardus Ullathorne, Episcopus Birminghamiensis, ad genua Sanctitatis Vestrae provolutus, humiliter repraesentat quod in Civitate Oxfordensi nulla existat Ecclesia Catholica praeter parvam atque humilem Capellam in loco viliori suburbano abscondite positam, ubi temporibus difficilioribus Catholici conveniebant, atque etiam in hoc istud tempus

Barnabò has implied or asserted, in consequence of applications I made to him, that I wished to bring other Oratorians under me, contrary to the Rule of St Philip. It will be wonderful, if your letter, clear as it is, does not prevent his doing so a third time.

One only real difficulty remains in our undertaking a house at Oxford — and it is the pecuniary difficulty. We are even at present much straitened here for means. Our school has required large sums, which it does not enable us to replace; and our Fathers have not private means sufficient to meet the current expenses of a House such as this. It will be some years before we get clear of these embarrassments; and meanwhile, we cannot increase them by undertaking a new establishment at Oxford, without some clear prospect of meeting its liabilities. We consider that the expenses of an Oratory House, including rent, wages, board, coals, lights, washing, journeys from Birmingham cannot be brought under £200 or £250 a year. An Offertory can do nothing towards this sum, for it has its own objects to provide for, viz 1. salary of Missioner ⟨(say £40)⟩. 2. outlay of Sacristy — 3. music in Church. 4. poor school. Some means then must be found to meet this £250.

Your Lordship's reference to the 'Diocesan Administration' leads me to ask you the following question:– Would the Administrators take into their hands the management of the three following items of Mission property — 1. the £537 raised or promised for a new Mission Church. 2. the £745 which was made over to you by the Jesuit Fathers. 3. the St Clement's property, (House, Church, ground) valued at £1000, and pay us in turn out of it an income of £150 a year? These three items amount only to £2282, but the Oxford Catholics might increase their £537 by several hundreds, and the St Clement's property might let for a higher rent than the interest of the sum it would fetch if sold. If this could be done, we would risk the remaining £100 of the £250 ourselves; and we would engage, that, if the Offertory rose to more than that £100 above the expense of the four objects above set down, we would deduct that excess from the £150 which we received from the Diocesan Administration — e.g. if we gained by the offertory £20 over and above the

congregantur. Unde Revds Adm. Pater Newman Oratorii Birminghamiensis Praepositus, zelo animarum actus, proponit Oratorii Domum in celebri illa civitate, cum approbatione sui Episcopi, incipere et Ecclesiam modestam, suis atque amicorum impensis, super terram jam obtentam, erigere; cum intentione non solum, quae Oratorii sunt functiones peragendi sed insuper missioni illius civitatis inserviendi.

Cum vero Patres Oratorii pauci sunt numero, necesse erit ad effectum istius propositi ut ad tempus Domus Oxfordiensis inserviri possit a Patribus Oratorii Birminghamiensis, uno vel duobus ad illud opus deputatis, cum spe ultimè stabiliendi Oratorium distinctum apud Oxford; crescentibus scilicet numeris, atque mediis temporalibus, cum progressu temporis, auctis. Opus vero adeo pium, et non parvis sacrificiis instruendum nullo modo procedere possit, nisi Domus parvulus [sic] apud Oxford, usque dum robustior a teneris incoeptis insurgat, omnino atque in omnibus a Domo Birminghamiensi et ejus Superiore dependeat.

Proinde idem Episcopus Birminghamiensis humiliter supplicat Sanctitatem Vestram, ut dignetur modum expositum erigendi Domum et Ecclesiam Oratorii apud Oxford approbare, et cum conditione, quatenus vita Revdi Patris Newman durante, et saltem per tres annos post ejus decessum, Domus Oxfordiensis Oratorio Birminghamiensi atque ejus Superiori subjiciatur in omnibus, haud secus ac si haec duo unum Oratorium constituerent.' This letter was sent on 11 June. For the reply see the letters at 25 July.

£100 for the House, and the cost of Missioner, sacristy, music, and poor school, we would take from the Administration £130 instead of £150 — and so on[1]

Begging your Lordship's blessing I am,
Your Lordship's obt & affte Servt in Xt
John H Newman of the Oratory

The Rt Revd The Bp of Birmingham

TO EDWARD BADELEY

The Oratory Birmingham June 5. 1866

My dear Badeley

I meant before this to have written to you on a matter in which you have been so very kind, on Bellasis's suggestion, to anticipate me. It was only in consequence of the many engagements which pull me about, and the many letters which I have had to write, that I did not write to you days ago. You know what it is I mean, and I find from Bellasis this morning that you are really giving time to it and that he is to see you again tomorrow.

Walford, as perhaps he told you, is brother of Edward Walford, who has made a mess of his Catholicity — but perhaps this brother, who has lately been received, will set him right.[2] He has been a prominent Tutor at Eton — and we are very glad to have him in our school. Whether he is able from circumstances to retain his fellowship or no, it would be a great point to prove that he has the legal right.[3] It might influence the determination of the question at Oxford and the position of Catholicism in Oxford would be wonderfully changed, if it could have its professors among the resident and governing body of the place. As it is very likely that the Oratory after all may be going to Oxford, I look forward to your view of Walford's case with special interest, not only for his sake, but on our own account.

I hope before long to have the opportunity of putting my head into your chambers, and taking the chance of your being at leisure for a gossip. It is a long time since I saw you. I wish you could have seen our play last week — it would have been as good as a week at Scarbro' to you, I am vain enough to think. Of course spectators are lenient, and look at exhibitions of the kind on their fair side but they seemed very much pleased, and I think with reason

Ever Yours affly John H Newman of the Oratory

E. Badeley Esqr

[1] See letter of 8 June.
[2] See letters of 13 May and 19 Aug. 1860 to Edward Walford.
[3] J. T. Walford was a Fellow of King's College, Cambridge, 1855–66.

The Oratory Bm June 5/66

My dear Bellasis

I am ashamed to think that your zeal for me should have exceeded my attention to my own promise of writing to Badeley. I did not at all forget it, but I had so many letters to write that I had not yet done it. I have done it now. I was very glad of the opportunity to write, since it is so long since I have seen or heard of him.

Some time this month I am coming to Town on business — I don't yet know when — but I shall ask to take advantage one night of your hospitality at the Lawn.[1] Thank you for your great promptness about Walford — it is most kind of you, considering all your engagements. We sent in yesterday what may be called a final letter to the Bishop on the subject of Oxford — our taking the Mission now turns simply upon the money question — for we cannot lay out a penny in housekeeping there, which is not by hook or by crook, found for us. When this is arranged, we shall have the great difficulty come upon us, who is to go there. I don't think I asked you to thank Mrs Bellasis for her very kind letter to me — so I will ask you now.

Yours affly In Xt   John H Newman of the Oratory

Mr Serjeant Bellasis

The Oratory Birmingham June 5 1866

My dear Child,

Fanny [Frances Jane Bowden] told me about you, as doubtless she has told you. I will not forget the Masses — they will help you, and you must simply put yourself into God's hands. As I understood F. you have no call on you to do any thing, or to decide on doing any thing, at this moment. Do you know, though this is of course a trial, yet I have ever felt it a great mercy. One of the greatest of trials is, to have it cast upon one to make up one's mind, — on some grave question, with great consequences spreading into the future, — and to be in doubt what one ought to do. You have not this trial — it is also a trial to wait and do nothing but how great a mercy is it not to have responsibility! Put your self then, my dear Child, into the hands of your loving Father and Redeemer, who knows and loves you better than you know or love yourself. He has appointed every action of your life. He created you, sustains you, and has marked down the very way and hour when He will take you to Himself. He knows all your thoughts, and feels for you in all your sadness more than any creature can feel, and accepts and makes note of your prayers even

_____
[1] Bellasis's house at Putney.

247

before you make them. He will never fail you — and He will give you what is best for you. And though He tries you, and seems to withdraw Himself from you, and afflicts you, still trust in Him, for at length you will see how good and gracious He is, and how well he will provide for you. Be courageous and generous, and give Him your heart, and you will never repent of the sacrifice

Ever Yours affectionately in Xt   John H Newman

FRIDAY 8 JUNE 1866   finally resolved in Congregation to undertake the Oxford Mission.

TO BISHOP ULLATHORNE

The Oratory Birmingham June 8. 1866

My dear Lord,

We thank you very sincerely for the great pains you have taken to remove our difficulties in undertaking the Mission of Oxford. After your letter of this morning, we consider them now to be at an end.[1]

Accordingly, having no doubt that the Holy Father will sanction the arrangement which you are so kind as to propose to lay before him, we accept the Oxford Mission from your hands, with our best acknowledgements for the confidence you place in us.

We will show you first any statement which we may put out with a view to raise the necessary funds for building. Would you think it suitable to give us a letter of recommendation to go with it?

Begging your Lordship's blessing on us and our new work, I am,

My dear Lord Your obt and affte Servant in Xt
John H Newman of the Oratory

The Rt Revd The Bp of Birmingham

SATURDAY 9 JUNE 1866   J. B. Marshall came back to pack up etc and go.

TO SIR FREDERIC ROGERS

The Oratory Bm June 10/66

My dear Rogers

If all is well, I propose to go to Bellasis's on the 18th, tomorrow week — then I shall come to London with one of my friends here, who is to take care of me. We shall go to the Langham or some such Hotel. I am very well, but am not so strong as I should like to be — and do not feel up to a ten days in

---

[1] Ullathorne on 7 June explained in detail how the income of the Oxford Mission would amount to £160 a year.

London, with the chance (tho' I trust not a great one) of being knocked up. He will keep his eye upon me, tho' this will not hinder his going his own way, and I mine. It is William Neville, whom you have seen here. He is a capital nurse, and has the sharp eyes and affectionate heart which belong to women rather than men. The distances are so great in London, and there are so many persons I wish to see, and June is so warm a month, that I am not sorry to have one who will see, as the day goes on, that I am not overfatiguing myself.

After all, it is all but certain that we are going to Oxford. Our Bishop proposed it to me three successive years — and I could not refuse — but I look on the prospect of being there with extreme dismay. I have parted with it for once and all, and it is opening wounds which are quite healed. And I want to be in peace, when, for what I know, I may not have many years more. It is a great mark of confidence in him, and that alone makes it almost a duty in me to accept it, considering the various controversies going on around and about me.

My medical man is sending me to Switzerland for a month, where I am to drink in as much mountain air as ever I can.

When I am in London, perhaps you will let me come and dine with you some day.

Ever Yours affectionately John H Newman

P.S.   I shall take the chance of Lady Rogers being at home — and giving notice of my arrival by calling.

MONDAY 11 JUNE 1866   boys went to Bishop's chapel for confirmation.

TO W. J. COPELAND

The Oy Bm June 11/66

My dear Copeland

I get quite anxious at the thought of the protracted trial which your brother's sad illness brings upon you — to say nothing of your sister's. I go to Town next week — and from what you say shall put off the hope of seeing you at home then. Here I am engaged in examining the boys Friday and Saturday — and on (no matter whether) Wednesday or Thursday, I shall be in retreat. It seems no invitation to ask you here tomorrow and Wednesday — though you may be sure it would give us much pleasure to see you. Edward Caswall has gone off to his brother who is uncomfortably unwell.

In your present unsettlement you cannot be thinking of your 'History of the Movement.' I do wish you could go on with it

Ever Yours most affecty John H Newman

The Revd Wm J. Copeland

249

TO EDWARD BELLASIS

The Oratory Bm June 12. 1866

My dear Bellasis

From what Richard tells us, I think I may propose to you and Mrs Bellasis my paying you a visit with Fr Neville on Monday next the 18th. We would come down to you to dinner and say Mass next Morning; and then take leave of you. It will be a great pleasure to us; was not the last time of my dining at your house, on occasion of the Achilli matter? how many things have happened since!

Ever Yours affly in Xt   John H Newman of the Oratory

Mr Serjeant Bellasis

TO JAMES HOPE-SCOTT

The Oratory Birmingham June 14. 1866

My dear Hope Scott

I hope it wont take you many minutes to look over the inclosed, and mark in pencil any thing you don't like.[1]

I am coming to Town next week, and want to send it to the Bishop before I start. I will dine with you any day you name after next Wednesday the 20th.

Ever Yours affly John H Newman of the Oratory

J. R. Hope Scott Esqr

FRIDAY and SATURDAY 15 and 16 JUNE 1866   examined the boys

TO JAMES HOPE-SCOTT

The Oy Bm ⌈June 17. 1866⌉

My dear Hope Scott

⌈You have let my Paper off very easily — I hope the Bishop will be as lenient.

I will gladly dine with you on Thursday at half past seven — I forgot to tell you that I bring up Father W. Neville as my nutrix — or pedagogus — may I bring him with me to you as my umbra?⌉ — Don't have any difficulty in saying No — for he has come up to amuse himself and I should send him elsewhere

Ever Yours affly John H Newman

P.S.   ⌈We mean to be at the Westminster Palace Hotel — having been drifted into that atmosphere of law and politics by the reflection of other places of sojourning. Shall we be able to breathe there?⌉

[1] This was a draft of a new circular about the Oratory at Oxford.

TO BISHOP ULLATHORNE

The Oratory Bm June 17. 1866

My dear Lord

Before I go away, I send for your inspection the Advertisements I propose to issue. Should your Lordship have occasion to write to me, the letter will be forwarded on to me from this place to London. I hope to say Mass for Mother Margaret's religious works tomorrow morning before starting — and beg you to say every thing kind from me to her and the nuns at Stone[1]

Your obt and affte Servt in Xt   John H Newman of the Oratory

The Rt Revd The Bishop of Birmingham

P.S.   I expect after Monday to be at the Westminster Palace Hotel.

MONDAY 18 JUNE 1866   J. B. Marshall went for good.   Wm [William] and I went through London to Bellasis's Putney.   Mr Weld Blundell to dinner

TO W. J. COPELAND

The Oratory Bm Monday June 18/66

My dear Copeland

Your letter distresses more than it surprises me. I am now starting with Neville for Bellasis's at Putney — tomorrow we go to the 'Westminster Palace Hotel.' If you have any place to put up at in London, we might pass Friday together.

Ever Yours affly John H Newman

TUESDAY 19 JUNE 1866   went out first sitting to Woolner's — established ourselves in the Wr [Westminster] Palace Hotel

TO WILLIAM MONSELL

The Westminster Palace Hotel June 19. 1866

My dear Monsell,

Here I am close to you, yet cannot find you, or learn where you dwell. I have in vain attempted you at the House of Commons. But the postman *must* find you, so I leave the matter to him. I would come and breakfast with you, (if you *can* eat or drink during this crisis,) on any morning you name[2]

Ever Yours affly John H Newman

[1] Ullathorne replied from Stone on 19 June, 'Might I suggest the change of the phrase "representatives of another faith" — to representatives of another communion . . . I have nothing else to suggest, although I have an impression that many Protestants will shake their ears and construe some of the expressions as a challenge.' See letter of 15 July to Ullathorne.
[2] On 18 June Lord Russell's Government was defeated on an amendment to their Reform Bill. On 26 June they resigned, and Lord Derby formed a Conservative ministry.

23 JUNE 1866

WEDNESDAY 20 JUNE 1866 I breakfasted with Gladstone.[1] I dined with Rogers Every day but Sunday at Woolner's

THURSDAY 21 JUNE called on Mrs Ward, Simeons, Duchess [of] Argyll, H. Bowden's, Mrs Bowden. We dined with Hope Scott

FRIDAY 22 JUNE we dined at Sir J. Acton's

SATURDAY 23 JUNE breakfasted with Monsell lunched with Mrs Towneley we dined at Hope Scott's

TO AMBROSE ST JOHN

⌜Westminster Palace Hotel Saturday June 23/66⌝

My dear A,

I would write you a long letter, had I not just returned from an excursion of 8 or 9 hours, consisting of chapel, a breakfast at Monsell's, a sitting at the Sculptor's, and luncheon at Mrs Towneley's and some calls, and am very tired.

⌜Hope Scott has sent William to Oxford this morning to see about buying more land. He is to return by dinner time, and we dine with Hope Scott at ½ past 7.⌝ At luncheon today I met Mr Higgins and the boy who is to come to us; and after dinner came in Monteith, the O'Connor Don, Mr Maxwell, Blennerhassett etc. On Thursday we met at Hope Scott's the whole Kerrs. At Gladstone's at breakfast I met the young Lady Lothian, Lord Lyttelton, General Beaurégard and others.[2] Tomorrow we lunch with the [F.R.] Wards and dine with Bellasis. On Tuesday I am to dine with the Simeons to meet Mr Chichester Fortescue, Stanley, and perhaps Gladstone.⌝[3] I have made many calls and have more to make.[4] ⌜On Monday we shall breakfast with Badeley. So

[1] Acton wrote: '15a Hill St. Wednesday
My dear Father Newman
                    Yesterday, Gladstone, learning that you were in town, but not knowing where to find you, charged me to convey to you his most pressing and cordial invitation to breakfast with him tomorrow, Thursday, at 10.
    He has, I know, been long anxious to see you. He never speaks of your writings without great warmth, and I am sure that he will be much disappointed if he loses the opportunity of seeing you during your present visit to London.
                    Believe me Dear Father Newman Ever faithfully Yours J D Acton
    If you dislike or are prevented from accepting, may I ask him to meet you at breakfast here on Friday?'

[2] Pierre Gustave Toutant Beauregard (1818–93), of French ancestry, and one of the Confederate generals in the American Civil War. After his surrender in April 1865, he was for five years president of the New Orleans, Jackson and Mississippi Railway, and later Adjutant-General of Louisiana.
[3] Chichester Samuel Fortescue (1823–98), went up to Christ Church, Oxford in 1841, and took a first in Classics. He sat as Liberal Member of Parliament for County Louth, Ireland, from 1847 until 1874, when he was made Baron Carlingford. He was Chief Secretary for Ireland from Nov. 1865 until 26 June 1866. Always in favour of conciliation, he was responsible for the Irish Land Act of 1870, and supported Gladstone to the full, until the latter adopted the policy of home rule.
[4] A letter of 29 June from Stanton shows that one of the places where Newman called was the London Oratory.

you see in my old age I am learning to be a man of fashion. Today I went to Paget, and he comforted me even more than Dr Evans — and he said that commonly the pain of getting rid of that particular calculus was very great.[11] I *fear* I shall not be back by St Peter and St Paul

Ever Yours affly J H N

SUNDAY 24 JUNE 1866   said Mass at Oblate church   I called on Mr ... North.[2]   Miss Holmes called.   we lunched with the [F.R.] Wards   called on Lady Rogers   we went down to dine at Bellasis's

TO T. W. ALLIES

Westminster Palace Hotel June 24. /66

My dear Allies,

I ought to have written to you on your kind proposition before now — and can only plead in excuse that I hardly have been indoors at all, except when dressing or sleeping. Thank you for your offer, which would have been very acceptable to me, could I have promised myself the pleasure of seeing anything of you in consequence, but, as I have said above, I am out of doors from morning to night, — and so is Father Neville too, and therefore, since we are here for so uncertain a time, we think it best to stay here. Joining his thanks to mine,

I am Yrs affly in Xt   John H Newman

TO MRS J. W. BOWDEN

Westminster Palace Hotel June 24/66

My dear Mrs Bowden,

I have not answered your kind note, not knowing my own movements, or how long I should be in London. Now, however, unless meanwhile you are engaged, I am able to ask you to let me come to lunch with you and Emily on Wednesday next the 27th

Ever Yours affectionately in Xt   John H Newman

P.S.   I have not answered your kind wish to receive me altogether, while I am in London — but I can't profit by it, thank you. I am here with a friend and I am obliged to be in London itself.

[1] [[the pain of getting rid of what I had got rid of was commonly very great.]] See diary for 17 Jan. 1866.
[2] Probably William Henry North (1836–1932), at Eton and Christ Church, and an officer in the Life Guards, who became a Catholic with his wife in 1867, and succeeded his mother, a peeress in her own right, as eleventh Lord North in 1884.

MONDAY 25 JUNE 1866   we breakfasted with Badeley   called on Jesuits — we dined at Blennerhassett's

TUESDAY 26 JUNE   called on Mrs Bowden   I dined at Simeon's — met Gladstone etc etc.

WEDNESDAY 27 JUNE   we breakfasted at Wegg Prosser's   called on Mr Hutton   we dined with Hope Scott

THURSDAY 28 JUNE   H. Mozley to breakfast   called on A. Mozley   called on Acland   Miss Monro   came down safe and well to Birmingham

FRIDAY 29 JUNE   Hurrell Froude here for the day

SATURDAY 30 JUNE   Funeral of A. Pope.   dreadful storm.[1]   Ambrose remained at Rednall till next Wednesday

TO AN UNKNOWN CORRESPONDENT

[July 1866?][2]

You ask me whether it is an article of faith that the voice of the Apostolic see is per se the infallible word of God. I answer that it was certainly not so in Bellarmine's time, and if it has been made so by the Church since, it must [have] been without any one knowing it. Once of a time Christendom is said to have suddenly woken up and found itself Arian, but not thus silently are doctrines slipped in to that Faith extra quam nemo salvus esse potest. We are bound to accept as from God what the Church categorically declares to be divine truth, but her declarations are ever direct and precise, and mere acts of ecclesiastical authority such as are involved in the teaching and governing of the faithful must not be taken for definitions of faith.

I speak under correction, as indeed I wish to speak about the clearest things, but in their number I place the above statements; and to deny them seems to me to disturb consciences and to imperil souls.

J.H.N.

MONDAY 2 JULY 1866   Mr Kelke came
TUESDAY 3 JULY   Mr Kelke went
WEDNESDAY 4 JULY   Mr Everard came
THURSDAY 5 JULY   Mr Everard went

[1] The funeral was that of John Archdale Taylor Pope, a boy at the Oratory School, who died on 26 June, aged sixteen. He was the son of Thomas Alder Pope, and the boys of the School attended his burial at Rednal. A granite cross was later erected under the trees there, with the inscription, composed by Newman: 'LAUS DEO In thankful remembrance of June 30, 1866, when Divine Providence saved our school-boys, all collected round their Father Prefect [St John], under the adjacent shed, from a sudden thunderstorm, when the lightning playing round them, struck with death as many as ten sheep about the field and trees close by.'
[2] This undated draft has been filed with the last letters concerning Pusey's Eirenicon.

TO WILLIAM CHARLES LAKE

The Oratory Birmingham July 5, 1866

My dear Mr Lake,

The July number of the 'Contemporary Review' has been sent to me from the Publisher by your direction; and I thank you very much both for your Article in it and your kindness in sending it to me.[1] I read your remarks on Keble with great interest, and was exceedingly touched by your notice of myself. It is very pleasant to have thus brought to me the recollection of my Oxford days, and in particular of one whom I so liked and respected as yourself. I do not wish to claim a nearer acquaintance with you, than I was allowed to have, but I knew you enough then, to feel very kindly towards you, and to be much gratified to find now by your present word and deed that you feel kindly towards me.

Let me take the privilege of an old man in expressing my earnest wish and trust that God will ever bless you, and believe me to be, my dear Mr Lake,

Very sincerely Yours John H. Newman[2]

TO WILLIAM BENHAM

The Oratory, Birmingham. July 7, 1866.

Dear Sir,

No apology was necessary for your letter, which I answer without delay.[3]

1. It is false that I was first of the College of the Propagation of the Faith at Rome, and afterwards of Oriel College, Oxford.

2. It is false that I was educated at the College de Propaganda Fide at Rome, partly at Oxford. I was educated wholly in England. I first went to school when I was seven years old. There I remained, viz., at Ealing, near London, from May 1808, to December 1816. In the same December, 1816, I was entered at Trinity College, Oxford. There I took my B.A. degree, and I remained there in residence till April, 1822, when I was elected Fellow of Oriel.

3. It is false that I had an interview with Dr. Wiseman in 1832. It is false that in the interview which I had with him in 1833, in company with Mr.

[1] 'Mr Keble and the "Christian Year,"' the *Contemporary Review*, (July 1866), pp. 314–37. In order to illustrate the life and outlook of Keble, Lake relied largely on *Apo.*, which he used with obvious sympathy.

[2] Lake replied on 8 July with a letter of profuse thanks, and said that Newman's teaching 'has been, and still is, a blessing to the Church of England, in giving to many that conviction of the reality of Christian Faith and Love which is their best safeguard in an age of doubt.'

[3] C. H. Collette's book *Dr. Newman and his Religious Opinions*, London 1866, was severely criticised in the *Churchman*, 31 May 1866. Collette sued the Editor, William Denton, for calling his accusations against Newman 'foul'. Denton asked Newman to assist him by writing to deny them. The action between the *Churchman* and Collette was submitted to a referee, William Benham. Collette argued that Newman had not specified the statements he denied and so Benham asked for this present letter, which was published, with a supporting letter of his own in the *Churchman*, (12 July 1866). See letter of 24 July to Benham.

Froude, I was formally ordained a Priest of the Roman Church, or ordained at all, or that I was then, in fact, a member of that Communion.

4. It is false that I was ordained a Priest of Rome before I had publicly renounced the Communion of the Church of England.

5. It is false that I was not ordained a Priest of Rome in Rome after I had publicly renounced the Communion of the Church of England. I was ordained Sub-deacon of the Catholic (Roman) Church in May 26, 1847, by Cardinal Fransoni; Deacon, May 27,[1] 1847, by the Cardinal Vicar; Priest, May 30, 1847, by Cardinal Fransoni. I said my first Mass on June 3, 1847.

6. It is false that I spent the early part of my life in the College of Propaganda. I never left England in my life till I was nearly thirty-two, viz., on December 9, 1832.

7. It is false that the ceremony of my ordination at Rome was deferred.

8. It is false that I was a Priest of Rome while officiating in the Anglican Church.

I am, dear Sir, faithfully yours, John H. Newman.[2]

SUNDAY 8 JULY 1866   went out to Rednall?

TO WILLIAM DENTON

The Oratory Bm July 8/66

My dear Sir,

I inclose my answer to a letter Mr Benham addressed to me.

As I do not recognise any one but yourself in the matter about which he writes to us, I think it best that my answer should come to him through you. I hope he will not think this uncivil in me.

Very truly Yours John H Newman

TO T. W. ALLIES

[The Oratory, Birmingham.]
July 9, 1866.

My dear Allies,

Thank you for your pages, which I return.[3] That man, Collette, who is some kind of lawyer, has been ever since Christmas trying to get me into controversy, in various ways. Now, after sending his volume against me to the Churchman, he is bringing an action against the Churchman for reviewing it unfavourably, or what he calls libellously. His one object, I believe, is to get

---

[1] A mistake for 29 May.

[2] In sending this letter to Benham Newman added, 'As I write to you in Mr Denton's behalf, not my own, I think it will make this clearer, if I send this to you through him. JHN'

[3] These appear to have been the pages slandering Newman in Collette's *Dr. Newman and his Religious Opinions*.

his volume sold, or himself known. And actually, in order to defend the Churchman, I am obliged formally to declare that I was *not* educated at Propaganda etc, etc.

As to the line taken by my Objector against your Pamphlet, I think it comes to this, that there is a step which you have not actually named.[1] Simple schism does not break unity, he says, but that schism which is heretical, but then it would not have been difficult to show that both Donatists and Anglicans *are* heretical.

I forget whether I said so to you before, but I should wish to distinguish between active and negative schism. The latter is such (as) St Mellitius's, who would say, 'It is no fault of mine, things are at a dead lock. I suppose they will get right in time.'[2] And in the 15th century 'I do my best to find out the true Pope. I have no theory to maintain. It is a simple question of fact.' But the Anglican says 'I am *not bound* to be united to the Holy See. The Pope's claims are usurpations.' Here is a definite, active opposition, a doctrinal opposition, which must be of the nature of heresy.[3]

Every yours affectly in Xt, John H. Newman of the Oratory

TO BISHOP ULLATHORNE

The Oratory July 9. 1866

My dear Lord,

I should have written to you before this, if I had any thing to report to you of a positive character about the Oxford matter. Now, as I am starting for Rednall, and after that am going abroad, I will not at least delay to send you the letter you were so kind as to give us in 1864. You will see what alterations have to be made in it, to suit our present circumstances.[4]

When I was in London, I found my friends would not hear of my building without securing more land, or without arriving at a larger sum total of contributions than I had fixed upon. Accordingly, we have been ever since engaged in rummaging out the owners of the properties contiguous to ours, the character of the tenures etc. and this is very slow work — though we have done our best to expedite matters.

I am, My dear Lord, Yr affte & obt Servt in Xt
John H Newman of the Oratory

The Rt Revd The Bp of Birmingham

[1] A paper written by Ignatius Ryder shows that he was the objector to Allies's *Dr. Pusey and the Ancient Church,* London 1866. Allies was maintaining that the grace of the sacraments was not given outside the unity of the Church. To this Ryder objected that not every schismatic was a formal heretic.

[2] St. Melitius, Bishop of Antioch 360–81, was at the head of one of two rival orthodox parties during the struggle against Arianism.

[3] Allies replied on 19 July, accepting Newman's distinction, but saying that 'negative schism, if it continued long, would be sure to make itself a heresy . . .'

[4] Newman was preparing the new circular about the proposed Oxford Oratory. See letters of 17 June and 15 July to Ullathorne. His letter of 1864 was that of 27 October, placed before Newman's of 28 October 1864.

THURSDAY 12 JULY 1866   BBC [Birmingham Banking Company] stopped payment.[1]

TO WILLIAM NEVILLE

The Oratory Bm [Rednal] July 12, 1866

My dear William

I am far from unwilling to buy Mallam's property at a good price — tho' one need not at once come in to his terms — but then it must be on the credit of the *Contributions generally* — not as promised by you, or Edward, or any of us. Hope Scott contemplates our being able to give £5000 for land — I should run the land at the back *against* Mallam — i.e. I would get whichever I could. Mallam's is not so valuable with the St Aldate's piece thrust in.[2] I think our game would be to say to Mallam 'Buy the St Aldate's piece, or get a long lease of it — and then your land would be worth a good sum.' Are you not *sure* that Hope Scott (as a sensible person) would indefinitely prefer the land at the back, rather than Mallam's *without* St Aldate's? I would say to Mallam 'I will give you three thousand for yours or St Aldate's.'

As to Mrs Benson's ground, unless it is very dear, we *must* get it.[3] But the *land at the back*, running from street to street, from Brewer's Lane to the water course, is far the best to spend money on.

I think of coming back for Saturday evening — preaching the Sunday morning sermon, and then returning here

Ever Yrs affly J H N

TO J. WALKER OF SCARBOROUGH

Rednal July 12/66

My dear Canon Walker,

Nothing is altogether settled about Oxford. The step wanting is the consent of Propaganda, which the Bishop, who knows of course, says will come without any trouble — but, as Cardinal Barnabo has already on three distinct occasions acted uncomfortably towards me, I will begin nothing and will spend nothing, till I have his leave so distinctly that he cannot undo it. Nothing can be kinder or more considerate than the Bishop has been.

And besides since I know that there were powerful influences from home which were especially directed against the Oratory going to Oxford in 1864,

[1] There was a financial crisis in England and the Birmingham Banking Company was among the casualties.
[2] Mallam's land had a long frontage in Brewer Street, which leads into St Aldate's, Oxford.
[3] Neville has left a note that 'Mrs Benson's ground was two or three houses at the end of Broad Street and looking up that street and close to the corner of New College Lane.'

the event will alone decide whether or not those influences will remain in a quiescent state now.

Very sincerely Yours John H Newman of the Oratory

The Very Revd John Canon Walker

P.S. I am going abroad for a time at a doctor's orders for refreshment.

FRIDAY 13 JULY 1866 Returned from Rednall
SUNDAY 15 JULY Went out to Rednall?

TO FRANCIS TURNER PALGRAVE

The Oratory Bm July 15. 1866

My dear Mr. Palgrave,

I feel greatly obliged to you for your proposed present.[1] Your Father was the first literary man who took notice of me, and there could not be a more handsome compliment than that he paid me in his well-known work.[2] It will be very pleasant to receive such a memorial of him, presented to me by his son. Do me the additional kindness of writing in it, how it comes to me. I am not possessed of volumes 1 and 2; but it would be hard, if I were not contented with those which are in your hands already.[3]

As I was not the best sitter in the world, I am glad to have your judgment

[1] This was evidently the third and fourth volume of *The History of Normandy and England*, London 1864, by Sir Francis Palgrave, who died in 1861. They were published posthumously by his son.

[2] Sir Francis Palgrave, in *Truths and Fictions of the Middle Ages: The Merchant and the Friar*, London 1837, introduced quotations from Newman, without mentioning him by name. He pictured Friar Bacon speaking to a friend. 'Instead of the Friar in his study, discoursing with a friend, imagine yourself in the neighbouring Church of St. Mary the Virgin. Suppose you have before you a Preacher addressing this University of Oxford, in an age when, by the permission of Providence, those sciences which I now recommend, shall be pursued with intoxicating vigour: when the Handmaid, instead of waiting with humility for the commands of her Mistress, shall rudely endeavour to usurp her authority. Consider this Preacher as one, who, never forgetting the prerogative derived from his high and sacred commission as a member of the Apostolical Hierarchy, is equally preserved from the delusions of spiritual pride, and the chill of worldly wisdom, and he might answer arguments like yours in the following words:-

"The heavens do declare the glory of God, but not his will . . . perverts the whole tenor of Scripture." [*P.S.I.*, 'The Religion of the Day,' pp. 317–18]

Such might be the sentiments of the Preacher whom you may picture to yourself as living in after-ages, and happy will this our country be, if, the error prevailing, so faithful a minister should arise.' *Op. cit.*, pp. 370–2.

Palgrave continued to quote and paraphrase the same sermon. 'Let me continue my anticipation of the Preacher, who may be heard in this seat of learning, when centuries shall have rolled away . . . we may imagine him describing our sins and errors in the following guise. — "The adversary of mankind devised a new Idol, to be adopted by the world as the true Christ . . . patterns or the tyrants of a beguiled people."' [*P.S.I.*, pp. 310–11]. *Op. cit.*, pp. 374–5.

Palgrave, who had been influenced by Tractarianism and became friendly with Newman, did not mention the source of his quotations.

[3] The first two volumes of *The History of Normandy* are with the last two in Newman's room. There is no inscription in any of them.

that the anxious pains, which Mr Woolner took with me, are not likely to be thrown away.[1]

> Very truly Yours John H Newman

F. T. Palgrave Esqr

P.S.   As I am leaving home for some weeks, I fear I shall not be able to acknowledge the arrival of your packet in person; but I will leave word for its acknowledgment.

TO BISHOP ULLATHORNE

> The Oratory July 15/66

My dear Lord

I thank you very sincerely for your most kind and effective letter.[2] We are still negociating with Oxford — and though it seems we can get more land, we do not yet know how much, or at what price

> Your Lordship's obt and affte Servt in Xt   John H Newman

The Rt Revd The Bp of Birmingham

TO JAMES CASTLE

> sent in substance   Rednall   July 16. 1866

Sir,

Mr. Neville has told me of the zeal with which you have prosecuted inquiries which he suggested to you on the subject of the properties adjacent to my house and stables in St Aldate's. We should be desirous at all events to purchase Mrs. Bensons — and should be glad if she named a price — and if we were able to purchase hers and Mr Micklem's, we should be willing to treat for Mr Mallam's. Any how we are anxious to hear about Mr Micklem's. You may offer him £2500. Or we would treat with Mr Mallam's representatives, in case they would first themselves purchase the property of St Aldate's parish. We would give them a good sum for their own and the St Aldate's property together. But, unless we were secure either of the St Aldate's, or of Mrs Benson's and Mr Micklem's, we do not feel disposed to treat for Mr Mallam's piece by itself. We do not wish you to give over your inquiries about the properties adjoining Mr Laken's

I have only just heard that you had been engaged by Mr Comberbach in preparing plans for a Church at Oxford. We knew nothing about it — indeed till now I did not know you were by profession an architect. Had I known it I should have taken care to inform you at once of our previous engagements.[3]

Mr James Castle

[1] See diary for 19 June.

[2] Ullathorne's letter of 12 July was inserted in Newman's Circular of 13 Jan. 1867. It will be found in note to letter of 14 Jan. 1867 to the Duchess of Argyll.

[3] i.e. with Henry Clutton. Castle accepted his disappointment with good grace.

July 16. 1866

My dear Ignatius

I send you another paper. I wish I could bring out clearly what I am at.[1]

Primarily, I am attempting to put on some intelligible ground, of reason, of philosophy, what has to be said about the Church's (Pope's) infallibility. To say that it is a gift, to guarantee to the end of time the integrity of the original revelation, made once for all through the Apostles, is *perfectly* intelligible — and, I suppose, till the utterances of these modern schools, sufficient as well as intelligible. Now if we are to believe more, it ought to be placed on an equally intelligible basis. E.g. supposing the Church, by the voice of Pope or General Council, declared that there *were* certain other respects or subject matters, in which she was infallible, that would be a perfectly intelligible basis — because what she so said, would, by her saying it, have the guarantee of its being part of the original revelation:– from the first she *would* have been infallible in those certain respects, though she had not *declared* it till a late period. But there has not in fact been any such formal definition from the Church, through any organ. Again, even if there be a consensus of divines on the infallibility of the Church on these certain matters, I conceive this does not *prove* her infallibility. Though one and all said, 'What the Pope says is certain though not infallible,' this would not oblige me to accept their opinion. For first, what the Schola says is never, as such, a point of faith, or de fide — next, all that the consent of divines binds us to, is *silence* — we must not oppose it — not internal assent — thirdly, the Schola actually has before now changed round, e.g. on the point of the Immaculate Conception — according to the passage in de Lugo, which Stanislas [Flanagan] spoke of to Henry.[2]

I cannot then decide the point in question by authority — whether of Church or Schola — in neither do I find the 'intelligible ground' which I am seeking. Hence, I must betake myself to the reason or philosophy of the matter, and here the way of arguing adopted by our friends is not such as to command my assent. They say the Church *has* infallibly defined her power, (viz of being certain beyond the revelation) in her ruling that she may pronounce on dogmatic facts — but if she has jurisdiction over dogmatic facts, therefore she may have the same jurisdiction (i.e. power of pronouncing authoritatively and certainly or infallibly,) on other matters; and thus we have a whole field of

---

[1] Ryder had written on 16 July from the Oratory, 'I am delighted that you have begun. It is to me like a waft of fresh air . . . Ward has been a positive nightmare to me for some time past . . .' On receiving Newman's present letter, Ryder wrote on 17 July, 'Many thanks for your letter and the accompanying paper on Dogmatic facts. It certainly satisfies me more than anything else I have seen on the subject.'

Newman's various papers on Infallibility will be included in the volume of his Theological Papers.

[2] See de Lugo, *De Fide*, Disp. XX, iii, 128, Venice 1751, Vol. III, p. 327.

matters, over and above the original depositum, on which the Church is infallible, and which we must believe in order to salvation.

Then, these writers, when urged to reconcile their teaching with the old and received view that the Church is infallible only *in ordine ad* the original depositum of faith, make these verbal and unintelligible distinctions, which to me sound like shuffles. Oh, they say, we don't absolutely say that the Church is infallible in such matters, but she is certain, errare non potest. Next, we don't say that the faith that receives them is divine faith (that is, I suppose, from *grace*) — we only say it is not human — that is, it neither is from grace — nor is it not from grace, and therefore we will call it 'ecclesiastical.'

I cannot then acquiesce in the notion that such a view of the matter ought to satisfy me — for, to my mind, it is utterly *un*intelligible.

I want then some better ground than the ipse dixit of Cardenas, Fénelon, and Muzzarelli,[1] before I receive the doctrine that what the Pope says, (that is, what the Church says, for no one says that the Pope is infallible except as being in himself the Church) is certain, when he is not professing to explain or declare the Apostolic depositum which has [come] down to him by tradition. The Church (or Pope) can determine the sense of the depositum — she can declare its implicit meanings — she can declare what contradicts it — she can declare what in its nature subserves it (i.e. pious opinion) or is prejudicial to it, (i.e. what is erroneous, false, near heresy, savouring of heresy, etc) — she can declare its concrete manifestations, as that the inspiration originally given at Pentecost is carried out in the *particular* Epistle to the Hebrews (i.e. that it is canonical) or that certain five truths of the depositum are contradicted in the Augustinus of Jansen (i.e. a dogmatic fact.) — but all these enunciations are to be received by Catholics BECAUSE they *directly* relate to the depositum, *not* as being mere utterances of the Church or Pope. Next, I have said, 'they are to be received; — ' but *how* received? as *infallible*? I have no difficulty in so receiving them myself, but I have yet to discover that it is de fide, or that there is a consensus scholæ, that they *are* infallible. E.g. Lambertini says that it is doubtful whether it is de fide that the Pope is infallible in the Canonization of Saints — and the Jesuits, I think deny it. Chrissman denies that it is de fide to believe in the Church's infallibility as to dogmatic facts, and so on.

However, *I* do not deny that in all these enunciations the Church is infallible and certain; — and is to be believed fide, not humanâ sed divinâ — divinâ *et* ecclesiastical. But while on the one hand I would destroy the distinction between infallible and certain, divine and ecclesiastical, as unintelligible, so on the other I would deny that the Church's infallibility stretches beyond those matters which are related to, which bear upon, the depositum.

E.g. Muzzarelli, I suppose, would say, You are bound to believe under pain of damnation that 'the Pope's temporal power is necessary towards the

---

[1] Juan Cardenas (1613–84) and Alfonso Muzarelli (1749–1813) were Jesuit theologians who maintained that the Pope's prerogative, of preservation from error in teaching, extended beyond the sphere of revealed truth. For Fénelon's views see *DTC*, Église, IV, 2190–2.

spiritual in these times', because in saying so he is infallible or at least certain
— [1] but, according to my present information, I am not bound so to believe,
unless 1. the Church in Council or at least ex Cathedra Petri said it — and 2.
said it, with the *profession* that it came from tradition from the Apostles, and
with the other formal requisites of a definition. Till this was done, I should
not think the Church or Pope infallible or certain in saying it, because it did
not *intrinsically bear upon* the depositum or was *in* the depositum implicitly
(according to my apprehension) and it had not the extrinsic proof of it, arising
out of the Church's authoritative declaration that it *did* bear upon or was
implied in the depositum.

And if, to go back a step, as to what I have said above, it be asked me *why*
I believe that the Church is infallible in her declarations as to what *subserves*,
prejudices, and concretely *exhibits* the depositum, I answer that I do so on the
general principle, that in all creatures nature is sufficient for herself, or is
gifted with a self-conservative power — and thus that the Church has a true
divine instinct as to what is good or bad for the depositum, which in fact is her
life, as well as her charge.

As I have not put down before, what I mean so much as [sic] length, I
wish you would be so good to keep this.

I write it that you may see what my difficulty is, and how you can help me

Yrs affly John H Newman

WEDNESDAY 18 JULY 1866   came in from Rednall
THURSDAY 19 JULY   prizes given away etc   Mr Ware came
FRIDAY 20 JULY   Boys went   Mr Ware went

CIRCULAR LETTER TO PARENTS

The Oratory July 20th 1866

Dear Sir,

In consequence of the high price of meat, and the steady advance of prices
generally we are compelled to make it a weekly charge in our future terminal
account, when any of our boys are allowed meat or eggs at breakfast.

In case of such allowance being the wish of their parents we shall be
obliged to them to signify it to us in writing

I am, dear Sir Very truly Yours John H Newman[2]

[1] Muzzarelli wrote separate works on the Papal Primacy, on Papal Infallibility, and on the
Temporal Power.
[2] Only the signature is autograph.

TO JAMES HOPE-SCOTT

The Oratory Bm ⌜July 20. 1866⌝

My dear Hope Scott

⌜I don't know how far you heard that I had last winter a very serious illness — the anxieties of which, however, passed off in a wonderful way, and left me quite well.

My medical adviser in consequence wished me to go abroad for some months, in order, if possible, to throw back my life some years, and to set my constitution on a new basis.[1]

He has urged me to go at this time to Switzerland. There is one plan he likes better, viz my going for some months abroad in winter.

This led me to think of Hières — for two reasons — first, because, being a place where John Bulls were to be found, it would have an additional attraction to me to find myself near you — next, because your being in the neighbourhood would be a guarantee to my friends here, that I was safe in point of health, since you would be able to let them know, if any thing was going on wrong with me. Else, they would have to send out some one with me.

I am too much of an old batchelor to think of coming under your roof, even if you could offer to have me. All I think of is being near you. And my reason for writing is to ask you, is Hières a good place for me? what of the climate and the people? shall I get a comfortable lodging? are the expenses very great? etc etc All which questions your knowledge of the place will enable you to answer.⌝

Fr St John will be in town next week — and, if you would give him a quarter of an hour, he would explain every thing to you, and hear what you had to say.

⌜We are anything but idle about the Oxford matter — but inquiries into property move slowly⌝

Yours affly John H Newman

J. R. Hope Scott Esqr

TO THOMAS KEBLE, JUNIOR

The Oratory Birmingham July 21. 1866

Mr dear T. Keble,

Mr Mozley has sent me word that you have inquired of him about your dear Uncle's poems in the Lyra Apostolica.[2] *Whoever* owns the Lyra, of course

---

[1] [[Footing]]

[2] John Mozley, the publisher of *Lyra Apostolica,* wrote to Newman on 20 July that Thomas Keble Junior had inquired as to the copyright, wishing to publish all his uncle's poems, including those in that volume.

it is plain that his friends may do what they will with those poems, because, since he was never paid any thing for them, they were always his property.

However, I am glad to have an opportunity of writing to you about the Lyra, all the writers in which, my dearest friends, are dead except myself, Bowden⟨α⟩, Froude⟨β⟩, Keble⟨γ⟩, R. Wilberforce⟨ε⟩ and Williams⟨ζ⟩.

I was the original editor, and owner of the volume. The contributors gave me their poems. In 1845 I made over the ownership to your uncle. As *I* had paid the bills and received the profits up to that time, so has *he* since. When I saw him at Hursley last Autumn, he volunteered to speak to me on the subject, and said, self reproachfully in his way, that I ought to have had part of the profits. This idea *never* had come into my head, and of course I told him so as forcibly as I could.

Now, however, when every one else but myself is gone, it would be a pleasure to me, if your uncle's representatives thought the ownership of the work might return to me. If they think otherwise, I readily give way — only I should consider (as I dare say they would) that, as you, for instance, might publish your uncle's Lyra poems in a collection of his works, and as Isaac Williams's representatives might publish his, so I, if I wish, may publish mine.[1] With my best respects to your Father and Mother

                    I am, Very sincerely Yours John H Newman

The Rev. T. Keble Jun.

TO CHARLES RIDDELL

The Oratory, Birmingham July 21. 1866

My dear Mr Riddell,

I must not let your son leave us without sending you a line about him, and thanking you and Mrs Riddell for the kind confidence you have shown us in putting him into our hands.

He has ever been a well conducted boy, and has given us satisfaction and we trust he will make progress in the special studies to which he is now to be introduced.[2]

As time goes on, he will have perhaps to take care that his amiableness and popularity may not become a snare to him. We are not sure that he has all the self-command necessary for a young man entering life. But this opinion may possibly be over anxiety on our part — anyhow, I hope you will excuse my mentioning it out of the interest I take in his future.[3]

---

[1] Thomas Keble Junior on 25 July thanked Newman for his 'kind letter,' and ended his own, 'Pray do not think me wanting in kindness or courtesy if I ask for a little time to consult with others whose opinion I feel bound to take, before I reply to the latter part of your note.' See letters of 9 and 13 Sept.

[2] Charles Edward Riddell was to be a civil engineer.

[3] The conclusion and signature were cut out, before the autograph was copied.

TO RICHARD SIMPSON

The Oratory Bm July 22. 1866

My dear Simpson

You must have thought that I had in mind to purloin your number of the Études.[1]

Till now I have not had time to make the extracts, which I wished.

I do trust you have not needed them. They shall come back to you by Book post.[2]

There is a fair chance of our founding an Oratory in Oxford after all. The proposal has gone to Rome. I *suppose* there will be no difficulty there — but I cannot forget that the Archbishop exerted himself there against my going in February 1865 — and I do not know why he should have changed his then sense of duty by this time.[3]

Yours affectly in Xt   John H Newman of the Oratory

MONDAY 23 JULY 1866   went out to Rednall with Wm [William]   Ambrose went

TO WILLIAM BENHAM

[24 July 1866]

My dear Sir

I had already thanked you through Mr Denton for the trouble you had taken about me, before your letter of the 23rd came to me.[4] And now let me thank you with my own hand, and also let me express how much I feel the kindness you have shown me in the great interest you have taken in my Apologia.

I trust as you say that those absurd reports about me are now brought to an end. Still nothing has such vitality as a lie — and I have often been astonished how it is capable of being cut in pieces, like some reptiles, yet without substantial injury to its power of action — and this is especially the case with those of the old Orange and Presbyterian stock.[5] However, as you say, I have

---

[1] See letter of 25 March 1866 to Simpson.

[2] Simpson had evidently sent Newman *Études* for April and May 1866, which contained the second and last instalments of his article 'Le Docteur Pusey et son nouveau programme d'union avec l'Eglise Catholique.' See letter of 2 Aug. 1867 to Simpson.

[3] Simpson replied, 'I am charmed to hear of the renewal of the Oxford scheme,' and promised to send the second instalment of his contribution, once Newman's proposal was approved.

[4] Benham, the referee between Collette and the *Churchman*, wrote on 23 July to thank Newman for his letter of 7 July to its editor. Benham said he could not be sorry for having troubled Newman, 'for I am sure your letter is a most valuable supplement to the Apologia, which I had read through five times.'

[5] Benham wrote that Collette gave as his 'authorities' for his accusations against Newman, a daily paper (Dublin) an Orange Weekly, the Saint James' Chronicle, and "the Church and State Gazette."'

now put a statement on record which may be used should these reports revive. There was a misprint (the omission of a 'not') as the Times and Guardian gave my letter, which I have mentioned to Mr Denton.[1]

Again thanking you for your kindness.
J H N

FROM BISHOP ULLATHORNE
Birmingham July 24th 1866

Dear Dr Newman

Yesterday evening's Post brought me a letter from Propaganda, apropos of the petition respecting the proposed Oxford Oratory.

The letter informs me that the Holy Father directs the reply to be delayed until I have furnished information as to whether the apprehension which existed two years ago that the establishing of an Oratory might indirectly influence the attracting of Catholic students to the University has ceased, and from what cause it has ceased.[2]

I am trying to find the letter in which Cardinal Barnabò, whilst approving of my having requested you to withold the once contemplated circular, expressed equal approval of your going to Oxford, or at least some *dignus et doctus vir*.[3]

To this I propose to add the substance of your letter, which guarantees against any mixing on the part of the Oratory with University Education.

I shall further add a statement that it is chiefly through the wish of others that you have been induced, and that with some reluctance, to take up the burden of founding an Oratory and Church at Oxford.

I shall also point out the need of the mission.

Of course it cannot be denied that indirectly, and *praeter intentionem*, the establishing of an Oratory in connexion especially with your name, may act as an encouragement in some persons to send their sons to the University.

In case you should wish to offer any remarks before my reply is sent, I will delay the transmission until I hear from you.

Wishing you every blessing I remain Dear Dr Newman your faithful and affectionate Servt in Xt

✠ W. B. Ullathorne.

[1] In paragraph 5 of the letter of 7 July, 'It is false that I was not ordained a priest of Rome . . .' Newman wrote to Denton on 23 July, 'I am obliged to you and Mr Benham for the trouble you have been at with my letter.
There was one mistake in the report of it in the Times . . .'
[2] Barnabò's letter of 14 July to Ullathorne said: 'Mens autem Sanctitatis Suae haec est, ut in tui memoriam revocentur quae anno 1864 delata fuerint ad Sanctam Sedem circa erectionem domus praedictae Congregationis Oratorii in Civitate Oxfordiensi, cum videlicet Sacra Congregatio prudentiam tuam laudarit eo quod ita egeris cum R. P. Newman ut ex proposito illius nullum sequeretur periculum ne Catholici etiam indirectè ad Universitatem Oxfordiensem adeundam allicerentur. Vult itaque nunc Summus Pontifex ut A. Tua significet an et quomodo timores duobus ab hinc annis concepti evanuerint.' Ullathorne's *Facts and Documents*, p. 14. See also Archives of Propaganda, *Lettere e Decreti*, Vol. 357, f. 644, where it is followed by a letter of the same day to Manning, asking for his views.
[3] Barnabò's letter of 8 Feb. 1865. Ullathorne found the letter and quoted the relevant part in his letter of 30 July to Barnabò; see Ullathorne's letter of 31 July, placed before Newman's of 12 Aug. Cf. letters of 17 Feb. 1865 to Ullathorne and 21 April 1865 to St John.

TO BISHOP ULLATHORNE

Projected letter — not sent, because my friends objected to it.

July 25. [24] 1866.[1] Rednall

My dear Lord,

I think I foresee that the Holy Father is getting me out of a toilsome and anxious undertaking, for which I never offered myself, but which, when offered to me, I did not dare to decline.

It grieves me to think of the trouble and odium you are bringing on yourself for me.

Is it not better, my dear Lord, to end a matter at once, which seems so sure to fail, and to close the correspondence with Propaganda, by saying that I have begged your leave to withdraw from the proposed plan? Indeed, how could I comfortably proceed with it, even if allowed, encountered as I am already in the outset, with distrust and suspicion in those quarters whence I can least bear it, and beset, as my every act would certainly be, by illwill and hostility?[2]

Is it worth while to exert your influence to force me into a position which I neither covet myself, nor others wish for me, and to bring me into hot water which will be too much for me at my time of life, when I might remain as I am, in peace and tranquility?

Yours &c J H N

WEDNESDAY 25 JULY 1866   Wm [William] went to Oxford and London to Hope Scott

TO JAMES HOPE-SCOTT

⌐Rednall July 25/66⌐ morning

⌐My dear Hope Scott

Yesterday was an eventful day, and, since we were here, the telegraphic messages were delayed, and crossed in delivery.

1. A letter from Fr St John, saying you disapproved of buying Mrs Benson's piece for £600. Nothing had been settled, and I sent a telegram to Oxford to stop the negociation, tho' some of us were so warm in its favour that they wished to buy it on their own hook. For myself, I certainly thought it a mistake not to buy it.⌐ The telegram by mischance did not go from Birmingham till the evening, and I have not heard in answer.

⌐2. A telegram from Oxford from Castles asking whether he should bid for Mallam's land, which had been priced by the owners at £1600.

---

[1] The letters which follow show that this draft was drawn up on 24 July.

[2] In the first draft Newman continued: 'I am not surprised at this result of your application — it is part of a whole. As I have already anticipated the contents of your letter, so now I anticipate.' This he erased.

3. Before our answer could be given, though we did send one in the negative, a second telegram to the effect that Castles on his own responsibility had bid for Mallam's land and got it for us for £1040 — and asking us for the deposit £104 at once. This we did not get here till 10 at night.

4. Meanwhile a letter had come to me from the Bishop, of which I send a copy, which seems to me to show that *we shall not be sent to Oxford* at all.

5. Before the telegram had come about Mallam's property, I had written (not sent) my answer to him to the effect that he had better let me withdraw from the scheme,⌐ and not tease himself and me any longer with further attempts. On second thoughts ⌐however, I shall wait to know what you think, considering myself in the hands of yourself and others⌐ who have contributed towards my Oxford plan.[1]

⌐6. This morning, (sent in to Birmingham last night), goes a telegram to Castles, simply disowning our having any thing to do with the purchase of Mallam's.

Fr Neville is now leaving this place first for Oxford, then for you⌐[2]

Ever Yrs affly J H N

TO AMBROSE ST JOHN

Rednall. July 25. 1866

My dear Ambrose,

I write this for a record — and wish you would send it back. Yesterday was a day of events, of letters and telegrams, of messages crossing and contradicting each other.

1. First came your letter, containing Hope Scott's strong disapproval of Mrs Benson's piece, especially at £600

2. William was strong for it — said he *would* buy it himself — I consented to Edward's buying it, if so sharp a fellow *would* — but I wrote a telegram for William to take to Birmingham, telling Castle that *I* would not offer her beyond £300.

3. William went in to Birmingham. Edward not at home — he did *nothing* — did not send my telegram — and came back.

4. Yes, one thing he did — he found a telegram at Birmingham, asking him (from Castle) whether he (C.) should bid for Mallam's land, the auction

---

[1] Neville made a note for Hope-Scott, 'The Father [Newman] had not time to say that he thinks there is no chance of his going. He does not want to go without being recognised by Propaganda — he thinks they may let the Bm [Birmingham Oratory] do it but will not recognise his going. This would not do since he is spending so much money W N.'

[2] Neville sent Hope-Scott's reply: '9.45 p.m. Wed.
H. S. says you must not be the person to break off — you must not break it off with the Bishop — the Bishop wishes it.
Much has been done to bring it to an end, but those who have tried to do so have not had success — the thing is still going on — you are in the hands of Providence — let the act of stopping you be theirs, if so it is to be.'

coming off at one o'clock. He telegraphed back '*No*' — very properly, for what would Mallam's house be without Mrs Benson's piece?

5. Also, he found in Birmingham a letter for me from the Bishop. I inclose a copy. We both considered that it showed the Oxford matter was virtually at an end; and we were very glad that we were not further involved in purchases.

6. In consequence I sent in a telegram to Castles by one of the orphans to the effect that he must suspend all negociation with Mrs Benson, till he heard from me. This telegram did not get off from Birmingham till after the Oxford telegram came to *Birmingham* which I have next to tell you of.

7. I had made up my mind that every thing was at an end, and had sketched the letter which I inclose, as a basis of a letter to the Bishop, when at ten o'clock at night, when I was partly undressed, comes Godwin with a telegram from Castle, to the effect that he and Hanley had bought for us Mallam's at £1040, a great bargain, and bidding us send the deposit £104 at once.

8. We sent back a telegram by Godwin, which would go the first thing this morning, and ran thus: 'Our telegrams have crossed. We are in the country, and did not receive yours till late last night. Thank you for your activity, but we did not wish the auction property, and we shall not be able to take it. Give over Mrs Benson's, as we said.'

9. Then, after Godwin went, we determined that William should go to London this morning taking with him a copy of the Bishop's letter to Hope Scott; that, as to what answer I should make to it, I should put myself in H.S's hands — and that if *he* chose to buy Mallam's and Benson's, he might. *I* could not, in the great uncertainty which is thrown over the future by the Bishop's letter. And he will explain to H.S. the probability of his (H.S.) being able to exchange Mallam's piece for the St Aldate's piece. William will take Oxford in his way, and ask Castle to give him 12 hours before he sells Mallam's to any one else — (not that he will sell it.) William left this place before Mass this morning.[1]

Thus we stand. I wish you directed your letters here instead of to Birmingham. I shall not get your conversation with Hope Scott about Hyères till tomorrow.

Ever Yours affly J H N

P.S. You must *now* direct your letters to me at Birmingham — at least, I leave this place for Birmingham on Saturday *morning*.

[1]Neville made a note, 'J.H.N. came to my room at 4 o'clock in the morning with a letter he had just written to Mr. Hope Scot — also a telegram to Mr Castles. He got me to get up directly and hurry off to Birmingham as best I could and then hasten on to Oxford. . . .'

TO BISHOP ULLATHORNE

Rednall July 26. 1866

My dear Lord,

I did not answer your letter at once, because I could not at once determine whether I need avail myself of the opportunity you have given me to offer remarks upon its contents.

You may be sure I read it with great interest, and with much gratitude for the trouble to which you are subjecting yourself on my behalf. But nothing occurs to me to say besides, except that I shall have no difficulty in acquiescing in the Holy Father's decision, whether it be in favour of my taking the Oxford Mission or against it

Your Lordship's obt and affte Servt in Xt
John H Newman of the Oratory

The Rt Revd The Bp of Birmingham

TO AMBROSE ST JOHN

⌐Rednall July 27/66⌐

My dear A

It is very doubtful whether I can start for Brighton till Tuesday.

It is the delay in selling our stock. Had you been here, it could have been done at once — by writing to Mr Giles — but I had no one to send to. So first, I applied to the London and Westminster Bank, which had bought in for me and had a power of attorney for me — but they answered they could not now the Bm B. C. [Birmingham Banking Company] had stopped —this lost time — time was lost before it; and I really don't know when the money will come down — I must wait for it. It *may* come tomorrow. I must telegraph to you on Monday, if I CANNOT come.

⌐William has bought Mrs Benson's piece for £570. Wm or Edward, Mallam's for £1040. Hope Scott said what was done could not be undone. They are trying to exchange Mallam's for the Corporation piece. Hope Scott as every one else thought the Bishop's letter very unfavourable to the project. I think it is decisive against it, and am in peace. H. S. would not let me write such a letter as I sketched to you. I *thought* not. He says I must stick out to the end, and throw all the failures on others.⌐

I am quite sure you could get the tickets simply by writing up to London for them. But as I go through London, *I will get them.* The name is Cook — I will find his direction in London. *Now,* if *you* get them, *we shall get them twice over,* so you *must not* get them.[1] I hope you are well.

Ever Yrs affly J H N

[1] The tickets were those for Switzerland. Thomas Cook moved the head office of his tourist agency from Leicester to London in 1865.

P.S.   William has just come from Bm [Birmingham] and, *as things stand*, I can't [lea]ve till Wednesday morning — but I shall be in Birmingham tomorrow, and I will so alter things, that (if possible) I may start on Monday. He also has in the Town rummaged out one of Cook's papers — *so I will write for them at once.*

SATURDAY 28 JULY 1866   came in with Wm [William] from Rednall

TO WILLIAM LEIGH, JUNIOR

The Oratory Bm July 29. 1866

My dear Mr Leigh

I am very sorry I missed you, when you called here and I write a line to tell you so. It is very many years since I saw you as a schoolboy at Oscott — but I have not forgotten the occasion — and I should have been pleased to renew my acquaintance with you.

Pray give my best respects to your Father and Mother
And believe me to be, Very truly Yours in Xt

John H Newman of the Oratory

W. Leigh Jun. Esqr

TO W. A. WEGUELIN

The Oratory, Birmingham. July 29th. 1866

My dear Mr Weguelin,

You must not think me uncertain or inconsiderate — but I am very sorry to say I cannot fulfil what I undertook about your boy. Something has happened within this week, which makes me see I must not take a *direct* part in sending a youth to Oxford. Till I am forbidden to give advice, I shall do so as each case comes before me in which my advice is asked. But I must not be so much a principal in getting any one entered at Oxford, as I should be if I actually went between a parent and a head of a College.[1]

I am very sorry thus to disappoint you, though it is no very difficult matter, as you must know, to get an introduction to the Dean of Ch: Ch: [Christ Church] We will gladly add any testimonials about your Son which he requires.

I am sorry too to say that our prospect of establishing an Oratory at Oxford is not so clear as it seemed to be 2 months ago.

I am my dear [Sir]
Sincerely yours in Christ John H. Newman.

P.S.   I am going abroad tomorrow for some weeks.

[1] See letter of 28 April to Weguelin, whose son John Reinhard did not go up to Oxford, but after being an underwriter at Lloyds for three years, became an artist.

MONDAY 30 JULY 1866   left Bm [Birmingham] for London — joined Ambrose, and travelled to Calais, and thro' night

TUESDAY 31 JULY   to Paris, thence to Macon where slept

WEDNESDAY 1 AUGUST   to Geneva, and thence to Vevey

THURSDAY 2 AUGUST   Went over in boat to see Glion

FRIDAY 3 AUGUST   remained [returned] to Glion, where remained

SUNDAY 5 AUGUST   very rainy — could not go to Vevey to Mass

TUESDAY 7 AUGUST   went up the Rochers de Noye[1]   fine day

FRIDAY 10 AUGUST   went to Champéry   very rainy

SATURDAY 11 AUGUST   Bishop's letter to Cardinal Barnabò sent me from home

TO MRS GOLDSMID

Champery August 11, 1866.

Dear Mrs Goldsmid,

I left Glion on the morning after your letter came to me, or I should have had great pleasure in calling on you at Vevey as you wished. Indeed, I did make an attempt the same evening, but the rain came on so heavily, as to make it impossible.

Mr St John, who had, as well as myself, the pleasure of seeing you at Rome, joins with me in every kind of remembrance to you.

I am, Dear Mrs Goldsmid, Sincerely Yours John H Newman

Mrs Goldsmid

SUNDAY 12 AUGUST 1866   said mass — answered the Bishop's letter

TO WILLIAM NEVILLE

Champéry. Val d'Illiez Canton Valais August 12. 1866

My dear Wm

Thank you for your packet. I return the Bishop's letter with my answer. I am going to give you the great trouble of copying my answer. You have already copied the Bishop's letter. Please send them both to him.

Ambrose put into this morning's box a letter for you. We had a most glorious walk this morning. The place is full of walks — but, alas, the weather is sad. This morning we took advantage of a few hours of comparative brightness — not that the sun came out. Now clouds float close around us — we have both been on, almost *in*, our beds, to get a little warmth after the exhaustion of

---

[1] '7000 feet high; as Glion is 2500 we had a pull of over 4500 and a very neat pull it was in a broiling sun the hottest day we have had. We started about 9 and were at the top at 1½. The last part very steep, a regular Jacob's ladder, up which the Father ran almost without stopping like unto a very active lamplighter . . .' (St John, 11 Aug. to Neville.)

our walk. I am sitting with three under garments on, a waistcoat, a coat, and my great rug over my shoulders, and my worsted cap on, and am just tolerably warm. The fare is fair here — the bread, butter, honey, cream, good. They won't give us cheese, though it is the pride of the country — the wine and brandy bad. I am very suspicious of the water, as having lime in it. The meat tolerable — dinner, alas, at one; a nice, clean house; about 40 inoffensive inmates, most of them women and children. The Church quite close by, we said Mass there this morning. Ambrose walks famously; has no asthma. I have done some certitude — little enough in quantity — but, (unless my whole theory be a maresnest, of which I am not sure) good in quality. I can do it when lying down, or travelling. It is a work of analysis, not of many words.[1] Ambrose thinks of taking up his sermons but work we both must have, for the weather keeps us indoors. It has been so for many weeks.

You will see I have been somewhat sharp in my answer to the Bishop — but I have written as carefully as I can — any one who likes can see your copy of my answer — not my own, lest it should get fingered

Love to all Ever Yrs affly John H Newman

Thank Austin for his letter. Tell him the Bankers only can suggest a remedy for my want of signature on the back of cheques. I will do what they tell me.

P.S.   Your letter of the 9th just come with my nephew's letter.[2] Thank you.

P.S.   8 P M. pouring rain again.

FROM BISHOP ULLATHORNE

Birmingham, July 31st 1866

Dear Dr Newman

I send you the copy of my letter in reply to Cardinal Barnabo, requesting its return. You will see that I have found the missing letter, and have quoted the important passage from it. Wishing you and your brethren every blessing I remain

Dear Dr Newman Your faithful St & affectionate friend ✠ W. B. Ullathorne.

Birminghamiae die 30 Julii 1866

Eminentissime et Reverendissime Domine

Litteris die 15 Julii datis, Eminentia vestra mihi significavit mentem esse Summi Pontificis ad differendam adprobationem in meo supplici libello petitam, quoad domum et ecclesiam Oratorii erigendas in civitate Oxfordiensi, donec respondeatur ad quaestionem; — an et quomodo timores, duobus ab hinc annis concepti, ne Catholici etiam indirecte ad Universitatem Oxfordiensem adeundam allicerentur, cessaverint?

Huic questioni vix satis respondere possim, nisi totum rei statum aperiendo, et motiva quae me inducebant ad petitionem Sanctissimo humiliandam. Omnia vero imprimis S. Sedis judicio libenter subjicio. Et Pater Newman, cui tenorem litterarum vestrarum intimavi, si forsitan aliquod haberet suggerendum, respondit simpliciter,

---

[1] This was preparation for *A Grammar of Assent*. See letter of 31 Aug. 1870 to de Vere and *Ward* II, p. 245.
[2] This was from Henry Mozley.

se nihil habere suggerendum, eo excepto, quod facillime absque ulla difficultate acquiescere vellet decisioni Sancti Patris, sit in favorem vel in adversum propositi de onere missionis apud Oxford sumendo.

Duo veniunt distinguenda in hac quaestione, videlicet, civitas et Universitas. Oxford est civitas 28,000 animarum, quarum circa 2,000 alumni sunt vel magistri Universitatis. Habet ista civitas 28 templa Protestantica, quorum 13 sunt parochialia, caetera vero ad Collegia Universitatis pertinentia. Habet insuper 12 alia templa a variis sectis aedificata, quae satis numerosae sunt inter populum civitatis. Dum vero omnes ferè sectae inter quas populus iste Angliae scinditur, habent earum templa et cultum omnibus accessibilem in illa civitate; soli Catholici non absque ratione erubescunt nullam habentes ecclesiam publicè et conspicue omnibus intrare volentibus expositam. Et majus rationabiliusque erubescunt, cum civitas ista adeo celebris sit sola inter omnes in hac Diocesi positas, quae nullam ecclesiam Catholicam habeat.

Parvulam quidem vilemque habemus capellam, a populo frequentiori remotam, in loco surburbano, ad dorsum residentiae sacerdotalis ignominiosè absconditam. Et haec missio per longum tempus a sene vel infirmo aliquo sacerdote aegre administrata fuit. Unde accidit, ut Catholici apud Oxford decem ab hinc annis non fuerunt numerosiores quam, ut scriptis patet, in anno 1775: quando 150 cujusque aetatis enumerati fuerunt. Hoc etiam numero constabant anno 1856, quando vix septem pueros puellasve invenire potui doctrina christiana erudiendis. In visitatione autem facta hoc anno currente, Catholici inventi sunt ad numerum 373 animarum. Baptizati per annum fuerunt 12, et conversiones ad fidem similiter 12. Et intra duos ultimos annos decem alumni Universitatis in gremium Ecclesiae recepti fuerunt. Et licet ista miserabilis capella congregationem non capit, licet locus in quo stet refugium sit notorium mulierum impudicarum quae juvenes Universitatis in domus suas alliciant, adeo ut qui hanc partem frequentent, in suspicionem facilè veniant; hoc tamen non obstante, nunquam desunt aliqui inter alumnos Protestanticos, qui capellam nostram intrent et sacerdotem visitent, ut de religione Catholica inquirent. Et patet quidem ex conversionibus.

Facile proinde ab Eminentia Vestra intellectum erit, quantum sit cordi Episcopi, quantum et populi fidelis, ut ecclesia in ipsa civitate, decorè posita et facilè accessibilis, erigatur. Notandum est etiam ingenium civitatis, ab Universitate diversum, ubi, sicut in aliis Angliae civitatibus, omnes religiones libere exercentur, et aeque tractantur. Et quidem in Universitate ipsa ii semper inveniuntur qui nostras doctrinas, nostra solemnia a nobis scire volunt.

Itaque ad opus missionis simpliciter respectum habui, cautelis interpositis de non interveniendo iis quae ad educandos Catholicos in Universitate spectant, quando propositum mihi factum fuerit pro ecclesia et oratorio ibidem aedificandis. Ortum primò habuit hoc propositum a quibusdam Catholicis apud Oxford commorantibus, qui impensis suis provisionariè terram amplam obtinuerunt, quo facto, Patrem Newman adierunt omni modo eum precantes, ut, potentia sui nominis assistente, in adjutorium eis adveniret; aestimantes quod nullus alius potuit subscriptiones pecuniarum operi adaequatas obtinere. Interea amici zelosi Patris Newman urgebant, eumque, quantum potuerint, inducere conebantur, ut opus propositum assumeret. Notio etiam proferebatur, ut ecclesia construenda in monumentum conversionum ad fidem evaderet quae intra 30 ultimos annos effectae sunt. Tandem mihi venit iste Pater, rem exposuit, et cautelis, uti dixi, interpositis, opus suscipiendum approbavi; et terra, provisionariè obtenta, impensis Patris Newman, in ejus proprietatem translata est. Approbationem dedi, capitulo prius consulto, et exactis conditionibus de non se immiscendo in iis quae educationem Catholicorum in Universitate respiciunt, quarum tenorem Eminentiae Vestrae litteris communicavi.

Cum vero post aliquod tempus audirem, Patrem eumdem litteras circulares ad subscriptiones pecuniarias invitandas paravisse, ubi non solum de missione sed aliquantulum de Catholicis in Universitate educandis tractavit; eum ergo adivi, et documentum, antequam in publicum deveniret, suppressum fuit. Crescentibus vero rumoribus de instantia facta apud Sanctam Sedem hac de re, et sub impressione partim erronea, quod Praelati quidam Romae aestimati, contra hoc opus ibidem viriliter agerent, cessit ab incepto, et terram obtentam vendidit aliis.

Haec omnia Eminentiae Vestrae communicata fuerunt, et die 8 Februarii 1865, dignata est mihi istis infra citatis verbis respondere: scilicet —

'Dum enim prudenter admodum impedivisti, quominus per litteras a laudato sacerdote praeparatas patres familias Catholici vel indirectè allicerentur ad filios Universitatibus Angliae committendos, apprime cum illo egeras de Missione in Civitate Oxfordiensi erigenda, qua fidelibus inibi existentibus opportuna subsidia religionis non deessent. Quod si P. Newman propositum illum missionis statuendae, dimittendum putavit, sollicitudinis tuae pastoralis erit providere ne civitas Oxfordiensis docto aliquo ac digno viro ecclesiastico destituatur, ad quem supradicti fideles in necessitatibus spiritualibus confugere valeant.'

Haec, aliaque in favorem P. Newman in illa occasione ab Eminentia Vestra scripta, non potui non quantum ad substantiam ei communicare, ut aliquo consolamine refrigeretur. Unde ideam missionis Oxfordiensis succurrendae non omnino deseruit, et quando ultima in visitatione illius missionis, necessè venit ut propositum ejus scirem, paratus fuit, quibusdam expositis, ad onus iterum suscipendum aedificandi ecclesiam et oratorium.

Planè autem intellectum fuit inter nos, ut nihil ageretur in causa studiorum Universitatis, et quod ad opus missionis curamque animarum solummodo intenderetur. Ne vero pecuniae ab illo et amicis proferendae, labores anxietatesque exantlandae in opus adeo arduum, in nihilum, ex aliqua nova oppositione, devenirent, proposuit ut supplex libellus Sanctissimo humiliaretur, cujus curam libenter suscepi. Et dum haec in via fuit, quidam zelosi in hoc opus eidem Patri persuaserunt ut ecclesiam ampliorem contemplaret, fretus bonis dispositionibus amicorum ad eum adjuvandum, quapropter, alia terra priori adjacens nuperrimè coempta fuit.

Iis igitur expositis, haud negari potest quin, aliquo modo, et indirecte, et ultra intentionem, si ecclesiam missionariam erigamus apud Oxford, attractio erit major pro Catholicis versus hanc civitatem et Universitatem. Et nomen Patris Newman cum attractivum sit ad media adducenda pro edificanda ecclesia, neque sine aliqua indirecta attractione erit pro iis patribus familias qui dispositi sunt ad filios Universitati mittendos. Non tamen proponit Pater Newman residentiam suam a Birmingham mutare, sed aliquos e suis fratribus ibi disponere, et civitatem de tempore ad tempus visitare.

Haec omnia, quanto potui candore, et partium studio secluso exposui, de caetero questionem judicio Sancti Patris humiliter submittens; et Pater Newman aequè se submittit, volenter acquiescens ejus decisioni, quaecunque et quomodocumque in sua sapientia determinaverit.

Eminentiae vestrae manum deosculans, et omnia feliciora precans Servus sum Humillimus, devotissimus, obsequentissimus

Guglielmus Bernardus Ullathorne Epis. Birminghamiensis[1]

Eminentissimo et Revdmo Cardinali Barnabo
S. Congr de Propaganda Fide Praefecto &c &c.

TO BISHOP ULLATHORNE

Champery. Val d'Illiez Aug 12. 1866

My dear Lord

I feel very much obliged by your Lordship's letting me see your letter to the Cardinal, which I herewith return.

Your kindness in showing it to me leads me to think that you will not be displeased at my making a remark upon one part of it

Your Lordship says, 'Itaque ad opus missionis simpliciter respectum habui, *cautelis interpositis* de non interveniendo in iis quae ad *educandos*

---

[1] For the reply from Propaganda see letter of 26 December 1866 to Ullathorne.

Catholicos in Universitate spectant, quando propositum mihi factum fuerit pro ecclesiâ et Oratorio ibidem aedificandis.'

And then: 'Cum vero post aliquod tempus audirem, Patrem eundem litteras circulares ad subscriptiones pecuniarias invitandas paravisse, ubi non solum de missione, sed *aliquantulum de Catholicis in Universitate educandis tractavit*. Eum ergo adivi, et documentum, antequam in publicum deveniret, suppressum fuit.'

My own recollection of what passed on my part is as follows:— When I first thought of purchasing Mr Smith's five acres, it was with no intention at all of having in consequnce any part myself in any work at Oxford of any kind. I entertained the idea of purchasing it, because I hoped to resell it to Bishops or laity, taking on myself the immediate responsibility of the purchase. Whether it was to be used at once, or some time afterwards, whether for an Academical College, or for an Oratory, or for both, or for a Monastic house, or for an inclosed nunnery, or for training schools, or for a Church and Mission, or for several of these, I left for the future. It did not come before me that I was to have a personal part in any plan.

To my surprise your Lordship called at the Oratory, and offered us the Mission; and thus for the first time my thoughts were turned to Oxford as a place in which I was personally concerned.

I wrote you word, after consulting with the Fathers, that, if I took the Mission, it would be solely for the sake of the young Catholics, then and in time to come at Oxford. And in conversation afterwards I suggested that I might provide lodging for some of them within an Oratory, if erected there. This, according to my recollection, is the very whole of what I suggested as to any plan of educational work, if it so deserves to be called. Your Lordship replied, however, that to lodge undergraduates would be putting myself in relations with the University authorities.

In consequence I wrote to you a second letter, in which I said I would take it simply as a mission.

These two principles, that I took it from your Lordship as a mission, and that, as my own personal motive, I undertook it for the sake of the Catholics in the University, actual or to be converted, I have never given up, nor hidden. I profess them now; and his Eminence should clearly apprehend that I feel no calling whatever to go to Oxford, except it be in order to take care of Catholic undergraduates or to convert graduates. Such care, such conversion, is at Oxford the chief and most important missionary work. If in future there are no undergraduates to care for, at least there will be graduates to convert.

It was in reference to the first of these two objects that I drew up the Circular which at your wish I suppressed before publication. It would have been very 'bellicose', (to use your Lordship's word of my recent one not yet circulated,)[1] to have referred *there* (unnecessarily) to the second.[2]

[1] See letter of 17 June to Ullathorne.
[2] For the circular of 1864 see letter of 27 Nov. 1964 to Ullathorne.

In the proposed circular I said *only* what I had *already* said to you, viz that I took the Mission of Oxford, especially for the sake of the Catholic youth there; this being at a time, when there was not only no discouragement from authority, but no talk of discouragement of their going there.[1]

Not a word did I say in that circular, not a word did I mean to say, much less did I 'tractare de Catholicis in Universitate educandis.' What I did say, I will transcribe from a rough copy which I have here, which is (I know) substantially as I prepared it for the press.

'Father Newman, having been entrusted by his diocesan with the Mission of Oxford, has it in contemplation, with the blessing of God, to proceed to the establishment there of a Church and House of the Oratory.

Some such establishment is at this time especially required, as a provision in behalf of the Catholic youth, whom the *Colleges of the University*, in accordance with a kinder and more liberal policy than they have hitherto pursued, are beginning to admit *within their walls*.

It need scarcely be shown that a measure like this, conceived in however good a spirit, is nevertheless fraught with spiritual danger to the parties for whom it is designed, unless the inexperience incident to their time of life and the temptations of the place are met with some corresponding safeguard of *special religious superintendence*.

The Priests of St Philip Neri may attempt, it is hoped, without presumption to supply *this imperative need*, considering that the Oratory has ever made the care of young men its primary object, and that the English Congregation in particular, by virtue of the Apostolic letters constituting it, is sent to those classes of society above others to which the members of an Academical body necessarily belong.

Moreover, educated as they have been themselves at Oxford and Cambridge, they bring to their undertaking an intimate acquaintance with the routine and habits of University life, which furnishes a reasonable hope of their being able to discharge such duties as are involved in commencing such a work, without giving umbrage to the authorities of the place, . . . '

So far my copy here allows me to go; but I am sure no words followed, suggestive of any educational plan, or work, ever so little. I guarded myself all through upon this point, keeping in view St Philip's Oratorium parvum as the type of the instrumentality by which we were to act upon the Catholics under education at Oxford, after the manner, (as we understood) of what the Jesuits have done at Bonn.

I will add, that, when after the December meeting of the Bishops (in that year 1864) I withdrew from the contemplation of any Oxford scheme, I did so on the avowed ground, which I got mentioned at Rome to a Cardinal (I think Cardinal Reisach) that the very fact of my going there would encourage parents to send their children to the University.

Moreover, I told every one, what I said to your Lordship in a letter of

[1] See last note to letter of 31 Oct. 1864 to Hope-Scott.

February 1865 (I think), that the Oxford scheme was, as far as I was concerned, entirely at an end.[1]

If I bought fresh land at Oxford, it was, as I both meant and said, for the future, not for any personal purpose.

I was not prepared for your Lordship's reviving the project of my having the Mission, as you did, in the spring of 1865, though I felt the kind confidence in me which it betokened. I have no anxious longing to be laden with so heavy a responsibility;[2] though, if I was once engaged in it, certainly there would be no intention on my part, when the church was built, of keeping aloof from the practical working of the Mission.

It may surprise Cardinal Barnabo to master the fact, which your Lordship puts before him, that I am thus indifferent how the Holy See in its wisdom decides; but it is quite true, to use the words of one of your late letters to me, though his Eminence does not know it, that I undertake the Mission of Oxford with 'reluctance'.

There is only one thing which would be more trying to me than accepting it; viz. to be allowed to build the Church there, and, as soon as that preparatory work was over, to be told from Rome that I had now done my part, and might retire.

You have always allowed me to write so freely to you, that I have not been able to bring myself to disguise any feeling which has risen in my mind from the light which your Lordship's letter throws upon the Cardinal's view of the whole transaction.[3]

I am, My dear Lord, begging your Lordship's blessing Your obt and
affte Servt in Xt   John H Newman of the Oratory

The Rt Revd The Bishop of Birmingham

P.S.   I should be much obliged to your Lordship to send me the proper form to enable me to say Mass in these parts. I am sorry to give you the trouble. Any letter, sent to Father Neville at the Oratory, would find me, wherever I am. We have sadly rainy weather.

TO A BIRMINGHAM ORATORIAN

[Middle of August 1866][4]

Also thank Wm [William] for forwarding me my draft of the Oxford circular — which, as he has seen, was of great use to me in my letter to the

[1] Letter of 10 Feb. 1865.
[2] In his draft Newman first wrote, instead of this phrase, the following: 'Now, if I were left to myself, if it were not for your Lordship and for my friends, I should certainly decline having anything to do with it. It is no effort to me to leave the disposal of it, (as I explained to you,) to the Holy Father, especially as I see he is inclined to decide in the negative.'
[3] For Newman's further comment on this episode see next letter, Memorandum of a conversation with Ullathorne on 23 Sept 1866, and letter of 9 Dec. 1866 to him. Hope-Scott wrote on 13 Nov., 'I suspect my Lord thought that proof of his vigilance with regard to Catholics frequenting the University would help his case — and so he put forward this as a prime topic.'
[4] This extract from a letter, probably to Caswall or Bittleston, is preserved in a copy made by William Neville.

Bishop. I am glad you like the letter. It seems to me that he has set me wrong with Cardinal Barnabò, and cannot set me right without setting himself wrong, by unsaying his words. And, if I were the Cardinal, I should be very suspicious of a person, who, as the Bishop has represented me to have done, after having received a 'cautela' not to speak a word 'de Catholicis educandis' in the University, proceeded to prepare a circular for publication in which he distinctly 'tractavit' though 'aliquantulum' 'de Catholicis educandis'. Again it seems to me quite clear that the Bishop *only* wants the *Church built*, by my name and influence — and he has no *wish* at all that I should have any thing more whatever to do with Oxford, though of course he would not oppose my being there, if it was the price of the Church being built — he throws out to the Cardinal this very thing, viz — that, after building the Church, I may probably do nothing more. I now understand various things he said to me in conversation, which puzzled me. I thought he meant that he did not wish us to have the Mission — but I see now, he wished me to build the Church, and do nothing more. Not that *he himself*, as I have said, would be against my being at all at Oxford, but he thinks I am very unpopular at Rome, and he does not wish to get into the scrape of placing me there; so he apologises to the Cardinal on the ground that it is very desirable to have a good church there and that I have friends who will build one for me.

WEDNESDAY 15 AUGUST 1866   said mass   very indifferent weather — but good enough to take walks some days and parts of days good

TO MARIANNE FRANCES BOWDEN

Champéry Valais The Assumption 1866.

My dear Child

I seldom say Mass here — but I have today — and I said it for you and for your sisters — and I write to tell you so. You are ever in my mind, and I am only sorry that, being from home, I cannot say Mass for you oftener.

Since I have been ordered abroad, I am doing all I can to make myself strong — but I am very sceptical that any better place could be found for me than Rednall. I never was in Switzerland before — and of course am much struck with the mountain scenery — but the weather is very bad — incessant rain, except as far as a few hours interval now and then enables us to snatch a walk. Fr St John is with me.

I suppose you are all from home likewise; and from what the English papers say, I fear your weather is as bad as ours. Except as regards the weather, everything has gone well with us. We are at present in a wonderful valley — one of those which branch off towards Savoy from the valley of the Rhone —

the Val d'Illiez — The Dent du Midi is over our heads. If the weather per-
mits, we hope to walk from here to Chamouni, and so proceed to Geneva, and
Lucerne, but everything is uncertain; — to be home by the end of the
Vacation.

My love to Papa and all of you and believe me Ever Yours affectly in Xt

John H Newman of the Oratory

Miss Bowden

SUNDAY 19 AUGUST 1866   said Mass

MONDAY 20 AUGUST   said Mass

TUESDAY 21 AUGUST   went off suddenly to Monthey, Lausanne and Fribourg where
slept

WEDNESDAY 22 AUGUST   went on to Berne and Interlaken, where stayed

THURSDAY 23 AUGUST   went up to the Murren   fine weather

TO HENRY BITTLESTON

Interlaken August 24/66

My dear Henry

You, with your love of scenery, would be much delighted with this place
— and in short, when you are told to go abroad you should come here.

We had on the whole very bad weather, while we were in the Vaud and
Valais. That was not the cause of our leaving Champéry suddenly — but the
vile stinginess of the fare. The whole house was in arms against the Maitre
d'Hotel — One family (Catholic) left the day after they came — and the
gentleman was so disgusted that he actually would not come down to the
second day's dinner. So it was with various others. The morning we left, a
lady with whom we got well acquainted, had had a serious interview with the
landlord on the subject — Ambrose had spoken to him some days before, but
with no success. The dinner we had at Lausanne the day we left at a third
rate hotel was the first dinner I had eaten for three weeks, i.e. the last dinner at
Edgbaston. We determined to leave Champéry the first fine hour, and we did,
viz on Tuesday. Yesterday and today we have been revelling in substantial
feeds. The cream and honey were capital at Champéry — but there was no
meat. This was not observable at first, but it grew upon one. First what meat
there was, was so abominably tough that few could eat it — and there were
running complaints made by the feasters all through the dinner. Next, there
were pasties, and the paste only contained and concealed heads and tails, and
drumsticks and backs of chickens, the leavings apparently of other dinners.
The best thing was a seagull, which we had one day. This, added to the one
o'clock dinner, knocked up Ambrose, to say nothing of myself — so, in spite
of the beautiful walks, which are more beautiful than I can describe, and the
really good company (which was the difference between this place and Glion)

281

suddenly on Tuesday morning we walked down to Monthey on the Rhone Valley rail-road (9 miles) and crossed the lake of Geneva to Lausanne. We slept at Freiburg [sic], and yesterday morning went on, crossing the beautiful lake of Thun to this place. The weather is now glorious, and the place looked so beautiful on our arrival, with the Jungfrau in most perfect view that we determined to stay here a day or two. There is a Catholic chapel here with daily Mass. The number of large and grand trees overshadowing the road, the splendour of the weather and (pro pudor) the gaiety of the shops took me — and I said 'Let well alone; here we are in a nice place, and we cannot be better than well'. So we shall stop till Monday or Tuesday (August 27.28) We have told the people at Champéry, as we told you, to direct our letters to the Poste Restante, Lucerne — where we shall find whatever are due.

We have been a wonderful walk today, which has been cloudless. We have been to Mürren. It is a very stiff walk, but not to compare in difficulty to our walk to the Rochers de Noye above Glion. We went in a char to and from Lauterdrunnen, where the walk begins. I dare say Edward has been there, and will describe it to you. We did not rise above 2500 feet from the point we started at — but it was still a stiff walk.

We are at the German Hotel (Fischer's) — however, I suspect it is Catholic rather than German. The Fitzherberts were here — and just now a French lady came up to me and asked me, whether I was Dr Newman, though we did not arrive till near candlelight last evening and been out the whole of today, and Ambrose had not yet put down our names in the Hotel Book.

I shall like to rest the next day or two, and return to Certitude — I have done little enough, but have made my ground (to my own apprehension) very much more clear and natural.

Love to all. Ever Yours affly John H Newman

P.S.   Dr Evans told me to go up aloft; so we have ever counted the number of 100 feet above the sea. Now I think it is next to impossible to combine such country pensions with good fare, which is the characteristic of great towns.

MONDAY 27 AUGUST 1866   bad weather again
TUESDAY 28 AUGUST   much rain at night
WEDNESDAY 29 AUGUST   went off to Lucerne — a good day

TO WILLIAM NEVILLE

Hotel de Lucerne Luzerner hof Lucerne September 3 1866
My dear William

Your note for £15 has come safely. It is not certain we shall want it — I trust not your kind additional £5 of it.

I fear I shall disappoint you much when I say that this trip has done me no good except what change of air *must* do. That I trust will show itself hereafter. As far as fidgetty symptoms go, I think I should have had them less at home, and have been able to meet them better. However, I have very little, thank God, to complain of here — though I certainly should have been better at home.

But what we both feel is want of good meals and want of sleep. I think neither Ambrose nor I have had more than two good nights' rest since we left England. It is all the same for that whether we are at Glion, Champéry, Interlaken, or here.

For myself, it arises, I think, from the food. I cannot digest such a nagging meal as a table d'hote dinner is. As to a restaurant's, I manage well enough. You order your two dishes and have as much as you can eat — but first a small piece of boiled, then a cold lobster salad, then a wing of a pigeon, then some hard beef, then an impossible sweet bread, then some beans, and, to finish, some cruel ice, which simply destroys the working power of the stomach — and all these at vast intervals, and then the uncertainty, when it is put before you, whether you should be able to manage the particular dish or not, the suspicion with which you begin to eat and the impossibility of your getting your will to cooperate with your jaws, which is a great secret of food digesting well, the disgust at what you don't like, and the desire to get rid of it off your plate into your stomach as soon as you can, all this, in the event, not only does not answer the purpose of food, but murders sleep, when night comes. I have now (7 a.m.) my inside all disarranged by yesterday's dinner still — and as to sleep, I woke in discomfort at 12, and again at 2 — and then, at half past 3 I woke for good — except a little dozing between 5 and 6. Then the beds, though new and good, are intolerable to me, and I cannot tell why. They make me restless. I wake with a crick in my neck — or a pain in my shoulders — or with my foot bare, from the blanket etc being pulled too much over my shoulders — and above all, they are so wonderfully hot. At this time my mattress lies against my wall, as I take it off my bed, before going to bed — the under mattress being harder. The upper mattress is springy, and I can't lie even — At Champéry I had to lie like a serpent in and out — and to sleep is impossible under such circumstances. The mattresses are new, filled with hair — there is no fault to be found with them, except that I cannot sleep on them. I have said nothing of the wine. It is all acid, Yvorne and all; and this I have been drinking now 5 weeks. I have tried to obey Dr Evan's order implicitly, but in vain. As to brandy, I have sometimes gone to it — but it is no support, and wishy washy. The only point in which we went out of Dr E's directions is in our coming down from our altitudes to Interlaken and Lucerne, but we have been brought down against our will by bad fare and bad weather. We were not high enough to get rid of fogs and rain — and if we had gone higher we should have got out of the Catholic region, except at Zermatt. Also I am sure that a high place like that would be most dreary for any length of time. Then again in high places such as Champéry, there is no competition in hotels — and you are at the mercy of a stingy land lord.

Ambrose has been lamish — and Dr de Mussy who is here, assures him it is nothing more than a little sprain.

We were going to see Seelisberg today, the place which the poor [F.R.] Wards liked so much – but I am too tired.

You must not be surprised, if we come home a day or two earlier — for we are not doing much more than spend money. Our rooms had better be ready. I don't suppose we should start hence at once — but I doubt whether it will be prudent for you to write again. We have got all your letters from the Poste Restante.

Ever Yrs affly J H N

WEDNESDAY 5 SEPTEMBER 1866 set off suddenly at 1 PM for Bale, travelled thro' the night
THURSDAY 6 SEPTEMBER and through the day by Paris and Calais to Bm [Birmingham], where arrived at 1 a.m.

TO JAMES FITZJAMES STEPHEN

[7 September 1866][1]

As to the treatment of the subject of lying (and of all moral offences) in our books of Moral Theology, in saying what follows, I am not differing from what you have said, but (as I conceive) illustrating it.

If Catholics have to go to confession, they must not be left at the mercy of the individual priest whether they get absolution or not. If he is to declare his intention not to commit an act again, he must be sure that it is a sinful act — and who is to decide between him and the priest?

There a general standard is [of] right and wrong in detail is necessary. The Church does not supply one, except in great questions of morals — as the ten commandments etc. but its divines in all countries, or the Schola, as it is called, supply a body of precepts — which are the individual Priest's rule in those cases in which there is a unanimous consent of divines — but when there is not, e.g. as regards lying, the penitent has the benefit of the discordance of opinions so as to be allowed to take the laxest view entertained by any divine of the details of morality, if he will, and may *insist* on the priest's giving him absolution, on that lax view, as [it] is generally considered, or at least may obtain absolution from another confessor.

[1] Stephen wrote on 6 Sept., 'Some time ago I was looking over my contributions to the Saturday Review with a sort of notion of collecting some of them for publication when I happened to come across an article which may interest you. It is called "Lying" and is an attempt to give a definite answer to a question which you ask in the Apologia as to the cases in which men of the world consider a lie justifiable. You will see that I have tried at all events to state your view fairly, and that my own does not widely drift from it.'

Stephen did not include this article when he reprinted his contributions to the *Saturday Review*, in *Horae Sabbaticae*, three volumes, London 1892.

This view of divines *in the Church* answers to that public opinion on morals, the view of society or the world, which in the passage you quote from me I wished to exist on the subject of veracity. While Society was Catholic, the view of divines was the view of Society, but now of course it is so no longer. This does not matter to us as regards our duties to God and to ourselves — but it does matter in our intercourse with others, our neighbour, so far as our neighbour is not Catholic. Hence on the whole subject of justice, law, honesty etc etc we have great difficulties at this day, because

SATURDAY 8 SEPTEMBER 1866   Ignatius returned.

TO T. W. ALLIES

The Oratory Birmingham Sept. 9. 1866

My dear Allies,

I got back a day or two ago. Your letter just caught me before I set off, and was very useful. We had put aside the four places you mentioned from there being no Catholic church in any of them. However, in consequence of what you said, we went up to Glion for a week, and found it all that you said, in point of extreme beauty and grandeur. We went up the Rochers de Noye on foot, (7,000 ft.) which lie behind Glion, and had a most splendid view of Bernese Valais, and Savoy Alps, ranging from the Wetterhorn to Mont Blanc — so fine, that I did not care to go up the Righi. We were driven from Glion (besides the want of church) by the fare and the company, and I went to Champéry in Valais, where the company was as quiet and pleasant as could be, and the people as Catholic with a church at our door, and the walks superb, but the fare worse than Glion, and the fogs and rain cruel. Thence we steamed and railed to Interlaken, where we remained a week in perfect content, with a Chapel close to us, a quiet hotel, excellent fare, and glorious weather, and we walked up the Mürren, the view from which is certainly sublime. We should have remained at Interlaken, I think, till the end of our time, had not we had our letters directed on to Lucerne, so at the end of a week off we went to the latter place, where we found a grand and a comfortable Hotel (the Lucerner-hof), all but its table d'hôte delicious, which, though as good as such dinners can be, never can please me, and we had splendid weather again. We did nothing great there in the way of walking. I should have liked to have gone up the [Neisen?] from the Lake of Thun, from which you see both Mont Blanc and the Jungfrau, but I had no great desire to mount the Righi. We suddenly settled one morning at breakfast to start home, after a break at Lucerne, putting ourselves in the train at one p.m., and found ourselves next night at Birmingham, after a very easy and prosperous journey.

So we have been to two out of your four places, and have kept your letter as a memorandum for future travellers.

Ever yours affly John H Newman

TO THOMAS KEBLE

The Oratory Birmingham Septr 9. 1866

sent

Dear Thomas Keble,

I am not pained at all at your declining to accede to my request, for there might be good reasons; but I cannot call the reasons you do give good or kind.[1]

I had not a dream of suppressing one word of the Volume, or I should have told you so.

As if I should ask you for it, and then, as soon as I got it safe into my hands, at once quietly commit an act which would stultify the gift, and of which I had given you no warning!

As if I should have written a letter expressing much affection towards the memory of its author as my dear friend and then proceed to extinguish the very memorial of them.

As if I had any need of condescending to such sliness [sic], had I determined to be so hard, seeing that legally I could for 20 years past have withdrawn my verses from the volume without asking leave of any one, since, when I gave it to your brother, of course, I took no payment for them.

As if, had I wished to suppress them, I should voluntarily have given the volume to him in 1845, as I did, at a time when it was mine in the very same sense in which it was after that day his.

I asked of you the favour, because I thought it a very gracious thing for you to grant. I should have felt it a sort of legacy of his to me, without harm to any one, a legacy which I *could* not transmit to others, for, I suppose, the copyright expires with me, if not with him. No one after my death would have legal power to suppress what in my life time I should have much enjoyed, as coming to me from him, as it had gone to him from me.

If it was a duty to refuse me, the refusal might have been given graciously, without gratuitous imputations.

I cannot be sorry for having asked; I cannot but be sorry to be so answered.[2]

Very truly Yours John H Newman

The Revd T. Keble.

[1] See letter of 21 July to Thomas Keble Junior. The substance of his eventual letter in reply, which Newman thought came from his father (to whom he returned it — see letter of 13 Sept.), may be gathered from the present correspondence.

[2] Thomas Keble senior replied on 12 Sept. 'I do assure you, I have not written to you or any one else, on the subject of your letter.' Mrs John Keble had given all her husband's copyrights to her nephew Thomas Keble junior. His father continued, 'I did not see your [original] Letter to my son, but I understood it was an exceedingly kind one, and that he was *very* desirous to fulfil your wishes — only he was afraid (in which feeling, I confess, I sympathized with him) you might think it your duty, as a loyal member of the Church of Rome. to suppress your own portion (at least) of the L.A. [*Lyra Apostolica*] — and we all shrank from this thought, as you may well suppose.' Thomas Keble added that he had not seen his son's letters to Newman, and ended, 'I hope you will still allow me to subscribe myself Your's always gratefully and affectionately'.

MONDAY 10 SEPTEMBER 1866 about now Edward returned
TUESDAY 11 SEPTEMBER school met
THURSDAY 13 SEPTEMBER Edward went for his holyday again.

TO THOMAS KEBLE

The Oratory Birmingham Septr 13. 1866

sent

My dear Thomas Keble

I sincerely beg your pardon for attributing to you a letter which is not yours. And I assure you I reciprocate the kind words you use about me. I have admired and loved you ever since I knew you, nay before; ever since your Long Vacation Sermons in St Mary's pulpit in 1822. I have never forgotten the visits I paid you in 1834 and 1837 — or my meeting the Bishop and his Chaplain — and carrying little Tom on my back from the valley to the neighbourhood of the Parsonage.[1]

I send you the letter which so much pained me, as I had rather be without it.[2]

Let me send my kindest remembrances through you to Mrs Keble and believe me to be

Ever Yours affectionately John H Newman

The Revd Thos. Keble

TO DAVID DOUGLAS

The Oratory, Birmingham, 14 th September 1866

Dear Sir

On my return from abroad I found on my table your letter and the September Number of *The North British Review*, and I have read, I need

---

[1] Newman visited Thomas Keble at Bisley, Gloucestershire, from 16 to 27 July 1834. On 26 July the Bishop of Gloucester, James Henry Monk, came with his chaplain and held a confirmation, staying the night with Thomas Keble.
Newman's second visit was from 8 to 10 June 1837.
[2] Thomas Keble replied on 15 Sept., 'Your note received yesterday is a relief and comfort to me.
I have not written to my son upon the subject — but may I hope, that, if he asks you to regard the copyright of the L.A. [*Lyra Apostolica*] as your own, you will kindly comply with his request.'
Thomas Keble junior only heard of Newman's letters to his father at the end of Sept. and wrote on 1 Oct. 'to crave your forgiveness for the awkwardness of expression,' and said he would write to John Mozley, the publisher of *Lyra Apostolica*, 'and ask him to consider you as the sole proprietor of the Book.' The matter was not finally settled until Aug. 1868. See letters of 1 and 10 Aug. to Liddon. On 7 Aug. 1868 T. Keble junior wrote to Liddon, 'The fact is that in July 1866 Dr N. wrote very kindly to me, and asked to have the copyright of the book returned to him. I had a (perhaps mistaken) feeling that it had been left to me in trust, and . . . arrived at a decision which I have since regretted — viz. to decline giving up the trust.' Newman eventually transferred the copyright to Keble College.

scarcely tell you, with extreme interest, the article on Mr Keble, to which you direct my attention.[1]

I feel very grateful to a reviewer, as the writer of it, who describes with so much real sympathy and truth the characteristics of a religious movement, of which, naturally, I have such vivid recollections, and such affectionate though mournful remembrances.

And it is an extreme pleasure to read a critique on *The Christian Year* which speaks with such depth and exactness, both of the work itself, and of the character of its author.

As to what the writer says of me, I wish I deserved only half the praise he gives me; but still I cannot help being much grateful at it, though I am not quite pleased with myself for being so. Anyhow I can thank him for what is more than kind, though I do not feel it right to appropriate it.[2]

I am, dear sir, very faithfully yours, John H. Newman.[3]

David Douglas Esq.

FROM GERARD MANLEY HOPKINS

Oak Hill, Hampstead, N.W. Aug. 28, 1866.

Reverend Sir,

I address you with great hesitation knowing that you are in the midst of your own engagements and because you must be much exposed to applications from all sides. I am anxious to become a Catholic, and I thought that you might possibly be able to see me for a short time when I pass through Birmingham in a few days, I believe on Friday. But I feel most strongly the injustice of intruding on your engagements or convenience and therefore, if that is the case, I shall think it a favour if you will kindly let me know that you are unable to see me. I do not want to be helped to any conclusions of belief, for I am thankful to say my mind is made up, but the necessity of becoming a Catholic (although I had long foreseen where the only consistent position would lie) coming upon me suddenly has put me into painful confusion of mind about my immediate duty in my circumstances. I wished also to know what it would be morally my duty to hold on certain formally open points, because the same reasoning which makes the Tractarian ground contradictory would almost lead one also to shrink from what Mr. Oakley calls a minimising Catholicism. I say this much to take from you any hesitation in not allowing me to come to Birmingham if duties should stand in the way: you will understand that by God's mercy I am clear as to the sole authority of the Church of Rome. While much in doubt therefore as to my right to trouble you by this application, I would not deny at the same time that I should feel it the greatest privilege to see you. If it were so, I should hope not to detain you long. I may perhaps in some way introduce myself by reminding you of an intimate college friend of mine, William Addis, who once had the pleasure of spending an hour with you at the Oratory; I think also he has written to you since: I have little doubt that in not a very long time he will become a Catholic. If I should be so happy as to hear

---

[1] The *North British Review*, (Sept. 1866), pp. 229–64. Douglas, who was the editor and publisher, sent the *Review*, with a covering note, on 1 Sept. The article on Keble was by J. C. Shairp and was republished in his *Studies in Poetry and Philosophy,* first edition Edinburgh 1866, second edition with additions 1872, third edition 1876, fourth edition 1886.

[2] The passage about Newman, which comes at the beginning of the article, is printed in the Appendix to *Campaign,* pp. 4–15.

[3] Douglas sent this letter to Shairp, who replied, . . . 'It is a great privilege to have the opportunity of saying to Dr Newman how much we of a younger generation here owed him for the high and unworldly lessons he has taught.'

before Friday that you could spare time to see me, I should hope to be at Birmingham that day and sleep there, of if you had any convenient time in the two or three weeks after that I should like to come over from Rochdale where I shall be staying at Dr. Molesworth's. But in ending I would again say that I beg you will have no hesitation, as I have no doubt you will not, in declining to see me if you think best.

Believe me, Reverend Sir, your obedient servant, Gerard M. Hopkins.

TO GERARD MANLEY HOPKINS

The Oratory Birmingham Septr 14. 1866

My dear Sir

I am sorry I was abroad when your letter came. Now I am returned and expect to be here for some weeks. I will gladly see you as you propose, if you will fix a day

Very truly yours John H Newman

G. M. Hopkins Esqr

WEDNESDAY 19 SEPTEMBER 1866 Mr Lynch's letter about now[1]

TO LADY HERBERT OF LEA

The Oratory Birmingham Septr 20. 1866

Dear Lady Herbert,

I thank you very much for your most kind letter. It will be a great pleasure to me to receive the call with which you purpose to favour me at the beginning of October.[2] You may be sure I should be only too happy to answer any question you may put to me to the best of my ability — but every one has his own gift — and I feel sincerely that I am a bad person to consult in a practical difficulty.

A lady whom I think you know, Miss Holmes, told me you wished to see me in London. I should most gladly have availed myself of the opportunity of so great a pleasure — but I was not there at the time when your Ladyship was

I am, My dear Lady Herbert, Sincerely Yours in Xt

John H Newman of the Oratory

The Lady Herbert

TO J. R. BLOXAM

The Oratory Birmingham Septr 21. 1866

My dear Bloxam

I send you a line in anticipation of tomorrow, and to say that, if all is well, I shall then say Mass for you, and Copeland, and all connected with

[1] See letter of 28 Sept to Lynch.
[2] Lady Herbert became a Catholic in 1865, after the death of her husband. During their honeymoon they had called on Newman at Rome, see diary for 1 Dec. 1847.

289

Littlemore, living and dead, that God may be merciful to them 'granting them in this world knowledge of His Truth, and in the world to come life everlasting.'[1]

Also I owe you a letter in return for your call. As you know, I was abroad — I was very sorry, but it could not be helped. Medical men and my friends here sent me abroad, thinking to make me stronger, which was my sole ailment just now — I never expected good from it, nor as I think, have I got it, though I am very well. At my age the bustle of travelling is not a diversion but a fidget, and I hope they will be wiser another time.

I have nothing to write to you about — we have just begun school again. I have emendated and printed a play of Plautus for the boys, and am teaching them to construe it. This is my daily task just now — and will last for many weeks. Daily duties come and go — friends flit to and fro — and thus the year glides by, after other years which have glided by, on to future years which will glide by still faster, till one gets upon the brink of the Eternal Year.

God bless you, My dear Bloxam,

I am with kindest wishes, (you know what that means)[2]
Ever Yours affectionately John H Newman

The Revd Dr Bloxam

TO R. W. CHURCH

The Oratory, Bm Septr 21, 1866

What wonderful events have taken place lately! quite a new world is coming in; and if Louis Napoleon were to fall ill, the catastrophe would be still more wonderful. I don't quite like our being thrown so much into the background. Twenty-five years ago Rogers said one ought to go abroad to know how great England was — it is not so now — some foreign papers simply leave out the heading 'Angleterre' in their foreign news. And the fate of Austria, a state in some striking points like us, though in others different, is a sort of omen of what might happen to us in the future.[3] Then, I am quite ashamed at the past ignorance of the *Times* and other papers and at myself for

[1] Littlemore church was consecrated on 22 Sept. 1836. Bloxam was present and he and Copeland worked at Littlemore as Newman's curates. See *Newman and Bloxam*, pp. 34–7.
[2] Newman always hoped that Bloxam would become a Catholic. Bloxam replied next day, 'Your most welcome and kind letter reached me this morning. Though unexpected, the subject matter of it did not take me by surprize. All day yesterday (the 22d) I was full of recollections of Littlemore. How well I remember thirty years ago the consecration of the little chapel — Isaac Williams reading the prayers — your text and sermon — the little child getting its head fixed in the altar rails — Ward of Baliol walking back with the Warden of Wadham etc etc. and what I now look back to with the greatest satisfaction was an accidental walk to Littlemore a day or two before the consecration — and finding the chapel door open, and entering just as you were placing the Cross over the altar. You spoke to me then, a stranger, a few kind words which have been treasured ever since. — I have good reason to remember Littlemore and the 22d of September — and be sure that your kind prayers for me now are duly appreciated.'
[3] The defeat of Austria at Sadowa on 3 July brought the Austro–Prussian War to an end and cut her off from Germany, leaving Prussia supreme there.

having been so taken in by them. Think of the *Times* during the American civil war! And again on the breaking out, and in the course of the Danish War.[1] Really we are simply in the dark as to what is going on beyond our four seas — even if we know what is going on within them. How dark, as even I could see, we are as to Ireland, from having been there. Some four years ago I met a man, he seemed some sort of country gentleman, at the inn of a country town — we got into conversation. I told him the hatred felt for England in all ranks in Ireland — how great friends of mine did not scruple to speak to me of the 'bloody English' — the common phrase — how cautious and quiet government people simply confessed they would gladly show their teeth if they were sure of biting; but he would not believe me — and that has been the state of the mass of our people. Even now they are slow to believe that Fenianism is as deeply rooted as it is. Every Irishman is but watching his opportunity — and if he is friendly to this country, it is because he despairs.

Don't think I am tempted to despair about *England*. I am in as little despair about England as about the Pope. I think they have both enormous latent forces; and if, as they now talk, he goes to Malta, I shall think it is caused by some hidden sympathy of position. Misery does indeed make us acquainted with strange bedfellows. And, whatever the Pope will have to do, at least England must make some great changes, and give up many cherished ways of going on, if she is to keep her place in the world.

However, much all this is to an old man like me.

TO MARK PATTISON

The Oratory Birmingham Septr 21. 1866

My dear Rector

I was very sorry to find that you had called on me during my absence from home. Medical men had sent me abroad. I am very well, but had had a bad time of it last Christmas and they thought I might be made stronger. I am very well still, but am very sceptical as to the good of such remedies in my case, unless indeed I were to go for as much as a year or two to New Zealand or the Moon — that indeed would be a renovation of one's constitution.

There was a fair chance some months ago of the Oratory coming to Oxford after all — our bishop wished it — but I thought a spoke might be put in the wheel. Nothing is settled yet, nor will be for some time — but, as I do not mean to come except on my own terms, I am not sanguine that the project will come to any thing.

I have been in Switzerland. The weather was not good — that and the German war made tourists scarce. For the English were kept away by the

---

[1] *The Times* backed the Southern States of America and then Denmark, over the question of Schleswig-Holstein.

weather, and the poor German students had been cut off by the war. The Americans, however, were in great force.

Yours, My dear Rector, Ever affectly John H Newman

The Revd The Rector of Lincoln

TO MRS F. R. WARD

The Oratory Septr 22. 1866

My dear Mrs Ward,

Your letter is most touching and long to be remembered. May we all be as ready for death, when our time comes, as that dear boy was. He could never be more fit to die than now, and so God took him.[1] And for what, my dear Mrs Ward, was he given you, what was your mission in cherishing and rearing him up so carefully, except to bring him to heaven? That was your very work, — not to gain him a long life and a happy one, but to educate him for his God. That was your work, and through God's grace you have done it. You have carried it home. What can you want more? Your loving Lord has fulfilled all your largest prayers — and now your dear boy will pay them back to you a hundred fold by praying for you and for all who are so dear to him. And one of his first prayers, be sure, will be that his Mother may be able to bear his loss well.

I am so glad to have seen him for a few minutes on that Sunday in June[2]

Ever Yours Very affectionately in Xt   John H Newman

MEMORANDUM   Sept 23. 1866

The Bishop went half an hour ago. After a conversation of near an hour he said:

'By the bye, I received your letter from Switzerland.

I have not written to Cardinal Barnabo to set right the point to which you directed my attention, because I thought [[if I did so]] it would give him an impression that you were anxious [[for a favourable answer]] about the Oxford matter.

[1] Francis, the eldest son of F. R. Ward, at the Oratory School from 1 May 1859 until the end of 1861, went in 1865 to the Royal Military Academy at Woolwich, where he was held in high estimation. He died of diphtheria at his parents' house on 18 Aug. 1866, aged 20. Mrs Ward wrote on 20 Sept. that he received the last sacraments the day before he died. After the ceremony, his mother said to him, '"now, my dearest, if God is very good He will let you stay —" He did not speak directly, and I thought he was not going to answer — then he said very slowly "yes, and if God is very good He will let me go — too," that was the first thing he said that gave me a clue to how he felt about dying; after that his joy was more and more apparent — and he seemed at last to be watching with a bright expectation of seeing the veil removed . . .' Mrs Ward added, 'he was always very moderate in his expressions of pleasure at the events of life — and I can truly say that I never saw him as glad to do anything as he was to die; it took me by surprise for he was very happy and his life was full of promise.'
[2] Francis Ward ended a letter he wrote on 15 Feb. 1865 to Newman, 'Believe me I shall always try to follow your advice as to making God my friend, and not being ashamed of my religion.'

It is best not to seem anxious. But, as time is now going on, I shall address a letter to Mgr Neave on the subject, which he will read to the Cardinal.'

I said I quite agreed with his Lordship that it was not well to seem anxious — and that I was quite satisfied he should do just what he thought fit, for in writing my letter to him I had done all that I cared to do or to be done.

JHN

[[The Bishop said the above fixing his eyes steadily upon me and smiling in a gracious way, meaning (as it seemed to me) 'So you felt I had kicked your shins in my letter to his Eminence, — well you may have borne it pretty well.']]

N.B. I think Bishops fancy that, as justice does not exist between the Creator and His creatures, between man and the brute creation, so there is none between themselves and their subjects. So that they [[do inconsiderate or strong acts, and]] only look out *how* clergy and laity accept those acts of theirs which in one *not* a Bishop *would* be unjust,[1] e.g. whether the aggrieved accept them as an opportunity for gaining merit ⟨(Vid Bowyer's case)⟩, with humility, cheerfulness, submission, resignation, etc. The Bishop's manner was, as if he was *testing* my spirit.[2]

MONDAY 24 SEPTEMBER 1866   Mr Browning, Walford's friend came and slept[3]

[1] [[On whom those acts tell, will accept what in one]]
[2] [[as if he had had an opportunity of testing my spirit]] Sir George Bowyer was engaged in a long dispute with the Archbishops of Westminster about the Church he had built in Great Ormond Street.
   Neville wrote an account on 23 Sept. to Caswall: 'The Bishop called upon the Father this afternoon. Evidently the Bishop was a little fluttered as also did the Father so feel when first he went to him. However the Bishop began at once with gossip and carried it on a very long time, until the Father mentioned Dr Neave's name: whereupon the Bishop looking at the Father and assuming a polite style of smile and voice and inclination of the head and as if suddenly reminded of something by the mention of Dr Neave's name said: "I received your letter to me" (i.e. the letter written at Champéry on Aug. 12) "I have not thought it worth while to do any-thing about it yet — I thought that you would not wish to seem to Cardinal Barnabò to be eager about Oxford and had I written to him yet about your letter to me, it would have seemed as though you are eager about Oxford and, I thought that you would not like that and therefore that you would quite approve of my not doing any thing. But now the vacation in Rome has commenced I am writing a letter to Dr Neave, which he will read to Cardinal Barnabò and that letter will set you quite right with the Cardinal when he has heard it read."
   His Lordship having said that much, and by the bye, as it were, continued to talk about other little matters and presently went away.'
   In *Letters and Documents,* which he published in April 1867, Ullathorne wrote that 'after reading it [Newman's letter of 12 Aug. 1866], he [Ullathorne] saw that he ought to have been more definite in expressing his meaning,' p. 21. He then quoted from Newman's letter of 9 Dec. 1866.
[3] This was Oscar Browning, then an assistant master at Eton. 'On my first visit to Newman at the Oratory, Edgbaston, I was not permitted to dine in the refectory, lest the legend which was being read at the evening meal might excite the risibility of a novice. I joined the Fathers in the parlour after dinner, where tea was served instead of wine. The conversation was most interesting and turned largely on Swiss travel. I was struck with Newman's marvellous copiousness of language and his abundant fluency, also with his use of harmless worldly slang, that he might not appear priggish or monkish. Next morning I met him in the library and had a memorable conversation with him. He showed me a large collection of Dante literature which had been left him by a departed friend; he spoke of Dante as one of the foremost Catholic teachers. He also called my attention to a large collection of bound pamphlets which he had

TUESDAY 25 SEPTEMBER   Mr B went.   H. Mozley came and dined in his way to Eton.
F. Henry went away.

TO E. B. PUSEY

The Oratory Bm Sept 25/66

My dear Pusey

I do not know whether it is worth while writing to you, but it can be no harm. I hear there is in the last Number of the Roman Analecta, (which is to be got, or used to be) at Dulan's Soho Square, an article, quasi authoritative, on Private Revelations; and that the drift of it is to disown extreme sayings about the Blessed Virgin.[1]

I would send it to you, if I had got it. My informant was a man of ability, but I cannot answer for his impression of the work being what yours would be. He thought it was in a way apropos of your Eirenicon

Ever Yours affiy John H Newman

P.S.   Have you heard (I don't wish my name mentioned) that Faber's translation of de Montfort is *very* incorrect. He did it when he was too near death to be able to be accurate. De Montfort does not say some of the things which are most startling in the English.[2]

THURSDAY 27 SEPTEMBER 1866   Mr. Hopkins called about this time[3]

given to the library, and to his own works. This led to his inclusion of Thomas Aquinas amongst the greatest writers of the world, a judgment then entirely new to me, which later study has convinced me to be true. Being attracted by a number of editions of the Vulgate, he told me that he had been commissioned by Pope Pius IX to make a new translation of that work, but had been prevented from doing so by his inability to understand the Latin, some parts of which were to him unintelligible and untranslatable. He said that he had applied to his brother Francis, formerly Professor of Latin at University College, and that he was unable to help him.' Oscar Browning, *Memories of Sixty Years at Eton, Cambridge and Elsewhere*, London 1910, pp. 269–70. Browning's memories were not always accurate, since at the end of this passage he describes a visit to Newman's room after his death, when he saw 'the last sermons he had written and the hair shirt which he wore.'

[1] *Analecta Juris Pontificii*, Neuvième Série, LXXV, Paris 1867, Vol. V, i., pp. 22–53, 'Révélations Privées.' The article took a severe line and showed that private revelations could not be part of the formal object of divine faith.

[2] *A Treatise on the True Devotion to the Blessed Virgin*, by the Ven. L. M. Grignion de Montfort, translated from the French, with a preface by F. W. Faber, London 1863. See *A Letter to Pusey, Diff*. II, p. 98.

[3] On 22 Sept. Hopkins wrote his account to Robert Bridges:

'Dr Newman was most kind, I mean in the very best sense, for his manner was not that of solicitous kindness, but genial and almost, so to speak, unserious. And if I may say so, he was so sensible. He asked questions which made it clear for me how to act; I will tell you presently what that is: he made sure I was acting deliberately and wished to hear my arguments; when I had given them and said I could see no way out of them, he laughed and said "Nor can I": and he told me I must come to the church to accept and believe — as I hope I do. He thought there appeared no reason, if it had not been for matters at home of course, why I should not be received at once, but in no way did he urge me on, rather the other way. More than once when I offered to go he was good enough to make me stay talking. Amongst other things he said that he always answered those who thought the learned had no excuse of invincible ignorance, that on the contrary they had that excuse the most of all people. It is needless to say he spoke with interest and kindness and appreciation of all that Tractarians reverence . . . .

TO HENRY J. LYNCH

Septr 28. 1866

Dear Sir,

I inclose you a copy of a letter addressed to our Secretary by the Revd
J. S. Flanagan on occasion of your Statement which we sent to him for his
remarks upon it.[1]

I have to add that we do not give our consent to your printing as you propose to do our private letters which went to you in past years in the name of
the Oratory, and we hereby make our *protest* against your doing so.

J H Newman

H. Lynch Esqr

TO E. B. PUSEY

The Oratory Bm Septr 28/66

My dear Pusey

A friend of mine, Mr Morell, the bearer of this, has asked me by means of
it to introduce him to you. I have told him you are very busy with press work
just now (of which I know well the anxiety) and that you wrote to me from
London — but still he thought he should like to have it. He has corresponded
with you before now.

I think he wants introductions to Oxford people through you quite as
much as to see you personally

Thank you for your letter. I have seen scarcely more than the outside of
Harper's book yet.[2]

Ever Yours affly John H Newman

SATURDAY 29 SEPTEMBER 1866   Edward returned

MONDAY 1 OCTOBER   Mrs Bellasis called and Combs and Captain Mousley

I am to go over from Oxford to the Oratory for my reception next term — early in the
term I must make it, and since a Retreat is advisable for a convert, Dr. Newman was so very
good as to offer me to come there at Xmas, which would be the earliest opportunity for it. He
thought it both expedient and likely that I should finish my time at Oxford . . .' *The Letters
of Gerard Manley Hopkins to Robert Bridges,* edited by Claude Colleer Abbott, London 1935,
pp. 5–6.

[1] Lynch wrote on 11 Sept. about the sale by the Oratory of an estate at Rathtarman to
Stephen Woulfe Flanagan, and enclosing a long Statement objecting that it should have been
offered to him. See letter of 10 July 1857, and those addressed to Lynch in 1859. The estate
had always been held in the name of J. S. Flanagan, and had been sold in 1861, Lynch's brother
acting as agent. Flanagan's letter refuted Lynch's claims, and in a private letter of 21 Sept. he
said that while it was dishonourable of Lynch to print private letters, his Statement would do
no harm to the Oratorians. At first Lynch said he would not print it, see letter of 11 Nov. to
him, but in 1867 it was printed for private circulation.

[2] This was Thomas Harper's *Peace through the Truth : or Essays on subjects connected with
Dr Pusey's Eirenicon* first series.

The Oratory Birmingham Octr 2. 1866

My dear Jemima

Thank you for your kind present which Harry delivered quite faithfully, and which I was very glad to have. He gave me a good account of your health, and said you played the piano again just as well as you used to do.

He had some doubt, however, whether you played at sight so well, but I attribute that to that weakness of sight, of which I was sorry to find you complaining. I feel it in playing the violin — my eye cannot follow the notes so quickly, and besides that my head gets a little confused, and I find if difficult to recollect the key I am playing in, when modulations are frequent, or the continuation thro' the bar of accidental sharps and flats.

I came back quite safe from Switzerland without accident, and in spite of the bad weather managed to get some fine days.

This wretched paper will try your eyes

Ever Yours affly John H Newman

WEDNESDAY 3 OCTOBER 1866   Mr Bigg called[1]
THURSDAY 4 OCTOBER   The Duke [of Norfolk] and Lady Mary H. [Howard] called
FRIDAY 5 OCTOBER   W. Palmer came and slept
SATURDAY 6 OCTOBER   Renouf here again   Henry returned
SUNDAY 7 OCTOBER   Service for the Pope[2]   Palmer went   Fr Suffield came

TO E. B. PUSEY

The Oratory Bm Octr 7. 1866

My dear Pusey

On reading your letter of September 26 again before putting it away, I understand it to say, which I did not make out on first reading, that you have not seen de Bandeli's book. *I* have not certainly — but if you have not, and it is not too late, I think Mr Jenkins, incumbent of a place (Lytham?) near Hythe has got it — at least he quotes it freely.[3]

---

[1] Probably Charles Bigg (1840–1908), the historian of the early Church, who left Oxford in 1866 to become a classical master at Cheltenham College.

[2] The French garrison was being withdrawn from Rome by Napoleon III, and Garibaldi was threatening all that remained of the temporal power. Ullathorne ordered special prayers, and said that the sermon on this day must 'instruct the faithful on their obligations to the Holy See, and on the duty . . . of praying for the Pope.' Newman preached 'The Pope and the Revolution', which he printed separately at once, and included in the third edition of *O.S.*, pp. 263–98, in 1870.

[3] Pusey wrote that after his *Eirenicon* was completed he found his quotations used by de Bandelis, (who attacked the Immaculate Conception), had long ago been disputed. He was consulting the copy in Christ Church library.

They say that both you, Archbishop Manning and Mr Harper have made mistakes upon Cardinal Turrecremata; and that in particular your quotation in the Irenicon is not to be found in him.[1]

Ever Yours affly John H Newman

MONDAY 8 OCTOBER 1866   Mrs Hervey called and went.   Lady Herbert called   Fr Suffield went

TO MISS MUNRO

The Oratory Bm Octr 8. 1866

My dear Miss Munro,

I wished to have answered your welcome letter before now — but all last week, and to the very moment of delivering I was occupied with a Sermon on the subject of yesterday's solemnity

A report had come to me that you had not been well — but I did not know what it meant. I grieve indeed for what you tell me of yourself, but hope it is all over now. You must have had a good deal of pain.

I hope you are not teasing yourself with such metaphysical questions as 'Where are we?' if the Pope loses his temporal power. First I consider we must be somewhere, even if he did — and next, I think he won't. No one, but the extreme reds, wish him to lose it — no one but extreme ultramontanes think he can lose no part of it. Bishops speak as strongly as they can — because they consider that the more they claim, the less he will lose — Protestants too on their side speak as strongly against him as they can — because they think that the less they profess to give him, the less he will retain. I think the Archbishop and Times would come to a compromise, whatever they may think right to say, if they had a conference. Each side is trying to make the best terms for itself[2]

What you say about your book is very good. I don't see why you should hesitate about going on with it

I am glad you talk of coming down here.

Do you know that I give you a Mass every now and then together with some other ladies? I said Mass for you last Friday

Ever Yrs affly John H Newman of the Oratory

Miss Munro

TUESDAY 9 OCTOBER 1866   Austin went away

[1] Pusey replied that his quotation from Turrecremata had also been used by Perrone.
[2] Manning's forceful pastoral in support of the temporal power was read in the London churches on 30 Sept. *The Times* also published it, and attacked it violently in a leading article. Cf. the *Tablet*, (6 Oct. 1866), p. 632.

TO CHARLES MEYNELL

The Oratory Bm Octr 11. 1866

My dear Dr Meynell

I fear I have led you to think that I am acting as a critic towards your Sermons[1] — but that is not the case — I have taken them up, when I have had a leisure five minutes, from the pleasure of reading them. I have not yet read a great many — but however many I read, I see clearly my present judgment of them will not be altered. They seem to me exceedingly well adapted for the purpose which has occasioned them, viz to make an impression upon boys — they are short, clear, pointed — enough matter, and not too much, — suitable to their intellectual wants — and, to me at length, new either in argument or in handling argument.

I am very glad you have published them

Very sincerely Yours in Xt   John H Newman of the Oratory

The Revd Dr Meynell

FRIDAY 12 OCTOBER 1866   sent up Sermon for Press.   Renouf went
SATURDAY 13 OCTOBER   Mr Wegg Prosser to dinner   J. B. Marshall came   Austin returned

TO SIR JUSTIN SHEIL

The Oratory Birmingham October 13. 1866

My dear Sir Justin,

I hoped to have managed the gymnastics before this— but we could not learn of any except those exercised by young ladies. In a little time we shall have them in our own grounds.

It pleased me to hear you say that your boy [Edward] was going on well in his Latin. I was very glad you examined him. His place in the examination I suppose was determined by the accidents of the moment. Boys often fall below what they can do, most unaccountably. Sometimes they take fright at questions, and will not calmly take hold of them — at other times they mistake them. Then, they, too often, will not read over what they give in — transcribe their rough copies incorrectly, or make other mistakes, which they could set right, if they did but think twice on the subject.

He is in Plautus this term with me — and its taking great pains with it

I am, My dear Sir Justin, Sincerely Yours
John H Newman of the Oratory

Sir Justin Shiel K C B &c &c.

[1] *Short Sermons on Doctrinal Subjects,* London 1866. Meynell was a professor at Oscott College.

The Oratory Birmingham Oct. 14. 1866

My dear Frank,

I am glad to hear of your whereabout; and your account of Maria is most pleasant and encouraging. Your troubles in your new house are among the ordinary miseries of Human Life.[1] Every one has to go through them, till his house, like a snail's shell, has become part of himself. I am surprised you say nothing about chimneys smoking. They are the opprobrium of this scientific age. They and sea-sickness are universal evils, the latter left incurable — the former left to settle themselves by experiment, and the force of usage. Chimneys almost seem testimonies in favour of Darwin's theories — for instead of being made for use as a final cause, they seem to grow into comfortable use by using

I have been sent into Switzerland to be made young again. I have no faith in such recipes except under very exceptional circumstances. The Antipodes are said to renovate the infirm or old. Perhaps a perch on the Himalayas or a rock in mid ocean, might do the same, if one did not die in the process — but this was not the recipe. I am not fond of the trouble of travelling — And, though I will not say it did me no good, yet I was not unwell before I went, nor am I in extraordinary health and vigour now. I was so well, and am so well, that I would gladly compound on the terms of being never better and never worse.

Arabic in European type — it would be a great step in literary and social intercourse to have a common alphabet every where; but it seems at present impossible. Think of Greek — one should have to begin Greek again, if it were written in Roman type: even the Germans won't give up their exclusive alphabet, tho' they could do it so easily.[2]

With love of [sic] Maria

Ever yours affectly John H. Newman

The Oratory Birmingham Octr 14. 1866

My dear Stewart

I have written to Monsell by this post in your behalf. I hope you will succeed. I had fancied the Bishops were nearly as much opposed to the Supplemental Charta as the Queen's University graduates; but you give a different view of things.[3]

[1] F. W. Newman had moved to 1 Dover Place, Clifton.
[2] F. W. Newman published in 1866 *A Handbook of Modern Arabic*. He replied on 22 Feb. 1867, 'I have no thought of *superseding* the Arabic character, which is a short hand; but only to introduce a long hand side by side with it. Arabs *must* learn European letters, if they are to use maps; i.e. if they are to be educated.'
[3] This Charter was intended to bring the Catholic University within the state system.

It is a pleasant thing for Ornsby that you should be his successor in house and furniture — and, I suppose, in Professorship. You don't say any thing as to how you are, and Mrs Stewart and all of you. You have had, I think, as trying a Summer as we have

> Yours affectly in Xt   John H Newman of the Oratory

Jas Stewart

MONDAY 15 OCTOBER 1866   Mr King to dinner
TUESDAY 16 OCTOBER   J B Marshall went   Edward and Wm [William] went to Oxford about Wm's purchase.

TO WILLIAM MONSELL

The Oratory Birmingham. Oct 16. 1866

My dear Monsell

Mr Stewart, one of the Professors in the Catholic University, has written to me to send to you and Lord Dunraven a testimonial in behalf of his fitness for the place of Matriculation Examiner in the Queen's University.

I do not know what the subjects of examination are — so I can do no more than give you my general opinion of Mr Stewart's qualifications for such an office. But so much I do heartily. He is a very deserving man, a hard worker, and now for twelve years acting as a classical Professor in the Catholic University. He is a graduate of the University of Cambridge. He is very popular, I believe, among both students and professors, and I don't think you will find a better man.

His writing to me shows that the new System is really to be tried — but, from what I had read in the Papers, I fancied that both the Catholic Authorities and the graduates of the Queen's University were against it.

I hope you are going on well in Limerick and Ireland in this anxious time. You will be somewhat exposed at Tervoe, if the Fenians are to invade you from America this winter

> Ever Yours affectly John H Newman of the Oratory

The Rt Honble W. Monsell. M P.

WEDNESDAY 17 OCTOBER 1866   Serjt and Mrs Bellasis passed thro.   Mr J F Stephen called in evening

18 New Inn Hall Street, Oxford. — St. Theresa, [15 October] 1866.

Very Reverend Father,

I have been up at Oxford just long enough to have heard from my father and mother in return for my letter announcing my conversion. Their answers are terrible: I cannot read them twice. If you will pray for them and me just now I shall be deeply thankful. But what I am writing for is this — they urge me with the utmost entreaties to wait till I have taken my degree — more than half a year. Of course it is impossible, and since it is impossible to wait as long as they wish it seems to me useless to wait at all. Would you therefore wish me to come to Birmingham at once, on Thursday, Friday, or Saturday? You will understand why I have any hesitation at all, namely because if immediately after their letters urging a long delay I am received without any, it will be another blow and look like intentional cruelty. I did not know till last night the rule about *communicatio in sacris* — at least as binding catechumens, but I now see the alternative thrown open, either to live without Church and sacraments or else, in order to avoid the Catholic Church, to have to attend constantly the services of that very Church. This brings the matter to an absurdity and makes me think that any delay, whatever relief it may be to my parents, is impossible. I am asking you then whether I shall at all costs be received at once.

Strange to say of four conversions mine is the earliest and yet my reception will be last. I think I said that my friend William Garrett was converted and received shortly after hearing of my conversion;[1] just before term began another friend, Alexander Wood, wrote to me in perplexity, and when I wrote back to his surprise telling him I was a convert he made up his own mind the next morning and is being received today;[2] by a strange chance he met Addis in town and Addis, who had put off all thought of change for a year, was by God's mercy at once determined to see a priest and was received at Bayswater the same evening — Saturday. All our minds you see were ready to go at a touch and it cannot but be that the same is the case with many here. Addis' loss will be deep grief to Dr. Pusey I think: he has known him so long and stayed with him at Chale in a retreat.

I shall ask F. William Neville to open and answer this in your absence.

Monsignor Eyre seemed to say that I ought not to make my confession by means of a paper as I have been used to do. Will you kindly say whether you wd. prefer it so or not?

Believe me, dear Father, your affectionate son in Christ, Gerard M. Hopkins.

P.S. And if you should bid me be received at once will you kindly name the day? The liberality of the college authorities will throw no hindrance in the way.

The Oratory Bm Octr 18/66

My dear Mr Hopkins

It is not wonderful that you should not be able to take so great a step without trouble and pain.

There is no reason you should not travel on Sunday, if, as you seem to say, it would be a convenient day for you

There would be no difficulty in granting you leave to continue for a time

---

[1] Alfred William Garrett (1844–1929), at Balliol College, Oxford, 1863–7, was confirmed by Manning on 8 Oct. 1866. He was in the Indian Education Service until 1884, and then in that of Tasmania.

[2] Alexander Wood (1845–1912), at Trinity College, Oxford 1863, B.A. non-collegiate 1870. He went to live in Sussex, where he knew Coventry Patmore.

attendance at the College Chapel, if the authorities did not at once give you leave to absent yourself. In that case you would say your own prayers there.[1]

But I can explain all this when I see you. Meanwhile you have my best prayers that He who has begun the good work in you may finish it — and I do not doubt He will

Yours most sincerely John H Newman

TO MARK PATTISON

The Oratory Birmingham Octr 19. 1866

My dear Rector

Thank you very much for your invitation. It would give me great pleasure to accept it, were I coming to Oxford as you suppose — but in fact it never was less likely.

I forget whether I mentioned to you, when I wrote the other day, that our Bishop here renewed to me his offer of the Oxford mission last Spring — I told him I thought there would be some difficulty at Rome, in consequence of representations which would be made there by good English friends of mine. My anticipation has proved correct, for, though nothing is determined there, yet the affair is likely to linger on, or conditions will be annexed to the leave which I am not likely to accept.

Besides, of course I am older every year — and cannot reckon on my health.

I think the report you mention must have arisen from friends of mine, on their own hook having lately bought some land at Oxford. They have done this certainly in hope of my going there — but their buying does not overcome the real obstacles

Yours very sincerely John H Newman

The Rector of Lincoln

SUNDAY 21 OCTOBER 1866   Mr Hopkins came from Oxford and was received

TO T. W. ALLIES

The Oratory, Bm Oct. 21. /66

My dear Allies

Of course I am very much gratified at what you say about Mr Dewar's conversion.[2]

---

[1] See Hopkins's letter of 16 Oct. to his father, *Further Letters of Gerard Manley Hopkins,* edited by C. C. Abbott, second edition Oxford 1956, p. 91.

[2] Allies wrote at the end of his letter of 19 Oct., 'There is residing close by me now a Mr Dewar who has just resigned a living in Lincolnshire, and become a Catholic with his wife and family. He tells me that your Letter to Dr Pusey was the first thing to do away with his difficulties as to the worship of our Blessed Lady.'

As to my Sermon, I am publishing it, since so many reports are circulated about me, but I have seen nothing in the Papers about this sermon which was not *in the main* accurate.[1] The account of it in the Guardian (taken, I think, from the Daily News) was singularly fair. But of course I know nothing of what kind friends and enemies say about me privately without foundation.

Certainly, the tone of Dr Cullen, almost giving up the Church, if the temporal power went, shrieking as if he were on the edge of an abyss, and saying that it was all the Emperor of the French, did not recommend itself to me.[2] And, though I have no difficulty in saying that the temporal power is necessary, while it lasts, nothing can make me say that it is necessary, if it be clean taken away, — and I am quite as sure that, when it is clean gone, if that ever took place, no Pope would say that it was necessary, as I am sure no Pope will say that Our Lord is a mere man.

Ever yrs affly John H Newman

TO HENRY JAMES COLERIDGE

The Oratory Bm Octr 21/66

My dear Fr Coleridge

H. Wilberforce fancies in his kindness that some pages I wrote for the French Translation of my Apologia, by way of explaining to foreigners the state of things in the Anglican Church, would be of use in England. I cannot see this. I have said nothing in them but what every one here knows very well. I have no objection at all to its being published in English, but I don't think it worth publishing. You are quite welcome to it, but (if you take it) it would be better to say that it is translated from the French.[3]

It has pained me to find that in the Month the Anglican sacrament has

David Erskine Dewar, at Winchester and then New College, where he was a Fellow 1845–53. He was Rector of Friesthorp, Lincs., until his conversion in 1866. He became a priest after his wife's death.

[1] The *Pall Mall Gazette*, (8 Oct. 1866), thought that Newman's views on the temporal power 'appear to fall considerably short of those entertained by Dr. Manning and the Irish bishops.'

Allies began his letter, 'The Pall Mall Gazette, and I believe other papers, have given a perversion of your sermon on Rosary Sunday [7 Oct.],' and asked Newman to publish it. Allies continued, 'But what makes me further desire it is the account which an auditor, W. Palmer, has given me of it. Its publication will probably put an end to many false impressions as to your sentiments on so important a subject as the Temporal Power.'

[2] In his pastoral letter read in the Dublin churches on 2 Sept. Cullen spoke of how Napoleon III had allowed no other power than France to be the protector of the Holy See, and was now about to withdraw his troops. 'Thus Rome will be abandoned to the tender mercies of the infidel and excommunicated ministers of Victor Emmanuel.' The *Tablet*, (8 Sept. 1866), p. 571.

[3] Newman's note on the Church of England was published in the *Month*, (Dec. 1866), pp. 623–7, without mention of his name but with an explanation that through the kindness of a friend of the French editor, the original English text had been obtained. It appeared in *Histoire de mes opinions religieuses,* Paris 1866, Appendix I, 'Notes inédites composées par le P. Newman, pour la traduction française,' pp. 437–444. Wilfrid Ward retranslated these notes into English and published them in the Introduction to his edition of *Apo.*, London 1913 (reprinted 1931), pp. xxii–xxx.

been said to be probably a slice of a quartern loaf, and nothing else. What good such expressions can do, I know not — but I feel keenly what harm they do.[1]

Then as to the Pusey controversy, of course (to take the lowest ground, and without reference to the *duty* of a Catholic periodical) you are in for it, and must go on. But you are in for it for good and bad — and, as you (in consistency) must profess eagerly and confidently to be looking out for his promised explanation, and may fairly anticipate his failure, so again, while the controversy lasts in its identity and continuity, you must carry with you in your readers' thoughts, all you have said in your earlier papers on the subject, and necessarily have the burden of all those hard sayings against him, which now perhaps you might wish to smooth down if you could. They live in your fresh papers, tho' these may be written in a better spirit, because the controversy is *one*. I confess I wish you were not on what I think the wrong set of lines.

Yours most sincerely, John H Newman

TO HENRY WILLIAMS MOZLEY

The Oratory Birmingham Octr 21. 1866

My dear Harry

Thank you for your effort to get the Number of the Chr. Rem. for me. I fear it is hopeless.[2] It was as great a pleasure to me to see you, as you say it was to you to see me. You have been all in my thoughts and prayers, since you were born — and therefore at length to see your living faces is even a greater joy to me than yours can be.

God bless you, and believe me Yours ever affectionately

John H Newman

H Mozley Esqr

MONDAY 22 OCTOBER 1866   Lord Gainsborough called.   Sir Vere de Vere called with Mr Boyle

---

[1] An article, 'Unionist Essays,' in the *Month*, (Oct. 1866), p. 356 spoke of 'the probability that the "Eucharistic Sacrifice" of the Ritualists, in spite of chasubles, and lights, and incense, is only the manipulation of a piece of a quartern loaf.' A note to Newman's letter shows that Coleridge thought another Jesuit wrote the sentence, and he, the editor, allowed it to pass. See also letter of 24 Oct. to Coleridge.

[2] Newman evidently wanted to see the article which reviewed *A Letter to Pusey*, Pusey's republication of Tract XC, and works by Manning and Oakeley on Reunion, in the *Christian Remembrancer*, (July 1866), pp. 155–83. The July number was sent to him by Mrs John Mozley. See letter of 14 Dec. This High Church periodical was full of admiration for *A Letter to Pusey*.

TO T. W. ALLIES

The Oratory, Birmingham Oct. 23/66.

My dear Allies,

I fully adhere to the declaration of the Pope and the Bishops 'in *praesenti rerum* humanarum *statu*, ipsum hunc principatum civilem, pro bono ac libero Ecclesiae animarumque regimine omnino requiri.'[1] And I think that the 'praesens status' will continue throughout time, and that the Pope's temporal sovereignty (at least in Rome) will continue through our time. But I *may* be *mistaken* in thinking that the praesens status may not be suddenly superseded, by revolutions as violent as the rise of Prussia in a week last June. The Pope and Bishops have not said it will not be so, nor have they said that in that case, in the futuro rerum statu of human affairs, if a new world came in, as different from the present as the present is from the old pagan world, that then the temporal sovereignty will be necessary. Since then I have no light of prophecy about the future, and *may* be mistaken about the continuance of the praesens status, I am obliged to contemplate the possibility of the Pope's position in other states besides the present, and I say that to make his temporal power necessary in *all* states, when I have no word of Scripture, tradition, the Pope, or the Church to make me say so, is simply unbelieving. God can support His Church by every word that goeth out of His mouth, and it is well to tell Protestants this, that we do not depend upon man, and that, if they take away (by God's permission) the temporal power, still the Church is the Church still.

And you will see, from my saying this, how lightly I make of your argument about the consensus of infidels, lax Catholics etc that the Church depends on the Temporal Power — they think so because they have not *faith* in the promises.[2]

We ought to pray and to do our part for the preservation of the temporal power, but it is most undignified to shriek, most undignified to say 'it is all along of Louis Napoleon.' It may be so, but it does not become the Church of God to imply that mortal man can do us real harm, or be angry with those who ill treat her. All things will turn to good. The Apostles did not shriek when they were put into prison. The Pope has not shrieked when he has spoken of the temporal power. The Bishops at Rome in 1862 did not shriek — but now it is the fashion for certain persons to shriek, and say 'we are all being done for.' Our own Bishop in a dignified way has said 'Pius will suffer but his cause will gain,' but in the mouth of other prelates a sacred cause is lowered and disgraced by the appearance of abject fear.[3]

Yours affly John H Newman

[1] This was the Declaration about the temporal power, made on 9 June 1862 at Rome, at the gathering of bishops for the canonisation of the Japanese martyrs.

[2] In reply to Newman's letter of 21 Oct. Allies wrote next day how he felt the force of the argument 'that every enemy of the Church in every country, whether infidel, liberal, heretic, schismatic, bad liver, or shaky Catholic, is unanimous in desiring the extinction of the Pope's Temporal Sovereignty . . .' while all faithful Catholics supported it.

[3] Allies replied on 26 Oct. still unconvinced, but thanked Newman for his 'most beautiful sermon' on 'The Pope and the Revolution.'

The Oratory Bm Octr 24. 1866

My dear Fr Coleridge

The worst effect that could happen from any letter of mine to you, would be your giving up controversial writing, for I do not know any one who would write with greater taste and selfrestraint, to say nothing of higher qualities, than yourself.[1]

Of course I take a different view of Pusey from what you do — but for argument's sake I will allow that, as you say, he shuffles desperately — also, I take the very ground that you do, viz that his word is taken as law by numbers, when it should not be. Also, of course I think and desire, that for the sake of those numbers, and moreover (which it strikes me you do not so much consider) for the *sake of himself*, what he says incorrectly, should be set right, and brought home to him as requiring such right-setting.

And now, it is because I wish you so much to continue to write as controversialist in the Month, and hope you will, that I bore you about this matter — If I was sure you were giving up that Office, I would not say another word.

Well then, I think any thing like *abuse* is just as likely to effect your object with Pusey himself and his admirers, as the wind was likely, in contest with the sun, to blow off the traveller's coat. As to the quartern-loaf τόπος, if there is one thing more than another likely to shock and alienate those whom we wish to convert, it is to ridicule their objects of worship. It is wounding them in their most sacred point. They may have a false conscience, but, if they are obeying it, it is laughing at them for being religious. For myself, I can recollect myself firmly believing that what your friend calls a piece of a quartern loaf, was, not only that, but the body of Christ — and, to my own *consciousness*, I as truly believed it and as simply adored it, as I do now the Blessed Sacrament on Catholic Altars. And what I did then, I know many Anglicans do now. Moreover, as the writer confessed by saying that it was 'probably' nothing more than bread, it is possibly, or even not improbably, something more — or at least, though *I* may not think so, I cannot condemn another who does. Now I cannot see how laughing at a worship which has nothing laughable in it, and, which, if not well founded, has no *intrinsic* incredibility, but is invalidated by purely historical considerations and ritual facts, how such a polemic has any tendency whatever to weaken the worshippers belief in its truth and obligation. On the other hand I see that it would offend him just as much as the blasphemous bills upon the Dublin walls against Transubstantiation disgust and anger the Catholics who pass by. Such

---

[1] Coleridge made a note to this letter: 'I seem to have written to N. saying I thought of giving up that kind of writing in consequence of his objections, the truth of which I felt, and this letter is his answer. I think N. was quite right in the main point but he did not know how aggravated we were at Pusey's controversial methods — He seemed to us to live and write for the sake of preventing conversions to the Catholic Church by any means, fair or foul.'

ridicule is not the weapon of those who desire to save souls. It repels and hardens.

And now to go on to Pusey. In like manner, abuse of him will neither convert him nor any of his followers. I received an Oxford undergraduate the other day — he was speaking of Pusey, and took occasion to say how young men revered him chiefly for his very austere life, and his meekness in controversy. He said that they could not bear to hear him spoken against.[1] I do not call exposing a man's mistakes 'speaking against him' — nor do I suppose *any* one would. But if, instead of exposing those errors in detail, and as matters of fact, in simple grave language, a controversialist *began* by saying 'This man is absurd — he shuffles — he misrepresents — he is keeping men from the truth' — every word of it might be true, but I should say he was calling names, and indulging in abuse. For by abuse I mean accusation without proof — or condemnation before proof — and such a process of putting the cart before the horse defeats itself, and has no tendency to convince and persuade those whom it concerns.

I have not yet had an opportunity of reading Fr Harper's book —[2] I expect great instruction and pleasure in doing so; and I look with special interest at what comes from him from simple gratitude to him for some both kind and very seasonable letters I have had from him; but I cannot deny I have been distressed at the tone he takes about Pusey, and for this plain reason, because I think he defeats his object by adopting it. What the Guardian said of his work illustrates what I mean. It dismissed a learned and (I am sure) convincing work with the remark 'We need only say that this book is written in the controversial style of the 16th and 17th centuries,' or words to that effect.[3] This was a convenient, for it was a telling way, of getting rid of a formidable opponent. It was a very good excuse to its readers for not going into his arguments. It was just in the same way that Marshall's important work on Christian Missions was got rid of. His acrimony against Protestants was made the excuse for tossing it aside. Excuse all this and believe me

Ever Yours most sincerely in Xt   John H Newman

P.S.   I have no *English* of my notes. They are in French in the French Edition.

[1] Cf. G. M. Hopkins's letter of 16 Oct. to his father, 'In fact Dr. Pusey and Mr. Liddon were the only two men in the world who could avail to detain me: the fact that they were Anglicans kept me one . . .' *Further Letters of Gerard Manley Hopkins*, p. 94.
[2] *Peace through the Truth, Essays on subjects connected with Dr. Pusey's Eirenicon,* first series.
[3] The *Guardian*, (12 Sept 1866), p. 954. For Marshall, see letter of 4 Oct. 1862 to Daunt.

The Oratory Bm Octr 24/66

My dear Jemima

Pray offer John my best congratulations. From what I had heard from your boys, I thought Miss E. P. was destined for one of them, but I did not know which.[1]

My friend, Mr St John, has been much troubled with asthma. He finds paper dipped in salt petre and burnt, a specific when an attack is coming on. As it is a remedy immediately acting on the lungs, it is likely to succeed in one case as another.

I rejoice to see in today's Times, Alfred's success at Jesus.[2]

I heard by accident in London in June that Grace was in Australia, and had a little boy. I am glad you have a good account of her. Some time ago an accidental person spoke of my 'relations' in Australia. I could not conceive what he meant[3]

Yours affecty John H Newman

Mrs John Mozley

TO J. WALKER OF SCARBOROUGH

The Oratory Bm Oct 25. 1866

My dear Canon Walker

You must not expect any thing from my Sermon. It is a mere parish Sermon, which I publish because it has been talked about, and which I publish as I preached it. I won't say it is like *every* Sermon that the Archbishop has preached, because his Sermons are unlike each other — but it seems to me not unlike the one he was preaching just at the time that I preached mine, judging from the Newspaper account of it. For in it he said, that though it was our duty to maintain the Pope's temporal power, he did not mean to say that the Church would be extinguished, if the Pope lost it — and that is pretty much what I have said.[4]

I saw a notice of the new Catholic paper in the Guardian — but the paragraph did not say any thing of its being the Bishops' paper, but Mr Sheridan Purcell's — nor can I conceive that the Bishops would undertake the responsibility of one. The same paragraph spoke of a Paper from another

[1] John Rickards Mozley, Jemima's second son, had become engaged to Edith Merivale, daughter of Bonamy Price.

[2] Alfred Dean Mozley, Jemima's fifth and youngest son, was matriculated on 24 Oct. at Jesus College, Oxford, where he won a scholarship.

[3] Grace was the only child of Newman's sister Harriett, wife of Thomas Mozley. Grace, who married William Langford in 1864, emigrated to Australia. Her only child, William, was born in 1865.

[4] Manning's sermon was preached at St Mary Moorfields on 7 Oct. He treated the question of the temporal power historically, and admitted that for 300 years the Papacy had existed without it.

quarter — but in both cases the money question will be the difficulty. You cannot get good articles, unless you pay for them.[1]

Very sincerely Yours John H Newman

The Very Revd Canon Walker

TO MRS F. R. WARD

The Oratory Bm Octr 25/66

My dear Mrs Ward

I am very sorry for Richard's most unaccountable trouble. As every one did what he should do (except the Trinity authorities) there is nothing to be sorry about. That the old President and Catholicism are at the bottom of it, there can be no doubt — but this does not clear it all up. From what I have heard, Dr Wilson is simply disgusted with the new state of things in Oxford — and I dare say was most unwilling that Catholics should be admitted into College.[2] Again, the Tutors give out, I am told, that Richard is to try a third time, 'because he has improved so much —' which sounds so strange, as to show there is some other reason, and that they feel he has not been treated fairly. But how could the President affect the result? He of course can refuse to give rooms — but he does not take part in the examination. How many examiners are there? do any agree with him? If so, of course one bigotted examiner can manage to be unfair with great plausibility. I thought that they might have pitched on Richard's translation into Latin, and made it the reason for rejecting him; but Mr Adams says it is not that, though he is not at liberty to say what it is. There is something strange in his not taking him back — as if he found it would be disadvantageous to him to have a Catholic in his house. Mr Ward's letter seemed to me a very wise one. I suppose they will make up for their injustice, when next Richard presents himself. Mr Waite must be very much annoyed.

Thank you for letting me see the letter. Give my love to Richard

and believe me Yours affectly in Xt
John H Newman of the Oratory

P.S. I return the letters by this post.

Friday 26 October 1866

My Sermon on the Pope came down from London.

[1] The *Guardian*, (10 Oct. 1866), p. 1032, quoted the *Pall Mall Gazette*, which announced the appearance of two new Catholic peiodicals, one conducted by E. S. Purcell, the *Westminster Gazette,* and the other by T. F. Wetherell, the *Chronicle*, supported by those who had written for Acton's *Home and Foreign Review*. See letter of 1 Jan. 1867 to St John.

[2] Richard Ward wished to enter Trinity College, Oxford, and went up in Oct. 1867. John Wilson, who became President of Trinity in 1850, resigned on 12 Dec. 1866. He was succeeded by S. W. Wayte, a personal friend of the Wards. Mr Adams was Richard Ward's private tutor.

TO LORD CHARLES THYNNE

The Oratory, Birmingham, Oct. 29th. 1866.

My dear Lord Charles,

Thank you very much for your kind letter. I was very glad to hear from you, and about Charlie.

You will be sorry to hear that at present there seems very little chance of our going to Oxford. As you know, the Bishop offered us again the Mission last spring. We accepted it, but I told his Lordship there would be difficulty of getting the arrangement confirmed at Rome. He made very light of it — but Cardinal Reisach came over to inquire into the whole matter. I had known him at Rome, and would have waited on him, had I received ever so little encouragement, I received none. He was recommended to W. G. Ward, and remained with him three days. I suppose he learned enough from him to supersede the necessity of hearing any thing from any one else. While he was in England, I had a letter from our Bishop, saying that there were difficulties — When I was abroad, the Bishop sent me word that the difficulties continued — and since I have been back, the Vicar General has given his private opinion that the answer, when it comes, will be unfavorable to us.[1]

We have bought more than one piece of land opposite Ch. Ch. [Christ Church] — but I don't think any thing will come of it.

Towneley is still here, reading with Walford, who was, till he was received last spring, an Eton Tutor. His father put off his entrance at Ch. Ch. for a year — he was so young. Latin Verse tells in a competition examination — but I doubt whether it would in an examination for entrance.

With kindest remembrance to Lady Charles & Charlie, I am, My dear Lord Charles,

Sincerely Yours in Christ, John H. Newman of the Oratory.

The Lord Charles Thynne.

TUESDAY 30 OCTOBER 1866   Ambrose went to Rednall   Miss Ind came to Edgbaston
WEDNESDAY 31 OCTOBER   Eddy Froude came
THURSDAY 1 NOVEMBER   boys went out to Rednall   Wm Froude called

---

[1] 'At the middle of July came Cardinal Reisach, one of the Cardinals of Propaganda, to England, commissioned to examine the question on the spot. This was a practical and sensible measure, but its purpose was frustrated by the manner in which it was carried out. Reisach was the one Cardinal who, under the influence of Fr Coffin's representations, had at Propaganda advocated Manning's appointment to Westminster. It was therefore natural that Coffin should now act as his guide in England; but this resulted in his hearing only one side of the question.' *Butler* II, pp. 14–15. See letters of 11 Nov. 1866 to Emily Bowles and 15 April 1867 to Patterson.

The Oratory, Birmingham, November 1. 1866.

My dear Mrs. Bretherton,

Father Edward has already told you what we think as to Willie. I don't think much of his calling himself groom and gardener. Things are very different there from what they are here. I have heard of the daughters of an Anglican Colonial Bishop, who scrubbed the floors — yet no one would call them housemaids in the sense of the word at home. Rebecca kept the sheep — and so now in the Colonies a sort of patriarchal life goes on. The two Allies in Australia were simply shepherds and farm servants.[1]

Willie must stick on and not change. A rolling stone gathers no moss. If he has energy, he will in time make his way, of course he looked into books on New Zealand and consulted people, before he went. They would tell him just what he has found. A Colony is always a rough place. It is the place for young people. I was surprised to find the other day that I have a Niece out in Australia. She and her husband went there on their marriage. She complains of the climate — but they must rub on.[2] Willie is in an excellent climate, and in time will like the place.

Love to Eleanor & all your party, Ever yours affectionately
John H Newman, of the Oratory.

P.S.   Father Edward has got the letters.

The Oratory Bm ⌐Novr. 1. 1866

My dear Hope Scott

A telegram, we have just received from London from our Oxford man of business, leads me to write to you. I shall ask you a question, but, even if you can do nothing in the matter, at least I shall have put you au courant. Did I know our Oxford agent's address in London, I should be disposed to send him to take the chance of finding you in Parliament Street, that you might be able to ask him questions.

⌐I hope to inclose a little plan — but for the present

---

[1] William Bretherton emigrated to New Zealand in 1865. Cyril and Edward Allies went out to Queensland in 1863.
[2] See letter of 24 Oct. to Mrs John Mozley.

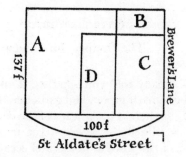

This only gives the relative location of the plots, not the proper size.

⌐A is Hanley's which I bought a year ago for £2000.

B is Mrs Barton or some such name which Fr Neville bought last July for between £500 and £600

C is Mallam's which he bought at auction for £1000 and odd.

D belongs to the St Aldates Feoffees, and is unsold.

The Incumbent of St Aldate's has gone to Canon Auriol (one of the Simeon Trustees) and he has gone to the Charity Commissioners, and got them to sanction the Feoffees selling it to him on condition he gives it in perpetuity to the Incumbent of St Aldate's. The price being a little more than £1000.

Our agent (Castles) wrote to us to advise us to bid against him £1500, considering the Trustees would not change their minds unless for a considerable addition.

Since that, as I learn from the Telegram just come, he has gone to London, seen the Commissioners, and they have determined to put the land *up to auction*.

I don't know more about it than that it has four small houses at the back, and one large (divided into two) house in front — bringing in certainly £50 rent, perhaps more.

What you said about my letting the St Giles's land go without writing to you, leads me to ask you this. Will you *bid* for the land (D)? and to what amount, and on what conditions, if so?⌐[1]

Ever Yrs affly John H Newman

TO WILLIAM MONSELL

The Oratory Bm Novr 1. 1866

My dear Monsell,

Thank you for the sight of the Draft Report, which I herewith return. I am glad so see you have got so far.[2]

---

[1] Hope-Scott replied on 3 Nov. from Abbotsford, 'I cannot undertake any further expense just now, even for so good an object as the acquisition of land D.'

[2] This refers to the draft proposals for linking the Catholic University of Ireland with the Queen's University.

And I am very glad to have your story of Fr Prost. Coming from a Redemptorist, it is specially valuable.[1] One of the Limerick Redemptorists wrote here to complain of some thing I had said in my Letter to Pusey; and Fr Coffin, I am told, speaks quite strongly against me. Also I believe they were some of those religious, who complained about what I said to Rome — though nothing has come of it. I have had a satisfactory letter from our Bishop on the subject of my Sermon — but he, like you, thinks what I have said about Italian and English Catholics will not please some of our Roman friends —[2]

FRIDAY 2 NOVEMBER 1866   sang High Mass   Ambrose returned from Rednall
SATURDAY 3 NOVEMBER   Mr S. Evans called

TO HENRY JAMES COLERIDGE

The Oratory Bm Novr 4/66

My dear Fr Coleridge

As to the MS of mine which H. Wilberforce has, my difficulty is, that I really am sure it is not worth publishing in England. It was written for France, where nothing is known about the Anglican Church. What would be useful there would be a series of absurd truisms here. Again I put down what to the best of my belief was true — was substantially true — but I did not verify by references every half sentence — therefore for what I know there are errors in detail, which, though not such as to invalidate the statements I have made, might serve to make Anglicans angry, and give ground for attacks.

These are my reasons — a publication which is gratuitous, ought to be at least harmless. Again, if it is worth while adding it, I wrote *for* a French translation — and, for what I know, the *English* may be very incorrect in point of style.

If you use it you must be so kind as to let me see a proof.

Have you heard the report that Canon Escourt was going to bring out an Essay against Anglican orders, and he came to some hitch which stopped him?[3]

Ever Yours most sincerely in Xt   John H Newman of the Oratory

The Revd Fr Coleridge SJ.

TUESDAY 6 NOVEMBER 1866   Eddy Froude went?

[1] In thanking Newman on 29 Oct. for his sermon 'The Pope and the Revolution,' Monsell described what he had heard fourteen years before from this Redemptorist, Fr Prost, who was then giving a mission in Limerick, and 'had given missions and heard confessions by thousands in America and almost every country of Europe.' He told Monsell it was 'a universal truth that every where the Catholics in Protestant countries were better than the Catholics in Catholic countries.'
[2] Ullathorne wrote on 29 Oct., 'The contrast between the actual condition, as a general fact, between [sic] the Catholics of Italy and those of England in this day is one which forces itself as a reflection on many minds. You alone, however, of devout men, would have the boldness to set it forth before the world. I scarcely think, however much truth there may be in it, that it will prove palatable to our friends in Rome.'
The second page of Newman's letter to Monsell has been torn off, and the last two words here, added from it in Monsell's hand.
[3] E. E. Estcourt's *The Question of Anglican Orders Discussed* was published in 1873. The preface explains that the book was begun more than ten years earlier.

The Oratory Birmingham Novr 7. 1866.

Dear Lady Herbert,

Thank you for the interest you show in our School. I hope we shall be able to take Mr Dunne's son. I inclose a letter to him, which I ask of you the kindness of directing.[1]

Whatever we have heard about the Oxford scheme, since you were here, is adverse to the prospect of its being carried out

I am, Dear Lady Herbert, Most truly Yours in Xt
John H Newman of the Oratory

FRIDAY 9 NOVEMBER 1866   Mr Gallagher called or on the 16th?

TO EMILY BOWLES

The Oratory Bm Novr 11. 1866

My dear Child

I got your July letter before I set out, though I had not time to answer it. You were the first to give me information of Cardinal Reisach being in England.[2] Had I had the slightest encouragement, I should have called on him, for I knew him at Rome. But, though he was at Oscott, I did not know of it, till he was gone. Mr Pope from this house went up to London, and saw the Archbishop and the Cardinal. Neither of them even mentioned my name. The Cardinal was sent, I am told, for three days to W. G. Ward's — where of course he would hear one side fairly and fully enough — but it is a one sided way of getting at the true state of things to be content with the information of a violent partizan. It is on account of things of this kind that I view with equanimity the prospect of a thorough routing out of things at Rome — not till some great convulsions take place (which may go on for years and years, and where I can do neither good nor harm) and religion is felt to be in the midst of trials, red-tapism will go out of Rome, and a better spirit come in, and Cardinals and Archbishops will have some of the reality they had, amid many abuses, in the middle ages. At present things are in appearance as effete, though in a different way, (thank God) as they were in the tenth century. We are sinking into a sort of Novationism, the heresy which the early Popes so strenuously resisted. Instead of aiming at being a world-wide power, we are shrinking into ourselves, narrowing the lines of communion, trembling at freedom of thought, and using the language of dismay and despair at the

[1] No boy of this name came to the Oratory School.
[2] In July Emily Bowles wrote urging Newman to see Cardinal Reisach who was in London. See also letters of 29 Oct. 1866 to Thynne, 15 April 1867 to Patterson and 22 May 1867 to Ullathorne.

prospect before us, instead of, with the high spirit of the warrior, going out conquering and to conquer. Can any thing be more unworthy of Christian Prelates than the laments of the Irish Bishops that no hope is left, that there is no earthly power to aid the Holy See, and that it is all along of that wicked Louis Napoleon? One is tempted to adopt the words of the blaspheming Assyrian, as capable of an allowable application to such craven conduct 'Lo thou trustest upon this broken staff of a reed, upon Egypt; upon which if a man lean, it will go into his hand and pierce it — so is Pharao '— so is Napoleon, so Francis Joseph, so Isabella, so King Bomba — so are all of them. Haud tali auxilio etc.[1] I believe the Pope's spirit is simply that of martyrdom — and is utterly different from that implied in these gratuitous shriekings which sorround his throne. But the power of God is abroad upon the earth — and He will settle things in spite of what cliques and parties may decide.

I am glad you like my Sermon — the one thing I wished to oppose is the coward despairing spirit of the day

Ever Yours affly in Xt   John H Newman of the Oratory
Miss Bowles

TO HENRY J. LYNCH

November 11. 1866.
Dear Sir,

I have to acknowledge your letter, informing me that it is not your intention to put into print the statement which you lately sent me.

I am glad that this has been your final decision.

Yours truly John H Newman
H. Lynch Esqr

TO R. W. CHURCH

The Oratory Bm Nov. 13/66
My dear Church

I have been going to write to you on the subject of your coming here, ever since November began; but you have anticipated me. I shall be here all next week, and shall rejoice to see you, if you can come. If you can let me have a line as to the day, when it is settled, I shall be glad

Ever yrs affectly John H. Newman
The Revd R. W. Church

[1] II *Kings* 18:21. 'Non tali auxilio nec defensoribus istis Tempus eget.' *Aeneid* II, 521.

The Oy Bm Nov 14/66

My dear Fr Coleridge

What you propose to do, both in itself, and in reference to my paper, seems to me very good. At the same time, I really think my paper will be an encumbrance to the Article.[1]

Very sincerely Yours, John H Newman.

TO DAVID MORIARTY, BISHOP OF KERRY

The Oratory, Bm Novr 14. 1866

My dear Lord

It was a great pleasure to me to get your letter.[2] The subject of the Temporal Power is one I have no pleasure in undertaking, as being semi-political and out of my beat. Especially these last years, after the failure of all that seemed probable about the struggle in the United States and in Germany, to say nothing of the Indian Revolt nine years back, I have felt that to predict the consequences of social and political changes might befit others, but not me. Therefore I have been glad to refer to the words of the Holy Father and the Bishops, that 'in the present state of public affairs the Pope's Temporal Power is necessary,' and so leave the matter.

Our Bishop's order, however, obliged me to preach on the subject, and, since I was to preach, I was glad to think that the Pope had so frequently said it was necessary for the free exercise of his Apostolical office, — and the Bishops too, — and Catholic reviews and newspapers, that there was no need of insisting on it myself. What is the good of examining a question and coming to a conclusion of one's own, when it has already been ruled one way by authority? Rome has spoken — let us be silent — it would be something like 'Ego et Rex meus,' to say 'The Pope has said the Temporal Power is necessary, and I think so too.' This will account for what you remark upon, viz. that I do not in my Sermon insist on this point — though in matter of fact I do mention it among the reasons for thinking that the Temporal Power will continue. I say 'All mankind are parties to the inviolable union between the Pope and his city. His autonomy is a first principle in European politics, whether among Catholics or Protestants.'

---

[1] The proposal was to append the note on the Church of England, written by Newman for the French edition of *Apo.*, to Coleridge's article for the December *Month*, 'The "Apologia" in France.'

[2] In thanking Newman on 12 Nov. for 'The Pope and the Revolution' Moriarty wrote, 'Looking at it in relation to those for whom at least it was printed I think it is calculated to do more good, that is, to conciliate more the English mind to the Pope's temporal power than the strongest pleadings or protests that have been made.' Moriarty added how he agreed with Newman's insistence 'that if the Pope was deprived of his temporal power he would still be as much a Pope as ever.'

I feel what you say about our letters to Rome being read by Ricasoli or Mazzini.[1] It puts in a striking light the miseries which the Roman Congregations would suffer, if a secular sovereign had sway over them. But there is no evil without its alleviation — it would cut off a great deal of unprofitable gossip sent to Rome from the orbis terrarum, and of crude answers sent back from Rome by men who seem to have authority, but have none — and it would throw power into the hands of the local Bishops every where.

Very sincerely Yours in Xt   John H Newman

TO THOMAS GAISFORD

The Oratory, Birmingham. November 15th. 1866.

My dear Mr. Gaisford,

I should prefer Ch: Ch: [Christ Church] to Balliol for many reasons. There would be more Catholics at the former — and at Balliol, say what they will, it is a competition examination which they propose for candidates for admission — and, though Horace would have a very fair chance, when it was his time to offer himself, still there are so many candidates that no one can be sure. Also, there is a good deal of lax, sceptical opinion at Balliol, which it is well to avoid.

Mr. Walford, who has the care of Horace's form, speaks of him very favourably.

Very sincerely yours, John H. Newman of the Oratory.

Thomas Gaisford Esq.

SATURDAY 17 NOVEMBER 1866   Carr Glyn came
MONDAY 19 NOVEMBER   Carry Glyn went

TO E. B. PUSEY

The Oratory. Novr 20/66

My dear Pusey

It pained me very much to learn from the Papers that your Book was on the Index — and took me by surprise.[2] Of course, as you say, the act originated

[1] Moriarty concluded his letter by saying, 'It is not fair to find fault with you for omissions, but in the circumstances it would have been well to bring out strongly and clearly the reasons on account of which we hold to the temporal power, especially that on which the Pope insists in the last encyclical — that it is necessary for the full liberty of the spiritual government of the church. Of course our Divine Lord may provide for this in some other extraordinary way or may abundantly compensate for the loss of it, but it is dreadful to think of the Roman Post office in the hands of a Ricasoli or Mazzini.'

[2] This widespread rumour was without foundation. Pusey wrote on 19 Nov. to ask, 'What is the real meaning of a book being put on the Index?' and wondered whether it would involve Newman in suspicion 'if one who is on the Index, writes publicly to you?'

in England, but the question is, why it was determined on at Rome; and, as you say, what it means; and what is its affect.

1. Why is your book on the Index, and not mine on the Prophetical Office? I suppose, because they did not wish at Rome to quench the smoking flax thirty years ago — but now they think there is a flame in the Anglican Church which severity will fan, not put out. But again, Cardinal Wiseman was the ruling spirit in England in 1840, and he was a man of genial temper and large mind, and was averse to harsh measures.

2. As to the meaning of the act, it does not go further than to imply, that there are things in your book which the Church disallows. Thus, I think, a work of Malebranche is on the Index, of Dante, of Machiavelli. I suppose what has joined the Eirenicon to their company, is, its doctrine that there is any ecclesiastical corporation or communion besides the Roman, which has any claim to be considered the successor of the Church of the Apostles, — that either Greek or Anglican Church is a portion of that Communion to which the promises are attached. The contrary doctrine to this is almost de fide.

3. The effect of the act is to discourage Catholics reading the Eirenicon.

Thank you very much for your kind anxiety lest I should suffer by your writing to me. But this is impossible — such an act as the censure of a book would not touch the author, nor any one else.

Ever Yours affly John H Newman

P.S.   Tell me if I have not answered enough what you wished to ask.

WEDNESDAY 21 NOVEMBER 1866   Church came for some hours

TO GERARD MANLEY HOPKINS

The Oratory Bm Novr 21, 1866.

My dear Mr Hopkins,

I had hoped to have a line from you to say how you were getting on and whether your difficulties were arranging themselves. About College Chapel, I suppose, was soon settled.

I know you are reading hard but give me a line some time

Yours most sincerely in Xt   John H Newman

TO HENRY JAMES COLERIDGE

The Oratory, Bm. The Oy. Bm Nov 22/66

My dear Fr Coleridge

No one can find fault with your mode of speaking of Pusey in the inclosed

318

article, if you are to be hostile to him, which you have quite a right to be, if you think you ought to be[1]

I have made some corrections in my own part of the Article, which I cannot help thinking are true to my own Ms. if I may trust my memory.

Ever Yrs sincerely in Xt   John H Newman of the Oratory

The Revd Fr Coleridge SJ

P.S.   Your article reads very well.

SATURDAY 24 NOVEMBER 1866   Miss Ind went

TO SIR GEORGE BOWYER

The Oratory Bm. Nov. 25/66

My dear Bowyer,

I dare say I am wrong in my hypothesis about the Irish Bishops — but as to speaking to Dr Ullathorne, depend upon it he knows more than I do, and, did I speak to him, would feel, if he did not say, Don't teach your Grandmother to suck eggs.[2]

Ever Yours affly in Xt   John H Newman of the Oratory

TO JAMES STEWART

The Oratory Bm Nov. 25/66

My dear Stewart

I fully think my letter to Monsell was a formal testimonial.

However, if Dr Woodlock thinks it will not do, I will gladly transcribe and sign any other one, which he is kind enough to send me.[3]

Ever yrs affly John H Newman

TO WILLIAM MONSELL

The Oratory Bm Novr 27. 1866

My dear Monsell

It took me quite by surprise to see an announcement of Lady Dunraven's death in the paper yesterday. When you write to Lord D. will you send him my

---

[1] 'The "Apologia" in France', the *Month*, (Dec. 1866), pp. 620-3. For Newman's part, the note on the Church of England, see pp. 623-7.

[2] This letter perhaps refers to the temporal power of the Pope, which was ardently championed by Bowyer.

[3] See letters of 14 Oct. to Stewart and 16 Oct. to Monsell.

truest condolence, and tell him that I will lose no time in saying a Mass for his intention on so great a trial.[1]

Professor Stewart writes to me, if I understand him, that he wants the letter of recommendation I sent to you in his favour some time ago. If you have got it at hand, and if it is suitable in its style for him to send in to the Committee, will you be so kind as to send it him? Perhaps it is too familiar or otherwise ill suited for the purpose.

Can you tell me the name and address of that *American dentist,* of whom you spoke of so highly several years ago?[2]

Ever Yours affectly John H Newman of the Oratory

The Rt Honble Wm Monsell MP

TO CHARLOTTE WOOD

The Oratory Bm Novr 27. 1866

My dear Miss Wood

I had intended before now to have acknowledged your kind congratulations on my having at length come of age.[3] I wish I could flatter myself I had come into such great spiritual goods on the occasion as an heir of this world does. I ought to thank God, and at least may do this, that, being born in middle age, I have lived long enough to come to my majority. Give me some good prayers that I may not be found an unfaithful steward of God's mercies.

It pleased me of course very much to hear from you so much about Gerontius — I knew the Bishop of N. had sometime ago spoken kindly of it — indeed you told me so — but to [it] took me by surprise to find that he had not yet ceased to praise it, when it was an old story.[4]

I have been publishing a sermon on the Pope. It has no great point, and it was circumstances which obliged me to do so. I don't know whether you will care much about it, but I shall take the chance and send it to you. The Papers now say that the Holy Father will be able to come to terms with Italy. Only the continual prayers offered for him and the grace given to Peter would support him, I think, and him an old man, under such cruel anxieties With kindest remembrances to Mrs Wood

Ever Yours affectly in Xt   John H Newman

[1] The Countess of Dunraven died on 22 Nov.
[2] See letter of 30 Dec. 1855 to Flanagan.
[3] Newman came of age as a Catholic on 9 Oct. 1866.
[4] See letters of 28 Aug. 1865 and 27 Feb. 1866 to Bishop Brown of Newport.

TO HENRY WILBERFORCE

The Oy Bm ⌜Novr 29/66⌝

My dear H W

I never had any correspondence with Whately on any subject of difference between us, except in 1834 — when four letters passed, two apiece, three of which are given in Miss Whately's work — and the fourth (mine) by some mistake omitted.[1]

In 1849–50 I had a correspondence with Mr Stanley Faber on the passage you refer to — not directly, but indirectly, in letters addressed by both of us to Frank Faber. Of these the principal one of mine occurs in my Apologia.[2]

⌜I have two explanations of the passage in print[3] — one in Loss and Gain, and one in Anglican Difficulties.⌝

I have not heard any thing about you and yours a long while. I hope you have got quite well after the illness you had some time ago. So William is going to Maidenhead; some one said so in conversation the other day. I was in Switzerland in the Summer — the Doctor made me go, but I don't see why — and it seems to me that, while (thank God) I am very well, I should have been quite as well without it.

With love to your wife and children, I am, Very affly Yours
John H Newman of the Oratory

SATURDAY I DECEMBER 1866   first snow
SUNDAY 2 DECEMBER   snow   Advent Sunday

TO MRS EDWARD BELLASIS

The Oratory Bm Decr 2. 1866

My dear Mrs Bellasis

I am glad Edward has gone to you. What you say explains why we had not been quite pleased with him lately. When he was younger, he could not command himself at times in little things — and we thought he really physically could not. I thought he had outgrown the infirmity, by growing stronger. But now I have no doubt that he is not quite well, and requires rest. His being

---

[1] See letter of 24 Sept. 1865 to Miss Whately.

[2] *Apo.* pp. 200–03. See letters of 22 Nov. and 6 Dec. 1849 to F. A. Faber, and *Apo.* p. 185. The passage about which Wilberforce asked, was that at the end of Newman's 'Retractation of Anti-Catholic Statements,' in the *Conservative Journal*, (Feb. 1843). It was reprinted in the Advertisement to the first edition of *Dev.*, pp. vi–x, and in *V.M.* II, pp. 428–33. It ran: 'If you ask me how an individual could venture, not simply to hold, but to publish such views of a communion so ancient, so wide-spreading, so fruitful in Saints, I answer that I said to myself, "I am not speaking my own words, I am but following almost a *consensus* of the divines of my Church. They have ever used the strongest language against Rome, even the most able and learned of them. I wish to throw myself into their system. While I say what they say, I am safe. Such views, too, are necessary for our position."' See also *K.C.*, pp. 202–04.

[3] [[about 'necessary for my position.']] The explanations are in *L.G.*, pp. 278–81, and *Diff.* I, pp. 140–2.

at home will do every thing for him. Will he be well enough to take a part in our play? We meant to have cast the characters at the end of this term. It will be a sad thing if we lose him in this — but I don't disguise from you, if he had any part, it would be a principal one — and would be, both in learning by heart and in getting it up, a considerable exertion. Will you, before Christmas, let me know your feeling on this point?

I am very glad indeed the Serjeant is going to Hope Scott
Ever Yours most sincerely in Xt   John H Newman of the Oratory

TO THOMAS HARPER, S.J.

The Oratory Birmingham Decr 2. 1866
My dear Father Harper,

I will gladly make your novena known. For myself, since Gladstone went to Rome, I have specially remembered him daily. It has struck me since he went out of office, how it may become a season of grace for him, in the breathing time of a public career.[1]

I hope you have quite recovered from the fatigue of your volume. Its length and variety show what a great strain it must have been on you, that is, judging from myself. I am reading it with great interest and profit, but have not got above a third part through it yet. It is beautifully written, and in a very kind spirit to the Anglicans. However, I am too great a friend of Pusey's, to like your tone about him, and I suspect too it will make his friends angry, which I know is far from your intention.

With my best respects to your Fathers at St Beuno, and begging their good prayers
I am, my dear Fr Harper, Very sincerely Yours in Xt
John H Newman of the Oratory.

TO MISS DUNN

The Oratory Birmingham Decr 6. 1866
My dear Child,

I was very glad to get your letter — I have had you in my mind and prayers continually. It is no doubt a great trial to you to go among strangers, and I felt it would be so

But you must be brave and cheerful. Beg our dear Lord to give you these gifts — bravery and cheerfulness. Such trials are worst at first — by God's

---

[1] Harper wrote on 29 Nov. from St Beuno's College, 'We are getting up here a novena, to commence tomorrow, for the English diplomatists now residing in Rome, especially Mr Gladstone.' Besides Gladstone there were in Rome at this time Lord Clarendon, Edward Cardwell and the Duke of Argyll, members of the Liberal Ministry, which had resigned in June. 'Gladstone fully held that the Holy Father must be independent.' John Morley, *The Life of William Ewart Gladstone,* cheap edition, II, p. 162.

mercy, the strangeness and desolateness will wear off. You will get accustomed to the people and things that you are among. It is a very pleasant thing to hear you say that your mistress speaks English, and is kind. In a little time you will gain some knowledge of French, and be on easy terms with the servants.

The character of the French is to be light hearted and cheerful — and they think English people gloomy. You must show them that they are mistaken.

You go at a time of year when every thing external is at the worst. When spring and summer come, you will find what a bright pleasant country France is.

May God and our Lady preserve and keep you — and St Philip not forget you

Yours affectionately in Jesus Christ   John H Newman of the Oratory

TO JAMES HOPE-SCOTT

The Oratory Bm ⌈Decr 6 1866
My dear Hope Scott

Charlie, the virtuous pony, which you gave us 14 years ago, has at length departed this life. He continued his active and useful habits up to last summer — bene meritus, but not emeritus. Then he fell hopelessly stiff, lame, and miserable. His mind was clear to the last — and, without losing his affection for human kind, he commenced a lively, though, alas, not lasting friendship with an impudent colt of a donkey — who insulted him in his stiffness, and teased and tormented him from one end of the field to the other. We cannot guess his age; he was old when he came to us. He lies under two sycamore trees, which will be by their growth and beauty the living monument, or even transformation of a faithful servant, while his spirit is in the limbo of quadrupeds. Rest to his manes! I suppose I may use the pagan word of a horse.⌉[1]

I hope you and Lady Victoria and your party are enjoying yourselves at Hyères.

Ever Yours affly John H Newman of the Oratory

⌈P.S.   No news about Oxford.⌉

TO GERARD MANLEY HOPKINS

The Oratory 6 Dec 1866

I am glad that you are on easier terms than you expected with your friends at home. . . . I proposed your coming here because you could not go home— but, if you can be at home with comfort, home is the best place for you.[2]

---

[1] Hope-Scott replied on 12 Jan., 'Bellasis brought me your lament over Charlie, which does credit to the feelings of your Congregation. Little did I think, when he left Abbotsford, that he would serve so long, and be so honourably remembered when he came to die.'
[2] i.e. during the Christmas Vacation.

Do not suppose we shall not rejoice to see you here, even if you can only come for Christmas Day . . . . As to your retreat, I think we have misunderstood each other . . . it does not seem to me that there is any hurry about it — your first duty is to make a good class. Show your friends at home that your becoming a Catholic has not unsettled you in the plain duty that lies before you. And, independently of this, it seems to me a better thing not to hurry decision on your vocation. Suffer yourself to be led on by the Grace of God step by step.

SATURDAY 8 DECEMBER 1866   sang Mass

TO BISHOP ULLATHORNE

The Oratory. Decr 9. 1866

My dear Lord

I had intended to come to day to the Exposition at St Chad's, and to have called at your House, but am afraid of the weather.

I am sorry to hear from Fr St John, that, in conformity with what you wrote to Cardinal Barnabò your Lordship still thinks, that, in my Circular of 1864 about our undertaking the Oxford Mission, I expressed some intention of taking part in the education of Catholics there. I had hoped to be able to explain to your Lordship's satisfaction the purpose of that Circular in the letter I sent to you from Switzerland.[1]

If it is true, as your Lordship thinks, that, after your distinctly telling me, that, in accepting the Oxford Mission I was not permitted to think of taking

---

[1] St John wrote out a 'Report of a conversation on Dec 8, between F. A. St J and the Bishop —

The Bishop began by complaining of the many delays arising at Rome in the way of business and then he spoke of Oxford, said he was determined to have an answer and should write again to Rome. On my saying that I was afraid the answer would be unfavourable he said, they had an unfortunate notion that the foundation of an Oratory was connected with education, and that there was some influence (he would not or could not say where) against such a foundation. I said, why the only notion Cardinal Reisach had when he went to Oxford was that there was to be a college there, and that the Oratory was a step towards it. This I had heard in London from Mr Hope Scott who had heard it from the Cardinal's secretary. He seemed astonished at this, said he had intended asking Fr Newman over to Oxford to meet the Cardinal, but had no proper intimation of the Cardinal's coming, and they had sent with him one of those Redemptorist Fathers. Yes, I said, Fr Coffin. Yes, said the Bishop, Him, and he always takes the most gloomy views of every thing, and put every thing in a bad light. (It seems to have been him who pointed out the proximity of Christ Church when the Father's ground was shown the Cardinal, who then said, "it will never do to have that great place just opposite." Well, I said, this showed that his animus was against Oxford, *as a recognised place of education* just as I had heard from Hope Scott. He seemed to see this for the first time, and said he would write at once to Rome and dissipate this impression; but he added the wrong idea has some how come to be fixed in certain minds from that *unlucky circular*. It gave the idea that Fr Newman was still mixing himself up with education. I stopped him and said, Why there was nothing at all in the circular about education. So, said he, Fr Newman told me in his letter from Switzerland [of 12 Aug.], and I wrote to Neve to set that right, but it was the tone etc. Well I have the circular here, said he, but it was the tone of it which displeased many persons. However, he was determined, he said, to have an answer from Rome one way or other, for it was too important a question to be set aside.'

any part in the education of Catholics at the University, I contemplated issuing a Circular, in which I did profess the intention of doing so, I do not wonder at Propaganda being unwilling to sanction our going there.

But I never did any thing of the kind. In my Circular I did but recognise the fact that Catholics were at the University, and I made that recognition, because I felt that in the fact of their being Catholics at the University lay my call for undertaking the mission. And this I told your Lordship from the beginning of the negociation in September 1864.

I should not be honest then, if I gave your Lordship reason to suppose that I retracted one word of the Circular in question. In undertaking the Oxford Mission, I adhere both to the letter and the spirit of that Circular.

I am sure you will understand, that in thus writing I am actuated by a desire of avoiding all possible misapprehension on your Lordship's part, as to the motives which prompt me to avail myself of so great a mark of confidence, as is contained in your intrusting me with the Mission in question.

I take this opportunity, having hoped that some opportunity would have occurred before this, of thanking you for the very kind and encouraging notice you took of my Sermon about the Holy Father a month back[1]

I am, My dear Lord, begging your Lordship's blessing
Your obt and affte Servt in Xt   John H Newman

P.S.   I inclose a transcript of my Circular of 1864.

TO CHARLOTTE WOOD

The Oratory Bm Decr 10 1866

My dear Miss Wood

I am sorry to say, as you must have conjectured from my silence, that I cannot negative the substance of the report you speak of. I knew Cardinal Reisach in Rome — and, had I had the slightest encouragement, should have paid my respects to him. But for a while I did not even know he was in England — then he even came to Oscott, and I did not know of it, till he had gone. He went to Oxford — and he was shown the ground I had bought there — but I was not suffered to show it him myself. I am told he was three days with Mr W. G. Ward, as his guest. From what I have heard I doubt not various false stories were told him about me.

As to Mrs Wood's little Godson, he is a good boy — but good little boys are often idle — and must become good great boys, before they learn to work.[2]

With every kind remembrance to her, I am My dear Miss Wood,

Most sincerely Yours in Xt   John H Newman of the Oratory

P.S.   No answer has come from Rome about our going to Oxford — but we expect it will be in the negative.

[1] See letter of 1 Nov. to Monsell.
[2] This was probably Edmund Charles Simeon who came to the Oratory School in 1866, aged ten, and whose home, like Mrs Wood's, was in the Isle of Wight.

The Oratory Birmingham Decr 13/66

My dear Pusey

Could you tell me the country or the convent where Mr Ferrette became a Dominican? I suppose the Dominicans in this country know nothing about him — and they know little or nothing, I suspect, of their brethren abroad. The difficulty in getting information of course, or at least of repeating it, is the fear of an action for libel.[1]

I went too far in my last, if I implied that Manning had to do with bringing your book to the notice of the Roman censors.[2] It is quite as likely to be the act of some individual member of a religious body in England — or some Englishman at Rome. I sometimes fancy, as I wrote a favorable article of the Ecce Homo in the Month, that the two books have been mentioned to some members of the Congregation of the Index by some one who is not over fond of *me*.

Ever Yours affectly John H Newman

P.S.   All kind Christmas greetings.

The Oratory Bm Decr 14. 1866

My dear Jemima,

I have received the Number of the Christian Remembrancer. It was directed, I think, in your hand-writing. If I am right, thank John for getting it for me, for I suppose it came from him.[3] I don't know whether I am right in understanding that the cost of it was 2/- This seems very little. I will not forget to send it to you.

I fear I saw in the Paper the other day the death of Mrs Rickards's sister[4]

Ever Yours affly John H Newman

SATURDAY 15 DECEMBER 1866   Mr Cornish came

[1] Pusey wrote on 10 Dec., 'Would any Dominican authority do you think, feel himself justified, or able to tell one of the circumstances under which Mr Jules Ferrette left their order He seems to be a mischievous person.' Jules Ferrette, after joining the French Dominicans and then becoming a Presbyterian missionary in Damascus, claimed to have been consecrated bishop by the Syrian Jacobite (Monophysite) Bishop of Emesa, at Homs, and appointed Bishop of Iona. He came to England in 1866, and was offering to reordain any Anglican clergyman who was doubtful as to his Orders.

[2] See letter of 20 Nov., about which Pusey wrote, 'Your letter did contain all the information I wished. This hostility has taken all heart out of me about it . . . The kindness of the French Bishops was very encouraging.'

[3] See letter of 21 Oct. to Henry Williams Mozley. Jemima's husband John was the publisher of the *Christian Remembrancer*.

[4] This was Harriett Wilmot, who married in 1821 the Revd George Cornish.

TO GERARD MANLEY HOPKINS

The Oratory, Decr 16, 1866

My dear Hopkins,

I was pleased to hear so much about you from Fr William Neville — who also was very much pleased to see so much of you the other day. You are quite right to go home, since they wish you — indeed, it would have been in every way a pity, had you not resolved to do so. But I don't mean to let you off coming here. How long do you stop at home? and when does Lent Term begin? Easter is so late that you will hardly be meeting at Balliol till February —could you come here for the week before term?

I want to see you for the pleasure of seeing you — but, besides that, I think it good that a recent convert should pass some time in a religious house, to get into Catholic ways — though a week is not long enough for that purpose.

Yours affectly in Xt   John H Newman of the Oratory

G. Hopkins Esqr

MONDAY 17 DECEMBER 1866   Mr Cornish went
THURSDAY 20 DECEMBER   Pattison called
FRIDAY 21 DECEMBER   Lord H. Kerr called

TO W. J. O'NEILL DAUNT

The Oratory Bm Decr 21/66

My dear Mr Daunt

I have received your pamphlet, and thank you very much for it. No one has a clearer right to be listened to on the very painful subject about which you write, than yourself who have such full knowledge of the matters of which you treat

Very truly Yours John H Newman

TO CHARLOTTE WOOD

The Oratory Bm Dec 21/66

Most Private

My dear Miss Wood

We are now so close upon Christmas, that I may fitly send you and Mrs Wood by anticipation my best and kindest congratulations on the sacred season, as I do most heartily.

I don't think it would be any good saying any thing to others on the matters about which I write to you. It would only lead to correspondence which might leave things worse than they are.

There has been from the first an animus against me — why, I cannot tell, though I may conjecture. Not because I have been strong for a Catholic College at Oxford, for I have never advocated it, feeling more might be said against it than for it. My opinion, however, has never been asked by *any* one in authority from the first day that the subject of Catholics going to Oxford was mooted. All sorts of people were consulted — the written opinions of several of the London Oratorians were sent to Rome — but mine has never been even asked, though from my connexion with the Dublin Catholic University, it would have been natural to have consulted me among others.

It is now more than three years since Dr Manning put an article in the Dublin Review about a Catholic University for England — in the course of it he enumerated all the English Catholic Colleges and Schools, first rate and second rate except one — that one was ours, he simply left out our school altogether.[1]

Two year ago (and since) at our Bishop's wish, I have thought of taking for the Oratory the Oxford mission. It has been carefully spread about in England and in Rome that I am contemplating *more* than an Oratory, namely a College. Manning is now opposing at Rome the Oratory's going there.

To strengthen this prejudice against the Oratory going there, they actually are now saying in London, by way of objection that, if I go there, I shall make too many converts, and create a row and so damage the Catholic cause. I have reason to think the Archbishop says this. It is not very long since it was objected to me that I was slow to make converts. Is it not a case of Dr Fell?[2]

When I published my Apologia, Dr Manning expressed his regret at it. Afterwards he qualified his reasons for it — he said he only meant my violence against Kingsley. Next, he wrote a pamphlet, which was mainly a covert attack on portions of it. One of the points I have mentioned in my letter to Dr Pusey — viz that I had said that the Anglican Church was a *bulwark* of the truth. That on this and another matter in it he was referring to me, I have the authority of a common friend to whom he showed the pamphlet either in MS or in the proof sheets.[3]

When I published the said letter to Pusey, he sent me two letters, one by his secretary, one in his own hand, expressing pleasure at it. Shortly after he secretly attempted to get parts of it *virtually* condemned by the Bishops. This fact I had from one of the Bishops to whom he applied.[4]

Two years ago, a lay friend of mine who was at Rome and saw various

[1] See last note to letter of 15 Aug. 1863 to St John.
[2] 'I do not love you Dr. Fell,
But why I cannot tell;
But this I know full well,
I do not love you, Dr Fell.'
Thomas Browne's translation of Martial, *Epigrams*, I, 32, in *Works* 1719, Vol. IV, p. 113.
[3] See letters of 17 and 28 Nov. 1864 to Walker, and notes there.
[4] See first Memorandum of 26 March 1866.

great people there said that he was sure Dr M, was more opposed to my going to Oxford than to Catholic youth going there, that *I* was the cause of his opposition.[1]

All this of course is in the strictest confidence.

If you ask my explanation of all this, I don't impute to him any animosity to me — but I think he is of a nature to be determined to *crush* or to *melt* every person who stands in his way. He has views and is determined to carry them out — and I must either go with him or be annihilated. I say this, because he long wished to get me made a Bishop (in partibus) — I believe because he knew it would be (as it were) putting me 'in the House of Lords'. When he found that I should not accept the offer, as feeling it would interfere with my independence, his only remaining policy is to put me out.

Now I have taken a great liberty with you. For I never wrote thus plainly and fully to any person yet

Ever Yrs most sincerely John H Newman

SATURDAY 22 DECEMBER 1866   Mr Outhwaite to breakfast

TO THE EARL OF DENBIGH

The Oratory Bm Decr 22. 1866

My dear Lord Denbigh

It is now so near Christmas, that I may offer you and Lady Denbigh our best wishes of the sacred season.

Thank you very much for the handsome present of game you have sent us and believe me

Most sincerely Yrs in Xt   John H Newman

TO HENRY BEDFORD

The Oratory, Birmingham. Decr 23/66

My dear Mr Bedford

My best thanks for your pamphlet on Venice. There was one before it, which I did not acknowledge, so let me now thank you for it too.

You have accompanied it with a very kind letter, which I assure you I value very much. It is so difficult to write without rousing, against one's will, all manner of antagonisms, that it is a real relief and encouragement to have a letter like yours, tho' far above my merits. I am ever tempted to say 'What's the good of writing?' and wonder at myself when I find I have after all ventured into print again.

We are now so near Christmas, that I may offer you and all your associates

[1] This was Edward Bellasis. See note to letter of 9 Feb. 1865 to Miss Holmes.

at Allhallows the best wishes of the sacred season, which I do with all my heart.

Very sincerely Yours in Xt   John H Newman

P.S.   Mr Marshall is studying law in London. His direction is 5 Richmond Villas, Bayswater W.

TO W. J. COPELAND

The Oratory Bm Decr 23. 1866

My dear Copeland

All best Christmas greetings to you. Your most kind present came yesterday, and was shown round the room at recreation as a beauty and a wonder. But it does not satisfy me for my not seeing you — and I can only grieve for the causes which draw you so imperiously in other directions. Your new affliction is quite tragical.[1] I assure you, my dear C not a day passes in the ordinary course of things, in which I do not think of you. I so dread lest your sorrows should be too much for your strength. Some one said you were not well. I wish you had said something about yourself.

If you came here, it might divert your mind. I am nearly sure of my own movements this vacation, but not quite.

Ever Yours affectly John H Newman

TO HENRI DE RAMIÈRE, S.J.

The Oratory Bm Decr 23. 1866

My dear Revd Father

We are all very much pleased and touched at your kindness in recommending our School to one whose future career seems to be so distinguished as the son of Count Lualt. And I assure you we shall be glad to do our utmost to promote his father's wishes respecting him.

There is only one question which we have to ask, and that relates to the young gentleman's *age*. The English system of education is so different from the continental, that we feel we cannot do youths justice, unless they come to us when they are boys. We have fixed *twelve* as the *highest* age at which we take them from abroad. You can easily understand what a disadvantage it is, and what a discouragement, for a young man to find himself in a junior class with boys, from the circumstance that he has not learned some of the things, of which we make most account.

Will you then have the kindness to satisfy me on this point, before I write to the Count

Thank you for your news of M. Barrow

I am, begging your good prayers, My dear Revd Father
Yours very sincerely in J.C.   John H Newman of the Oratory.

[1] For Copeland's afflictions see letter of 30 Dec. to Miss Giberne.

TUESDAY 25 DECEMBER 1866   sang the 5 oclock Mass
WEDNESDAY 26 DECEMBER   Ambrose went to Brighton

TO BISHOP ULLATHORNE

The Oratory Decr 26/66

My dear Lord

I had intended to call on you to day, to offer my congratulations on the Sacred Season, before your most kind letter anticipated me.[1]

Thank you for the copy of the letter of Propaganda; which we have already had a consultation about — but, unless you wish for an immediate answer, we should like to delay it[2]

Ever, My dear Lord Your obt and affte Servt in Xt
John H Newman of the Oratory[3]

The Rt Revd The Bp of Birmingham

[1] Ullathorne wrote on 25 Dec., 'As I shall not have time to call and see you today, and shall be from home tomorrow, I send a copy of the Letter of Propaganda enclosed.

You will perceive that the subject was brought before the Congregation itself on the 3d of Octob, [sic] and that the petition is substantially granted, the saving clause I look upon as a general precaution which is not likely to have practical consequences.

Propaganda has only just now replied to questions addressed to it by all the Bishops in April last, and as this case was opened in June, the delay cannot be considered as unusual, or owing to any cause special to this petition.'

[2] The letter from Propaganda to Ullathorne, as sent by him to Newman, ran: 'Illme et Rme Dñe.

In generalibus Comitiis habitis die 3 hujus mensis Emi ac Rmi PP. S. hujus Consilii jussu Ssmi D. N. Papae egerunt de petitione a Te missa ad Sanctitatem Suam sub die 11 junii labentis anni, de explicationibus circa ejusdem objectum expositis in literis tuis diei 30 Julii ejusdem anni. Itaque PP. Emi, omnibus mature perpensis censuerunt supplicandum Ssmo pro concessione gratiae a R. P. Newman optatae, erigendi videlicet domum atque Oratorium sui Instituti in civitate Oxfordiensi sub dependentia Superioris Oratorii Birminghamiensis durante vita laudati P. Newman ac per tres annos ab ejus obitu, ita tamen ut prohibitio cujuslibet communicationis catholicae juventutis cum Universitate Oxfordiensi confirmata intelligatur, ac nisi experientia constiterit pericula quae ex nova fundatione timentur devitari non posse, ita ut praesens concessio conditionata tantum ac provisoria censeatur.

Porro Smo D. N. |relata fuit sententia S. Congris in Audientia diei 9 hujus mensis, Bmus vero Pater eam in omnibus ratam habuit ac probavit. Quapropter de supradictis omnibus Te certiorem facio, precorque Deum ut Te diu sospitem et incolumen servet.

Romae ex Aed. S.C. de P.F. die 18 Decembris 1866.

Ampl. Tuae Uti Frater addictissimus Al. C. Barnabo, Praef.

R. P. D. Guillelmo Berno Ullathorne
Episcopo Birminghamiensi Birmingham.

A. Capalti Secrius.

Ullathorne omitted at the end of the first paragraph the so-called 'secret instruction': 'Praeterea Sacrae Congregationis mens fuit ut ad Te scriberetur ut P. Newman si forse de sua residentia in Urbem Oxfordiensem transferenda cogitantem videris, ab ejusmodi consilio, quo certe allicerentur Catholici ad filios suos illi Universitati absque ullo metu committendos blande suaviterque revocare studeas.' See the correspondence at 6 April 1867.

[3] Neve wrote to Ullathorne from Rome on 22 Dec. that he had seen Barnabò, who promised to send that very day the reply to Ullathorne's petition of July, and this had been done. Neve added, 'Of the nature of the decision on the Oxford question I could ask nothing, as I am a suspected person on that subject. The state of feeling of some persons who have influence at Propaganda is such that I should be much surprised if you find your answer too favourable.'

Newman replied on 1 Jan. to Ullathorne's letter of 26 Dec.

TO WILLIAM MONSELL

The Oratory Decr 27/66

My dear Monsell

We return with great sincerity the kind wishes which you send us at this Sacred Season, and thank you for them.

I am told that Mrs Monsell has a great bereavement. I have been saying Mass for the soul of her Father. She bears her loss well, I hope.

At length a letter has come from Rome about Oxford. I suppose we shall go there — but there are conditions annexed to the leave, which will make it a difficulty.

You have seen the remarkable letter of Ricasoli's to the Bishops exiled at Rome. It seems as if he was determined to carry out in his political system the principle of private judgment or religious liberty. How, except by miracle, can the Pope resist or supersede it? I wonder what will come of the collision.[1]

I have nothing to tell you and am My dear Monsell, very affly yours

John H Newman of the Oratory

The Rt Honble Wm Monsell M P

P.S. I send you the catechism by this post.

TO MARK PATTISON

The Oratory Birmingham Decr 28/66

My dear Rector

I attempted the letter you wanted from me the day after you were here — but I ought to have asked you more distinctly what it is you wish of me, and what I am, if I can, to aim at — how any thing I may be able to say is to bear upon your Pamphlet etc. I must of course have this clear to my mind, or I shall be writing what is beside the mark.[2]

We are somewhat interested here in the Trinity election, which is said to take place today.[3] I do not know how far Heads of Houses are united in one body now, or whether it much concerns, whether the other Heads or the University itself, who presides over the Colleges.

It gave me great pleasure to see you the other day

Yours very sincerely John H Newman

The Revd the Rector of Lincoln

[1] Baron Ricasoli, the Italian Prime Minister, wanted to bring about a reconciliation with the Vatican and allowed forty-five bishops to return to their sees. The Italian Chamber prevented further advances.

[2] Pattison wanted Newman to write on the subject of Catholics attending the universities. See letter of 4 Jan. 1867 to Pattison, who wrote various articles on university education.

[3] S. W. Wayte was elected President of Trinity College, Oxford, on 28 Dec. See letter of 25 Oct. to Mrs F. R. Ward.

TO AN UNKNOWN CORRESPONDENT

The Oratory Decr 29. 1866

Dear Sir,

I wish it were in my power to answer your questions fully. As to the translations into English made of certain of St Augustine's works, your best informant would be an experienced bookseller, such as Mr Stewart of King William Street West, who, I believe, has such matters at his fingers' ends.

About 20 or 30 years ago Dr Pusey published his great Library of Translations from the writings of the Fathers. It began with a translation of St Augustine's confessions — what other works of his the Library contained, I do not know — but any bookseller could give you the catalogue of them.

Your second question relates to the fidelity of the translations. Now here, first, I am quite sure that the translators meant to be fair — and I have no reason to suppose that they were not fair. Nor are they likely to be under temptation not to be fair — for there is only a passage here and there in the Fathers, in which Dr Pusey and his friends would not concur. And in such passages I think they would strive to translate as literally as possible — and, whether a *Catholic* would translate them otherwise or not, I think they would *consider* they had translated them rightly, though they would go as near to explaining away the meaning, as they thought they could go honestly. I think they would reserve any Anglican bias for their *notes*. I should expect they would put a note on any passage they did not like, and what Catholics would consider an unfair note. But I do not think they would be unfair in the *translation*. For instance, the word 'paenitentia' they might translate 'penitence' when a Catholic would translate it 'penance;' and then they might append a note saying that it was a *mistake* to translate it 'Penance.' But they would not slur difficulties over. I do not know their translations of St Augustine myself, but I judge of what I should expect of them

Yours truly John H Newman

TO MISS M. R. GIBERNE

The Oratory Bm Decr 30. 1866

My dear Sister Pia

A happy Christmas and New Year to you, in the best sense of the word. I have not written to you, because I knew Fr William had made a point of keeping you au courant.

Your prayers have succeeded — it seems certain we are going to Oxford — not *quite* certain, but almost. We have received leave from Rome, and have accepted the Mission from the Bishop — that looks like certainty — but the leave is coupled with a condition — and that condition hinders us from setting about to build a Church — and the Bishop may feel a difficulty in arranging with us, if we do not build a Church. However, I expect it will all go straight. We understand, it is so decided at Rome, against the Archbishop's and Cardinal's Reisach's wishes. Is it not strange that this two or three years past Dr M. should have taken this strong part against me? He is as bland and smooth as ever in word and writing.

I suspect a spoke has been put in the wheel of my nephews' coming to me. Herbert said he should come in his way to Derby — and that Frank should come to me in his way to Oxford — neither came. Harry came, and was very nice — but gave little hopes of his coming again. I must let things take their course. I shall be amused to see what Frank and Alfred do, if I go to Oxford.[1]

You know how ill Mr George Copeland has been. The account is very much worse the last day or two — and his spirits have failed him. All this sounds very bad. His poor brother has been sadly tried. His sister lies in Cornwall, struck with paralysis. Her son, a sailor, came home invalided, and almost dying — and then her husband died. Poor William C. has been running to and fro between Farnham, Cheltenham, and Penzance.

Pusey's Eirenicon has been put on the Index, in company with two heretical or unbelieving works.[2] This has pained him a good deal, and he has almost resolved to give up eirenicizing.

And now I have told you all the things which have to be told, as far as I know them   God and our Lady bless you.

Ever Yours, affectionately and most Sincerely in Xt, John H Newman

Sister M. Pia

P.S.   I hope you are well. The weather *here* is very rheumatic and *influential*. Have you proper medicines etc.

The names of the Three Plays Phormio — Pincerna (Cupbearer) — Aulularia (Money jar)

TO MOTHER MARGARET MARY HALLAHAN

The Oratory Decr 30. 1866

My dear Mother Margaret

I thought of you and your's specially on St John's day, because I well remembered your former kindness to me on my Feast, and I thought of you especially at Mass, though my Mass being engaged, I could not give you my intention.

What makes you say that I am not happy? This indeed is not the case. Once or twice of late years I have been cast down at thinking how little I have done for God, or how little I have the opportunity of doing — but the depres-

---

[1] Francis Mozley was at New College and Alfred Mozley at Jesus College.
[2] See letter of 20 Nov. to Pusey.

sion has not lasted, and I feel in my reason, as well as my heart, that I should be most ungrateful if I had any unhappiness at all On the contrary, I am quite in clover, and though I am not strong, I have no duties to try my strength. I only wish you were as strong as I am — and that I did the tenth part of what you do, and then the balance between us would be trimmed more to my satisfaction than it is at present

I am such a stay-at-home except called away by stern necessity, that I know you will think it enough if I say Mass for Miss Wilson and you on the 23[1]

TO ROBERT ORNSBY

The Oratory Bm Decr 30/66

My dear Ornsby

I return to you and Mrs Ornsby your Christmas greetings with all my heart — I was very glad to hear the other day a good account of Fr Dalgairns. Your letter about Athens came in due course, and it was ungrateful in me not to acknowledge such interesting details. I had quite mourned over your exclusion from Asia Minor and Broussa, when in your absence I heard of it — for I knew how you would enjoy it.[2] To visit it would have been like being the first to visit a catacomb or unearth a Pompeii — for I suppose it is in statu quo (in which) Othman left it, and not very different from what it was under the Roman Emperors.

In return for your good news about Dublin, I have to tell you that a letter has come from Rome allowing the Oratory to go to Oxford; however, the leave is under a condition, and I am not clear the condition will not embarrass. At the moment, however, the decision rests with me.

Our Fathers send you their kindest thoughts — & I am,

My dear Ornsby, Yours affectionately in Xt

John H Newman of the Oratory.

P.S.   Have you many theological books in the Arundel Library? say, of the 16th century.

TO WILLIAM KIRBY SULLIVAN

The Oratory Bm Decr 30 1866

My dear Professor Sullivan

A happy Christmas and New Year to you. I am told that our University has doubled in numbers since its incorporation with the Queen's University. This is good news.[3]

[1] The copy ends thus.
[2] Said to have been founded at the suggestion of Hannibal, Broussa was the capital of Bithynia.
[3] This refers to the Supplemental Charter of 1866, which was ruled illegal on a technicality in 1868. See E. R. Norman, *The Catholic Church and Ireland in the Age of Rebellion*, pp. 236-8.

The inclosed explains itself — will you write to Messrs Longmans about it? I take this opportunity to say that I owe the University some shillings, not more than shillings, which Messrs Longmans have paid me in the course of the last few years on account of the sale of the Atlantis.

I was very glad to read your pamphlet on the University of last year and thank you for it[1]

Very sincerely Yours John H Newman of the Oratory

W K Sullivan Esqr

TO MRS F. J. WATT

The Oratory, December 30th. 1866.

My dear Child,

A happy Christmas and New Year to you, your husband, Mama, and all of you. Thank you for giving so good an account of yourself. We all send you our congratulations. It is likely after all, though not certain, we shall found an Oratory at Oxford, — I dread the work, and prefer to be idle here — but these things are beyond us —

I hope Willie will persevere in New Zealand. The other day I was talking to a sharp young man who has just come thence.[2] He says that, if a youth will but buckle to and be resolute, he is sure to succeed. And in this day nothing is done without patience and determination, and a country like New Zealand is a great field. Father Ambrose always says that, if left to himself, he should have gone out as a settler. It is a grand idea, and worth some roughing.

Ever yours affectionately in Christ, John H. Newman of the Oratory.

MONDAY 31 DECEMBER 1866   sharp frost and snow

TO CATHERINE ANNE BATHURST

The Oratory Bm Dec 31. 1866

My dear Child

A happy Christmas and New Year to you, I was very glad to hear from you, for you had vanished from the world, or at least my world. I have said a number of Masses for you during the year, but it might have been for your soul, for what I knew. The nearest idea I got of you was from a report that you had become a Beguine.

That day, when I called on you — was the beginning to me of a serious

---

[1] *University Education in Ireland, A Letter to Sir John Simeon,* Dublin 1866.
[2] See diary for 22 Dec. See also letter of 1 Nov. to Mrs Bretherton.

illness — December 22/65. I felt ill when I walked up to you, got worse as the day went on, and was so bad in the train going back, that I thought I never should have lasted to the end of the journey, and all but determined to stop at Rugby. I managed, however, to sing the Christmas morning Mass, and then took to my bed. On St Antony's day[1] I was set right almost by miracle — so that it quite overpowered me to think of it. And I have been well ever since, though there is always the danger of the evil returning.

Incomprehensible as it is, great ecclesiastics in England, friends of mine, have set themselves with a feeling quite personal against me in the Oxford matter, and for two years past have thwarted the plan. Our Bishop has just triumphed over them, and we are to go there. The leave has come from Propaganda. Still, the same influence which has been so violent against me will bother me when I am there, I cannot doubt. So you must give me some good prayers.

I grieve very much that disappointment should still go with you. These things are very mysterious — but, depend on it, those with whom all goes smooth are not the happiest persons, or most dear to God. I shall at any time be most deeply interested and rejoiced to hear about you, whenever you think it worth while to tell me of your movements. I have no particular news to tell you — Our school is in most excellent condition but I wish we had more boys — that the two ends might meet. You may have heard that the elder Ward, who had left us, died suddenly of diphtheria, a most happy and impressive death. One of our masters too, Mr Pope, lost an only and most promising son — he lies at Rednall.[2]

Ever Yours very affectly in Xt   John H Newman

TO EMILY BOWLES

The Oratory Bm Decr 31. 1866

My dear Sister Emily,

I thank you and Lady Lothian for your kind zeal — but you must not expect much. I don't expect any thing, for I am too old to be good for any thing, and, as I have been all along hoping and expecting that I should not go to Oxford, this decision has taken me by surprise.

As to the Romans, I said distinctly that only a *minority* were revolutionists, and that the rest were cowards.[3] So they are — nothing can make me think otherwise. *Who* is it that has inflicted on us all the opprobrium of 'foreign bayonets,' but the Romans? Why is it the Americans have power in Ireland and can get up Fenianism? It is because Ireland is discontented with our Government and people. Why is it that French revolutionists never could do

---

[1] 17 Jan. 1866.
[2] See letter of 22 Sept. to Mrs F. R. Ward, and diary for 30 June 1866.
[3] This refers to Newman's sermon, 'The Pope and the Revolution'.

much with the English people? because they are loyal. Unless the Romans were weak or wicked, foreign Mazzinians could never have done much — and we, the whole body of Catholics, are dragged through the mud because of the Romans. I shall be very glad if they are brought to be ashamed of themselves and to repent.

As to my 'invitation' to Rome, it was this — Mgr Talbot, who had been spreading the report that I subscribed to Garibaldi, and said other bad things against me, had the assurance to send me a pompous letter asking me to preach a set of sermons in *his* Church, and that then I should have an opportunity to shew myself to the authorities, (that, I think, was his phrase,) and to rub up my Catholicism. It was an insolent letter. I declined.[1] All that you report about 'the Pope having a great desire to see me, and receive me with warmth — and talk (!) of the state of things', and my refusing 'again,' is all moonshine. It is the first time from you that I hear it. As to my being in Birmingham, it is because the Cardinal put me here. Fr St John strongly corroborates me that he *never* asked me to go to London. The truth is people are obliged to get up erroneous statements to account for what has been done towards me.[2]

Yet I know other things worse still. You must continue praying for me, for since you have prayed me into this scrape, you must pray me out of it. I am tempted to say with St Benedict 'Parcat tibi omnipotens Deus soror! quid est quod fecisti.'[3]

TO AN UNKNOWN CORRESPONDENT

[End of 1866?][4]

.... Your question is, whether there may not be two classes of those who are exempted from damnation, the one who see the Face of the Eternal Trinity in Unity, and the other who only see the Humanity of our Lord. Or since our Lord is in heaven two classes of the saved or celestials.

I do not recollect any mention of such a doctrine in the Fathers; and for myself I do not feel that it is according to the analogy of faith, whether as set before us in Scripture or by theologians.

It is too large a subject to treat satisfactorily in the compass of a letter; but the following remarks will show the direction in which my thought lie in respect to it.

[1] See letter of 25 July 1864.
[2] In accordance with Newman's instructions on 3 Jan. the rest of this letter, which evidently referred to Manning, was destroyed. Emily Bowles wrote at the end of the page, '(The rest destroyed. Signed as usual Yours affly J.H.N.)'.
In her manuscript 'Memorials of John Henry Newman,' preserved at the Birmingham Oratory, she did copy out on page 47 the words which followed those Newman told her to destroy. They are inserted above.
[3] St Scholastica prayed that her brother St Benedict, who was visiting her, might not leave her, and a sudden storm prevented his departure.
[4] This draft is filed between one of the summer of 1866 and one of 1867.

1. I consider that the beati and the cælicolæ — or cælestes are commensurate and identical; but none are blessed but those who are in heaven, and none are in heaven but the blessed; according to the words of the Catechism of Trent '*Beati* qui in *cælesti patriâ* vivunt.' Symb. xii, 5.

2. All the cælicolæ see the face of God; that is, that none are in heaven who do not see the face of God, according to the words of Pope Eugenius, 'Animae à peccatis purgatae *in cælum* recipiuntur *et intuentur* clare Deum.'[1]

3. All the beati see the face of God; that is, that none are blessed who do not see the face of God; according to the very phrase, Beatific Vision, that vision being the only means of beatitude; (Hence Viva says, 'Ad objectum beatitudinis *essentiale* pertinet divina essentia.' p 45)[2] and according to the Catechism of Trent 'solida beatitudo, quam essentialem communi nomine licet vocare, in eo sita est, ut Deum videamus.' part 1. art 12. §7. And again, ibid §10 Beati Deum præsentem semper intuentur.

4. It seems to me then that being in heaven, seeing the Divine Essence, and being blessed, are convertible terms; and that these terms are equivalent also to the word 'salvation'; ⟨Beati qui intrant etc outside is the 'darkness' and hell. 'foris canes et venefici' etc Apoc. xii, 15

5. And equivalent also to 'eternal life;' according to our Lord's own definition; 'Hæc est vita æterna; ut cognoscant te, solum Deum verum, et quem misisti Jesum Christum.' Ioan xvii, 3

6. The same conclusion seems to follow from the consideration of the lumen gloriæ. This lumen is given to all the Blessed, and it is given to them in order that they may see God. Viva includes both these propositions in the following sentence. 'In patria datur lumen gloriæ *in ordine* ad Deum videndum, . . . quod communiter docent esse intrinsicum, et permanenter inhæreri intellectui *Beatorum*.' De Deo p 37. But if all the Blessed have the lumen gloriæ, and the lumen gloriæ enables them to see God, all the Blessed see God. And this is what is told us in the Apocalypse c. 22. 'Videbunt faciem ejus, . . . et non egebunt lumine solis, quoniam Dominus Deus illuminabit illos.' And hence the Prophet saw 'civitatem sanctam Jerusalem . . habentem claritatem Dei' etc. c xxi.

7. Further, every created intellect has the desire and the capability of fulfilling its end, i.e. of seeing God, (i.e. with the lumen gratiæ and the lumen gloriæ) and therefore there is nothing to hinder its attaining this its ultimate end, i.e. receives these means and this process being supposed. As all who are in heaven have washed their robes in the blood etc the blessed have attained the end of their being, therefore they see God.

8. As to the contemplation of our Lord's humanity, not only is it to holy souls on earth the means by which they learn to rise towards the contemplation of God and their support in contemplating him, but even to the blessed in

---

[1] The Bull, *Laetentur Caeli,* of 6 July 1439.
[2] The references are to Viva, *De Deo Uno*, Padua 1755.

heaven it fulfils a service of this kind. On this subject I quote a passage of Scaramelli Direttorio Mistico p 104.[1]

9. Hence lastly, the two contemplations of the Blessed in heaven of God and of God Incarnate, though two, are in effect one and the same. Thus St Francis de Sales unites then in the following passage — (the Love of God p 147) 'Nothing can be more amiable and attractive etc'[2]

These are the considerations which your question suggests to me, but of course, I speak under the correction of those who have thoroughly mastered the subject. I will make one more remark; — nothing is further from the view which you suggest than any approximation towards Pelagianism. You would say that those who have the secondary blessedness owe it to the grace of God as fully as those who have the higher. However, it so happens that Pelagius did hold two classes of the Beati; the higher, those who were admitted in the kingdom heaven, and that through baptism as the first step in their course; the secondary, consisting of those who in a general sense of the word gained vita aeterna, such were the heathen who were saved.

---

[1] G. B. Scaramelli, *Il Direttorio Mistico,* Naples 1773, II, xvi, 178.
[2] *A Treatise of the Love of God,* Book III, Chapter X. Newman used the translation published in London in 1835.

APPENDIX

Bishop Ullathorne's letter to the Tablet on Newman's Devotion to our Lady

TO THE EDITOR OF THE TABLET

Birmingham, April 4th, 1866.

Sir, — I had hoped that I should not have to write upon the remarks that have been so unjudiciously, as well as unfairly, put before the world respecting Dr. Newman's letter to Dr. Pusey; indeed I am ashamed of being forced into this act of justice and of charity. Little can they know of him on whom they pronounce their hasty and un-authorised judgments, who presume to tell the world that Dr. Newman has derogated from the devotion which good Catholics pay to the Virgin Mother of our Lord. Laymen, especially, ought to know that it is not within their competence to pronounce public judgments upon the teaching of priests. They are amenable to their ecclesiastical superiors, who alone are their judges; and when laymen have any complaint on this, or any other subject, against the clergy the order and rule of the Church requires that they should refer their complaints to those whose duty it is to examine and to judge. When the champion of Israel was made a sport for the Philistines we do not find that it was any of the children of Israel who first made their defender blind, and then brought him forth as a spectacle of derision; but it was the Philistines themselves who did this disgrace to him, and there are always a sufficient number of them for this kind of work, without needing help from the camp of Israel.

But another motive urges me to which I defer with a greater sense of respect. I have been told that, after all that has passed, there are not a few worthy priests who, in different parts of England, have expressed a wish to know what I should be disposed to say on the subject in question; and that some have even expressed an apprehension that Dr. Newman is encouraging a dry and formal devotion towards the Blessed Virgin and the saints. It has thus become a duty in me to remove these apprehensions, as well as to put facts in their proper light. But before I do so, I beg to invite attention to the wisdom of a saint which the Church has made its own, which the Popes have invested with their authority, and with which the prelates of the Church have every-where sought to imbue their own hearts, and those of the clergy, as well as of the devout religious and laity.

When St. Ignatius and his saintly disciples began to give the spiritual exercises they were assailed as innovators, and even as heretics; and his own experience of this readiness in Catholic men to suspect, and criticise, and take exceptions, even in what the Holy Ghost has inspired, led him to insert the following admonition, drawn from the maxims of our Lord, into the text of those spiritual exercises. He says:—

'That both he who gives, and he who receives the spiritual exercises, may be helped to their profit, it must be presupposed that every pious Christian man is in readiness of disposition to interpret any obscure sentence or proposition in a good sense, rather than to pronounce condemnation. But if he can in no way put a sound construction upon it, let him enquire of him who gave it utterance; and if then his sense comes short of what is right and accurate, let him correct him with love; and should this not succeed, let him try all proper ways to keep him sound and safe from error. It is not so unfrequent for those who proclaim the errors of their neighbours to have themselves committed the error, but common prudence requires, before we rush out before all the world with our discovery, that we should first ascertain whether we are correct in our conclusion or not; for, once before the world, there is no recovering those sentences which fly before every wind; whilst correction of the error, once blown abroad, is but a coy reluctant messenger to follow; unacceptable to those who have endorsed the mischief, it is slow of motion, and prone to drop upon the ground.'

For myself, I prefer solid facts to lightly flying assertions, and so I proceed to give them in historic order. When Dr. Newman entered the Church he took the name of Mary in confirmation. He went to Rome, and there placed himself under the most celebrated teachers. He had no sooner received the priesthood than he put himself under the guidance of the Oratory of St. Philip Neri, for Cardinal Wiseman had pointed out that congregation to him as the best adapted for the work he was called to do in England. When he had received the brief which authorised his establishing the Oratory, and was leaving Rome, ere he quitted the Roman territory, he knelt down and kissed the earth, in token of obedience to the Head of the Church. He selected the feast of the Purification for commencing the Oratory at Mary Vale. He chose the same festival of Our Lady, in the following year, for commencing the Oratory at Birmingham. He dedicated the house and church at Edgbaston to the Mystery of the Immaculate Conception. When sent by the Sovereign Pontiff to found the University in Dublin, he at once placed the University under the patronage of Mary as the Sedes Sapientiæ, and dedicated the church which he there built with his own funds to SS. Peter and Paul.

When you enter the Oratory, the first thing that meets your eye in the entrance hall, is a statue of the Blessed Virgin, raised upon an altar, as a sign of the patronage under which you enter. And on proceeding further into the church, you find it a complete representation of a fervid Roman church. The altars everywhere exhibit the cultus of the Blessed Virgin or of the Saints, and of their relics, where you have not immediately the representation of our Lord's Passion and Crucifixion. I repeat, that no other Church in England that I have ever seen, is so complete a representation, in all its appointments, of a fervid Roman church.

I will now enumerate the devotions practised at this day towards the Blessed Virgin, in this Birmingham Oratory. I say, at this day, because before the school absorbed so much of the time of the Fathers, the devotions were yet more frequent.

1. Every day in the year the Rosary is publicly said in the church.

2. Every Sunday the Rosary is said twice; once for the students, and once for the people.

3. A large number of the students meet their tutors daily to say the Rosary as an act of free devotion.

4. The Angelus is, of course, three times a day.

5. On Sundays, the children of the poor schools at mass and catechism, sing hymns and the Litany of Loretto, in honour of the Blessed Virgin.

6. There is a Novena before the feast of the Purification, the day on which the superiors of the congregation are elected, to place their election under the protection of the Blessed Virgin.

7. A Novena is made before the feast of the Assumption, and another before that of the Immaculate Conception, the patroness of the Church, and principal feast of the congregation, followed, as in all the churches of Birmingham, by the forty hours' adoration, when all that art and resources can do is expended on the adornment of the altar and sanctuary.

8. The month of Mary is celebrated with all the Roman devotions; and a picture of Mary Immaculate, painted at Rome, and framed in a costly manner by the devotion of the students, is set up in the middle of the church, with flowers and lights. There are two celebrations of the devotion each day of the month; one for the students, and one for the people.

9. The statue of the Blessed Virgin at her altar is always adorned with flowers and lights, and has ever attracted much devotion from the people.

10. There is a Holy Guild of the Immaculate Heart of Mary, which meets monthly in the chapel of the Sacred Heart for instruction, and whose communion days are the feasts of the Blessed Virgin.

11. Dr. Newman was the first to introduce this cycle of devotions to the Blessed Virgin, and from Birmingham they went with his disciples to London.

Of course I am limiting myself to an account of devotions to the Blessed Virgin exclusively, and every one will understand that other devotions are observed in due proportion. I might next go on to mention the works produced at the Birmingham Oratory in honour of the Blessed Virgin.

1. Dr. Newman's two sermons on the Glories of Mary.

2. The book of hymns written or translated by the Fathers at Edgbaston, to which Dr. Newman contributed Nos. 31, 32 and 38, in honour of the Blessed Virgin.

3. Father Caswall's translation of the Office of the Immaculate Conception.

4. The same author's poems, the Masque of Mary, the Mary Pageant, and his numerous hymns in general use throughout England.

5. Father St. John's translation of the *Racoltà*, containing all the indulgenced prayers and Novenas used at Rome in honour of our Lady.

This authentic statement must put all further questioning to rest touching Dr. Newman's idea of devotion towards the Blessed Virgin. He brought from Rome what he found in Rome, and I well recollect the pregnant answer which he wrote when it became my duty to interrogate each priest having cure of souls in this diocese, prior to the definition of the Immaculate Conception. The question sent to each asked the sense of the priest, and the traditional sense entertained in his congregation with respect to that mystery. And he wrote in substance: 'We are too young to have a tradition of our own, but we brought the doctrine of the Immaculate Conception of the Mother of God from Rome, where we imbibed it with our other teaching.'

What more exquisite, or more ample proof could we have of the depth to which the singular privileges and glories of the Mother of our Lord have been imbibed into the mind and heart of the person in question, than the exposition of the Mystery of the Immaculate Conception in the letter to Dr. Pusey; an exposition which, I have reason to know, has cleared away the difficulties that obscured the minds of several earnest inquirers with respect to the whole subject of the Blessed Virgin.

Is petty cavilling from Catholics without authority to be the present reward for a masterly exposition of the subject most difficult for a Protestant to comprehend, and which has made that subject classical in the English tongue?

In vain have I striven to find what Dr. Newman has written derogatory to devotion to the Blessed Virgin, or beyond the limits of theological prudence. The style, the aim, and the whole mind put forth by a writer require to be considered, in estimating the force of particular sentences, and the sentences of this author are often struck out with a concise vigour and a point, which detach them like proverbs, and fasten them like nails into the mind; and I apprehend that this sharp and incisive prominence of particular sentences so concentrates the attention of certain readers through their keenness, that they are wholly diverted from carrying in their minds that circle of qualifications which attends upon them. However that may be, I cannot myself fail to observe the ardour with which Dr. Newman defends every inch of the ground of Catholic principle from the attacks of Dr. Pusey, and the earnestness with which he puts forth his whole soul in exalting each glorious privilege of the Immaculate Mother of Our Lord. A book condensed as this is requires to be studied with patient attention to every sentence and clause, that the reader may carry forward what precedes into what follows.

There are some people, often in the first and tender green of their faith, who seem to think it impossible that there should be abuses or indiscretions in speaking of the Blessed Virgin. And I remember being utterly shocked at a letter which appeared in one of our Catholic papers some years ago, in which the adversaries of the Blessed Virgin were challenged to try if they could possibly think anything derogatory of her purity. That foolish writer must have been altogether ignorant of the prominence given to St. Mary Magdalen for a certain purpose in the Talmud; and of the conflict waged against Pagans as well as Jews on the ground of that very story from the day of Origen to the days of Epiphanius. He must have been altogether ignorant of certain Protestant historic theories on the subject of the family of the Blessed Virgin. I was thoroughly ashamed of that letter, and of whoever gave it insertion; and am ashamed of having to allude to it. But if so many evil things have been thought and uttered of our Blessed Lord, what wonder that they should be uttered of His Blessed Mother? We need not go to old errors in devotion to the Blessed Virgin condemned by the Church. De Montfort's book is a case in point. Whatever beautiful and devotional truths it embodies, it was written in express advocacy of an unsound devotion, which the Holy See condemned, and the instruments used in which were ordered to be broken and destroyed. When that devotion was introduced from abroad into a certain place in this Diocese, I condemned it before I knew that I had been anticipated by the Holy See. We are not the slaves even of God, but, as St. Paul says, our service is a free and reasonable service.

There can be no doubt that a certain prudence and measured wisdom of language is demanded, according with the genius of language and methods of thought which belong to a nation; and that under the penalty of having our doctrines and sentiments completely misconceived. Dr. Faber wrote to me a letter in the year in which the Immaculate Conception was defined, in which he says, referring to a book upon that mystery, that had he and some of his brethren always used the discretion of language which he thought characterised that work, they would have been saved from certain troublesome consequences. And greatly as I admire much which he wrote, I do regret that in a note to his translation of De Montfort, he should have said that the devotion, though condemned in confraternities, might be practised by individuals; since it was the principle of that devotion which was condemned as unsound. Let me give an instance out of several within my knowledge of the injudicious use of certain books. Quite recently, a lady had but one difficulty that kept her from entering the Church — it concerned the Blessed Virgin; De Montfort's book was put into her hands as the proper remedy, and it drove her away in terror. Had it been Dr. Newman's book, how different might have been the result.

When you make crude translations of books used by a people (we will say like the Neapolitans), with their hyperboles and superlatives, neglecting the conditions of thought in the language of the people for whom you render them; instead of fairly representing those books, you do them injustice, as well as the people whose devotions they express, and the faith which they embody, and the readers into whose hands they are liable to fall. Ardent and enthusiastic phrases, intense with life in the hearts of those who used them in their native tongue, the very burning summits of a lava flood of devotion, are extracted, cold and flat, out of the frigid translation and industriously circulated in a thousand prints through the Protestant world, for the purpose of showing that our Blessed Lord is taken by Catholics out of the economy of redemption, and our Lady put in His place. And thus thousands upon thousands are driven into gross and even blasphemous errors against the Church of Christ, and even against the Mother of our Lord. And all this comes from what in its own sense, and in its own place, is beautiful and true.

There is prudence of language especially needed in a country like this, and so long as we use the language of Popes, councils, fathers, theologians, and liturgies, as Dr. Newman had done, so long shall we be able as he likewise has done, to give the most perfect honour to the Mother of God. But even then, let us guard the truth from human misconception as far as charity requires, whilst we withhold not the whole truth nor cool in our own devotion.

This spirit characterises the Oratory of Birmingham, which is Roman in its devotions because it is Roman in the faith which its fathers believe and teach.

I remain, dear Sir, Your faithful servant, ✠ W. B. Ullathorne.

List of Letters by Correspondents

List of Letters by Correspondents

Abbreviations used in addition to those listed at the beginning of the volume:

A.	Original Autograph.
Bayswater	Oblates of St Charles, Bayswater, London.
Bodleian	Bodleian Library, Oxford.
C.	Copy, other than those made by Newman.
D.	Draft by Newman.
Georgetown	The University of Georgetown, Washington, D.C.
H.	Holograph copy by Newman.
Harrow	Dominican Convent, Harrow, Middlesex.
Lond.	London Oratory.
Magd.	Magdalen College, Oxford.
Pr.	Printed.
Pusey	Pusey House, Oxford.
Rankeillour	The Lord Rankeillour.
S. J. Dublin	The Jesuit Fathers, 35 Lower Leeson Street, Dublin.
S. J. Lond.	The Jesuit Fathers, 114 Mount Street, London.
Ushaw	Ushaw College, Durham.

The abbreviation which describes the source is always the first one after the date of each letter. This is followed immediately by the indication of its present location or owner. When there is no such indication, it means that the source letter is preserved at the Birmingham Oratory. It has not been thought necessary to reproduce the catalogue indications of the Archives at the Oratory, because each of Newman's letters there is separately indexed, and can be traced at once.

After the source and its location have been indicated, any additional holograph copies (with their dates) or drafts are listed, and then, enclosed within brackets, any reference to previous publication in standard works.

Lastly, when it is available, comes the address to which the letter was sent.

LIST OF LETTERS BY CORRESPONDENTS

Correspondent	Year	Date	Source	Location, Owner, Address
Acton, Sir John	1865	21 July	A	
Allcock and Milward, Messrs.	1865	3 July	D	
Allies, T. W.	1865	11 Oct	C	
	1866	19 Jan	C	
		31 Jan	C	
		19 Feb	C	
		9 Mar	C	
		13 Mar	H	
			D	(Two)
		15 April	C	
		24 June	C	
		9 July	C	
		9 Sept	C	
		21 Oct	C	
			D	
		23 Oct	C	(Two)
Arnold, Thomas	1866	28 Jan	C	(T. Arnold, *Passages in a Wandering Life*, London 1900, p. 204)
Badeley, Edward	1865	21 July	A	
	1866	5 June	A	
Bathurst, Catherine Anne	1865	6 Sept	A	Harrow
	1866	21 Jan	A	Harrow
		2 Mar	A	Harrow
		31 Dec	A	Harrow (*Trevor II*, p. 372)
Bedford, Henry	1865	4 Aug	A	Newman Preparatory School, Boston, Mass. *Ad.* Revd Henry Bedford / Foxcastle / Sudbury Suffolk
		10 Aug	A	Newman Preparatory School, Boston, Mass. *Ad.* the same
	1866	21 Jan	C	
		23 Dec	A	All Hallows College, Dublin
Bellasis, Edward	1865	4 Sept	A	
		26 Nov	A	
	1866	5 June	A	
		12 June	A	
Bellasis, Mrs Edward	1866	2 Dec	A	
Benham, William	1866	7 July	Pr	The *Churchman*, 12 July, 1866
		24 July	D	
Berdoe, Edward	1865	2 Oct	C	
Birmingham Oratorian, A	1866	after 12 Aug	C	
Bittleston, Henry	1865	29 July	A	(*Ward* II, p. 84)
		4 Aug	A	(*Ward* II, pp. 84–5)
		24 Aug	A	
Bloxam, J. R.	1865	14 Sept	A	Magd. Ms 307
		17 Sept	A	Magd. Ms 307
		28 Sept	A	Magd. Ms 307 (*Newman and Bloxam*, p. 228; R. D. Middleton, *Newman at Oxford*, London 1950, pp. 249–50)
		6 Nov	A	Magd. (*Newman and Bloxam*, p. 229)
	1866	21 Sept	A	Magd.
Bowden, Marianne	1866	29 Jan	A	Visitation Convent, Waldron, Sussex
Bowden, Marianne Frances	1866	17 May	A	*Ad.* Miss Bowden
		24 May	A	*Ad.* Miss Bowden/40 Prince's Gate/ London SW
		5 June	A	*Ad.* the same
		15 Aug	A	*Ad.* Miss Bowden/40 Prince's Gate/ London SW/*Angleterre*/to be forwarded

LIST OF LETTERS BY CORRESPONDENTS

Correspondent	Year	Date	Source	Location, Owner, Address
Bowden, Mrs J. W.	1866	24 June	A	Lond.
Bowles, Emily	1865	20 July	A	
	1866	18 Jan	A	(*Trevor* II, p. 373)
		16 April	A	(*Ward* II, p. 125; *Trevor* II, p. 381)
		23 May	A	(*Ward* II, pp. 126–7)
		11 Nov	A	(*Ward* II, p. 127; *Trevor* II, pp. 388–9)
		31 Dec	A	(*Ward* II, p. 47)
Bowyer, Sir George	1866	25 Nov	A	Catholic Church, Abingdon
Boyle, G. D.	1865	15 Sept	C	(*The Recollections of the Very Rev. G. D. Boyle,* London 1895, p. 216)
	1866	28 April	C	
			D	
		7 May	D	
Bretherton, Eleanor (Mrs F. J. Watt)	1866	21 Feb	C	
		21 Mar	C	
		2 April	C	
		28 May	C	
		30 Dec	C	
Bretherton, Mrs Peter	1865	3 July	C	
		9 July	D	
		28 Aug	C	
	1866	1 Nov	C	
Bristow, Miss	1866	15 April	C	
Brown, Thomas Joseph	1865	28 Aug	C	
	1866	22 Feb	C	
Burnand, F. C.	1865	5 Nov	C	
Castle, James	1866	16 July	D	
Chatterton, Lady	1865	27 July	A	Oscott *Ad.* Lady Chatterton/Finchden/Tenterden/Kent
		6 Sept	A	Oscott *Ad.* same
		10 Sept	A	Oscott *Ad.* same
			D	
		2 Oct	A	Oscott *Ad.* same
			D	
		10 Oct	A	Oscott *Ad.* same
		22 Oct	A	Oscott *Ad.* same
	1866	29 Mar	A	Oscott *Ad.* same
			D	
		5 April	A	Oscott *Ad.* same
		12 April	A	Oscott *Ad* same
Church, R. W.	1865	11 July	Pr	*Ward* II, p. 75 (*Trevor* II, pp. 336–7)
		6 Aug	C	
		Sept	Pr	*Ward* II, p. 96 (see last note to letter of 13 Sept. to St. John)
	1866	19 Jan	C	
		21 Sept	Pr	*Ward* II, p. 119
		13 Nov	C	
Circular Letter	1866	20 July	C	
Clarkson, Mr	1865	27 Nov	A	
Clifford, William	1866	17 Mar	A	Clifton Diocesan Archives
			D	
Coleridge, Henry James	1865	23 Aug	A	S.J. Lond.
		20 Oct	A	S.J. Lond.
		22 Nov	A	S.J. Lond.
		24 Nov	A	S.J. Lond.
		11 Dec	A	S.J. Lond.
	1866	28 Feb	A	S.J. Lond.
		15 Mar	A	S.J. Lond.
		3 April	A	S.J. Lond.
		9 April	A	S.J. Lond.
		13 April	A	S.J. Lond. (*Ward* II, p. 114)

Correspondent	Year	Date	Source	Location, Owner, Address
		18 April	A	S.J. Lond.
		20 April	A	S.J. Lond.
		1 May	A	S.J. Lond.
		22 May	A	S.J. Lond.
		21 Oct	A	S.J. Lond.
		24 Oct	A	S.J. Lond.
		4 Nov	A	S.J. Lond.
		14 Nov	A	S.J. Lond.
		22 Nov	A	S.J. Lond.
Combe, Mrs Thomas	1865	16 Oct	A	Keble
Copeland, W. J.	1865	28 Aug	A	Pusey
		30 Aug	A	Pusey
		1 Sept	A	Pusey
		3 Sept	A	Pusey
		4 Sept	A	Pusey
		7 Sept	A	Pusey
		1 Dec	A	Pusey
	1866	14 Feb	A	Pusey
		15 May	A	Pusey
		27 May	A	Pusey (*Ward* II, p. 130)
		11 June	A	Pusey
		18 June	C	Pusey
		23 Dec	A	Pusey
Crawley, Charles	1866	1 April	A	
Darnell, Nicholas	1865	16 Oct	D	
Daunt, W. J. O'Neill	1866	21 Dec	A	
de Lisle, Ambrose Phillipps	1866	7 Feb	C	(*de Lisle* II, p. 9)
		27 Feb	C	(*de Lisle* II, p. 10)
		3 Mar	C	(*de Lisle* II, p. 264; *Ward* II, p. 115)
		9 Mar	C	(*de Lisle* II, p. 271)
		28 Mar	C	(*de Lisle* II, p. 33)
Denbigh, Earl of	1865	9 Dec	C	
	1866	12 Feb	C	
		1 April	C	
		22 Dec	A	St John's Seminary, Camarillo, California
Denton, William	1866	8 July	C	
Dering, Edward Heneage	1865	6 Sept	A	Oscott *Ad.* E Dering Esqr/Finchden/Tenterden/Kent
		14 Sept	A	Oscott *Ad.* same
		17 Sept	A	Oscott *Ad.* same
		22 Sept	A	Oscott *Ad.* same
		18 Oct	A	Oscott *Ad.* same
		5 Nov	A	Oscott *Ad.* same
		16 Dec	A	Oscott *Ad.* same
	1866	26 Mar	A	Oscott *Ad.* same
		30 April	A	Oscott *Ad.* same
Douglas, David	1866	14 Sept	Pr	William Knight, *Principal Shairp and his Friends,* London 1888, p. 61
			D	
Doyle, Thomas	1866	15 April	D	
Dunn, Miss	1866	6 Dec	A	
Dupanloup, Felix	1866	25 Jan	D	
			C	Pierre Batiffol Archives
Editor of the Birmingham Daily Post	1865	9 Oct	Pr	The *Birmingham Daily Post* (11 Oct. 1865), p. 3
Editor of the Guardian	1866	23 Mar	Pr	The *Guardian* (28 March 1866), p. 333
			D	
Editor of the Tablet	1866	5 Mar	Pr	The *Tablet* (10 March 1866), p. 149

Correspondent	Year	Date	Source	Location, Owner, Address
Editor of the Weekly Register	1865	19 Nov	Pr	The *Weekly Register* (25 Nov. 1865) (Liddon's *Pusey* IV, p. 95, note)
Ellacombe, Henry Thomas	1866	19 Feb	A	Bodleian
Froude, Robert Edmund	1866	20 Apr	C	*Ad.* E. Froude Esq./Maison H de Mouléon/Mentone/Les Alpes Maritimes/France (*Harper*, pp. 182–3)
Froude, Mrs William	1865	7 Aug	C	(*Ward* II, p. 90; *Harper*, pp. 181–2)
		16 Oct	C	(*Ward* II, p. 96)
Gaisford, Thomas	1866	15 Nov	C	
Gallwey, Peter	1865	26 Feb	A	Anthony D. Bischoff, S.J.
Giberne, Miss M. R.	1865	21 July	A	
	1866	29 Jan	A	
		30 Dec	A	
Gladstone, William Ewart	1866	21 Feb	A	
Goldsmid, Mrs	1866	11 Aug	A	A. Oller y Arriaga, Barcelona
Gondon, Jules	1866	19 Feb	D	
Gordon, William Philip	1866	28 Jan	A	Lond. Vol 11
Gubbins, James	1866	19 Mar	D	
		7 April	D	
Hallaghan, Mother Margaret Mary	1866	14 Jan	C	
		31 Jan	C	
		30 Dec	C	
Harper, Thomas	1866	12 Feb	A	S.J. Lond.
		14 May	A	S.J. Lond.
		20 May	A	S.J. Lond.
		2 Dec	A	S.J. Lond.
			D	
Hawkins, Edward	1866	1 Jan	A	Oriel
			D	
		8 April	A	Oriel (*Newman at Oxford.* pp. 269–70)
Hecker, Isaac Thomas	1866	2 Mar	A	Paulist Archives, New York
Herbert, Lady of Lea	1866	20 Sept	A	
		7 Nov	A	*Ad.* The Lady Herbert/38 Chesham Place/London SW
Hewit, Augustine Francis	1866	16 May	A	Paulist Archives, New York
			D	
Hoghton, G. W.	1865	19 Nov	D	
Holmes, Miss	1865	2 July	A	
		27 Aug	A	
		15 Sept	A	
		3 Nov	A	
Hope-Scott, James	1865	25 Sept	A	Rankeillour
			H	1873
			H of D	
		23 Oct	A	Rankeillour
		26 Nov	A	Rankeillour
			H	
	1866	17 May	A	Rankeillour
			H	1866
		14 June	A	Rankeillour
		17 June	A	Rankeillour
			H	1873
		20 July	A	Rankeillour
			H	(two, 1873)
		25 July	A	Rankeillour
		1 Nov	A	Rankeillour
			H	
		6 Dec	A	Rankeillour
			H	(two, 1873)

Correspondent	Year	Date	Source	Location, Owner, Address
Hopkins, Gerard Manley	1866	14 Sept	A	Anthony D. Bischoff, S.J. (*Further Letters of Gerard Manley Hopkins*, edited by C. C. Abbott, second edition, London 1956, p. 404)
		18 Oct	A	Anthony D. Bischoff, S.J. (*Further Letters*, p. 404)
		21 Nov	A	Campion Hall, Oxford *Ad.* Gerald M. Hopkins Esqr/18 New Inn Hall Street/Oxford (*Further Letters*, p. 405)
		6 Dec	Pr	G. F. Lahey, S.J., *Gerard Manley Hopkins*, Oxford 1930 (*Further Letters*, p. 405)
		16 Dec	A	Campion Hall, Oxford (*Further Letters*, pp. 405–6)
Hostage, John	1865	17 Aug	A	John Hostage, New Haven, U.S.A.
Jenkins, Robert Charles	1866	19 Feb	C	
		26 Feb	C	
			D	
		4 Mar	D	
Keble, John	1865	4 Aug	A	(*Ward* II, pp. 92–3)
		1 Sept	A	(*Ward* II, p. 93)
		4 Sept	A	(*Ward* II, p. 94)
		7 Sept	A	(*Ward* II, p. 94)
		28 Sept	A	
		8 Oct	A	
		1 Nov	A	
		8 Dec	A	
	1866	17 Jan	A	
		7 Feb	A	
Keble, Thomas	1866	9 Sept	D	
		13 Sept	D	
Keble, Thomas, Junior	1866	21 July	A	
Kelly, Father	1866	15 Mar	A	St John's Priory, Thomas Street, Dublin
Kenny, Courtney	1865	7 July	A	Newman College, University of Melbourne, Australia
			D	
Knox, T. F.	1865	11 July	A	Lond. Vol. 15 *Ad.* The Revd/Fr Knox/The Oratory/Brompton/London SW
		15 Oct	A	Lond. Vol. 15 *Ad.* the same
Lake, William Charles	1866	5 July	C	(*Memorials of William Charles Lake*, edited by Katherine Lake, London, 1901, p. 210)
La Serre, H	1865	14 July	C	
		7 Aug	C	
Leigh, William, Junior	1866	29 July	A	Dominican Priory, Woodchester
Liddon, H. P.	1866	31 Mar	A	Keble *Ad.* The Revd H. P. Liddon/60 Upper Seymour Street/Portman Square/London W
Lockhart, William	1865	26 Oct	D	
		21 Nov	A	
Lynch, Henry J.	1866	28 Sept	C	
		11 Nov	C	
MacColl, Malcolm	1866	4 Feb	C	(*Malcolm MacColl Memoirs and Correspondence*, edited by G. W. E. Russell, London 1914, p. 289)
		25 May	C	(*Malcolm MacColl Memoirs and Correspondence*, p. 288)
Macmullen, Richard Gell	1866	11 Feb	C	
Manning, Archbishop	1866	9 Feb	A	Bayswater
		1 April	A	Bayswater
Maurice, R. R.	1865	9 Dec	D	

Correspondent	Year	Date	Source	Location, Owner, Address
Meynell, Charles	1866	11 Oct	A	
Monsell, William	1866	19 Jan	A	
		26 Jan	A	
		7 Mar	A	
		11 Mar	A	
		19 June	A	
		16 Oct	C	
		1 Nov	A	
		27 Nov	A	
		27 Dec	A	
Monteith, Robert	1865	22 Oct	A	Major J. B. Monteith
			D	
Moriarty, David	1866	23 Mar	A	
		14 Nov	A	
Mozley, Henry Williams	1866	21 Oct	A	J. H. Mozley, Haslemere, Surrey
Mozley, Mrs John	1865	27 Aug	A	J. H. Mozley, Haslemere, Surrey
		18 Oct	A	J. H. Mozley
		24 Oct	A	J. H. Mozley
		31 Oct	A	J. H. Mozley
			D	
	1866	21 Feb	A	J. H. Mozley
		8 April	A	J. H. Mozley
		12 May	A	Bodleian
		4 June	A	Oriel
		2 Oct	A	Oriel
		24 Oct	A	Miss Grace Mozley
		14 Dec	A	Bodleian
Munro, Miss	1865	20 Oct	A	
	1866	21 Jan	C	
		8 Oct	A	Lond.
Newman, Francis William	1866	14 Oct	D	
Neville, William	1865	7 July	A	
		10 Sept	A	
		24 Sept	A	
		1 Dec	A	
		2 Dec	A	
		5 Dec	A	
		12 July	A	
		12 Aug	A	(*Trevor* II, p. 385)
		3 Sept	A	
Noble, Daniel	1866	10 Feb	C	
Norris, John	1865	9 Aug	A	
Northcote, J. Spencer	1865	5 Sept	A	J. F. Bourke, Weswood House, near Droitwich
		10 Sept	A	Stoke
		24 Dec	A	Stoke
	1866	8 Feb	A	Stoke
O'Hagan, John	1865	27 Nov	A	S.J. Dublin
O'Neill, Simeon Wilberforce	1865	11 Aug	A	The Cowley Fathers, Oxford
Ornsby, Robert	1866	22 Jan	A	
			H	1873
		15 April	A	
		30 Dec	A	
Orpen, Miss	1865	18 Oct	A	Oscott
	1866	5 April	A	Oscott
		29 April	A	Oscott
Oxenham, Henry Nutcombe	1865	9 Nov	D	
	1866	17 Mar	D	
		20 Mar	D	
Paget, James	1865	14 Aug	A	Bodleian, MS. Autogr. b.13, fol. 376
Palgrave, Francis Turner	1866	15 July	C	

Correspondent	Year	Date	Source	Location, Owner, Address
Patterson, James Laird	1865	2 July	C	
Pattison, Mark	1866	21 Sept	A	Bodleian, Pattison Ms 56
		19 Oct	A	Bodleian, Pattison Ms 56
		28 Dec	A	Bodleian, Pattison Ms 56
Pététot, Louis Pierre	1865	3 Nov	D	
Poole, Imelda	1866	2 April	C	(*Ward* II, p. 133)
		27 May	C	
Prince Doria's Agents	1865	6 Sept	D	
Pusey, E. B.	1865	5 Sept	A	Pusey (Liddon's *Pusey* IV, p. 106; *Ward* II, p. 91)
			D	
		28 Sept	A	Pusey
		31 Oct	A	Pusey (Liddon's *Pusey* IV, p. 119; *Ward* II, p. 100; *Trevor* II, pp. 371–2)
		3 Nov	A	Pusey (Liddon's *Pusey* IV, p. 123)
			D	
		10 Nov	A	Pusey (Liddon's *Pusey* IV, p. 127)
		11 Nov	A	Pusey
		14 Nov	A	Pusey (Liddon's *Pusey* IV, pp. 126–28; *Newman at Oxford*, p. 251)
		17 Nov	A	Pusey (Liddon's *Pusey* IV, p. 128; *Ward* II, p. 101)
		19 Nov	A	Pusey (Liddon's *Pusey* IV, p. 128; *Ward* II, p. 101)
		23 Nov	A	Pusey (*Ward* II, p. 102)
		1 Dec	A	Pusey
		8 Dec	A	Pusey (Liddon's *Pusey* IV, p. 131; *Ward* II, p. 102)
		14 Dec	A	Pusey
	1866	19 Jan	A	Pusey
		22 Jan	A	Pusey
		12 Feb	A	Pusey
		2 April	A	Pusey (Liddon's *Pusey* IV, p. 137; *Ward* II, p. 113)
		20 April	A	Pusey
		29 April	A	Pusey (*Ward* II, p. 121)
	1866	31 May	A	Pusey
		25 Sept	A	Pusey
		28 Sept	A	Pusey
		7 Oct	A	Pusey
		20 Nov	A	Pusey
			D	
		13 Dec	A	Pusey
Ramière, Henri de	1866	23 Dec	A	Revue d'ascétique et de mystique, Toulouse
Reid, Charles Burton	1865	27 Aug	D	
Rhodes, M. J.	1866	25 April	C	
Riddell, Charles	1866	13 Feb	A	The Manuscript Society, East Oregon, N.J.
		21 July	C	
Rogers, Sir Frederic	1866	16 Jan	A	Divinity School, Spruce Street, Philadelphia
		18 Jan	C	
		13 May	C	
		15 May	C	
		10 June	A	
Russell, Charles	1865	5 Sept	A	S.J. Dublin
		4 Dec	A	S.J. Dublin
Ryder, Henry Ignatius Dudley	1866	16 July	A	
Sconce, Mrs	1865	15 Oct	C	
Seager, Mrs	1866	20 Jan	D	
Sheil, Sir Justin	1866	13 Oct	A	

Correspondent	Year	Date	Source	Location, Owner, Address
Shortland, John R.	1865	21 Nov	C	
		24 Nov	C	
		4 Dec	C	
Simpson, Richard	1866	25 Mar	A	
		22 July	A	
Stephen, James Fitzjames	1866	[7 Sept]	D	
Stewart, James	1866	14 Oct	C	
		25 Nov	C	
St John, Ambrose	1865	3 Aug	A	
		5 Aug	A	
		14 Aug	A	(*Trevor* II, p. 367)
			H	1875
		27 Aug	A	(*Ward* II, p. 123; *Butler* II, p. 13)
			H	1875
		13 Sept	A	(*Ward* II, p. 95; *Trevor* II, pp. 367–8)
			H	1875
		15 Sept	A	
			H	1875
		18 Sept	A	
	1866	23 June	A	(*Ward* II, pp. 130–31)
			H	1875
		25 July	A	
		27 July	A	
			H	1875
Sullivan, William Kirby	1865	25 Aug	A	
	1866	30 Dec	A	
Swanwick, Anna	1865	22 Aug	A	Walter R. Benjamin, New York
Taylor, J. P.	1866	8 Feb	A	Lond.
Thynne, Lord Charles	1866	29 Oct	C	
Thynne, Lady Charles	1865	12 July	C	
		29 Oct	C	
Ullathorne, Bishop	1865	23 Dec	A	
	1866	12 Feb	A	
		13 Feb	A	
		20 Mar	A	
		1 April	A	
		7 April	A	
		15 April	A	
		23 April	A	
			D	
			H	1867
		4 June	A	
			D	
		8 June	A	
			D	(Two)
		17 June	A	
		9 July	A	
		15 July	A	
		25 [24] July	D	(Three)
		26 July	A	
			D	(Two)
		12 Aug	A	
			D	
		9 Dec	A	
		26 Dec	A	
Unknown Correspondents	1866	17 Feb	A	
		13 Mar	Pr	The *Catholic Register* (Sept 1927)
		July?	D	
		29 Dec	A	
		[end of 1866?]	D	
Walford, John Thomas	1866	12 Mar	A	Georgetown *Ad.* J. D. Walford Esq/Miltown Park/Donnybrook Dublin

Correspondent	Year	Date	Source	Location, Owner, Address
		6 May	A	Boston
Walker, J. of Scarborough	1865	2 July	A	
	1866	18 Jan	A	
		17 Feb	A	
		5 April	A	
		12 July	A	
		22 Sept	A	
		25 Oct	A	
Walker, William	1866	10 Feb	A	Ushaw
		28 Feb	A	Ushaw
		6 Mar	A	Ushaw
		12 Mar	A	Ushaw
Ward, Mrs F. R.	1865	17 Dec	A	
	1866	5 Jan	A	
		25 Oct	A	
Ward, W. G.	1866	18 Feb	A	Mrs Sheed (*Purcell* II, 321–2; *Trevor* II, pp. 377–8)
			D	
Watt, F. J.	1865	30 July	D	
Watt, Mrs F. J.				*see* Bretherton, Eleanor
Wegg-Prosser, Francis Richard	1865	27 Aug	A	Wegg-Prosser Papers, Maryhill House, Belmont, Hereford
	1866	30 Jan	A	Wegg-Prosser Papers
Weguelin, W. A.	1866	28 April	C	
		29 July	C	
Wetherell, T. F.	1865	8 July	A	
		15 July	A	
			D	
		20 July	A	
		21 July	C	
		25 July	A	*Ad.* T. F. Wetherell Esqr/4 St James's Street/Pall Mall/London SW
		5 Sept	A	
Whately, E. Jane	1865	24 Sept	D	
Whitty, Robert	1865	25 Sept	A	
Wilberforce, Henry	1865	2 Nov	A	Georgetown
		3 Nov	A	Georgetown
	1866	3 April	A	Georgetown
			H	1873
		15 May	A	Georgetown
			H	1873
		29 Nov	A	Georgetown
			H	1873
Wilson, Lavinia	1865	27 Aug	C	
		29 Sept	A	
Wilson, R. F.	1866	28 Mar	A	
Wood, Charlotte	1865	11 Nov	A	
	1866	20 Jan	A	
		8 April	A	
		27 Nov	A	
		10 Dec	A	
		21 Dec	A	
Wood, J. O.	1865	24 Oct	D	
Woodgate, H. A.	1865	22 Nov	A	
			H	1872
			D	
		16 Dec	A	
			H	1872
		23 May	H	1872 Bodleian MS Eng. letters d. 102
Woodlock, Bartholomew	1866	28 Jan	A	University College, Dublin

MEMORANDA, ETC.

	Date	Source	Subject
1866	26 Mar (I)	A	W. G. Ward and *A Letter to Pusey*
	26 Mar (II)	A	Memorandum on the Oxford Mission
	17 May	A	Interview with Bishop Ullathorne on the Oxford Mission (*Trevor* II, pp. 382–3)
	23 Sept	A	(Two) Bishop Ullathorne's explanations (*Trevor* II, pp. 386–7)

LETTERS TO NEWMAN

		From	Inserted before Newman's of
1866	20 Jan	Bishop Dupanloup	25 Jan
	18 Feb	William Ewart Gladstone	21 Feb
	24 July	Bishop Ullathorne	25 [24] July
	31 July	Bishop Ullathorne	12 Aug
	28 Aug	Gerard Manley Hopkins	14 Sept
	15 Oct	Gerard Manley Hopkins	18 Oct

Index of Persons and Places

References are given always to *The Dictionary of National Biography* or *The Dictionary of American Biography,* and failing them, to Frederick Boase, *Modern English Biography* and Joseph Gillow, *Bibliographical Dictionary of the English Catholics*; also occasionally to other printed works. Much of the information is derived from the correspondence and other material in the archives of the Birmingham Oratory, and from various private sources.

Acheson (xxi), Lady A., 18.

Acland (xxi), Thomas Dyke (1809–98), 254

Acton (xxi), Sir John Dalberg (1834–1902), 15, 18, 252.

Adams, Walter Marsham, son of the judge Serjeant John Adams, went up to New College, Oxford in 1856, aged eighteen. He took his B.A. in 1861, and became a Catholic. In Nov. 1863 he took up law, entering the Inner Temple, and later wrote on early Egyptian religion. He published *Outlines of Geometry* in 1866, and a translation of the first book of *The Iliad* in 1873, 309.

Addis, William Edward (1844–1917), son of a Free Church minister in Edinburgh, was at Glasgow University, and then in 1861 a Snell Exhibitioner at Balliol College, where he was one of G. M. Hopkins's closest friends. He took a First in Classics in 1865, and in Oct. 1866 was received into the Church at St Mary of the Angels, Bayswater, a fortnight before Hopkins. He joined the London Oratory in 1868, was ordained priest in 1872, and from 1878 to 1888 was Parish Priest at Sydenham. He was a close friend of Baron Friedrich von Hügel, and in April 1882 was elected Fellow in Mental and Moral Philosophy at the Royal University of Ireland, but resigned six months later. In 1883 he published with Thomas Arnold *A Catholic Dictionary*. In 1888 Addis left the Church and married Rachel Flood of Sydenham. He became a Presbyterian minister in Australia and later a Professor at the Unitarian Manchester College, Oxford. In 1901 he joined the Church of England, and for the last ten years of his life officiated as a clergyman, being from 1910 Vicar of All Saints, Ennismore Gardens, 288, 301.

Allcock and Milward, solicitors, 5 Union Street, Birmingham, 5.

Allies (xxi), Thomas William (1813–1903), 45, 72, 94, 131, 145, 158, 174, 179, 204, 212, 253, 256, 285, 302, 305; Cyril and Edward, 311.

Ambrose, see St John.

Argyll (xxi), Duchess of, widow of the seventh Duke, 80, 252.

Arnold (xxi), Thomas (1823–1900), 19, 59–60, 140.

Auriol, Canon, 312.

Badeley (xxi), Edward Lowth (1803–68), 16, 246, 252, 254.

Barnabò (xxi), Alessandro (1801–74), 62, 223, 245, 267, 273–80, 293, 331.

Barrow (xxi), John (1810–80), 330.

Bathurst (xxi), Catherine Anne (1825–1907), 46, 123, 134, 168, 336.

Beauregard, Pierre Gustave Toutant (*DAB*, 11,111), 252.

Bedford (xxi), Henry (1816–1905), 135, 329.

Bedford, Henry (1824–1906), at Merchant Taylors' School and Emmanuel College, Cambridge, after studying law, took orders in 1854. He held a succession of curacies until 1876. In 1858–9 he was curate to W. R. Brownlow's father, at Wilmslow, Cheshire. In 1865–6 he was curate at Foxearth, near Sudbury, Suffolk. His later years were spent at Canterbury, 21, 28, 41.

Bellasis (xxi), Edward (1800–73), 42, 91, 111, 246–7, 250–3, 300; Mrs Bellasis, 295, 300, 321; Edward, Junior, 24, 321; Richard, 42.

Benham, William, 255–6, 266.

Benson, Mrs, 258, 260, 268–70.

Berdoe, Edward, a London chemist, educated for the Baptist ministry, became a High Church Anglican, but was drawn toward Catholicism through reading *Apo*. In Sept. 1865 he consulted by letter,

obtained a First in the Classical Tripos. In March of that year he wrote asking Newman to be his director. The latter refused on the ground that he was no longer exercising ministerial functions in the Church of England. On 17 Nov. Knox was received into the Church with F. W. Faber. In 1846-7 he travelled in America, and in 1848 he joined the English Oratory as a novice when it was set up at Maryvale. He was sent to London in 1849 and was ordained in the following year. He was Superior of the London Oratory 1865-8, and became known as a historian of the English Catholics. (*DNB*, XI, 333), 73.

Lake, William Charles (1817-97), after being at Rugby under Arnold, entered Balliol College as a Scholar in 1835. Among his friends were Stanley, Tait and Jowett, but he was a moderate High Churchman, and came under Newman's influence in his last year as an undergraduate. He became a Fellow of Balliol in 1838, and took Orders in 1842. He played a part in university reform in the fifties, and in 1858 left Oxford to become Rector of Huntspill in Somerset. In 1869 he was appointed Dean of Durham by Gladstone, and helped to found the College of Science at Newcastle. Lake left behind some chapters of autobiography, in one of which he described, in the highest terms, the influence of Newman's preaching and teaching during the Oxford Movement, Chapter III of *Memorials of William Charles Lake*, edited by his widow, Katherine Lake, London 1901. (*DNB*, XXII, Suppl. 950), 255.

Lambert (XXI), John (1815-92), 33.

Langford, Mrs William, Grace Mozley (1839-1908), only child of Newman's sister Harriett, and Thomas Mozley. Grace, who wrote two novels, *Werona, A Romance of Australian domestic life*, London and Sydney 1893, and *Tiffna's Revenge*, was an excellent pianist. On 4 July 1864 she married William Langford, an engineer, with whom she emigrated to Australia. They had one child, William. Newman had seen her when she was three years old, and did not see her again until she visited him a few days before he died, 308.

La Serre (XXI), Henri, 10, 26.

Leigh, William, Junior, succeeded to Woodchester Park on his father's death in 1873. He married Mary Victoria, daughter of Thomas Jarrett, and sent two sons to the Oratory School, 272.

Liddon (XXI), Henry Parry (1829-90), 195.

Lightfoot, John Prideaux (1803-87), was a Fellow of Exeter College, 1824-35, then Rector of Wootton, Northants, and from 1854 to his death, Rector of Exeter College. He was a member of the first Hebdomadal Council of Oxford University in 1854, and Vice-Chancellor. (*Boase*, II, 428), 140.

Liguori, Alphonsus, St. (XXI), 100.

Lingard, John (1771-1851), at the English College, Douay, returned to England in 1793, and in 1795 was ordained. He taught for a time at Ushaw College, and in 1811 went to the mission of Hornby in Lancashire, where he remained till death, studying and writing. He had already published the *Antiquities of the Anglo-Saxon Church*, Newcastle, 1806. His chief work was *History of England from the first Invasion of the Romans to the Accession of William and Mary in 1688*, London 1819-30. He was thought to have been created a Cardinal *in petto* in 1826. *DNB*, XI, 1199), 112, 204.

Lintott (XXI), William Henry (1810-77), 57, 123, 224.

Lockhart (XXI), William (1819-92), 84, 107, 109, 119, 121, 166, 183-4, 188, 193.

Lothian, Marchioness of, Cecil Chetwynd Talbot (1808-77), younger daughter of the second Earl Talbot, married in 1831 John William Kerr, seventh Marquis of Lothian, who died in 1841. Encouraged by Manning, she was received into the Church on 11 June 1851 by Fr Brownbill at Farm Street. On 16 Dec. 1851 she called on Newman in Birmingham, and wrote to her brother-in-law her impression. See diary for that day. The rest of her life was spent in bringing up her family and in works of charity and religion. (*Boase*, II, 500), 337.

Lualt, Count, 330.

Lynch, Henry (1824-70), a cousin of John Stanislas Flanagan, was from 1855 William Monsell's private secretary, while the latter held office in the Government, and in 1860 an Inspector of Schools. Through the intermediary of his cousin, he sold his Irish estate to the Orations in 1852, and in 1866 began a considerable agitation against them when he found they had resold to another cousin, Stephen Woulfe Flanagan, 289, 295, 315.

Lyttelton (XXI), George William, fourth Baron (1817-76), 69-70, 252.

MacColl, Malcolm (1831-1907), son of a tenant farmer in Inverness-shire, entered the Episcopalian College at Glenalmond in 1854, and received Orders from the Bishop of Glasgow. MacColl, owing to his championship of the Catholic teaching of Bishop Forbes and Patrick Cheyne on the Eucharist, found himself obliged to leave Scotland and the Episcopalian Church. Bishop Tait licensed him as a curate at St Barnabas, Pimlico, 1860, and then at St Paul's, Knightsbridge, 1861. Eventually in 1884, he became a residentiary Canon of Ripon. MacColl greatly